ALONG THE TRENCHES

ALONG THE TRENCHES

A JOURNEY THROUGH EASTERN EUROPE TO ISFAHAN

BY NAVID KERMANI

TRANSLATED BY TONY CRAWFORD

polity

First published in German as *Entlang den Gräben* © Verlag C. H. Beck ohG, München 2018. All rights reserved.

This English edition © Polity Press, 2020

The translation of this work was supported by a grant from the Goethe-Institute.

Polity Press
65 Bridge Street
Cambridge CB2 1UR, UK

Polity Press
101 Station Landing
Suite 300
Medford, MA 02155, USA

ISBN-13: 978-1-5095-3556-9
ISBN-13: 978-1-5095-3557-6 (pb)

A catalogue record for this book is available from the British Library.

Library of Congress Cataloging-in-Publication Data
Names: Kermani, Navid, 1967- author.
Title: Along the trenches : a journey through Eastern Europe to Isfahan / Navid Kermani.
Other titles: Entlang den Graben. English
Description: Cambridge, UK : Polity Press, 2019. | Includes bibliographical references.
Identifiers: LCCN 2019003897 (print) | LCCN 2019018326 (ebook) | ISBN 9781509535583 (Epub) | ISBN 9781509535569 | ISBN 9781509535569(hardback) | ISBN 9781509535576(pbk.)
Subjects: LCSH: Kermani, Navid, 1967---Travel--Europe, Eastern. | Kermani, Navid, 1967---Travel--Former Soviet republics. | Kermani, Navid, 1967---Travel--Iran. | Kermani, Navid, 1967---Family. | Europe, Eastern--Description and travel. | Former Soviet republics--Description and travel. | Iran--Description and travel.
Classification: LCC PT2711.E75 (ebook) | LCC PT2711.E75 E5813 2019 (print) | DDC 838/.9203--dc23
LC record available at https://lccn.loc.gov/2019003897

Typeset in 10 on 14.5 Adobe Janson by
Servis Filmsetting Ltd, Stockport, Cheshire
Printed and bound in Great Britain by TJ International Limited

The publisher has used its best endeavours to ensure that the URLs for external websites referred to in this book are correct and active at the time of going to press. However, the publisher has no responsibility for the websites and can make no guarantee that a site will remain live or that the content is or will remain appropriate.

Every effort has been made to trace all copyright holders, but if any have been overlooked the publisher will be pleased to include any necessary credits in any subsequent reprint or edition.

For further information on Polity, visit our website:
politybooks.com

CONTENTS

Cologne   1

First Day: Schwerin   2
Second Day: From Berlin to Wrocław   8
Third Day: Auschwitz   12
Fourth Day: Cracow   15
Fifth Day: From Cracow to Warsaw   20
Sixth Day: Warsaw   23
Seventh Day: Warsaw   30
Eighth Day: From Warsaw to Masuria   33
Ninth Day: Kaunas   35
Tenth Day: Vilnius and Vicinity   37
Eleventh Day: Via Paneriai to Minsk   42
Twelfth Day: Minsk and Khatyn   49
Thirteenth Day: Into the Chernobyl Exclusion Zone   55
Fourteenth Day: Kurapaty and Minsk   61
Fifteenth Day: Into the Exclusion Zone East of Krasnapolle   72
Sixteenth Day: From Minsk to Kiev   77
Seventeenth Day: Kiev   84
Eighteenth Day: From Kiev to Dnipro   88
Nineteenth Day: To the Front in Donbas   94
Twentieth Day: Via Mariupol to the Black Sea   98
Twenty-First Day: Along the Black Sea to Odessa   102
Twenty-Second Day: Odessa   104
Twenty-Third Day: Leaving Odessa by Air   111
Twenty-Fourth Day: Via Moscow to Simferopol   112

Twenty-Fifth Day: Via Bakhchisaray to Sevastopol   113
Twenty-Sixth Day: Along the Crimean Coast   122
Twenty-Seventh Day: From Crimea to the Russian Mainland   130
Twenty-Eighth Day: To Krasnodar   138
Twenty-Ninth Day: From Krasnodar to Grozny   141
Thirtieth Day: Grozny   150
Thirty-First Day: In the Chechen Mountains   158
Thirty-Second Day: From Grozny to Tbilisi   164
Thirty-Third Day: Tbilisi   171
Thirty-Fourth Day: Tbilisi   176
Thirty-Fifth Day: To Gori and the Georgian–Ossetian Ceasefire Line   182
Thirty-Sixth Day: From Tbilisi to Kakheti   189
Thirty-Seventh Day: From Kakheti to Azerbaijan   194
Thirty-Eighth Day: Along the Azeri–Armenian Ceasefire Line   199
Thirty-Ninth Day: By Night Train to Baku   206
Fortieth Day: Baku   214
Forty-First Day: Baku and Qobustan   223
Forty-Second Day: Leaving Baku by Air   228
Forty-Third Day: Yerevan   229
Forty-Fourth Day: Yerevan   243
Forty-Fifth Day: To Lake Sevan and on to Nagorno-Karabakh   257
Forty-Sixth Day: Through Nagorno-Karabakh   266
Forty-Seventh Day: To the Armenian–Azeri Ceasefire Line and on to Iran   273
Forty-Eighth Day: Via Jolfa to Tabriz   278
Forty-Ninth Day: Via Ahmadabad to Alamout Castle   286
Fiftieth Day: To the Caspian Sea and on to Tehran   295
Fifty-First Day: Tehran   299
Fifty-Second Day: Tehran   303
Fifty-Third Day: Tehran   308
Fifty-Fourth Day: Flying out of Tehran   314

Visiting Family in Isfahan   315
The Journey Begins   348
Acknowledgements   353
Notes   355
Bibliography   357

Cologne

Every day I walk through my neighbourhood behind the railway station. I hear some Arabic here, some Polish there, something Balkan-sounding to the left; Turkish, obviously; occasionally Persian, which makes me prick up my ears; I hear French spoken by Africans; Asian languages; also German, spoken in every accent and every quality, by blonds as well as by Asians, Blacks and Orientals. It is not always an unalloyed pleasure – the tramps, the many black imitation-leather jackets (or maybe they're real leather; what do I know?), my God, the gold front teeth of the black-haired women with their long, colourful skirts and their babies carried in slings, a second child led by the hand and a third running ahead, the young people hanging around, the drug addicts and the deranged who live in a home in Unter Krahnenbäumen – a street name referring to some long forgotten 'crane booms'; to round it off a few Muslims with suspiciously long beards. This is a reality that extends well beyond the area behind Cologne's railway station. In every city in Western Europe you can probably find the same mixture of Turkish green-grocers, Chinese supermarkets, Iranian specialities sold by a shopkeeper who used to be a director for Iranian state television before the revolution, traditional and self-service bakeries, rows of phone shops and Internet cafés – Iran, 19 cents a minute; Turkey, 9; Bangladesh, 24; the cheap hotels, sex shops, bridal shops, dives; tearooms and coffeehouses for Turks, Albanians, Africans; Turkish places that do or don't sell alcohol, chic restaurants and shabby ones, Thai massage studios, bookmakers that do or don't sell alcohol, import–export businesses, and here and there an antediluvian shop offering housewares or rubber stamps; on the main road the refugee shelter where the Roma have taken out the windowpanes to put satellite dishes in the open windows, and in the middle of it all, every winter, a shock troop of elderly gentlemen in blue or red uniforms with tricorn hats and rapiers, a band of Indians or a horde of half-naked Huns – the carnival societies, devotedly practising for their Pancake Day festivities from Epiphany on. What do merchants live on who all offer the same twenty batteries for one euro fifty in their oversized shops? Certainly not on the batteries, considering one after another of the old, well-respected specialist retailers can no longer afford the rising rents. International understanding takes place, with oom-pah and tata-ra-ta, at the beginning and at the end of the neighbourhood, where Cologne's most experienced whores stand at four long bars singing with fat Germans and with drunken Turks, always with the windows open. These

1

are the new inner cities, and the one behind the Cologne railway station is far less aggressive than others – no, it's idyllic beyond these or any other words. They are pure, nothing less. They have nothing to do with the history of the cities where they develop, although they cannot efface that history either – certainly not the 2,000-year history of Cologne. As if they wanted to restore Cologne to its name's etymological meaning, they are like colonies of foreigners, but of many different foreigners who are also foreign to one another as they sit between the blinds of their carrels in the Internet cafés or stand in groups in front of the call shops. I often wonder if they scrambled down an embankment into a boat one night near Tangier, a boat that neither sank nor got intercepted – walking success stories all of them, even if they're still sharing a room with four other people and afraid of the police? Iran, 19 cents a minute; Turkey, 9; Bangladesh, 24. These are not the margins of society. They surge out from the centre of town. It is the margins that still have the look of homogeneity. There the city is divided by income; in the centre, everything is jumbled together. I walk through the neighbourhood; I hear some Arabic here, some Polish there, something Balkan-sounding to the left; Turkish, obviously; occasionally Persian, which makes me prick up my ears; also French spoken by Africans, Asian languages, and German, spoken in every accent and every quality. I don't understand half of it, and I mean half. And of the half I do understand, I usually understand only half again, because it's already slipped away behind the window or into a shop, it's poorly enunciated or too far away, I walked by too fast or the speakers were walking past me. I finish the sentences in my head, or I guess how they began; I imagine stories set, not across the Rhine in Deutz or during the Second World War, but in provincial Chinese cities, at Nigerian universities, in boats, freight containers and departure lounges where hearts race.

From the novel *Dein Name*

First Day: Schwerin

'Are there really no problems at all?' I ask the woman who directs the Sunday school for Syrian children in the concrete high-rise housing estate.

'No,' the woman answers, 'nothing serious.' Once in a while an unfriendly word about her headscarf, she says, but nothing worth mentioning compared to what her family went through in Syria, in the war. The child she is carrying in her womb will be born in peace.

Ghadia Ranah is forty years old and was already a teacher before she left

2

Syria. Now she is responsible for 136 Syrian children who practise their Arabic every weekend in Dreesch, Schwerin's largest housing estate, to stay connected with their home country. The children I question on the playground of the community centre during the break have no intention of going back, however. I can hardly believe how well they already master German; they've been here just eight, nine months and they already inflect their verbs in the subjunctive, as required for hypothetical clauses, to explain what their day-to-day life would look like if they still lived in Syria: no school, no playing outdoors, the fear of bombs, tanks, fighters. Here in Germany, everyone is nice to them.

In September 2016, my trip barely begun, my expectations are already being challenged: my idea was to talk to the refugees themselves before hearing in the afternoon how Germany's new anti-immigration party, the AfD, talks about them. Naturally I assumed I would find them in God knows what horrible circumstances; as a West German, after all, I had pictured the formerly communist East as punishment in itself for any refugee: xenophobic neighbours, overstrained bureaucracies, isolation, possibly assaults. What I actually encounter are cheerful helpers, industrious refugees, playing children – as if the 'welcome society' were showing me its image video in the middle of the high-rise housing estate.

Word has got around among the Syrians, one of the volunteer Arabic teachers explains, that conditions in Schwerin are particularly advantageous for refugees. Come again? Yes, here you get your papers after two, three months, and you can work, maybe not in the profession you've learned, not as a chemist or an engineer, but as an interpreter for a social-welfare organization perhaps, or on a building site. Besides, the teacher explains, with so many flats vacant in the estate, the refugees aren't housed in shelters, the language courses aren't overcrowded, and there are no queues at the government offices. Soon the association the Syrians have founded will be offering free Arabic classes to interested neighbours; they've also been helping in the allotment gardens to show their gratitude.

It's not as easy as all that with the neighbours, says Claus Oellerking, who was a school head himself earlier in life, and is a co-founder of the refugees' aid association in Dreesch. The Syrians are very unusual, he says: middle class, highly motivated, good education, so they adapt much faster than the problem cases, of which there are some too of course among the refugees, especially if the influx is completely uncontrolled because there are no official ways to flee. On the one hand, most of the original residents of the estate once left their homes themselves, whether on expulsion from Germany's eastern territories after the war or as ethnic Germans 'returning' from the former Soviet Union, or as workers who moved to Schwerin when the factories were built in the 1970s. Accordingly, the willingness to help is widespread, especially among the older residents – in the beginning, the refugees hardly knew what to do with all the gifts they received. At the same time, Oellerking continues, many Germans here have the feeling they've been left behind: the sudden unemployment when the heavy industries shut down after unification, a meagre pension or benefit, the disproportionately high numbers of single households and people over forty, not enough children; add to that the welfare-state mentality left over from East Germany – and now hundreds of Syrians are moving into the estate, young men and, most of all, young families who, after having been lucky enough to escape with their lives, are determined to make something of them, and who are perhaps a bit more hot-blooded, have different customs, speak a different language, and also wear headscarves. Obviously that produces rejection, although mostly in private. There is hardly any violence in Dreesch, according to Oellerking, whatever the newspapers may say about a so-called flash point; not even graffiti or playground vandalism. But whether anyone will come to Arabic classes, or even just to an international barbecue – Oellerking has his doubts.

I ask about the allotment gardeners. Yes, that was good fun, Mr Oellerking immediately recalls, fun and at the same time a bit sad. Like so many other aspects of life here, the allotments are in gradual decline; the old gardening enthusiasts die, not enough new ones take it up, so that the allotment fees go up, which in turn keeps young families from taking one on – a vicious circle. Worse still, the sense of community is slipping away, the solidarity. It used to be that you only had to hang up a notice and the neighbours would be on hand at the appointed time and pitch in. But now, the steering committee put out an appeal to make the garden of an unwell pensioner shipshape – and except for only one allotment gardener, an AfD member to boot, only the Syrian refugees turned out, who have been seizing every opportunity to make themselves useful in Dreesch ever since the assaults by other migrants against merrymakers in Cologne on New Year's Eve, 2015. The man from AfD looked glum, then he made some frenzied phone calls to find German helpers, but the German allotment gardeners don't help each other any more. Certainly the ailing pensioner was pleased to have the Syrians' help, Oellerking recounts; getting the leaves raked and the branches pruned was the main thing.

Crossing the flower-bedecked city centre, where every historic brick seems to have been carefully restored, I pass the AfD's billboards warning of the 'destruction of Germany'. I have barely stepped inside the wood-panelled banquet room of the restaurant Lindengarten, where the party has invited citizens to 'coffee and cake on the topic of pensions', when I hear a woman complaining that German girls are being 'desecrated'. They're off to a good start, I think as I begin to look around. About fifty, maybe sixty people are standing in the room or sitting at the tables, which have been pushed towards the two side walls, as if to leave room for dancing in the middle. There's nothing unusual about the people, no insignia, no shaved heads, no high boots; their ages are well mixed. One young woman, the only one wearing a German traditional costume, looks somewhat lost. As I sit down at one of the tables, I too am served coffee and cake.

First, the candidates for directly elected seats in the state parliament of Mecklenburg–Western Pomerania introduce themselves, each in turn giving assurances that they are ordinary citizens. The one who acts the most house-wifely is the blonde lady who until recently was running an escort agency for an Arab clientele, as everyone in the room no doubt knows, since she has been dropped for that reason from the party's list of candidates for proportional seats. But she has nonetheless prevailed as the candidate for her district's direct seat, and she now smiles down from the posters in Dreesch, in her historic dress or astride a splendid horse – perhaps an Arabian. The speaker, Andreas Kalbitz, the vice-chairman of AfD's parliamentary group in the neighbouring state of Brandenburg, is counted among the right wing of the party; he is an alumnus of the nationalist student fraternities; the fake-news media say he also has connections to a right-wing extremist group. Myself, I made his acquaintance earlier by telephone when we arranged to meet in Schwerin: at that time he seemed – sorry, dear leftist friends, but I have to write it – not the least bit aggressive.

In his speech, Kalbitz emphasizes again and again that of course we have to make distinctions – but then no distinctions are forthcoming, only the next blanket statement about the establishment parties, the media and the asylum seekers. The illustrative examples too are strictly limited to just one side of reality: the housing estate in his district that was renovated for the refugees while the Germans go on living in their dilapidated flats; the annual shortfall of 200 million euros to bring Eastern pensions up to Western levels, while 90 billion are allocated for the asylum madness; the 12,000-euro pension paid to a broadcasting director and the helplessness of the authorities to deal with fare-dodging refugees, who are now given free passes in Berlin while pensioners and the unemployed have to pay for their discounted tickets. And so on: the parallel societies, Islamic justices of the peace, our German women who are afraid to go out at night – but naturally we must make distinctions. The premise of every argument is pensions: everyone, no matter what their political inclination, wants to live out their old age with dignity. And the unvarying conclusion is that someone else is getting the money that you will lack in your old age. Frankly, that seems a little too facile to me; the audience don't look that simple at all.

Only during the question-and-answer session do I realize what is going to bring the new party its 20 per cent in the state elections: not what they say, but what the people who come here are at last allowed to say. Everyone in the Lindengarten has their worries: for one, it's his pension; for another, it's the private health insurance that he daren't cancel at his age; for a third it's the foreigners in the streets, and besides that it's the high fees for the allotment garden; and all of them read the same best-sellers that warn against Islam. It's not hate, it is fear that speaks through their words – fear that they are the losers in their own country and that everything is going to come crashing down on them just as it did after the fall of East Germany. This group is not the neo-Nazi NPD; a skinhead would look more out of place and probably be more unwelcome than a black-haired person like me. These people really are ordinary citizens with ordinary jobs or insufficient pensions, at least those I get a chance to talk to after the programme: tradesmen and contractors, computer technicians, even a former OSCE election observer with international experience; an older gentleman who gave the Pirate Party a chance last time out and, with his long beard, looks more like a hippie. At the outside, Andreas Kalbitz has something of – no, not a Nazi – but with his little wire-rimmed spectacles, his blond moustache and his rousing diction, more something of Kaiser Wilhelm's Germany. And that Germany, the old Germany that was nationalist but not driven to its doom by Adolf Hitler, is perhaps the best point of reference for a *Burschenschafter*, an alumnus of the German student fraternities with their nationalist traditions – back when all was right with the world.

'We want everything to stay how it is,' says a young man in hiking trousers, who is as friendly and as curious as all the others who come over to talk to me after the event, without my having to approach them. 'You can want whatever you like,' I reply, 'and you can fight for your ideas – but so can I; you don't have priority over me.' His jaw drops: this point – the fact that

6

a man whose parents are immigrants has the same rights as an indigenous person – doesn't make sense to him. It does to the gentleman who used to work for the OSCE, of course, and immediately a discussion breaks out among the AfD supporters themselves. Even the right to political asylum now has its defenders, and there are repeated reminders that Germany needs an immigration law; it says so in the party's platform, after all. Only the events of autumn 2015 – when Chancellor Merkel opened the borders to refugees languishing in Hungary and further south – the chaos, that's not right, they're all unanimous, as is Mr Oellerking of Schwerin Refugee Aid. It goes without saying that none of them, apparently, has ever talked to a refugee, much less visited the Sunday school, nearby though it is. But, fair enough, who of my own 'left-red-green scruffy sixties Germany', as the AfD leader called it, ever goes to talk with members of his party?

As the room empties, I sit down at Kalbitz's table: he is exhausted, the heat, the many campaign appearances, and now getting a cold from the flight in; he would rather be spending a sunny Sunday with his family, his three children, he says, but the people's passiveness troubles him, the resignation, the low election turnout. The AfD is leading people back into politics, giving them a voice; as believers in democracy we should all be glad of that, don't I agree? In that case, I ask, doesn't it strike him as absurd when the AfD's billboards announce that Deutschland is threatened with destruction? After all, we in Germany know what destruction means, and, in case we do forget, we can look at the pictures coming from Syria and Iraq. But here in the picturesque city centre of Schwerin, in the wood-panelled banquet room – the destruction of Germany? To be honest, I can't think of any country that is much safer, more prosperous and more free – Sweden, maybe, or Norway.

He didn't make up the slogan, Kalbitz says, and besides it expresses only a concern, not a factual occurrence. Really? I ask. Yes, of course, Kalbitz assures me, a concern, not a fact, and then, in conversation, he actually does begin to make, one after another, the distinctions that he announced but didn't deliver in his speech. Suddenly there is not just that New Year's Eve, but the real victims of persecution who obviously have a right to asylum; not just the terrorist attacks but also the many well-integrated Muslims. In the end, all of his fellow AfD members' most provocative claims have been cleared away – from the concern that Germans wouldn't want the national football team's Black player Jérôme Boateng as a neighbour to the demand that Germany's borders be defended with firearms – and the only unique selling point that remains, more or less, is the call to prohibit minarets, although Kalbitz can't quite explain to me how people are supposed to identify with a new country if they can't naturalize their religion too.

This is exactly what the AfD has often been accused of: its representatives provoke an outcry only to claim afterwards that they didn't mean it that way. Thus the limits of outrage are gradually pushed back. But, as I sit facing him, I really couldn't say whether the real Andreas Kalbitz is the one who mocked refugee helpers like Claus Oellerking in his speech as 'plush-toy throwers' or the one who would have no qualms about a vice-chancellor of Turkish descent, as long as he was well integrated – his objections to the Green Party's Cem Özdemir are purely on political grounds. Recently a few Croatian businessmen told him they approved in principle of everything the AfD advocates but couldn't support the party because it is opposed to foreigners. Somehow, Kalbitz says, he can understand how they got that impression – which is completely wrong, mind! – and he wishes me a pleasant journey.

Second Day: From Berlin to Wrocław

On the roof of East Berlin's famous theatre in Rosa-Luxemburg-Platz, the Volksbühne, three giant letters glow red: *OST*, 'East'. This alone is a statement – more; it is meant as a protest – in the reunified Berlin, perhaps even in united Europe: EAST. Many of the theatre's major productions of the past two decades – physically exhausting productions because of their length alone, five, six, seven hours – have been adaptations of Russian novels, and its series of discussion events was at first titled 'Capitalism & Depression', and later 'Politics & Crime'. The city government has just decided to make Germany's most important dramatic theatre into a multimedia venue of the international festival circuit in which the primary language will be English. No doubt the topic of refugees will come up.

The taxi towards Berlin's main railway station takes me past a plastic cube that is bigger than any other building along Unter den Linden – the cathedral, the university, the opera, the Brandenburg Gate. It is still hard to believe that behind these plastic sheets the façade of the Prussian royal palace, the residence of the Hohenzollern kings and emperors, is being reconstructed brick by brick, as if history could be reversed. 'Do Bigger Things' commands the advertisement that covers the whole front of the building site. Did the ad agency choose that poster deliberately? The image is nothing less than subversive: a landscape framed in the screen of a smartphone, a stylus resting on it, about to retouch reality. Soon an imitation of Prussian imperial splendour, of all things, is to become a museum of international scope, a showcase for the cultures of the world, and no one knows how that's supposed to work. One floor has already been reappropriated for a better celebration of Berlin's local history. All that's needed now is to restore the gold cross on top of the palace, rising like a flag out of the colonial collections – the cross initially intended, after the failed revolution of 1848, to demonstrate the divine right of kings – then the cosmopolitan mask would be completely torn away.

In front of the Reichstag, whose cupola was also replaced after the fall of the Berlin Wall – but not with a reactionary reconstruction – I get out of the taxi. Because I'm a few minutes early, I roll my suitcase not to the right towards the station but left, to the Memorial to the Murdered Jews of Europe. Although I think the central site is right for the memorial, and its dimensions too, I find the walk-in landscape of concrete prisms awkward because it tries to create an empathy that can never be. Now I approach the memorial from the north for the first time, and I am surprised to see how the steles rise to form a greyish-black hill of gravestones, the trees of Tiergarten behind it becoming a cemetery garden, the surrounding office buildings metamorphosing into administrative tracts whose lines and colours coincide with those of the concrete cubes, the Brandenburg Gate suddenly a portal through which no one walked voluntarily. The sight, transforming the atrocity into an abstraction, since it is beyond imagining, leaves me reconciled with the memorial for a few minutes. But then I walk in between the steles and am immediately bewildered once more. The taller they get, the more remote the city, the more lost I feel, the angrier I am at the gimmick. The pronounced unevenness of the ground, apparently intended to simulate the faltering life force of the victims, yet to me the most trivial impediment imaginable, even with my wheeled suitcase, strikes me as impudent. The safety railings where stairs lead down to underground doors marked 'Emergency Exit' make a more honest impression than that.

Are the eastbound trains always this empty? I am embarrassed to admit it, but I have never been to Poland before. Born and raised deep in the west of Germany, we always looked towards France, Italy, the United States; we knew even the Middle East better than the east of our own country. Now the train is crossing the Oder, which seems to be a real river still, not built up and channelled; the banks are left to themselves. Not thirty seconds into Poland, the East already looks as unspoiled as in Andrzej Stasiuk's books. But naturally the concrete-slab housing estates appear right away, thirty seconds later.

In Poznań I almost miss my connecting train to Wrocław because, in spite of all my travel experience, I can't find my platform, and I don't understand what anyone says to me when I show them my ticket. And then, too, I pull up short at the bakery in the station: if there is anything I would have thought was typically German, it's the whole-grain bread, and now I realize that the Poles, or at least those in Poznań, bake their bread just as dark, and Germany's culinary culture belongs more to the east than to the west of Europe, and still less to the south, which never entered German cuisine before the past few decades. Although the Germans amongst themselves perceive a division between North and South, along the imaginary line delimiting the range of the Bavarian white sausage, in fact the European continent is historically divided between East and West along a border separating brown bread and white. Before the world wars, Germany was naturally classed with Poland, Bohemia and Hungary as belonging to Central Europe, and German intellectuals were quick to explain what distinguished their country from the West. When I finally find a seat in the train, I am surprised to find it completely full, even the first-class carriage, as if the Poles travelled only inside their own country.

In Wrocław, still called Breslau in German, the historian Krzysztof Ruchniewicz, director of the Willy Brandt Centre, explains that the more recent ex-chancellor Helmut Kohl is far more popular in Poland than the idol of my West German peace-movement generation. True, Brandt recognized the Oder–Neisse border between East Germany and Poland, but later he failed to support the anti-communist opposition, and during his visit to Poland in 1985 he refused to meet with the Nobel Peace Prize laureate Lech Wałęsa. If I were to ask around on the square in front of the synagogue, where we are sitting at one of the cafés, hardly anyone would be able to place Chancellor Brandt's name, and the people around here are educated. Hardly anyone in Poland heard about Brandt's kneeling at the Warsaw Ghetto memorial in 1970, Ruchniewicz notes: the photo was printed only once in a Jewish newspaper, and after that it was published only in retouched or cropped versions – a Brandt with no knees.

And more elementary facts that you don't realize if you grew up a few kilometres further west: every inhabitant of Wrocław, without exception, has what Germany is currently calling a 'migration background', and the entire population of the city was replaced in 1945, all 600,000 German inhabitants expelled – more, to be exact, because Silesia had been thought of as Germany's air-raid shelter, and many refugees from further west lived in Breslau at that time. The Jews were expelled twice – no, three times: first by the Germans, who jammed them into trains going to Auschwitz, Theresienstadt or Majdanek; then the few Jews who had survived in Breslau were expelled after the war as Germans; and finally those who had been resettled in the city along with other Poles were expelled as Jews once more. We know this only vaguely, since our history lessons in school referred to the territories that are no longer German ashamedly, if at all. But in Poland, too, Ruchniewicz points out, the remembrance of the country's past is only hazy and sees Poles exclusively as victims. Especially since the new, conservative government avoids any word about the expulsion of the Jews, not to mention that of the Germans.

I try to imagine how the Poles arrived in Wrocław, most of them after having been expelled themselves from what is now Ukraine; how they entered the homes the Germans had abandoned in haste, opening the wardrobes and the drawers; how the shoemaker kept an eye out for a cobbler's shop, the doctor searched for a suitable surgery; in the schools the drawings of the previous classes still hung perhaps, the caretaker's work coat, the headmaster's hat, with a German label inside it – and if it happened to fit the new head? One would think it impossible for life to go on if a city loses all its inhabitants, and with the inhabitants its history, and then a few decades later it looks as if no other people had ever lived in Wrocław.

Krzysztof Ruchniewicz recounts how German expellees once drove up in his wife's village near Bystrzyca Kłodzka, formerly Habelschwerdt, an extended family, or maybe more than one family, in a bus. The insistent German grandmother was dragged back by her daughters each time she asked about property prices and was finally pushed back into the bus. After a little tour, the bus stopped again in front of Ruchniewicz's in-laws' house. Someone handed a little present out of the door beside the driver, a packet of coffee, before the bus drove away. 'It was an odd feeling,' says the director of the Willy Brandt Centre, 'a very strange feeling: should we have given them something too, we wondered – but what for?'

In the evening, as I send Andreas Kalbitz an e-mail to thank him for the friendly reception, I close with a greeting – a cheeky one I admit, but sometimes our fingers are faster than our brains – 'from Breslau, where not cosmopolitanism but nationalism has reduced the German population to zero'.

Third Day: Auschwitz

The procedure that makes me fully German, with no ifs, ands or buts, takes less than a second. Because of the high number of visitors, I can visit Auschwitz only in a group, have to register in advance, ideally online, and must choose a language: English, Polish, German, et cetera. The system is not much different from that of an airport: the visitors, most of them with backpacks, short trousers or other indications that they are just passing through, hold up a bar code to check in, receive a sticker indicating their language, and go through a security check fifteen minutes before their tour begins. In a narrow waiting room they spread out along insufficient benches until their group is called. After holding my ticket under one more scanner, I am standing, from one step to the next, in the concentration camp, facing the barracks, the guard towers, the fences that all of us have seen in photos, reports, documentaries.

The groups have already sorted themselves, although the guides are not here yet. While the young Israelis are – or am I only imagining this? – somewhat louder and more self-assured, the Germans – no, I am not imagining it – huddle silently against the wall of the visitor centre. And then I stick the sticker on my chest bearing a single word in black and white: *Deutsch*, 'German'. It is that, this act, the legend on my chest from then on like a confession: German. Yes, I am one of them, not by descent, blond hair, Aryan blood or any such nonsense, but simply by my language, and hence my culture. I go to my group and wait, also silent, for our guide. Each group in turn lines up for a bizarre photo in the gateway surmounted by the motto *Arbeit macht frei*. Only our group is ashamed.

The three-hour tour is designed so that the horror escalates continuously, from the bunkhouses to the various sites of execution by hanging or firing squad, torture chambers, laboratories for experiments on humans, to the gas chambers, whose walls show the scratches of fingernails. When the gas chamber was opened again after twenty minutes, the guide explains through the wireless headsets that all the visitors are wearing, the bodies were often entangled – as if the living had embraced one another one last time, I think. In fact, there must be nothing more lonely, even in that tangle, than the death struggle, and the bodies lashed out uncontrollably in all directions in pain, panic and grief. But that too is only a surmise, for anyone who survived Auschwitz did not look into that deepest black. The Jewish workers who entered the chamber after each gassing waded through blood, urine and faeces. They pulled the corpses apart and laid them on their backs to remove the gold crowns from their teeth, which the German Reich saw as its property. Many jaws were clenched so tightly that opening their mouths was hard physical work, requiring tools – as if the last act of the dying had been to resolve to keep silent. The idea that no more poems could ever be written after Auschwitz has so often been misunderstood, ridiculed, dismissed; yet Adorno himself was a vigorous defender of avant-garde poetry after the war. In the gas chamber, the statement takes on a natural self-evidence, not as a proscription, but as the expression of an immediate feeling: how can civilization go on at all after such a thing; what is the good of it? What can a human being say, having seen this work of human beings? My jaw clenches too. And just when we think we have begun to grasp the dimensions of the camp, a bus takes us a couple of kilometres further to Birkenau, the second Auschwitz camp, which is simply immense. Himmler wanted to make Auschwitz a model of a kind of slave economy, an imposing sight for visitors; it had at least the appearance of a labour camp, of order and function. But Birkenau was obviously a death factory.

The different groups cross paths again and again, but in spite of the many visitors there is almost never a wait in front of the various buildings. Auschwitz has long since taken its place among Europe's top sightseeing destinations and offers the obligatory spots for selfies. Of course I constantly have a feeling of impropriety, yet I can't think of any other way to channel the masses of people through the camp. There cannot be a proper way of presenting to tourists the industrial annihilation of human life. I would like to break away from the group, to be alone and take off the headset, helpful as our guide's explanations are. But everyone has to maintain order to some extent so that it doesn't break down. And we do want Auschwitz to be seen by as many people as possible.

At the very back of the Birkenau death camp, I find the Israeli groups gathered in an assembly, several hundred young people in white T-shirts, with accompanying adults, on a terrace. Broad-shouldered security guards, probably flown in with them, make sure no onlooker comes too close. Individual members of the group stand up in front of a wall-sized flag of Israel to sing or recite. They close with a group prayer.

As the young people are on their way to the exit, I strike up a conversation with some of them. The trip lasts eight days and takes them to the major sites of the extermination of the European Jews. It is not mandatory, but it is subsidized, and most Israelis take it around the end of their schooling.

'And does it change something for you?' I ask somewhat awkwardly.

'Of course it changes something,' a seventeen- or eighteen-year-old girl answers. 'Before, the Holocaust was just another thing we read about in school. To be honest, it didn't interest me any more than algebra. But here it becomes real to us.' The first three, four days were almost a normal school trip; she didn't really get what it was all about. But then at some point it clicked, and she understood where her roots are, and how few of her ancestors survived, and what a salvation Israel is. 'I understand what it means to be a Jew, to be an Israeli; I really wasn't even conscious of it before.'

When the young people ask me in turn what Auschwitz has changed for me, I tell them about my sticker bearing just one word: 'German'. It is hard for them to believe that I feel guilty the moment I stick it on – or, perhaps, not guilty, but a member of the perpetrators' group, not the victims. I try to explain to them what Willy Brandt's kneeling in Warsaw meant to me, although I have to explain first who Willy Brandt was. To carry the burden of history, to sink to his knees under its weight, was a matter not of personal guilt – Brandt had fought against Hitler – but of responsibility for the country he happened to live in.

Auschwitz, one of the young people interjects, obligates every human being, no matter what country they belong to. He is still more surprised when I mention that my parents are not even German. The murders in Auschwitz were committed in German, I answer; all the orders posted on the walls, all the commands and all the duty rosters exhibited in the display cases here, even the instructions on the chemicals stacked in front of the gas chambers, are in German. Anyone who speaks this language, especially a writer who lives with it, makes his living by it, instinctively falls silent when he reads the posters of the camp commandants: *Ihr seid hier in einem deutschen Konzentrationslager*, 'You are in a German concentration camp …'. And he understands why none of the present-day signposts is in German. A German in Auschwitz will never be an uninvolved visitor. To myself, I add that the sentence about the poetry that can never be written after Auschwitz has another meaning, a special meaning, for that literature which is written in the language of the perpetrators: I read in Primo Levi that it was a matter of survival for the prisoners to know German so that they could understand the rules, the barked commands and abstruse decrees straight away. 'It is no exaggeration to say that it was their ignorance of these languages [German and Polish] which caused the very high mortality rate of the Greeks, the French and the Italians in the concentration camp,' Levi writes. 'And it was not easy to guess, for example that the hail of punches and kicks which had suddenly knocked you to the ground was due to the fact that the buttons on your jacket numbered four, or six, instead of five, or that you had been seen in bed, in the middle of winter, with a hat on your head.'[1]

The young people ask why they haven't seen a single German school group. The time of year, the distance – there will be some reason, I answer. If even to them, the young Israelis, Auschwitz was just something they read about in school, they can imagine how it is in German schools, especially since so many young people today come from other countries. That makes it all the easier, of course, not to see Auschwitz as a part of one's own history.

I think back to my visit to Schwerin, to the optimistic refugees and the alarmed citizens: if there was anything specifically German about the 'core culture' that is invoked every few years as a standard for the integration of Germany's immigrants, it would not be human rights, equality, secularism and so forth, because all these values are European, if not universal. It would be Germany's consciousness of its guilt, which Germany has gradually learned, and ritually rehearsed – but what the nationalist idea wants to abolish is precisely this achievement, which neither France nor the United States but only the Federal Republic of Germany can claim, alongside recycling and good automobiles. Conversely, though, those who oppose a nationalistic conception of the 'nation' must not set narrow ethnic limits on historic responsibility. If they want to be integrated, the Syrians, or at least their children, who have already mastered the German subjunctive, will also have to bear the burden of being German. In Auschwitz, if not before, they will feel that burden the moment they step outside the visitors' centre.

Fourth Day: Cracow

An exhibit in the Cracow Museum of Contemporary Art, which occupies what was once the site of Oskar Schindler's enamel factory, shows the photograph of a friendly-looking and very pretty young visitor laughing gaily by the fence of the Birkenau death camp. The shadow of the barbed wire lies across her face.

The photo was the subject of a local scandal: the Jewish community demanded its removal. Yet it shows a situation that can be observed every day in Birkenau: visitors smiling into the camera in front of the fence, the guard towers or the railway cars, sometimes taking the photographs themselves. When a woman buoyantly and confidently displays her beauty in Birkenau

15

today, is it a triumph over barbarism or a mockery of the victims of that barbarism? As if in defence, the catalogue emphasizes that the young woman in the photograph is a Jew – but does the propriety of smiling before the fence of the concentration camp depend on one's ethnic group? The catalogue also reproduces images from a 1999 video in which people, old and young, dance and cavort naked in the gas chamber. That time, the protest was not just local. Although, or because, the images are almost unbearable, they etch themselves into my memory, something video art rarely achieves.

The Schindler museum, which tries in three dimensions to elicit empathy with the forced labourers, has me bolting for the door after twenty minutes. In a colourless grey-beige room decked out as a mine, visitors walk on original gravel. I imagine some take off their shoes to feel the victims' travail. Outside the museum grounds, taxi drivers advertise an excursion with posters: 'Auschwitz Salt Mine Cheap!'

You can read how beautiful Cracow is in a travel guide, or more strikingly in the poems of Adam Zagajewski, the most famous of this city's many poets. The backdrop of Renaissance, baroque, Art Nouveau and neo-Gothic architecture has escaped all damage from the war and the communist wrecking ball. And yet it seems to me, the longer I meander through the city centre, to be only a backdrop, a backdrop containing the same 'Coffee Shops', 'Quality Hamburgers' and branches of the established fashion chains as Seville, Pisa or Avignon, the same pedestrian zones and separate rubbish and recycling bins, an identical selection of restaurants with a sprinkling of 'Local Food', the same cycle hire stations and wheeled boards with handlebars on them rolling helmeted tourists through the alleyways, the same football jerseys – Real, Barcelona, Bayern, Manchester – worn by children from every European country. Even the itinerant artists' pop songs, arias and magic tricks are the same everywhere in Europe. An ordinary urban life, on the other hand, with shop window displays addressing the locals, with tradespeople, business-people or hurried passers-by, is not to be found in the leisure parks which many European city centres have become: instead there is 'Carrefour Express' with exactly the same provisions as in any Spanish seaside town; there are the notorious bare-chested, beer-drinking young Englishmen – how uncanny that they are able to be in Seville, Pisa and Avignon at the same time.

Passing an inconspicuous church, I hear a female choir and open the door. There are nuns in white habits, not as old as elsewhere in Europe, scattered among the pews, each one by herself and yet all of them together. Seen from behind, they look all the same – after all, their clothes are a kind of uniform.

16

The scene, which I had not anticipated – although I might have expected it in Poland, if anywhere in the world – perhaps the scene seems so odd to me because the day-to-day life of the convent is the starkest possible contrast to the polyglot entertainments that dominate the environment outside. For a moment, the nuns' daily routine strikes me as more individual than the lifestyle in any 'Organic Café'.

As in every city where no Jews survived, the Jewish quarter of Cracow is particularly trendy. Perhaps kosher dining 60 kilometres from Auschwitz is also a kind of empathy, only with the illusion of a happy ending. The Hebrew letters are accompanied here by most of the signs indicating 'Vegan Cuisine' and 'Free Wi-Fi'. Even the cigarette adverts extol the 'Feel Good' lifestyle: low in harmful substances, multilingual, and easy on the conscience. In this 'Easy Jet' world that is making the cities as interchangeable as the beach resorts already are, no one has anything against gays, the disabled, Blacks, the headscarves of the Arab tourists, whose men wear the same Bermuda shorts as all the tourists in the world; everyone communicates in English; the baby-changing rooms are labelled for both sexes, and the visit to the Schindler museum is followed by a smoothie, enjoyed while simultaneously surfing the wide world of the web. No wonder Europe has made some people's homes feel strange to them.

But Cracow, the poet Adam Zagajewski counters, has benefited enormously from Europe, and especially from tourism and the subsidies from Brussels. The city used to be black with the toxic soot of the steel mills, black with the coal heaped in front of the buildings every autumn and washed onto the pavements with every rain, the Vistula, too, black with dirt. And it was not only the streets that were sombre: under communism the city stiffened 'in a weary grimace', as one of Zagajewski's books phrases it, 'in the catatonic stupor of a patient in the psychiatric ward who awaits the end of the world while clad in his blue-striped pajamas.'[2]

Adam Zagajewski, the poet of protest against the dictatorship in the years after 1968, was banned from publishing and emigrated first to Paris and later to the United States. In his poems, essays and diaries, he uncovered a kind of European consciousness, an empire of the mind, carefree and multilingual in its disregard for national borders, free of ideological compulsions in its view of the inevitably bloody past. Today, over seventy years old and translated into many languages, he doesn't want to leave Cracow again, yet he is horrified by the new nationalist-religionist government which, like the communist regime, obscures the society's real problems under an ideological veil: nation, church, family, tradition. The government would align the whole culture with patriotism, funding only patriotic plays, patriotic films, patriotic museums. The result, of course, is unspeakable kitsch.

'Being against communism was something,' he sighs over lunch in one of the old, now genteel literary cafés. 'It wasn't just risky, it was also intellectually worthwhile. You were taking on a whole edifice of ideas.' But the new right offers only fragments of a world view, he continues. The nation is not enough to make a political platform; after all, it is different everywhere you look, so that the Polish emigrants in Great Britain, for example, are victims of the same rhetoric that is used to inflame opinion against immigration in Poland – with, of course, the ridiculous twist that there are hardly any immigrants in Poland. 'And then a Catholic nationalism to boot: it's a contradiction in terms. This kind of thinking makes a heretic of the pope himself!'

The renationalization has many causes, Zagajewski says: there is the poorer population who have no share in the growing wealth of the middle and upper classes; there is the longing for community brought about by the atomization of the liberal system. At the same time, very old conflicts are still active, conflicts that date from the eighteenth and nineteenth centuries, when the landed aristocracy wore Sarmatian robes in rebellion against the French fashion. Today the cut of one's coat is no longer an issue, says Zagajewski; no one in Poland wants to dress in Middle Eastern clothes, least of all the nationalists, who are obsessed on the contrary with warning against the East; but the fear of losing the substance of 'Polishness' to modernization and Western influence is already rampant.

'And what is that substance?'

'Well,' Zagajewski sighs, 'it's a popular Catholicism in combination with pierogi and borscht; not much more than that, really.'

I have often wondered, although without thinking any further about it, at the fact that so many Poles have the typically Persian name Dariusz. Only during my preparations for this journey did I realize that the Sarmatians constantly referred to in Polish Romanticism are an Iranian ethnic group who settled in Crimea long before the Greeks, and who were thought to have migrated northwards from there. In reality, it was mainly Turkish-speaking Tatars and Mongols who spread throughout Eastern Europe from the Black Sea, and only from the twelfth or thirteenth century. While the Muscovites hid from the Mongols in the forests of the north, Poland was open to the oriental influences. Thus the division of the society into *herby*, or clans, could have its origins in nomadism, just as the relations between Polish lords and foreign merchants' colonies mirror the coexistence of Iranians and Greeks on the Black Sea coast. Sarmatia was a traditional, mythic term associated with the lifestyle of the old Polish aristocracy and the Polish-Lithuanian Commonwealth, the *Rzeczpospolita*, to explain its fundamental difference from Western culture – hence the men's robes in old portraits, the Middle Eastern pomp, the richly ornamented weapons, the bushy hair and moustaches; hence the Persian names. Sarmatianism was meant to express superiority, not inferiority. To enlightened Western rulers and philosophers, however, Sarmatia stood for backwardness, anarchy, intrigue and irrationality.

The revival of Sarmatianism in the nineteenth century was largely the work of the Polish national poet Adam Mickiewicz. In the decades that followed, whenever Germanization threatened to get out of hand under the influence of the Habsburg Empire and the German cultural canon, literature went back to glorifying the old Polish aristocratic culture, and the Sarmatian robes repulsed the fashions of Paris and Vienna. Do those who want to lead Poland back to its roots today still remember that their ancestors placed those roots in Iran – even though it was a mythical country they had in mind? Today many Poles see the election of past Polish kings by a mass assembly of aristocrats as a precursor of the parliamentary system: proof of their country's Western identity and inherent difference from Russian despotism. In reality, the custom, now constitutionally established in the form of the Sejm, arose in the late sixteenth century and was modelled after the Kurultai, the assembly in which Tatar nobles and tribal chiefs elected a new khan. The last mayor of Lviv to be appointed by Vienna, who bore the beautiful German name Franz Kröbl, underscored his Polish identity by having himself buried in Middle Eastern robes. Nothing could be further from the mind of Jarosław Kaczyński, the leader of Poland's governing PiS party.

'No, no one remembers the Sarmatians any more,' Adam Zagajewski confirms, stirring his coffee, which ... well, even a Jarosław Kaczyński knows where coffee comes from.

After the national-religious party won the elections, Zagajewski wrote another protest poem, his first in many years, satirical, angry, caustic, advising the new government to execute some movie directors and to set up penal camps, which 'should be lenient, so as not to provoke the UN'.[3] For a moment he was an activist again, drawing the nationalists' ire, becoming a hero of the pro-European movement. Since then, however, Zagajewski has abstained from political remarks. You can't be constantly fighting against the bigotry, the narrow-mindedness, the fear, he says; it would make you silly in the long run. What you need to do is to show – in the society, in the culture, in books, in day-to-day relations – that openness has value, is fun, is beautiful, that it is more advantageous than withdrawal. Europe can't be saved by boredom.

In the evening, Maria Anna Potocka, the very spirited and incisive director of the Museum of Contemporary Art, takes me to a real Polish restaurant, where she is amused to find that, to my Iranian taste, everything Polish tastes very German: ham hocks, red cabbage, and so on. And, to an ignoramus like me, the famous pierogi too turn out to be just Slavic ravioli.

We talk long about what would be an appropriate museum treatment of the Holocaust and disagree about the Jewish Museum in Berlin, whose 'Holocaust tower', simulating the victims' anxiety, I find ridiculous and indecent. Maria Anna Potocka thinks I am very dogmatic and that the Shoah is the most interesting challenge to art.

'And Auschwitz itself?' I ask.

There's not much that could be done differently there, she answers; there are so many visitors, the organizational challenges are so complex: just think of the many older people who can't walk around with the regular groups. 'The Nazis in the concentration camp faced the task of murdering one and a half million Jews,' she adds with the defiant tone of her exhibition, 'but it is no less a challenge to guide one and a half million tourists through Auschwitz every year.'

Taking up Adam Zagajewski's idea about the danger of boredom, I ask whether Cracow didn't use to be more exciting.

'Nonsense. Anyway, we locals see the city centre only once a year.'

Fifth Day: From Cracow to Warsaw

We take the longer route to Warsaw, driving through the countryside, which is far removed from the bittersweet image of rural Polish poverty that I expected as a reader of Stasiuk. The roads are excellent not only along the Vistula, which attracts many holiday-makers; the houses are freshly painted, nearly all of them have new doors; the window frames are synthetic; the lawns are impeccably mown and equipped with porch swings and ornamental plaster figures, some even with German garden gnomes; almost all the cars are current Western makes; the petrol stations are spotless and ultramodern.

And the barbecue equipment that's for sale at the petrol stations! No cheap stuff; strictly quality designs; prices from 100 euros upwards. Here too, then, people are frequent and enthusiastic meat eaters. I'm no economist, but Poland's landscapes certainly look more like they're flourishing than large parts of East Germany. And part of those landscapes are the blue signs that indicate funding from the European Union.

'The Poles know exactly what they have Europe to thank for,' says the journalist Igor Janka when I meet him that evening in Warsaw. I wrote to him because he had written a sympathetic, almost reverent biography of the Hungarian prime minister Viktor Orbán which was translated into German. I assumed he would be best able to explain to me what it is about the European Union that bothers so many Poles.

'Bothers?' Janka asks in his excellent English. 'If there were a referendum here, at least 70 per cent would vote to remain in the Union. At least.'

Nor is the PiS against Europe, by any means, Janka continues; it is mainly against Russia – unlike the FPÖ in Austria, the AfD in Germany or Le Pen in France, all of which are sympathetic to Putin; also unlike Viktor Orbán in Hungary, who would likewise push Europe eastwards. The Poles, Janka says, have not forgotten the NKVD's 'Polish Operation', one of the bloodiest chapters of the Stalinist purge: about 100,000 Poles were executed as alleged spies in the years 1937 and 1938 alone – of a total of 600,000 Poles in the Soviet Union.

'Is that the reason why Poland's right-wing populists are oriented neither towards the West nor the East?' I ask.

What the PiS advocates isn't right-wing populism, Janka corrects me. It's conservative, and, unlike the FPÖ, the AfD and Le Pen, it really is religious: against abortion and cultural diversity; for traditional marriage and devout Christianity. For his part, Janka says, he is against capital punishment but, if the majority wants to reintroduce the death penalty, making the subject taboo won't help. Poland doesn't consist only of cosmopolitan poets like Adam Zagajewski; in the countryside especially, hardly anyone even knows a foreigner. So they appreciate the prosperity that Europe has brought them, Janka continues, but in day-to-day life they don't see the positive aspects of diversity; instead they see the news of conflicts that diversity generates. Yes, that's provincial and backward, but, without this perseverance in its unique identity, Poland would not have survived the German occupation as a state, nor would its language and culture have endured. 'We're not against Europe,' Janka repeats, 'we're just allergic to being patronized; we have a reaction when someone talks to us condescendingly, especially someone who's German. We have this voice in our ears, even my generation, from films. And then when Martin Schulz talks! Honestly, I can't stand hearing Martin Schulz badmouth Poland, in that aggressive, preaching tone, with that stern face and those – watch him sometime – those protruding lips.'

I have a high regard for Martin Schulz, the president of the European Parliament, especially for the pugnacity, the passion with which he talks about Europe. But suddenly I imagine what he might look like getting worked up if I was Polish and didn't understand German.

And the garden gnomes? Andrzej Stasiuk is travelling abroad, so I can't visit him in his village; I am limited to carrying his books with me. 'We have always existed in the shadow of others,'[4] he writes in a passage I come across in my hotel, a passage that concisely explains both the garden gnomes and Poland's fear of Russia.

Poles lived in the shadow of Germans and Russians, Slovaks of Czechs and Hungarians, Hungarians in the shadow of Austrians and Turks, Ukrainians in that of Poles and Russians, and so on and on down to the paranoia of the Balkans and of Serbia, imagining sometimes that all other peoples on its borders are traitors denying their Serb nature.

My own country is scarcely any better. Poland would like to be at least as great and strong as America, so that Russia would finally be afraid of it. Sadly, it is not. Instead, my country travels to Germany to earn money, even though it was Germans who sent it up in smoke, turned it to ashes and murdered a large proportion of its population. And still my country goes to Germany to work. And what's more, as well as cash, it brings home German ideas about a better kind of life. Hence the notion that a lawn must be permanently well mown, displaying a range of plastic gnomes, clay dogs and miniature windmills. At present, Poland is Europe's leading producer of garden gnomes and exports them to Germany.

That sounds like gallows humour, but the surprising thing – people always talk about the unbelievable crimes of the twentieth century, but not about the equally unbelievable ethnic persistence of peoples – the surprising thing is that Poland still exists as a nation, as a culture, as a language community. Because after the Hitler–Stalin Pact and the occupation, the Soviets took action against everyone who belonged to Poland's elite to 'decapitate' the society. The NKVD, the Soviet Union's political secret police, decided who besides officers made up that elite by reading the Polish *Who's Who*. The same thing took place in the German-occupied part of the country, where Hitler wanted to make the Poles a malleable mass, to be enslaved, not governed: 'The leadership class we now have in Poland is to be liquidated.' Between September 1939 and June 1941, the Soviet Union and Germany in coordination murdered 200,000 more Polish citizens, most of them academics, officers, politicians, writers, musicians, artists. And that was before the actual war, the destruction of the cities, the Holocaust, the expulsion. 'We despise Russians for having developed our characteristics to monstrous, inhuman proportions. We despise Germans for not having any traits that we recognize as human, that is to say, as our own. Such – in simple terms – is the complex psychology situation of the descendants of Sarmatia in modern Europe.'[5]

Sixth Day: Warsaw

In the centre of Warsaw, on the widest boulevard, is a stele bearing the order given by Heinrich Himmler after the outbreak of the uprising in 1944: 'Warsaw shall be levelled to show Europe what it means to undertake a rebellion against the Germans.' Systematically and thoroughly, the German army destroyed one district after another, following Himmler's further orders to shoot all inhabitants, regardless of age and sex. In August and September 1944 alone, 150,000 civilians were killed in Warsaw. During the entire war, half of the pre-war population of about 1.3 million died. The rebuilding of the historic city centre, although practically not a single building had been left standing, was nothing but an act of self-affirmation, indeed of spite, and ultimately of triumph. In Stare Miasto, the 'old town' of Warsaw, none of the buildings is old. And every travel guide praises them the more highly for that. Other standing stones bear photos of fallen rebels.

I have never walked through a city with so many memorials. Just 200 yards from the martyrs of the war, another open-air exhibition shows Warsaw in the 1950s and 1960s, the modern buildings, the new vitality. Fifty yards further on – still on the same central boulevard – is the statue of a soldier from the Second World War. I follow the street and read on an ordinary signpost that the Monument to the Warsaw Uprising is 600 metres to the right, the Monument to the Heroes in the Ghetto 300 metres to the left, and the Monument to the Poles Fallen and Murdered in the East 500 metres straight on. Besides the memorials, only the National Library and the Chinese Embassy are indicated.

I choose the Warsaw Uprising Monument, which for all its monumentality captures fairly well the energy with which the irregulars burst forth from the destruction, their figures gaunt, their gaze resolute, though not hopeful. They knew they would face a superior force, and fought nonetheless for sixty-three days. An additional plaque near the monument mentions explicitly that the Red Army, which had by then advanced close to Warsaw, left the Poles in the lurch. It does not mention that the Warsaw Uprising critically delayed the liberation of Auschwitz, because the Russians were waiting for one enemy to subdue the other. For the other Allies too, although the heads of government were relatively well informed about its progress, the Holocaust was never a *casus belli*.

In the Museum of the Polish Resistance, a bomber hangs from the ceiling; it is dark, and the propellers shine in the blinking light, accompanied by the sound of explosions. It is hard to imagine aerial bombardments being projected in an endless loop on a cinema-sized screen in any museum in Dresden or Cologne. But in Warsaw, pain is omnipresent. At the same time, however, many memories are being junked at this moment: on the sixtieth anniversary of the bloody suppression of the 1956 protests against the Soviet-dominated Polish government, the National Memorials Institute announced that 220 Soviet monuments would be transported to Borne Sulinowo in the northwest of the country, where they would be stored in a park. The Russian foreign ministry compared the last such operation with the destruction of historic sites by the 'Islamic State'. The PiS in turn described the Russian–German pipeline project Nord Stream as a new edition of the Hitler–Stalin Pact.

New plaques have been erected at many war monuments in Poland, and at the Museum of the Polish Resistance, to commemorate the crash of the presidential aircraft in Smolensk on 10 April 2010. This places Lech Kaczyński and the other ninety-five government officials in the ranks of the national martyrs, the murdered elites, and in particular the 4,000 officers who were shot by the NKVD in Katyń, near Smolensk. At the same time, the new memorial plaques also suggest that the resistance against usurpation continues – the Kaczyńskis' father took part in the Warsaw Uprising – but that the enemies are now internal: according to the conspiracy theory, the Polish government of the time covered up the fact that Russia had shot down the aircraft. This is the logic at work when Jarosław Kaczyński, Lech's twin brother, calls his critics un-Polish and wages a personal campaign against the current president of the European Council, Donald Tusk, who was prime minister in 2010. To the opponents of the PiS, the plaques commemorating Smolensk are a monstrous provocation. The opposition points to the results of the official investigation which found that the crash was an accident, not an assassination. But, in Poland as everywhere else, the winners write their own history. 'The whole truth' is the promise of the film *Smolensk*, which has just opened in cinemas. The entire government attended the premiere; the Ministry of Education organizes screenings for school groups. 'We used to be kept ignorant of who committed the murders in Katyń; today we are afraid to ask what really happened in Smolensk,' says the film.

I visit a man who is currently on the side of the winners in Poland: Paweł Lisicki, editor in chief of the government-aligned magazine *Do Rzeczy*. Igor Janka recommended I look him up if I want to meet a real representative of the national-religious movement. When Lisicki took over as editor of a different publication a decade ago, he instructed his staff to search the Internet daily for negative news about the Germans. In his newest book, *Krew na naszych rękach?* ('Blood on our hands?'), he interprets the Second Vatican Council's decision to give up proselytizing the Jews as the beginning of a disastrous relativism that would cut Europe off from its roots.

Lisicki too speaks excellent English; he appears urbane, polite and smart, like an Internet company executive. Yet the first things he has to criticize about Europe today are a lack of respect for the Christian tradition, individualism, and secularism in general, which is 'going too far'. In Poland, religion is a real political factor, he says – admittedly less so in the cities, but in the countryside, 50 per cent of the people still go to Mass on Sunday – 50 per cent! The liberals, the intellectuals, the poets who profess a passion for Europe don't know this Poland; they are estranged from their own country. They have no sense of the fact that most people want to preserve their Polish and Catholic identity, and therefore reject immigration from other cultures.

'But you have the effects of nationalism,' I object, 'the quest for homogeneity, for a uniform identity – no country has suffered under it more than Poland.'

'On the contrary,' says Lisicki, 'without nationalism, positive nationalism, there would be no Poland today.'

I mustn't lump everything together, he says; nationalism per se is not necessarily aggressive. Well, I reply, I'm afraid I would call it aggressive when the leaders of the PiS rant that refugees and Muslims are urinating in the churches all over Europe. Ah! That's just political rhetoric; the other side does the same when they talk about totalitarianism and threaten to go underground; Lisicki tells me I'm just not used to the strident tone because the Germans, for historical reasons, force themselves to temper their words. The important thing is that no one here wants to redraw the borders, no one is being persecuted; free speech and personal liberty are the order of the day. The constitutional court that has Brussels worried at the moment, he continues, was already instrumentalized by the previous government, which appointed five judges at the last minute before the transition. The intellectuals are only nervous because they're afraid of losing their privileges. If Marine Le Pen became president of France, the French intellectuals would be nervous too – so what?

'But maybe there are reasons to be nervous,' I comment. 'The Muslims, at least, would surely see their fundamental rights curtailed under a President Le Pen. And maybe that would be just the beginning.'

'I reject any infringement of freedom of religion,' Lisicki insists. 'I only think the extremist mosques should be kept under observation, that's all. Fortunately, though, we have only very few Muslims in Poland so far.'

Among the intellectuals who are nervous about their privileges Lisicki would probably count Adam Michnik in particular, Poland's most famous intellectual: a dissident, a Solidarity advisor, and today the editor of Poland's largest newspaper, *Gazeta Wyborcza*. His namesake Adam Zagajewski has described how he first met Michnik in 1973, when, wary of the secret police with their snitches and bugs, people talked about politics only in quiet, carefully modulated voices, or with a hand over their mouth. But Michnik spoke out loud, unafraid, Zagajewski wrote; he made jokes, glowed with courage and love of life.

Adam was then, I think, one of the few happy people in Poland (and perhaps, in all of Eastern Europe). I don't mean the kind of private happiness that consists of finding a nice, pretty wife and an interesting, well-paid job, the happiness that comes from the consciousness that you are a healthy, decent, and useful individual. I have in mind the much rarer form of happiness that arises when you locate your true vocation with pinpoint precision, when you find the perfect outlet for your talents, not in the private, domestic sphere, but in the larger human polis.[6]

When I confess to Michnik at the beginning of our conversation how moved I am to be sitting face to face with him, having admired him on television in my youth, he replies drily that I have evidently learned my trade well.

'My trade?'

'Yes: you want to start your interview by flattering me.'

With his hair falling untamed across his forehead, the broad stripes of his polo shirt stretched across his stomach, four cigarettes plus a fresh pack stuffed into his shirt pocket, and keys hanging from two synthetic ribbons around his neck, Michnik doesn't look nearly as urbane as the editor in chief of a national-conservative newsweekly or Viktor Orbán's biographer. Nor does his office look aseptically modern: dangerously high stacks of unbound manuscripts, posters, photos, and just a few gaps between the books for guests to sit. Michnik doesn't speak English, but he does speak French – old school in this as in other respects – and his glasses are set in metal frames that he might have bought before Lech Wałęsa won the Nobel Prize. Whether he believes me or not, he was really a hero to me back then.

'Of course it's a problem for us that we no longer get any advertising from state businesses or from the public sector,' Michnik says in answer to my question about the new government curtailing privileges. In the first six months of the new government alone, the newspaper's advertising revenue dropped 21.5 per cent, he continues, while the weekly *Gazeta Polska* for example, which has ties to Jarosław Kaczyński's family, increased its advertising income by 300 per cent. In other words, every issue of it is funded with 40,000 euros out of the public coffers. The ministries of the PiS government and the courts have been explicitly prohibited from subscribing to *Gazeta Wyborcza*, which has responded by distributing enrolment forms for the 'Committee to Preserve Democracy'.

'The head of the moneyed press is also costing us a lot of energy and money by suing us because we exposed a case of corruption,' Michnik continues stoically, as if he were talking about a spell of bad weather. 'But, then, I am relieved to see that we are not completely irrelevant. Otherwise they wouldn't keep pounding us.'

What else Michnik has to say about the new government can be summarized for the most part as the opposite of everything Lisicki said: obviously the government suspends the rule of law, and it's ridiculous to compare earlier governments' judicial appointments with the current frontal attack on the supreme court. Ultimately, the same thing is at stake in Poland as in all the other countries over which 'the brown cloud is looming', including Turkey with Erdoğan and the United States with Trump: it's a matter of replacing a liberal democracy with an authoritarian (and, in Poland, a fundamentalist religious) nationalism in which elections are nothing but a farce.

'But doesn't that show that liberal democracy is at a crisis?' I ask. 'After all, the PiS won the parliamentary majority.'

'Liberal democracy has been in crisis throughout its existence,' Michnik replies; 'just think of the 1930s, Hitler, Mussolini. And yet democracy won then, and it will win again.'

'But at what price?'

'It won't get that bad in Poland. The Poles' democratic sense is too robust, and a government based on lies will not prevail. People will see through it.'

'But they've grown even more popular since the election.'

'Hitler and Mussolini were much more popular, and Stalin was as popular as anything. The PiS, I tell you, will lose again as early as the next elections.'

And in any case, Michnik continues with what seems like an unshakable optimism, we mustn't see just one side; we have to see not just Trump, but also Obama; not just Poland's Catholic Church, but also Pope Francis; not just Brexit, but also London's Muslim mayor, Sadiq Khan. Worldwide, the signals are by no means only negative, and Poland in particular has developed remarkably well in recent years; there's been a positive leap forward, in economic terms naturally, but also in terms of civilization. Of course the PiS play on fear, but it is by no means certain that they'll win the game. Poland used to have anti-Semitism without Jews, and today it has Islamophobia without Islam, a refugee crisis without refugees; there's nothing new about it. And the religious fervour is not nearly as strong any more as the right wing claims; in the cities especially, the churches are emptier all the time, and the majority in Poland, as in Catholic Spain, votes for liberal abortion rights.

I ask Michnik whether he understands what Igor Janka said to me about the feeling of being patronized and the rhetoric of Martin Schulz.

'Of course there is a memory of the occupation; of course we hear the German language in our minds. But to associate that with the Germany of today, the Germany that makes the case for Europe, the Germany that opens its door to refugees, is complete nonsense. Martin Schulz, honestly! But you know fools are born every minute, all over the world.'

The nationalists, Michnik continues, instrumentalize the past to fend off accusations from Berlin and Brussels. But isn't it understandable, I persist, in view of Poland's history, that people are afraid of foreign rule? No, Michnik replies: all the countries in this region have the same victimhood complex; in every country everything is always Germany's fault. 'We Poles don't like to be reminded of the crimes against the Lithuanians, the Ukrainians, the Jews, and most of all we dislike any mention of the crimes against the Germans. The expulsion may have been unavoidable in the special situation of the time, yes. But it was definitely barbaric.'

'You would call the expulsion of Germans after the war barbaric?'

'What else?'

'If anyone in Germany said that, there would be an outcry.'

'That's why I have to say it, as a Pole whose relatives died in the Holocaust: the expulsion of the Germans was barbaric.'

'And that doesn't provoke an outcry in Poland?'

'Only a little one,' Adam Michnik laughs, picking up a cartoon that's lying on his desk, one that just came in today, but of a kind that appears every day: it shows him raping Polish children. 'People have always tried to pressure me to emigrate to Israel. The communists couldn't do it, and the nationalists today certainly won't be able to do it.'

I ask Michnik what Willy Brandt's kneeling in Warsaw means to him: whether it changed his relation to Germany.

'Yes, that was something great,' he says, 'his kneeling for one thing, but also the recognition of the Oder–Neisse border. Those were very crucial milestones. And yet the criticism of his Social Democratic Party's *Ostpolitik* was also justified.'

'How so?'

'Of course it was necessary to talk to the communist elites. Perhaps the treaties also had to be signed. But they should also have talked to the opposition. At least talked to them. Instead, the SPD stood radically aloof from us civil rights activists. That's how we felt then. There was not only Brandt's refusal to meet with Lech Wałęsa during his visit to Poland in 1985. As early as 1977, there was supposed to be a meeting with me in Germany, and Brandt cancelled that too.'

'And did you meet him later?'

'Yes, I met Brandt in 1989 at a meeting in Hamburg which was also attended by his successor as chancellor, Helmut Schmidt, and by the West German president Richard von Weizsäcker.'

'And?'

'I expressed my gratitude for his kneeling at the Ghetto memorial.'

'And you didn't mention that you had been disappointed in him?'

'Why should I have said that? Just to score a point? By the time we met, I was already the winner. Criticizing him would have been malicious, as far as I'm concerned.'

Seventh Day: Warsaw

In an unassuming brick church on the south side of Warsaw, I am welcomed by the priest Adam Boniecki, who publishes a liberal Catholic magazine, although he personally is no longer allowed to give interviews because of his critical remarks on the Church. He comes across as anything but rebellious, though: an older gentleman who walks carefully with a stick and chooses his words more carefully still. 'As long as you don't publish our talk in the form of an interview, I am abiding by my prohibition,' Boniecki explains with a mischievous smile.

For the Poles, he says, the Church has always been a space of freedom, independent of the state. Moreover, when there was no Poland, it was Catholicism that defined the Poles, distinguished them from the Protestant Prussians and the Orthodox Russians, and preserved the Polish language. But today, many people have the impression that the Church is allied with the government, no longer autonomous, and in that way is undermining its own authority. The younger Catholics in particular, Boniecki continues, increasingly join lay congregations, because the priests have nothing more to say, in their preaching tone, that doesn't admit of questions, doubts. If the Polish Church distinguishes itself primarily by wanting to ban abortion, assisted reproductive methods and contraception, without turning its attention to the society's real problems, then sooner or later it will lose the people. Certainly, there are priests here and there who take the side of refugees, but there has not been a single statement by a bishop or a cardinal questioning the government's refugee policy. All they ever say, to avoid displeasing either the government or the pope, is that we need to do everything within our means to help. 'Isn't it shameful when a church can't unequivocally profess the Christian message?'

Naturally many Poles are afraid of terrorism, Islam, the refugees; the news from Germany is not always very encouraging; everyone is thinking of the New Year's Eve assaults in Cologne. But, in that case, it is the Church's job to promote understanding, allay fears and talk about precisely those topics that the people are worried about. In fact, many of the faithful, and especially younger people, have more comprehension for Pope Francis than for their own Polish Church, says Father Boniecki, and then he tells me a joke: the pope likes to use public transport to get to his appointments; when the Polish Church resolved to follow his example, each bishop bought his own bus.

I ask about Father Boniecki's magazine. He is still allowed to publish it, after all. Yes, Boniecki answers, and it is widely read too, even in the upper echelons of the hierarchy, as he can tell from the reactions. But, at the same time, the Church ensures that the magazine is not displayed for reading in the parishes.

'Isn't that frustrating?' I ask.

'To me, the important thing is not to get depressed but to do as much as I can. Ultimately everything is in God's hands anyway.'

As we walk to the car park, the interpreter, an altogether modern-looking young woman whom I have just met at this appointment, bursts out with the declaration that she is actually very religious and a Catholic, but for years she has gone to church only at Christmas because so few priests are like Adam Boniecki.

'Do you mean they don't share his opinions?'

'No, mostly I mean his doubts,' the interpreter answers. 'That he accepts them, and in doing so accepts ours too.'

My family is visiting over the weekend, and before we take off for the Masurian lake district, Michael Leiserowitz guides us through the new Museum of the History of Polish Jews, which illustrates the past through playful activities for children as well as adults – through didactics rather than empathy. I realize once again how little I know about the life of the European Jews before the Holocaust – but I am not the only one, says Leiserowitz, himself a German Jew who guides groups visiting Poland; for many Jews, too, the history of their people starts with their persecution. And yet Jewish life, in Poland especially, was diverse, and sometimes materially affluent by the way – in fact, before modern anti-Semitism, Poland was something like the America of Europe. Having escaped discrimination during the Spanish Reconquista and in the German-speaking countries, the Jews had found a safe home in Eastern Europe for many centuries – history must remember this too, Leiserowitz says, not just persecution and death.

I tell Leiserowitz about the young people I talked to in Auschwitz. Although he has devoted his life to teaching Jewish history, Leiserowitz has mixed feelings about the eight-day tour of the historic sites of genocide that most Israelis take near the end of their school years. After all, finishing school also means that these young people are about to start their military service: what does that do to Israel?

'I as a Jew never had the strength to go to Auschwitz until I was fifty. In hindsight, I'm glad it wasn't earlier.' Of course it's important, he says, to cultivate a Jewish and an Israeli identity. But perhaps it's not healthy for it to be based exclusively on the Holocaust. Although they have built such a fantastic museum of Jewish history in Eastern Europe – Europe's Museum of the Year 2016, as Leiserowitz proudly remarks – some of the youth tour organizers can't be persuaded to include it in their itinerary. 'Many Israelis don't find out anything about the successful history, a history of exchange, a history in which Jewish life flourished in Eastern Europe.'

We leave the museum and walk the few steps across the square to the Memorial to the Warsaw Ghetto Uprising. Where was the swing ride that the eyewitness and later Nobel Prize winner Czesław Miłosz wrote about in his most famous poem? Throughout the rebellion, it ran just outside the ghetto wall, and became a symbol of the Jews' abandonment:

At times wind from the burning
would drift dark kites along
and riders on the carousel
caught petals in midair.
That same hot wind
blew open the skirts of the girls
and the crowds were laughing
on that beautiful Warsaw Sunday.[7]

And where was the concentration camp to which, after the uprising had been defeated, the SS transferred prisoners from Auschwitz who were assigned to burn down the last buildings, salvage the valuables of the dead Jews, and burn the bodies of the Varsovians executed in the ruins of the ghetto? The conditions in that camp were so bad that some prisoners asked to be sent back to Auschwitz and gassed. Perhaps because almost nothing of the surroundings is visible in the photos of Brandt's genuflection – only the square with soldiers and officials in the background – I had always imagined that there must still be a ghetto there, something from that time. But of course there is not a single historic building, not even a wall; I should have known that. 'The previously existing living quarters for 500,000 subhumans, absolutely unsuitable for habitation by Germans, must disappear from the scene,' states another of Himmler's orders, issued eighteen months before the order to level the rest of the city. The square is surrounded only by postwar prefab blocks. That makes the memorial all the more important, because there is hardly any other trace of the Jews who once felt themselves abandoned by the world, and probably by God too. 'Before the abyss of German history, and under the weight of the millions murdered, I did what people do when words fail,' Willy Brandt said in explanation of his act.

Leiserowitz leads me behind the museum to a brick monument which bears a bronze plaque commemorating Brandt's 1970 visit – a rarity: a monument to a gesture at a monument. And there we stand, a Jew and a son of immigrants, and, for both of us, Brandt's kneeling in Warsaw is the incisive image of our West German socialization. Paweł Lisicki would probably not think it healthy to take a confession of guilt as the foundation of a national identity. But would he, the nationalist, think a nationalist Germany healthy?

Eighth Day: From Warsaw to Masuria

I don't need to describe the country that used to be East Prussia or the Masurian lake district. It is exactly as I have seen it described so often in German literature, most prominently in Günter Grass or Siegfried Lenz: rolling hills, wide fields of grain, apple orchards, and between them lakes whose shores are mostly overgrown, a village here and there, isolated farmhouses. Strange to be driving through a landscape I feel I know well but am seeing for the first time. Of course it was barbaric – what else? – to drive out a whole population, men, women, old people, children. We heard little in school, read little in the postwar literature about the circumstances of the expulsion. How exactly did it take place? Did a government employee come to the house, or a soldier or a neighbour, and give the family a month, a week, a day to pack up their belongings? How many belongings? Were there cars, trucks? Or could the people take only what they were able to carry? Did anyone have a hand free to lead the children out of the house? Did the children have a hand free? What explanation were they given? What thoughts may have gone through their minds? How deep was the shock that stuck in their souls?

I am sure it is all written down somewhere, in books, biographies, published diaries. Nevertheless, it is no doubt typical that someone like me who has no relatives from the East has hardly ever wondered about all these questions. In school there would have been at most an embarrassed mention of the territories that used to be German. We learned about the reasons for the expulsion but never talked about the pain of the people expelled. The expellees themselves only rarely gave voice to their pain – or perhaps not rarely, but they went largely unheard. We thought Siegfried Lenz was a restitutionist because he wrote about East Prussia. We schoolchildren, at

33

any rate, we readers of the postwar literature, heard practically nothing about the screams, the fears, the neighbours' taunts, the rapes of practically all the women, the privations on the march, the calluses on the feet and hands, the dead who were buried by the wayside. It cannot be healthy when a society is not allowed to express its pain. 'But we've got to go back,' says a character in Siegfried Lenz's novel *The Heritage*:

> 'But we've got to go back, Zygmunt, we've got to, because everything's there waiting for us: the trees and the lakes and Castle Hill and the fields, and the old river with the log floats.'
> 'No, Simon,' I replied, 'nothing's waiting for us there any more. The people who could have waited for us are gone, lost and gone, and that's why the moment you're waiting for will never come.'[8]

No doubt the German Expellees' Association did not always find the right words to express it delicately. But as we travel by car through East Prussia, getting out to walk along country lanes, swim in lakes, take a boat ride with a couple of sailors, check into a hotel with a German passport, I realize that the rest of society, not least we who considered ourselves somehow left of centre, wouldn't have listened anyway. Naturally there could not have been and cannot be any question of redrawing borders. Before Masuria was Polonized, it had been Germanized: colonially in the nineteenth century, and violently during the Nazi period. As everywhere in the world, something had gone before. As everywhere in the world where nationalism has displaced people or torn them apart, what is needed is to make borders irrelevant. Europe, not revisionism, has made it possible to speak German again in East Prussia, if only temporarily, in the restaurants and hotels. And Zygmunt and Simon, if they are still alive, can come back to Masuria at least to visit.

We stop near Mikołajki, formerly Nikolaiken, to see what's going on in a village church on a Sunday. Who was right: Paweł Lisicki, who said the rural population in particular is deeply religious, or Adam Michnik, who said the progress of secularism in Poland is inexorable? Well, so many of the faithful have trooped to the little town's church, young, old, children, that there is not even standing room for all of them, and the Mass is being broadcast through loudspeakers outside. No printed sheets are needed for the songs; everyone knows them by heart and sings along. And, to top it off, I learn that four masses are celebrated every Sunday – four! – and the church is just as full for each of them. And two masses are said every weekday, with the pews packed fuller than in German churches at Christmas. The idea that Western culture is Christian sounds different in Mikołajki, less outlandish, than in Dresden or Berlin.

Ninth Day: Kaunas

Ah, so this is where the Neman is, the river mentioned as the Memel in the first verse of the German national anthem to denote the eastern end of German lands – one of the verses, written in 1841, that no one sings any more. Of course I vaguely knew it was here, or I would have remembered it if I had thought for a moment. But when our guide casually mentions the name of the river we are following in Kaunas – a wide, powerful stream – I am nonetheless perplexed. I suddenly realize the river really exists – as if it could have been any other way. It flows through Lithuania, so far away from Germany.

Kaunas is a very idiosyncratic city, like a movie set. A uniform ensemble built between the wars to serve as the provisional capital of the new state of Lithuania – since Vilnius still belonged to Poland – its centre radiates a modernism that belongs in a museum today: lots of Bauhaus, Soviet architecture filling the gaps, and a three-kilometre pedestrian zone tracing a straight line through the city. We go into a doughnut shop where the whole interior, down to the loud polyester aprons, looks like an original relic of 'actually existing socialism', the sales clerks' blonde perms, bad tempers and girth all faithful to the period. The shop is full to bursting in spite of that – or perhaps because of it? Apart from this shop, numerous cafés, the usual fashion chains, plenty of young people because of the major university, and a memorial plaque to a Japanese consul, Chiune Sugihara, who helped several thousand Jews flee Lithuania. Emmanuel Levinas was born in Kaunas, but luckily – for him and for twentieth-century philosophy – he emigrated to France as early as the 1920s.

The churches in Kaunas are still not all repaired and hence look as though they are from another era, as if enchanted; in Soviet times, they were used as warehouses or for drying parachutes; the cathedral was a radio factory. To a German they look outwardly Protestant because they are made of brick like those in Lower Saxony or Schleswig-Holstein; inside, however, they are neo-baroque and full of frescoes. Two play corners have been set up for children, cheap plastic cityscape rugs rolled out exactly like the ones our Matchbox cars used to drive on. For children to play during Mass is probably unimaginable in Lower Saxony or Schleswig-Holstein; it is rather an indication of an older concept of religious practice, one not based on empathy and edification but more like those still found today in the orthodoxies of Christianity, Islam and Judaism. The example that made the deepest impression on me was the rabbis I saw at the Wailing Wall talking on the telephone while simultaneously reciting the Torah.

When we find the orthodox synagogue closed, we call the chairman of the congregation at the number printed on a notice. Until the German occupation, a third of the Lithuanian population was Jewish. Today there are only two active synagogues left in all Lithuania, one for the Orthodox and one for the Reform congregation, and the two are said to be on worse terms than the Jewish congregations in Berlin. Moses Beirak, the chairman of the congregation, comes to meet us, and when he hears that I speak German he switches to Yiddish, which almost brings tears to my eyes: it is the first time I have heard it as a living language. And, yes, between German and Yiddish we can communicate to some extent.

Beirak tells us he is a watchmaker, born in 1953. His father was the only one of eleven siblings to survive the Holocaust, his mother the only one of nine. Their parents rarely spoke of their experience in the concentration camps; in another five generations it will still be difficult to talk about it. But naturally he has often thought about what might have been going on in their minds when they returned to Kaunas, instead of emigrating to Israel or the United States like the other survivors. Actually, relations between ethnic Lithuanians and Jews were good, his father always said. Makabi, the Jewish football club in Kaunas in which Beirak's father played, had three Lithuanians on the team, and no one thought anything of it. But then those three, their own teammates, had stood by with white armbands when the Beiraks were carted off to the concentration camps. 'Why did my parents return? If they had been communists, all right, but they were adamantly anti-Soviet. Today everyone is anti-communist, but in those days it was dangerous, and my parents were persecuted for it. And yet they stayed. Why, I don't know. But I never want to leave here either.'

People who live in Germany, travel through Germany, immigrate to Germany, can hardly comprehend the proportions of the genocide perpetrated against the Jews. In Germany, the Jews were a tiny minority, one per cent of the population when Hitler became chancellor of the Reich, a quarter of one per cent at the outbreak of the Second World War. And the few Jews who lived there were hardly visible, did not wear black coats or long beards, did not speak Yiddish, and, in their customs, habits and opinions, many of them were particularly loyal, indeed decidedly patriotic Germans, the finest connoisseurs and the best exponents of German culture. Furthermore, in the first six years of Nazi rule, the German Jews were allowed to emigrate, although they were humiliated and robbed in the process. Few Germans live in houses that Jews lived in, walk through streets in which every shop and every business had a Jewish owner, see a former Jewish quarter on their city map, remember the sound of the old people's Yiddish. The golden 'stumbling blocks' that are now set in the pavement here and there to commemorate the victims in front of the buildings they lived in reinforce the impression, at least in naive, childish, ignorant or malicious minds, that there weren't that many after all. No, there weren't: 165,000 Jewish victims, among almost 80 million Germans, are not 'many', when at least 30,000 Jews were murdered in Kaunas alone – out of not even 100,000 inhabitants. But the young West German republic's westward orientation, forward-looking as it was, erased the Holocaust from its topographical consciousness. The preponderance of the genocide against the Jews had taken place in the East, where you didn't look if you were growing up in the German West. As an adolescent in Germany you learn the numbers, of course. But it is something else again when you encounter the ghosts of the people murdered at every step. If there were 'stumbling blocks' in the asphalt in Kaunas, or in Minsk, Lviv, Odessa, Brest, Riga, they would not be isolated paving stones – half the city would be paved with gold, like the New Jerusalem.

We drive to the Park of Peace, where the religions of Kaunas are peacefully united and Judaism is not so conspicuously absent: not only the Catholics, the Orthodox and the Lutherans have their churches, but the Tatars too have a very beautiful little white mosque, built in 1930. As we enter it, we hear women's voices from the gallery. A young woman with a headscarf comes down the narrow staircase and explains to us that the Arabic class is in progress. Today there are still 300 Muslims in Kaunas, including some students from Asia. Yes, Islamophobia has been increasing in Lithuania, but she herself has not yet been directly affected by it. Her biggest problem is the imam, who was sent from Turkey and, sadly, speaks only Turkish. None of the Muslims understand his sermons.

Tenth Day: Vilnius and Vicinity

For a long time Vilnius has been at the edge: at the edge of the Russian Empire, at the edge of Poland, later at the edge of the Soviet Union, now at the edge of the European Union. Outwardly at least, that has been marvellously good for the city: grandiose baroque and nineteenth-century architecture, not yet renovated into a theme park; idyllic courtyards, old trees, parks, a wide river; quiet, almost secluded streets right in the city centre, peaceful churches, good restaurants, lots of retail; a Europe in which time would seem here and there to stand still if the people weren't dressed in the latest styles. Of course, this is only the outsider's view. Just as no German is spoken in the formerly German Breslau, Polish has disappeared from Vilnius – once the heart of the Polish national Romanticism personified by Adam Mickiewicz and the home of the Polish Nobel laureate in literature Czesław Miłosz. And, in the city once called the 'Jerusalem of the East', Jewish culture has been extinguished. As in so many cities of Eastern Europe, life in Vilnius came to an end and yet goes on. The city is the northernmost link of a chain of baroque Central European cities – Lviv, Czernowitz, Bratislava, Ljubljana, Trieste, and so on – that were multilingual, multiconfessional and cosmopolitan.

The 1914 assassination of Archduke Franz Ferdinand in Sarajevo, the southernmost link of the chain, marked the beginning of the brutal clarification, which continued through the Balkan wars, that people no longer live in parallel societies, switch between languages, or have several nationalities at the same time. Of those cases which the age of extremes trimmed down to today's homogeneity, Vilnius was one of the most complicated. Lviv and Riga were each claimed by only two ethnicities for their new nations: Lviv by Poles and Ukrainians, Riga by Latvians and Germans. But Vilnius was considered the natural capital of a nation-state not only by Poles and Lithuanians but also by Belarusians. Immediately before the First World War, Vilnius had thirty-five Polish newspapers, twenty Lithuanian ones, seven in Russian, five in Yiddish and two in Belarusian. And some newspapers appeared in several languages. In the course of the twentieth century, Vilnius passed from hand to hand no fewer than thirteen times.

In the covered market, I am amazed at the origins of the fruit for sale: much from Lithuania, of course, but after that, it comes mainly from such countries as Moldova, Armenia, Georgia, Abkhazia, Azerbaijan, Ukraine – the continent of Europe is much larger when seen from Vilnius. Only the bread is still as dark, nourishing and delicious as the bread I know and love from Germany. Czesław Miłosz writes that the most metropolitan street in the Vilnius of his childhood was ulica Niemiecka, 'German Street', so called because only Jews lived there.

The little city museum is showing an exhibition about the 23rd of August

1989. Does that ring a bell? And if I add the 'Baltic Way': still no recollection? Don't worry – my own memory is jogged awake only when I see the photos of the human chain from Tallinn via Riga to Vilnius, 595 kilometres through three countries, on the fiftieth anniversary of the Hitler–Stalin Pact, 2 million people singing, hand in hand, for their freedom. They are powerful, uplifting images, an astounding demonstration of what nations can achieve, without violence, when they stand together in brotherhood. The western part of the continent has already forgotten the courage, the desperation and the sacrifice with which the East fought for its affiliation with Europe – not just in 1989 in the Baltic, or against the Securitate in Romania, but in 1953 in East Berlin, 1956 in Budapest, 1967 in Prague, 1981 in Gdansk, and most recently in Maidan Square in Kiev. The Soviet general who refused to fire on the unarmed demonstrators, Dzhokhar Dudayev – many streets are named after him in the Baltic states – was later elected president of Chechnya and killed by a Russian drone in 1996.

We have lunch in a Russian restaurant with Soviet decor as authentic as that in the doughnut shop in Kaunas. Originally a jazz café and an intellectual hangout, the restaurant was the favourite meeting-place of functionaries before the collapse of communism. Today, the stroganoff and the vodka are ordered mainly by tourists, diplomats and business travellers – by *Wessis*, as they would say in East Germany, who patronizingly taste the local foods like conquerors after their victory.

For the rest of the day, we drive out of Vilnius to see something of rural Lithuania. Again and again, the books and newspaper articles I read in preparation mentioned the fabulous Lithuanian forests. 'Wilno, city like a wolf that broods / 'Mid bears and boars and bison in the woods,' wrote Mickiewicz in his great epic poem *Pan Tadeusz*.[9] But a large part of the forests had already been cut down when Mickiewicz was alive. The twentieth century did for the rest of them, not least because the alternating occupation forces during the two world wars systematically burnt down forests to drive out insurgents and partisans. Today, Lithuania is a country of fields and pastures: gently rolling hills, few cars, hardly any people in the villages, many windows shuttered in the middle of the day, lakes that look completely untouched; the few grocery shops have no display windows but barred fanlights and brown steel doors from the Soviet period. When I sigh how idyllic the landscape is, our driver interjects, 'The suicide rate here is the highest in Europe, and alcoholism is the number one national disease.' If we were to drive two, three hours further, the landscape would be deserted, he adds; the region around

Vilnius is at least inhabited by commuters. Not integration, but emigration poses a major problem for Lithuania: according to official statistics, 700,000 Lithuanians have left the country since independence; the unofficial figure is significantly higher and includes mostly young people, from a population of not even 3 million. Yet, historically, Lithuania has always been a country of immigrants. As early as the thirteenth and fourteenth centuries, tens of thousands from other Baltic countries fled before the crusaders to Lithuania, which was still safe. When the Grand Duchy of Lithuania expanded as far as the shores of the Black Sea, many more immigrants were brought into the country from the conquered territories and from the west: Ruthenians, Tatars, Jews and Germans. In the seventeenth and eighteenth centuries, thousands of Russian Old Believers, fearing for their lives after the schism of the Russian Orthodox Church, fled to Lithuania. And between the two world wars Lithuania again offered shelter to many Russians who had fled the Bolsheviks. We make a stop in Trakai, inhabited almost exclusively by Karaites, one of the oldest of all Jewish sects. They broke with rabbinic Judaism in the sixth century before Christ because they believed that the word of God is found in scripture, and considered the additions of the Talmud sinful. Driven out of Egypt and Palestine during the first crusade, the Karaites settled in Crimea in the twelfth century. From there, some of them wandered further to Northeastern Europe. During the Second World War, the racial bureaucrats in Berlin decided that the Karaites should not be subject to the 'final solution' because they were not racially Jews but descendants of Khazar converts to Judaism. That was nonsense, but it saved many Karaites from death, and was one of the more absurd twists of the Nazi delusion: because the Karaites wanted to be more purely and originally Jewish than other Jews, the Nazis considered them not genuine Jews, but lukewarm converts. Jewish scholars in the ghettos of Warsaw, Vilnius and Lviv, when asked by the German occupying forces, corroborated the myth in order to save their brothers although they had no way to save themselves. Today Trakai is a picturesque little town between two lakes, its terraces and streets populated mainly by day trippers from Vilnius. I meet Karaites in traditional costume only in the souvenir shops offering handicrafts and culinary specialities. The community seems to do a good business with the tourists; the wooden houses with their window boxes look prosperous in any case. The Karaites probably change into their jeans when the shops close. Somewhere I read that, of the 300 Karaites left in Lithuania, three work in the diplomatic corps: not a bad ratio.

We ask a young nun in a white habit walking along the country road if we can give her a lift. To our surprise, she speaks a strongly American English and is more dazzlingly cheerful than any person from the Old World could ever be. 'It's really cool,' she rejoices through her chin-high wimple in every third sentence – this Lithuania: 'really cool'; her convent of the Order of St John: 'really cool'; the sisters, three of whom are as young as she is: 'really cool; oh, my God, we have *so* much fun!' And, no, we don't need to give her a lift, 'thank you *so* much,' she's just taking a walk, the solitary lanes, the fresh air, 'you know, it's really cool.'

In one of the silent, virtually deserted villages, we stop by a big, circular church with most of the paint peeled off its white façade, its door chained with a rusty padlock. Does anyone still pray here? The rectory looks deserted, at any rate; even at this daylight hour, all the windows are shuttered. Our driver goes to see if he can find anyone who can give us information. He returns with a very small, grey-haired man wearing a thick green-and-purple checked shirt, equally heavy trousers, dirty from work, with a belt buckled above his navel, gold teeth in his mouth, blue plastic clogs without socks on his feet. Unfortunately, he doesn't speak Lithuanian any more than the American nun. This is a Polish village, I discover, since my guide is able to communicate with the man, more or less, in a mixture of Polish and Russian. His name is Michał; he was born in 1939 and grew up in the Soviet Union. When Lithuania became independent, he was too old to learn a third language. 'Isn't it odd,' I ask, 'to live in a state whose language you don't understand?'

'Yes, well, the children learn it, and we old folks just go on speaking Russian together. We're all simple people here, you know – Lithuanians or Poles, it's all the same to us. The politicians say there's a difference; we don't.'

I ask whether his home country is Poland or Lithuania.

'It used to be Poland, now it's Lithuania, and in between it was the Soviet Union.' Then Michał laughs, as if there were no difference except to the politicians.

'And when has it been better,' I ask, 'now, or under communism?'

'Now,' Michał replies without hesitation. 'Now you can buy everything.'

Finding work has become more difficult, however. He and his wife have been drawing their pension for years now, earning a few additional cents here and there, growing fruit and vegetables in their garden – that's enough to get by on. The young people, though … well, most of them have gone away.

41

'And what do you think of the European Union?' My guide gives me a look to express his doubts about Michał's expertise in foreign policy.

'Yes, well, the EU finances my pension of course; that's good anyway,' he answers after some hesitation. 'But, as I say, it's not creating any jobs here.'

'And Europe in general – what does Europe mean to you? Does Europe mean anything at all, besides your pension?'

'Europe means that the drunks stumble through the village in broad daylight and there's no one to punish them. That's what Europe means. You know, under communism there was more discipline. That's why the alcohol problem wasn't as bad. Back then, if you didn't show up at work because you were drunk, the police came round. Today, the police don't come, and the people have no work to go to either.'

Eleventh Day: Via Paneriai to Minsk

This is one of the places where the Holocaust, the so-called Final Solution, began: here in this parcel of forest near the suburb Paneriai, whose population was half Jewish, ten kilometres from central Vilnius. The Soviets had dug huge pits between the pines, 60, 70 metres across, to store heating oil. Then, on 22 June 1941, the German Army arrived. Truckload after truckload, the Jews were rounded up by the SS and the Lithuanian volunteer units, led or driven through the woods, and shot on the edges of the pits. The number of people buried in the pits grew over the next three years to more than 100,000, including not only Jews but also political prisoners and Soviet prisoners of war. Because it often happened that victims broke out of their groups or jumped from the trucks, the forest was the scene of monstrous manhunts which could not be hidden from the inhabitants. This was not a concentration camp with a gas chamber and a crematorium: the mass murder did not become industrial until late 1941. Paneriai was its comparatively disorganized beginning.

Auschwitz became synonymous with the Holocaust only because it was not just a death factory but also a labour camp at the same time: 100,000 Auschwitz prisoners survived. In Treblinka, where 700,000 Polish Jews were gassed, there were only fifty survivors. There were still fewer witnesses of Paneriai. And this site is representative of dozens, hundreds more, where the victims were not first registered, inspected by physicians, housed and enslaved, but were murdered on the spot. Some of these places are still unknown; we know they must exist, but the bones have never been found; in

42

some cases, they have not been searched for. Other mass graves have been discovered by chance but then forgotten again.

The pines in this wood stand unusually far apart, so that the view of the sky is hardly obscured. The ground, crossed by occasional trails, is soft. It is known that, before their retreat, the Germans forced Jewish prisoners to dig open the pits and burn the bodies. For the sake of German orderliness, the prisoners also had to count the bodies, one tally mark after another. Although literally nothing is left of the murder victims except their number, you grow dizzy with every step, almost as if you were sinking into the ground. The background noise we hear from the nearby motorway would not sound so eerie in any other place; aside from that, complete silence; not even birds twittering. But, most of all, we meet no other people. Although Paneriai was one of the first major sites of the Holocaust, we are the only visitors on an ordinary morning.

A young man emerges from the tiny museum, lanky, early or mid-twenties at most, blond pageboy hair, an unusually innocent face. He studied local history and now does volunteer service at the memorial. In school, Paneriai was not even mentioned, he reports; they dealt with the Holocaust only in connection with Auschwitz, without learning that many Lithuanians had been involved in the murders. Just this year, though, a change has occurred: as if all at once, memorial events for the murdered Jews took place all over Lithuania; the subject is being avidly discussed in Internet forums. But there are no school groups coming to Paneriai yet; few Lithuanians of any age for that matter – most visitors are from abroad, many of them from Israel.

'Are they descendants?'

'No, I don't think so. There are practically no descendants.'

Nowhere did a greater proportion of Jews die in the Holocaust than in Lithuania: 95 per cent. The country remembers only hesitantly its joyful reception of the German troops, unwillingly the numerous collaborators, only recently the execution sites which existed in practically every city, the blind eye that neighbours turned in Vilnius, although the Jews were transported out of the ghetto in broad daylight on open truck beds, the constant rifle salvos in the forest, the cries for help, the barking dogs heard in the village, the smell, said to have been unbearable, the tonnes of clothes that the farmers sold cheap at the edge of the forest. The portable toilet standing between two pine trees is an indication that crowds are not anticipated any time soon in Paneriai.

There are far more visitors in the KGB museum in Vilnius, which displays

43

the office's original furnishings, down to the paperweights, the heavy black telephones and the wiretapping equipment. The fact that the German Army met with little resistance in 1941 has to do with what went before: the invasion by the Soviet Union in 1940. That regime was so brutal that any other occupation had to seem at first like a liberation. The NKVD's agenda, of which 'only' 25 per cent had been carried out at the time of Hitler's invasion of the Soviet Union, called for the deportation or execution of one in seven Lithuanians. That is why I hear again and again, as if in excuse, that there were two genocides, one against the Jews and one against the Lithuanians themselves (as if the Jews had not been Lithuanians and no Lithuanian had been a perpetrator). This interpretation is apparently documented by numbers on a wall chart showing, side by side, the numbers of victims of deportation, forced labour, and murder during the German and the Soviet occupations. When will the haggling stop? The former KGB headquarters is terrifying enough without the comparison: the cells that are too small to sit down in; the round stool, 12 inches in diameter, in the water basin, on which prisoners had to balance for hours, probably days; the special interrogation rooms for the ill, the wounded, the starved brought in on stretchers; the execution chambers in the basement, the bare stone full of bullet holes. 'A single occupation can fracture a society for generations; double occupation is even more painful and divisive,' writes Timothy Snyder in his book on the *Bloodlands*, which has become almost a sort of travel guide on my trip. 'When foreign troops left, people had to reckon not with peace, but with the policies of the next occupier. They had to deal with the consequences of their own previous commitments under one occupier when the next one came; or make choices under one occupation while anticipating another.'[10]

Projected on a screen in rapid sequence are the photos taken by the KGB: men and women of all ages, intellectuals, simple people, priests too, each person full face and in profile. Most of those arrested are visibly making an effort not to betray their fright, their desperation, their anxiety: the blankness of their gaze is the last possible expression of their pride. Some even smile slightly in scorn. No way to dismiss the thought: a state that needed such a repressive machinery absolutely deserved its demise. The next thought: is there not something similar in Guantánamo, run by the leading country of Western civilization? Finally: when such a state falls, well and good – but what if the torture chambers do not become museum exhibits, if no one honours the victims and prosecutes, or at least ostracizes, the perpetrators?

At the train station I get the last ticket to Minsk. In the carriage, I understand why the Lithuanian railway sells the seats in this row only after the folding seats in the corridor are taken. All the rows are close-set, but in this one there is also an electric junction box under our feet, so that my neighbour and I travel to Belarus with our knees pulled up. At least my legs are shorter than his. When I offer him my aisle seat, I make my first Belarusian friend. In the trains of the Belarusian railway, he says, if I understand his English correctly, you're not squeezed in like sardines in a tin, but in Lithuania everything is privatized.

'The railway too?' I ask.

'No idea,' he answers, 'but in any case it's only profit that matters.'

For the passport check at the border – the first since I left Cologne – six female customs officers enter the carriage, smart jackets, tight skirts, snappy caps, their hair up, their eyes of a uniform inscrutability. They carry little desks strapped in front of their stomachs with a computer, rubber stamps and a magnifying glass to inspect the visas. For many centuries, the entire territory down to the Caucasus, the web of cultures, languages and religions, was a single state, the Grand Duchy of Lithuania, whose successors Belarusian nationalists claim to be, and today I need a visa to travel the 170 kilometres to Minsk, while I can go halfway round the world without a visa and all the way to Lisbon with no passport. The stern customs officer is still inspecting my passport when another official joins her and begins rummaging freely in my suitcase. Oddly, he is most interested in my books. He leafs photo by photo through a volume about the Holocaust that I picked up in Cracow.

'They make trouble about political topics,' says my seat neighbour when the border officials have left the train.

'And what is more important to you: comfortable trains, or the freedom to read whatever you want?'

A terminus! While I am fighting my way through the crowd of arrivals and those waiting for them, I think that terminus stations – all the arriving tracks ending in buffer stops at the concourse – always have something old-fashioned about them. Is it because they resist the efficiency of through travel? Or is it that they express the imperial presumption that all roads lead to Rome, or to Paris or Vienna, as the case may be? If ever a city was the hub of a whole country, it is Minsk: unlike Rome, Paris or Vienna, it is exactly in the geographic centre, nearly equidistant from every border crossing. And yet nothing could be more wrong than to infer from its geographical location that Belarus grew organically out of a centre. Even the name Byelorussia is derived from that of a different country – as if there had been no native name

45

available. And how arbitrary the state's present territory is can be seen in the fact that, after the fall of the tsar, Smolensk, Vilnius and Grodno all claimed the right to be the capital of the Byelorussian People's Republic – yet today Smolensk lies in Russia, Vilnius in Lithuania and Grodno near the border with Poland. In the event, however, the new nation was not recognized by anyone and was broken up by the Bolsheviks a year later.

On the dissolution of the Warsaw Pact, the window of opportunity for independence opened a second time. But while other peoples, from the Baltic to Hungary, celebrated their national sovereignty, Belarus was 'like a person who suddenly notices that he has no shadow,' as Valentin Akudovich put it in his essay on the Belarusian mentality.[11] The book's title is *The Code of Absence* because Belarus is a nation which lacks a people. In the rarely interrupted succession of wars and occupations of the modern era, the linguistic, cultural and religious community which Belarus nominally denotes has been almost completely annihilated: the 'bloody deluge' of the mid-seventeenth century for example, when the army of the first Romanov tsar invaded, killing half the inhabitants. The region had been first thoroughly Polonized, and after Russification it was occupied successively by the Swedes, the French and the Germans before falling permanently under Russian rule, interrupted only by the German occupations in the first and second world wars. 'Coercion and occupation became the natural condition of the Belarusians,' Akudovich writes. 'With time, they grew accustomed to the foreign yoke, and no more felt it than we perceive the pressure of the air.'[12] Belarusian, the chancery language of the Grand Duchy of Lithuania in the sixteenth century, and thus one of Europe's oldest administrative languages, survived only in the villages. But nations arise in cities, and the cities of Belarus had long since become a Babel of Russian, Polish, Belarusian, German, Tatar and, most of all, Yiddish, which would have been a more fitting choice as a national language: according to the census of 1897, Jews made up 57 per cent of the population in the urban areas. But Jewish was something the national movement did not want to be, and among the Jewish elites themselves, the national movement of Zionism arose.

And so the Belarusian nation was born of city-dwellers who swarmed out into the countryside, co-opting the Polish vision of the national history as one of European identity and resistance against Russian colonization – although those emancipation efforts had never really existed. Furthermore, although the Principality of Polotsk and the Grand Duchy of Lithuania, which the national movement claimed as its predecessors, had in fact been a kind of outpost of European culture in the Slavic world, they had no more to do with modern Belarus than the Seljuk empire with today's Turkmenistan or modern Macedonia with the empire of Alexander the Great. Like the Lithuanian nationalists, the Belarusians made their own task more difficult by adopting Herder's concept of nation. Even the language of the nation they aspired to had to be developed – like modern Hebrew – from the rural idiom and the archaic documents. And just when a Belarusian community had developed in the young Soviet republic, it was rubbed out again in the Stalinist purges. Of the entire team of linguists who worked on the five-volume Belarusian dictionary, not one survived the terror of the 1930s, and at least 100 Belarusian poets and writers, or 300 according to some accounts, were shot in just one night, 30 October 1937, in the camp at Kurapaty on the outskirts of Minsk. What remained of the Belarusian language was eliminated in the 1960s and 1970s, when teachers in the cities were allowed to teach only in Russian, the last Belarusian newspapers were closed down, and the Belarusian place names disappeared. Paradoxically, the head of the Byelorussian Communist Party of that time, the former partisan Pyotr Masherau, is more revered today than practically any other twentieth-century leader in Belarus – a politician who conducted the systematic destruction of everything Belarusian. Even the current president of independent Belarus, Alexander Lukashenko, addresses his fellow citizens only in Russian.

'Is the president unable or just unwilling to speak Belarusian?' I ask Valentin Akudovich, whom I meet in an evidently trendy café that evening. In Minsk too it seems as if those who are oriented towards Europe like to bask in the inimitable charm of a Soviet warehouse, with vegetarian snacks and electronic music from a DJ's turntables. Only Akudovich himself, born in 1950, a philosopher and a key figure on Belarus's tenacious cultural scene, looks a bit out of place in the hip surroundings with his grey beard.

'No doubt he masters a few scraps of it,' Akudovich says, 'but certainly not enough to give speeches.'

'Has he never tried to learn it? I mean, he could at least read his speeches.'

'Of course he could learn it; he's not stupid. But he wouldn't want to. Belarusian has become an exotic language. It's a kind of declaration that you're somehow in opposition. Besides, it's the language of misery.'

'Misery?'

'Yes, because in the Soviet Union Belarusian was spoken only in the villages. And the village was synonymous with poverty. Speaking Belarusian was a stigma. Any self-respecting person spoke Russian.'

In *The Code of Absence*, Akudovich recounts that his parents sent him to a vocational school near Moscow after the eighth grade. When he returned, speaking Russian with a Moscow accent, they glowed with joy – because they instinctively assumed that he was now destined for a better life. Masherau is honoured today for a similar reason, Akudovich says: along with the Belarusian language, he banned misery from the people's consciousness. When Stanislau Shushkevich, the chairman of the Supreme Soviet of the Belarusian Republic, wanted to reinstate the public use of Belarusian, he soon found himself out of office. 'Most Belarusians thought, or at least felt, that a man at the head of the Belarusian state speaking the language of misery could mean only one thing: the country was in for a great deal of suffering.'[13]

Throughout the existence of the Soviet Union, Georgia, the Baltic countries and Ukraine had always had an elite who spoke their own language, but Belarusian had to be relearned after independence. Nonetheless, the villagers barely understood literary Belarusian. In other words, their own national movement was linguistically foreign to most Belarusians. The new nation consequently decided, in a four-point referendum of May 1995, to maintain economic ties to Russia, to adopt Russian as a second official language, to reintroduce the Soviet state emblems, and to expand the powers of Alexander Lukashenko, who, twenty years later, is still president. 'We called together the "Belarusian people" to a country in which no one lived except historic and literary spirits and phantoms,' writes Akudovich, who took part himself in the national reawakening. 'Naturally no one answered such a convocation to nowhere.'[14]

'Perhaps,' I sigh, 'the modern nation-state was simply not such a good idea.'

'Why?' Akudovich asks.

'You're asking me? You yourself write that Belarus is such an artificial, arbitrary construct.'

'Germany as a nation is an even bigger figment.'

'But so many people have been murdered everywhere, so many cultures, all the organic diversity destroyed so that nations could form, and then these nations made war on each other because they felt either superior or threatened – or both at once.'

'No, I don't agree with what you're saying,' Akudovich objects, 'you're just projecting your German trauma onto other countries.'

'I don't mean just Nazism. I mean colonialism and its arbitrary borders, Stalin's resettlements, the expulsions and purges all over Europe – the fact that there are no more Greeks living in Izmir today and no Turks in Thessaloniki, no Germans in Czernowitz, no Poles in Lviv and no Jews in Cracow. I mean the Balkan wars, I mean Rwanda, I mean what's going on now in the Middle East: people are trying once again to impose homogeneity in places that are as motley as Minsk or Vilnius in the nineteenth century – aren't those also consequences of exaggerated or failed or imposed nation-building?'

'As if there hadn't been mass murders long before! Just think of the Mongol hordes, the conquest of America – please: the nation-state just happens to be the most appropriate organizational form for societies since the decline of the principalities and empires.'

'And doesn't nationalism scare you today?'

'Not as much as the uprooting, the levelling, the disenfranchisement.'

'And what about Brexit, Trump, Le Pen?'

'Those are only temporary phenomena; the progress of globalization is inexorable.'

'Then what do you think of the right-wing populist parties in Eastern Europe, such as the PiS in Poland and Fidesz in Hungary?'

'Where they don't get too radical, I support them. And I would also subscribe to the Brexit slogan "Take Back Control".'

'But you're contradicting yourself! You aspire to Europe and at the same time defend the nationalists who are threatening Europe.'

'No, it goes together: we want to join Europe, and at the same time we want to develop our national identity. We can't do that with Russia. Russia is swallowing us.'

Twelfth Day: Minsk and Khatyn

In Minsk things have reached such a state that a solitary person feels like an ant with no antennae. The city is growing, not upwards, as cities do in capitalism, which increases the value of real estate; Minsk grows in area, because the state alone possesses all the land. The streets are therefore as wide as our motorways, the pavements as wide as our streets, the buildings generally only four or five storeys high, but long; and the desolate stone squares are as big as whole neighbourhoods in old cities. Just crossing a junction of two streets can take a quarter of an hour in Minsk, and Lenin Square is so expansive that the city bus makes several stops there. The statue of Lenin, monumental in itself, is raised on a pedestal so that the revolutionary leader's feet are high above the heads of mortals. In the best Soviet style, most shops have no display windows, so there are no window-shoppers; besides, the distances are too great for strolling.

The Soviet city which has been epitomized in Minsk is no more a metropolis in the Old World sense than the American city with its uninhabited centre. Moscow at least has old buildings, alleys, squares where people meet instead of getting lost, buildings of different styles and eras. But in Minsk not a stone was left standing after the Second World War, so that the city has been completely rebuilt (in large part by forced labourers, by the way, whose German workmanship is still held in high regard today – the stereotype is so persistent, there may actually be something to it). The basic idea of the Belarusian capital minimizes the individual and maximizes everything that has to do with community. Even the River Svislach has grown so wide that it amounts to a lake, and its shores are lined with lawns in which the blades of grass are exactly equal in length. The lawns are hemmed in by multi-lane *prospekty*, as the thoroughfares in Russian cities are called, so that the vista, when you look from one row of buildings to the one on the other side, can extend a kilometre, if not two – and that right in the centre of a tremendous man-made landscape.

Xeniia doesn't think she lives like an ant: she finds Minsk beautiful. You have to take into account, she says, that the German Army left the city completely flat; you can't expect it to look like Heidelberg. Xeniia knows Germany because her husband works there; she herself studied German literature and now teaches German at the Goethe-Institut. Certainly she could go and join her husband, but a post-industrial suburb like Wanne-Eickel, in the Ruhr area, doesn't strike her, frankly, as all that attractive. All right, the concrete and the high-rise estates here are not exactly cosy either, she admits, but on the other hand practically every family has a dacha, so to that extent gardens, seclusion, natural surroundings are part of life in Belarus. And these days everything is available to buy, without waiting or queuing. Oligarchs? Yes, they have them, three to be exact, and all of them are in prison. 'Here you're not allowed to get too rich,' she laughs when she sees my startled face; 'naturally there are bigwigs, profiteers, fancy cars. But not like in Ukraine! Here there can be only one oligarch, and we call him president.'

If you haven't just been reading Svetlana Alexievich, you might easily imagine the Soviet citizen as being uncritical, docile, fatalistic. But Xeniia is not like that. She is only making rational choices: between the elections, which are a farce, and the war going on in the neighbouring country;

between her income, which is enough to live on, and the second job she'd have to take if she was a teacher in Lithuania; between the cleanliness of the streets; the safety, even at night; a state that offers basic services at affordable costs – and Wanne-Eickel, Germany. She doesn't need to resort to believing the reporting on state television, which portrays Germany almost as a failed state, flooded with fundamentalist and at the same time molesting and criminal Muslims; she needs only to remember her pension, the continuity and linearity of her career, to think her country is not so bad at all. As our taxi passes the headquarters of the KGB, which is unapologetically still called KGB in Belarus, Xeniia points her finger at the conspicuously inconspicuous men dotting the pavement, and sniggers. 'Of course, we still have the secret police,' she says, 'but we no longer have the fear.'

When I ask why the Baltic states turned towards Europe at the same time as they seized their independence, while Belarus remained Soviet in its outlines, Xeniia takes me to the museum of the Great Patriotic War: in no country did Germany cause worse havoc or make it easier for the Red Army to tout its victory as a liberation. The battles are reconstructed with life-sized mannequins like those you used to see in ethnographic museums, original tanks, a genuine German freight car, the partisans' printing press, a low walk-through tunnel representing the underground. In the last room, grateful Belarusians welcome the Red Army. The military parade running on big screens in the foyer is the same as the ones I saw on television as a child, except that it is not Brezhnev on the reviewing stand but the Belarusian oligarch.

That's all? I wonder; that's what the war is supposed to have been? A quarter of the population dead, another quarter abducted and enslaved; the cities levelled, the factories destroyed, the entire infrastructure crushed; over a thousand villages burnt down by the Germans; the Jews, the country's second largest ethnic group, exterminated – and all that's left today is the victory of the Red Army? I ask where in Minsk Stalag 352 is located, the infamous prisoner of war camp, the word 'camp' being almost a euphemism: on the eastern front, the Germans took prisoners to kill them; unlike concentration camp inmates, the prisoners of war – 3 million Soviet soldiers in the first year alone – were counted, but not registered by name. In Stalag 352, the prisoners were jammed in so tight between barbed-wire fences that they could only stand. When they were about to starve to death in late 1941, a few were able to escape into the neighbouring ghetto, which at that time was comparatively safe.

Xeniia has no idea where Stalag 352 was; she has heard of it, but she doesn't know of any memorial to what was probably the biggest and the most murderous POW camp of the Second World War. I should go to Khatyn, she says, if I want to understand Belarus better. She herself has to go home, however, because her daughter has a rehearsal for – Xeniia yawns demonstratively – the parliamentary elections, in which the government will be re-elected with a majority of 96 or 98 or 99 per cent, but you have to vote. At least her daughter enjoys the folk dance that her class performs, and Xeniia's colleague Vera spontaneously agrees to accompany me to the central memorial to the victims of the Second World War an hour north of Minsk.

Among the many stories that Vera tells me on the motorway about her parents, her in-laws and her grandparents, one anecdote about her mother-in-law engraves itself in my memory, although it is comparatively innocuous. The Germans set up a latrine in the courtyard, and the children occasionally tossed an apple over the door into it. Once a soldier stormed out of the privy with his machine gun in his hand, grabbed Vera's mother-in-law, who was then eight years old, and dragged her to her grandmother. He pressed the barrel of his gun against the girl's chest and said something like, 'One more time and I'll shoot her.'

And what did she have to say about Stalin? What her parents, in-laws and grandparents mentioned most often were the 'black crows', the NKVD officers' cars in which you could be taken away without ever knowing why, and without your family ever learning where. In the darkest times, a father or an uncle or a neighbour ended up in the black crow just to make up a quota, I read in *Bloodlands*. Order No. 00447 of 30 July 1937, for example – 'On the Operation to Subdue Former Kulaks, Criminals and Other Anti-Soviet Elements' – called for 79,950 Soviet citizens to be executed by shooting and 193,000 more to be imprisoned in the Gulag. It was up to the local NKVD officers how they fulfilled their quotas; the official guideline they followed was 'better too many than not enough'. Order No. 00447 therefore cost not 79,950 people their lives but five times that number. Nonetheless, when Stalin died in 1953, many people in her family wept, says Vera, although she doesn't understand it.

As the gigantic fields of the kolkhozy pass us by, Vera contradicts Xeniia, who has resigned herself to the system; she talks about dissidents who have been persecuted, the admittedly few but all the more courageous activists, the lies she grew up with. The Germans burnt down the villages? True, but

52

only because Soviet partisans were hiding in them, who had just as little concern for the inhabitants. The Germans destroyed Minsk? Nonsense; Minsk was captured by the Germans without a fight and then bombed by the Soviet Air Force during the four years of occupation. And after the war the communists tore down what was left to build their model of an ideal city. Stalag 352? For soldiers to have fallen into the hands of the Germans doesn't fit the triumphant image of the Red Army. Health care? If you don't have connections or money, you're better off not calling the doctor in Belarus. Free education? Parents have to provide their children even with toilet paper for kindergarten. Xeniia has her husband; she can send her children to Germany any time if there's no more future for them here. But she, Vera – will her children never live in Europe?

Khatyn is one of the villages burnt down by the German Army. Officially, it was selected as a memorial site because it is near the capital, easily reachable for visitors. But there may be another, unofficial reason: the name Khatyn is supposed to offset Katyń. Originally, the village was called Khotyn; the 'o' in the first syllable was changed to an 'a' only after the war. Be that as it may, soldiers herded the inhabitants of Khotyn or Khatyn into a shed, set it on fire and, when the people broke open the door, shot them with machine guns as they fled. At the entrance to the memorial stands the statue of a father holding his dead or unconscious son in his arms. Nothing heroic in his posture; only sheer despair in his face. The twenty-six houses stood, not close together, but scattered throughout a large glade. The foundations of each house are now marked by concrete beams and a stylized gate. The gate stands open in memory of the villagers' traditional hospitality. In the place of the chimney, a bell tower juts upwards, and a plaque on it bears the names of the murdered inhabitants, with the ages of the children. In the first house of air I enter lived three adults and six children, aged five, seven, eight, nine, ten and twelve. Fifty yards on, a house that belonged to a woman living alone. And so on: twenty-six bell towers scattered over the dead village.

Every thirty seconds, the little bells ring, but not quite simultaneously, making a drawn-out, high, childlike whimper that pierces the soul. Impossible to imagine that anyone could run around as they do at the Memorial to the Murdered Jews in Berlin, playing games like hide-and-seek. I have never walked through a memorial – back and forth through the village built of air – in which the violence, the grief, the emptiness are so physically tangible. And it is achieved not by Hollywood's methods, as in the Schindler museum in Cracow or the tower of silence in Berlin's Jewish Museum: not by empathy, original photographs, or the simulation of terror; it is achieved simply by the force of the artistic abstraction.

True, the murdered Jews are not mentioned at the national memorial, although the architect, Leonid Levin, who died in 2014, was himself a Jew. To the Soviet Union, all the victims were Soviet citizens, nothing else. Back in Minsk, Vera takes me to the monument in the former ghetto, erected as late as fifteen years ago: a sculptural group of emaciated naked people descending a stairway. The sculpture is moving, certainly – but, in a state that makes everything monumental, the Jewish memorial has turned out strikingly little, and then it is also crowded against a high-rise block and hidden by trees, practically impossible to recognize from the street.

Along a wooden wall behind which the third underground line is being built, we walk on through the former ghetto, which was forgotten after the war, although it had been the largest on Soviet soil, with some 70,000 Jewish inhabitants; even Valentin Akudovich, who is one of the most educated people in the country, mentioned yesterday evening that he stumbled only by chance on a book that told of Jewish life and death in Minsk during his studies at the Literature Institute in Moscow. Passing street pedlars, who may have taken up places along the building site because its wooden wall narrows the deserted *prospekt* to a busy alleyway, we come to a little park. No, it is not a park, I realize; it is a former cemetery, the Jewish cemetery. Some gravestones are laid close together, although it is unclear in the twilight whether this is still under construction or already a work of art. We strike up a conversation with an elegant woman who turns out to be – no, no reporter would dare invent such a coincidence – the daughter of Leonid Levin. Galina Levina is her name; she too is an architect; she speaks perfect English; her office also continues her father's life's work. Now she has been commissioned to redesign the cemetery, which is why she is here.

'We have a long way to go,' she says, 'before the people here understand, especially the young people, that the Jews were murdered because they were Jews.'

I ask her how her father was able to realize such a moving, silent memorial in the Soviet Union. Yes, it was hard, Galina Levina answers; in those days it was generally impossible to avoid the heroic mode. The fact that her father nonetheless got the commission was only because of Pyotr Masherau, the head of the Communist Party in Byelorussia: a politician, a high communist official, but a wise man with aesthetic sensibility. Masherau understood that art is more than propaganda and that the Belarusians needed a place of silent mourning, not triumph. What her father had to fight for most, says Galina Levina, was the use of bells, a Christian idiom, for this national commemoration. Although a communist, Masherau understood the bells too. He died in 1980 in a car accident under circumstances that are still uncertain today.

'I have visited so many memorials on this trip,' I say, 'seen so many memorials in Germany. In Khatyn was the first time I had the feeling: yes, this is fitting.'

'Yes, my father did that,' Galina Levina replies, 'but the work to be done is still tremendous.'

Because we are travelling on tomorrow towards Chernobyl, I equip myself with cheap clothes in the little shops. They said on the phone that everything we wear in the inclusion zone must be disposed of afterwards.

Thirteenth Day: Into the Chernobyl Exclusion Zone

Consequently, we look rather scruffy when we set out. Only the shoes I'm wearing are dear to me; I had best wait until we get there to put on the used pair I bought yesterday evening, because the soles are going to fall off them within a day. Along the motorway, and afterwards along the country road, we see one cemetery after another: a square bit of woods in the middle of a field, always enclosed by the same fence, always painted sky-blue. Under the birch trees, the gravestones huddle together like siblings, and the plastic flowers bloom even in winter. They are ordinary cemeteries, not mass graves, and yet every single graveyard in Belarus is at the same time a war monument, with a sculpture or an obelisk, with wreaths, also plastic, and the names of the fallen sons of the nearest village. And where there is no village any more because it was burnt down, and no cemetery because no one survived who could remember the relatives or neighbours, there is an isolated monument with no graveyard in the middle of the field.

Here, in this flat country, covered then with fens and forests, now made arable and hence lying as if naked, was the midpoint of the confrontation between the Third Reich and the Soviet Union; it was here that the terror of the two systems escalated: the Stalinist massacre starting before the war; the expulsion of hundreds of thousands of Poles after the Hitler–Stalin Pact; then the German Army's invasion, a matter of days; the partisan war, fought with such fierceness as nowhere else against both the local population and the occupiers; and, finally, the last stage of human barbarity, when the German Army command gave the order to leave behind 'dead zones' on retreating.

Other countries have monuments reminding people of the horror of the war and the Holocaust. Driving through Belarus, we get the impression that the whole country is one big monument – there are so many memorial stones, mass graves and signposts to the sites of death camps. Yet it is not permitted to commemorate all the victims without reservation: not the victims of Stalinism, not the Poles, not the prisoners of war and the returning forced labourers, not the Jews who were murdered as Jews, and not the victims of what Svetlana Alexievich has called 'the most important event of the twentieth century, despite the terrible wars and revolutions for which that century will be remembered': the victims of Chernobyl.[15] The reactor which exploded on 26 April 1986 was in the present-day territory of Ukraine, but 70 per cent of the radioactive fallout fell on Belarus. Although 485 villages and towns were abandoned, one out of five Belarusians today lives on contaminated soil. The people are 'living black boxes', the Nobel laureate wrote in her book on the nuclear disaster, the book that made her famous in the late 1990s; 'Belarusians are recording information for the future. For everybody.'

But what information are they recording? Alexievich described the effects of radioactivity on the psyche. But the numbers, the sheer numbers still diverge, thirty years after the catastrophe, by three zeroes – before the decimal point: when we research how many people have died of the effects of radiation, the answers range from 4,000 to 1.5 million. In Belarus itself, there is no access to data at all. What is more, a person who reports on the increased rate of cancer in children gets fired, like the director of the Institute of Nuclear Energy in Minsk, Vassili Nesterenko, or even arrested, like Yury Bandazhevsky, the researcher and director of the medical school in Gomel, the second largest city in Belarus, just 140 kilometres away from the reactor. And while private tour operators in Ukraine now offer day trips to Chernobyl, irresponsible as that may be, in Belarus it is hard even for scientists to visit the exclusion zone, euphemistically called the 'Radioecological Preserve'.

Khoiniki, a collection of concrete prefabs along six-lane streets with almost no traffic, is the administrative centre of the exclusion zone. When we arrive, the competent official is not at his post. Nor does he answer his mobile. The friendly woman in the anteroom tries to find a colleague who can sign the permit for our visit and, in the meantime, offers us tea. When it transpires that everyone in the agency says someone else is responsible, I lose my temper. The government is constantly complaining that that no one helps it manage the consequences of the reactor meltdown, and when a reporter actually does take an interest in Belarus rather than Ukraine, applies for a visa, which is bother enough in itself, travels to Minsk, obtains accreditation from the Foreign Ministry, makes an appointment with an official, drives out four hours by car – he gets sent back empty-handed?

Naturally I hope my blow-up will have the effect that the functionaries consider the possible consequences for their own careers if my reporting turns out all too negative, but in the end it is probably out of pity that a biologist volunteers with a sigh to guide us at least to the edge of the exclusion zone. Although he is wearing camouflage, he radiates good cheer, with his round belly, moustache, receding hairline, and look of mild surprise at our trek to this God-forsaken corner. For his part, he is studying the effects of radioactivity on the flora, he reports, as we drive through a 'can' zone, where the inhabitants are only advised to abandon their houses. However, he doesn't find any such effects.

'You don't find any effects?'

'That is, I don't see them, I mean. Naturally we find that the measurements are higher. But visible mutations occurred only in the initial years. By now, it's an ordinary natural landscape that's been left to itself. We even have wild horses now.'

'And what about the effects on people?'

'That's not part of my field of research. And there are no people there.'

'But what about you? I mean, you and your colleagues are in the exclusion zone every day, I suppose – aren't you afraid?'

'We always take a dosimeter along. Besides, we get regular tests.'

'And what if your test is positive?'

'Then I must have done something wrong.'

'Done something wrong?'

'Yes. Neglected the precautions. Spent too much time in the woods, for example. Or secretly eaten the berries or mushrooms. You can eat one or two, but if you eat too many berries, it shows; the measurements go up.'

'And what happens if a person exceeds the allowable dose?'

'They get suspended, or fired, depending. We're very strict.'

'They get fired because their exposure to radiation is too high?'

'Yes; after all, they must have done something wrong.'

What we drive through are not villages but individual wooden houses set at varying distances from one another, sometimes separated only by a fence, but usually by 30, 50 or 100 metres. Once they were villages. The abandoned houses have been torn down and the soil around them removed to a depth of several metres. Nobody moves here anyway, explains a man we meet on the street, a forester by profession. Here people only move away, and, if you don't move away, your house is torn down as soon as you die: 'No trace of us remains.'

Five hundred houses once stood here, densely packed; it was almost a little town, with its own school, with shops, an administrative building and a community hall. They even had a choir that was famous throughout the region. Now there are only thirty people left, and that house there ahead, the beautiful house with the ornamentation on the dormer windows, that's the next one that will be levelled; the old builder, who was buried a couple of weeks ago, built many of the houses in the surrounding villages. Then, for the last thirty years, he watched as one after another disappeared. The electricity still works, the running water doesn't; they get water from the well. They get their groceries from a merchant who comes with a van twice a week; the bus stopped coming here long ago.

I ask why he has stayed on. They offered him a flat in Khoiniki, the forester explains, but that's only 15 kilometres away; he doesn't see any difference, and in any case you get sick everywhere in the world. But hasn't the disease rate gone up here? The liquidators – hundreds of thousands of volunteers, or conscripted volunteers, who put out the fire in 1986 and built the concrete shell on the reactor – many of them have died, yes. But the locals – no, everything is average, they get tested annually. Sometimes the measurements are higher, sometimes lower; it probably depends on their diet. And the children? No, he hasn't noticed anything in the children; of course, there are only two left. That's how they first learned of the accident, he says: when the children and expectant mothers were suddenly taken away. He watched that going on from his tractor and immediately suspected something bad. The television reported on the accident only days later; even the May Day celebration went on with a parade the same as every year, just without children and expectant mothers.

An older woman joins us – green headscarf, gold teeth – and explains that many of the neighbours regret having moved away because they don't get on in the city, especially the old people. Sometimes they come back and kiss the ground where their house used to be. Many of them have taken to drinking, the woman tells us; to her that's worse than the radiation. Yes, the mushrooms and the berries haven't changed; the potatoes, too, taste the way they always have; did we think they'd grown horns or something? Okay, the dark berries have more radiation than the red ones; even she doesn't touch those.

Because I'm from Germany, the woman brings up the war – another, earlier division of life into a Before and an After. Many people from the village were carted off as forced labourers; others collaborated with the Germans, she recounts, pointing to the places where the houses of the ones and the others used to stand, the house of her aunt who had to go work in Germany and, two lots away, the house of the policeman who later fled with the Germans. Once her mother found a young soldier weeping bitterly in the cellar. What has happened here is going to happen to us, the soldier said. When the order came to burn down their village, the Germans discussed it among themselves. There was no point, some said. In the end the Germans retreated without burning the houses down; that's why the village still exists. There is nothing left of the neighbouring village but a memorial stone.

I ask whether we can see the memorial. The biologist hesitates because we would have to go through the woods, but the forester says there is a trail. 'Eternal Remembrance to the Victims of Fascism' is engraved on the stone, and below it the names. The wreaths were probably laid on the pedestal before Chernobyl, the plastic threads are so brittle, and the colours so faded. As on all the monuments, the 'Great Patriotic War' is dated 1941 to 1945, although for Byelorussia it began in 1939 with the Hitler–Stalin Pact.

We drive on and come to pastures and fields that have apparently been freshly planted. Here, too, the contaminated soil has been removed, the biologist reassures us, and, besides, all vegetables and dairy products are tested for caesium, strontium and other radioactive nuclides before they are sold. In the next zone, no planting is allowed, nor hunting, nor cutting trees. Barely 50 kilometres away from Chernobyl, we come to the checkpoint at which the actual exclusion zone begins – also a kind of 'dead zone', it occurs to me. The road is watched by two guards in camouflage uniforms, one of whom keeps watch from a wooden tower for forest fires. Apart from that, their work is limited to opening the barricade for one to three cars a day: the biologist's car, the forester's car, and the car of the two people who still live in the Radioecological Preserve.

'Two people still live there?' I ask, perplexed.

'Yes,' says the guard, and explains that the radiation is not evenly distributed everywhere. The dose is lower at the two people's houses, so the authorities yielded to their pressure and let them go on living there. 'I wonder myself what they do there. They don't talk very much.'

'To each his own,' says the biologist, 'and those two get by without discotheques.'

'Are they brothers?' I ask, because I have to imagine some kind of alliance to help them bear up against the isolation, the silence and the danger.

'No, just two men.'

'And they live together?'

'No, no, in two houses,' says the guard.

'Our people are not that depraved yet,' the biologist comments, laughing.

We are already driving back to Khoiniki when I realize I'm still wearing my trekking shoes. Do I have to throw them away now? The biologist said there was nothing to fear even working in the exclusion zone; he said the berries are edible too. The villagers didn't look as though they worried about every step they took either. And every summer, they told us, the people come from miles around to gather mushrooms in the woods. Surely the few yards I walked on the trail are nothing in comparison.

'What do you think?' I ask the biologist on leaving, 'Can I keep the shoes? They were rather expensive, to tell you the truth.'

'Throw them away,' advises the biologist who otherwise finds everything is average.

On the way back, we turn off at one of the signposts indicating a memorial: the Ozarichi camp existed for only a week, and consisted of nothing but a marshy forest that was fenced off with barbed wire, guard towers and mines. In the little car park is a car with its doors wide open and techno music turned up loud – probably the kind of music the biologist was thinking of when he mentioned 'discotheques'. When we park beside it, a pair of lovers creep out of the bushes, turn off the music and drive away looking bashful. A few yards beyond the monument with the colourful plastic wreaths leaned against it, the fence is still visible and, beyond the fence, the marsh where the German Army packed together 70,000 people who were not fit for labour – that is, mainly the old, the sick and the children – with no shelter, no sanitary facilities, no food, and only snow to drink. 'The decision to get rid of this burden, which is substantial in nutritional terms as well, in this way has been made after thorough consideration and examination of all the resulting implications,' says the German commander's log book. When the Red Army found the camp, more than half the prisoners had died of cold, starvation or disease – if they hadn't bled to death on the barbed wire or been shredded by a mine on trying to escape. I try to imagine what happened on the other side of the fence between the 12th and the 17th of March 1944, but all I can see is the marsh.

Fourteenth Day: Kurapaty and Minsk

The trees have already been felled. We are on the outskirts of Minsk: social-ist housing blocks, the motorway, beyond it a field so vast it couldn't possibly belong to a single farmer, and beyond the field a shopping mall with lighted signs advertising Adidas, Nike and Kentucky Fried Chicken. If the young people hadn't chained themselves to the bulldozers, and if the workers hadn't unexpectedly supported them, another shopping mall would have been built on this side of the motorway too. The motorway itself runs right through the middle of the site of the Stalinist death camp Kurapaty. The number of people who were shot here varies among different sources almost as widely as the figures on Chernobyl: officially, they were 7,000; the archaeologist Zianon Pazniak, who discovered the mass graves in 1988, calculates there were about 250,000. The inscription on the little memorial names neither the perpetrators nor the victims; it recalls in general terms only that Kurapaty was a site of extermination during the political repression between 1938 and 1941. Vandals will be prosecuted.

The discovery of the mass graves made Zianon Pazniak the most important leader of the national movement. Akudovich, who took part in the memorial marches to Kurapaty at the time, writes that Pazniak influenced the political situation so advantageously that everyone who was dissatisfied after the col-lapse of the Soviet Union marched under the Belarusian banners: 'Thus the paradox came to pass: over the heads of the hundred thousand workers who assembled for days on end in Independence Square in Minsk to demonstrate against the dissolution of the Soviet Union, against democracy and against rising prices, waved the white-red-white flags.'[16] But Pazniak's Belarusian Popular Front aroused expectations it could not fulfil. The majority of the Belarusians had not won democracy but had lost their social security. In that situation, the benefits Lukashenko promised were more seductive: the 'sau-sage ideology' was concerned more with wages, pensions and old customs than with liberation, separation of powers and national greatness. 'If you grab a mole by the fur and throw it up in the air, it will rightly perceive that as violence, not as a liberation and the gift of a chance to fly.'[17]

An underpass leads us to the other side of the motorway and into a pine forest where wooden crosses have been erected, bigger ones by activists, two, three metres high; smaller crosses for individual victims by their families; ones for the famous poets by their readers; there are also memorial stones erected by the various persecuted communities. The Jewish community's

61

has an especially beautiful inscription: 'To our Jewish brothers in faith, and also to our Christian and Muslim brothers in scriptural religion, who fell victim of the Stalinist terror, from the Belarusian Jews'. Although the earth was removed to a depth of several metres in the early 1990s, so that no one can count the bones, it is difficult to walk. Or is the reason why every step is disquieting because we do not know exactly where the pits were in which the people fell at their execution, and who fell when, on which spot? Each pit was filled with twenty to thirty corpses, I read, then they were covered with earth: thus I begin to calculate how big the pits must have been and how many, and how far the site must extend: a thousand, two thousand or ten thousand pits across.

The fact that the state yielded to the demonstrators' demands and now wants to build a memorial of its own to the victims of Stalinism may indicate an opening. Or the opposite: shortly afterwards, political protests throughout the country were brutally suppressed and many oppositional activists arrested. These demonstrations were set off by the so-called Parasites Act which, in the best Soviet tradition, reinterprets reality until it fits the concept: instead of admitting that there is rising unemployment, the state outlaws it.

Only a country like Belarus, where one trauma follows another like the cemeteries along the motorway, and where remembrance is at the same time so strictly regulated, could produce a writer like Svetlana Alexievich. For her work, unique in its form, consists of nothing but individual, taboo, sometimes unremarkable, often shocking contradictory memories. She is a quiet, you could even say inconspicuous woman whose courage and persistence are apparent in the power of her books. When I meet her at her favourite café, an Italian-styled place in the basement of a concrete block in central Minsk, she asks first for my impressions.

'It's incredible how present the past is, in every village, in every street and in every family – whoever you talk to, everyone has their history, which at the same time is a common history. Doesn't that give rise to a kind of collective memory, regardless of what the state dictates?'

'No,' says Alexievich roundly. 'In order for memory to be collective, the recollections have to be written down.'

In Minsk you need only look at the street names, she continues, to see the bandits, murderers, sadists who are still honoured. Anyone could know they are bandits, murderers, sadists; the information is not secret. It is merely limited to self-published books, the Internet, and grandparents' memories – the information is there; it just has no consequences. 'And when someone does mention something that must not be mentioned, the reflex answer is: But we won. If only victory is mentionable, then there is no room for the victims.'

I ask Svetlana Alexievich why she refused to chair the jury for the memorial in Kurapaty. Because none of the activists were included in the process, she answers. Besides, the application deadline was much too short, just one month, for anyone to submit serious plans. Still, the main reason: 'I have nothing in common with this government – what business do I have there?' When she won the Nobel Prize, the president himself accused her of slandering her country; two years later, she has to resist being co-opted.

And today, thirty years after the worst-case scenario, twenty years after her book, how does she assess the management of Chernobyl?

'There is no management,' Alexievich answers, recalling that, in the beginning, the state distributed Geiger counters and set up testing stations all over the country where people could have their foodstuffs tested: 'Everyone could see for themselves when the meters ticked. And what conclusions did the state draw from that? They shut down the production of Geiger counters and closed the testing stations.'

I ask whether the repression of Chernobyl in the public awareness is comparable with the repression of the Stalinist crimes or the Holocaust.

'Yes, definitely. The state's interest in both cases is to maintain its monopoly on the past. When it notices that the past has escaped its control and the people will not let go of their own memory, then it yields. Then suddenly the state wants to build a monument in Kurapaty. Just as it built a monument on the site of the ghetto when the inquiries from other countries got more and more urgent. But that's just tactical, to keep the pressure manageable.'

'What happens to a society if it can't speak about its traumas?'

'It gets sick,' Alexievich answers, and points to the rampant alcoholism, the high suicide rate, and especially the willingness to live with lies that anybody can see through, the political passiveness. Even in Kurapaty, which is about an event that only the grandparents remember, if anyone, it was almost exclusively young people who demonstrated against the trees being cut down. And when the older people do march, as they did in the most recent protests against the 'Parasites Act', it's because they are personally affected, not out of an interest in the general welfare. In her interviews, her experience has been that it takes a long time before people begin talking; sometimes she has to keep prying forever and ever. And when people have finally bared their souls, they often regret it the very next day and retract their statements. Her book on Chernobyl was only possible in the years following the collapse of the Soviet Union, before the old order had been restored. Furthermore, the effects of the radiation were obvious; there was no way for the state to suppress Chernobyl in the public awareness. Everyone knew someone who had got sick, died or been forced to abandon their home. But no one can live in fear for thirty years, and so people are happy to believe that the consequences of Chernobyl have been dealt with, and no one is surprised that, year after year, new areas are released for agriculture. And then they're grateful, Alexievich says, when the president gives tractors to the returning farmers. And now they're building a new nuclear reactor in Astraviets, near the Lithuanian border, without any local resistance forming – in an area that's already contaminated, where the people have already experienced for themselves the effects of radiation and how negligent the state's actions are.

'But, then, have your books not had a powerful influence?' I ask. 'After all, you've given a voice to the pain, the questions, the fears, a voice heard all over the world – that hasn't been silenced!'

'As a writer, you can't hope for too much,' Alexievich answers. 'Our achievements are modest. Sometimes when I read on the Internet what young people write, when I admire their boldness, I think, yes, maybe my books contributed to that. That's all.'

'The achievements of literature may be modest,' I say, 'but they are long-lasting.'

'How do you mean?'

'People will still be reading your books in a hundred years. Who in the world then will remember your current president?' Svetlana Alexievich lowers her eyes and smiles pensively, so that I am not sure whether she is pleased with the compliment or just can't take me seriously. In any case, I add, 'It's almost like the radiation.'

The photographer Dmitrij Leltschuk, who is accompanying me on this leg of the journey, knows someone who would be willing to talk about the past any time: Granny Frida, his brother-in-law's grandmother. As a young Jewish woman, she was captured by the Germans, and after her liberation she was condemned as a German spy. She doesn't hear well any more, says Dmitrij; actually she's as good as deaf; conversations with her are a bit one-sided as a result. But she's all the more glad of finding anyone who will listen to her. While we are on our way to see Granny Frida, the car radio broadcasts a speech by the president, who is upset about the 'parasites'. Suddenly Vera and Dmitrij laugh out loud.

'Did he make a joke?'

'No, he invented a new word again,' Vera explains. She and Dmitrij were already amused by the president's strong accent in Russian. The more he tries to sound like a Muscovite, the more you can hear him straining. But what's really funny is when, in his excitement, he doesn't find the word he wants: then he just invents one.

'The president invents words?'

'"Invent" is going too far perhaps,' Vera says, and goes on to explain that the president has just derived a noun from the verb for 'press', *nazhimat'*, to mean the 'pressure' he wants to exercise on the government. But there is no such noun. *Zhim* in Russian refers to an athletic exercise, as when a weight-lifter 'jerks' a barbell overhead. Furthermore, the president often begins a verb with a prefix that doesn't belong there, Vera says. You always understand what he means, but it sounds funny. And then he uses the familiar form of address with everybody, and uses strong language, really vulgar words. 'He's just a man from the kolkhoz.'

'The kolkhoz?'

'The countryside.'

'Then in the countryside they probably don't mind his Russian.'

'No, you're right; to country people his language sounds very familiar.'

I have barely sat down on the sofa when Granny Frida starts telling a story. Meanwhile her son, now a pensioner, takes his leave and goes into the next room, where he turns on the television set loud enough to drown out Granny Frida. She was twenty-one years old and working as a secretary in the staff headquarters of the 13th Front in Kursk when the position had to be evacuated in October or November 1941, only transport was lacking. Everyone had to flee however they could. Granny Frida was captured and driven, along with hundreds, thousands of others, back to Kursk, which was now occupied by the Germans. Fortunately she had been able to get rid of her uniform in time; some farmers had given her clothes. She had never practised the Jewish religion, nor had her parents before her; she was a dedicated communist and had been active in the Komsomol when she was young. But all the women in front of her and behind her knew she would be shot immediately if her Jewish origins were known. The Germans also gave short shrift to the wounded and injured.

'How could they have recognized you as a Jew?' I wonder, whereupon Vera shouts the question in Granny Frida's ear.

'By my black eyes and hair, my darker skin, my face, you could see that. A Jew or a Gypsy, one or the other.'

Granny Frida shows how she pulled down her headscarf to cover her eyebrows and kept her hand over her mouth as she walked. When they made camp, the other women put her in the middle so that none of the guards would notice her. That was also good against the cold. But she was afraid someone among the prisoners might betray her to butter up the Germans. Back in Kursk, she was put in a cell with fifteen women, with no room to lie down. Frida was the only one who never took a turn walking in the yard; the others brought her her food, too. Once in a while a young soldier came to the front of the cell and counted the prisoners; fortunately he never looked at them very closely. She learned two German words from him: *russisches Schwein*, 'Russian swine'. One of the prisoners, a nurse, recognized the different aircraft that flew over the prison. First they were German, then, a few days later, Russian; then the Germans began to panic. The prisoners had to line up in the yard to be inspected for their possible usefulness. Local policemen helped to identify the communist functionaries and the Jews among them. Whoever they picked out was shot on the spot, not twenty yards from Frida. But even the policeman, and the officer following him, walked past her without a word.

'But you just said you were recognizable as a Jew,' I interject.

'Maybe the policeman didn't want to recognize me. Or maybe he thought I was from the country. The Jews all lived in the city, and I looked like a farm girl in my clothes. The Germans laughed at me.'

'Weren't you scared to death when the two of them came past you?'

'Yes, of course; my heart was pounding,' Frida answers, and imitates the sound: 'Boom, boom'.

The same day, the women were taken to a big hall. There an officer stood in front of them, a good-looking man, Granny Frida recounts at the age of ninety-seven. Her heart was pounding again, but the officer sent the policemen out. He was an Austrian, the officer said in broken Russian, an Austrian and an antifascist. Austria itself had been annexed by the Reich, and so he was going to let at least the women go free. They were to go directly to the gate, which stood open, and run for it. Then he named the villages that were in Soviet hands and pointed the direction with his finger. The women should split up, he said, not march in a group.

'Did you trust the officer?' I ask. 'I mean, it was unbelievable, wasn't it?'

'We didn't know whether to trust him or not, but what else were we supposed to do? Go back to our cells?'

The gate was in fact open, there were no guards, and so the women ran in the direction the officer had indicated, and soon came to a village and asked what it was called. It was one of those he had named, and it was not held by the Germans. 'An Austrian saved my life,' Granny Frida says with amazement, three quarters of a century later. 'He was really a handsome man.'

Alone, she marched through the damp woods, hungry, freezing, and constantly afraid of falling into German hands again. She came to a little town where there was no one in the streets. Finally she discovered a woman carrying a bucket, and, heart pounding, she spoke to her. She learned that the town was called Ligov and was not occupied. She went to the command post and reported to the duty officer to return to service or be sent back to her parents. The officer said he was not competent and gave her tea until the competent officer came, and then another one besides. She sat in the office until evening, telling her story to one after another. The questions became interrogations; NKVD agents arrived. At night she spread out her coat on the floor of the office; in the morning the interrogation continued. Finally she was taken to a jail, and in early 1942 she was sentenced to ten years in Siberia as a spy.

'But why a spy?' I ask.

'The NKVD had no other explanation why the Germans would have let a Jew live.'

'Like the biologists in the exclusion zone,' Dmitrij says sardonically: 'If they get contaminated, they themselves are suspect.'

In the work camp she lost one tooth after another to scurvy, until she could eat nothing but soup; there wasn't much else anyway. Only in the second year was she allowed to contact her parents, who had thought she had been killed or abducted to Germany.

Whom does she resent the most, I ask: the Germans or the Soviets?

'The Germans,' says Granny Frida. 'The Germans started the war.'

'But the Soviets put you in the Gulag.'

'It was the Germans who made me a Jew. And if I hadn't been a Jew, the Soviets wouldn't have sent me to the camps.'

After her release – the war was long over; twelve members of her family had not survived it – she and her parents did everything possible to get her rehabilitated. But there were no documents, and she knew neither what had become of her fellow prisoners nor the name of the officer – only what he looked like and that he was from Austria. And, besides, Paragraph 124 prohibited rehabilitation in cases of treason: a traitor could not be believed no matter what evidence or witnesses she presented to prove her innocence. The more persuasive the defence, the more suspect the person.

Frida never gave up: not when Khrushchev was deposed, not when Brezhnev died, not when her parents died and not when the Soviet Union collapsed. She was finally rehabilitated in 1992. In spite of the effort it costs her to stand up, she has Dmitrij lead her to the living room cupboard and takes out a stack of letters and documents, on the top the certificate that she had been innocent when convicted. For a few years she received a monthly compensation from a German fund, from which she was able to pay for a carer who came once a day to wash her and cook for her. But the payments were stopped with the argument that she had not been persecuted as a Jew but condemned by the Soviets as a German spy, and that was not Germany's responsibility. As she looks for the decision she received from Frankfurt, she grows angry, her already loud voice almost cracks, and she pounds her hand on the stack of papers again and again.

'It's Germany's fault! It's Germany's fault! If I hadn't been imprisoned as a Jew, I wouldn't have had to fight my whole life long. Without my file, I would have had a better job. I would have earned a pension I could live on. Germany made me a Jew.'

'And Germany today?' I ask.

'That's different,' Granny Frida assures me, and calms down. 'I mean Hitlerism. Today it's a different generation, a different government. I'm ninety-seven years old. Who even remembers, now?'

Granny Frida shows me her photo album: family pictures, her wedding, her son's wedding, her grandchildren, snapshots. She stands out among her colleagues at work, that's true. Like Kafka, I think, the greatest German writer of the twentieth century, who noted that he was as dark as an Indian. Her husband, long deceased, was a Jew as well – what else? – although no one kept the Sabbath or went to synagogue – what synagogue, anyway? She wasn't discriminated against as a Jew, Granny Frida assures us, whereupon Dmitrij rolls his eyes. Never by people, she insists; only sometimes in government offices.

'Was the Soviet Union a good time, then?'

'Before the war it was good.'

'Was it with Stalin that it turned bad?'

'To me, he was Hitler's friend,' she says, and recounts that her mother, a simple librarian, wanted to speak to Stalin personally when she learned that her daughter was in Siberia. Everyone tried to dissuade her, because you couldn't just go and see Stalin, and if you tried, you never came back. But her mother went to Moscow anyway. Fortunately, no one at the Kremlin gate took her seriously.

'And did it get better after Stalin?'

'Oh, what do I know? We worked a lot, and we lived a little, that's all. Khrushchev, Brezhnev, Stalin, to me they were all the same.'

'And Gorbachev?'

Granny Frida thinks, and then says to my surprise that she can hardly remember Gorbachev. Apparently that's not long enough ago.

'Don't mention it,' she says when I go to thank her. 'I have so much time. If you hadn't come, I would just have slept.'

Back in the car, Dmitrij remarks that, in his childhood, he for one was certainly made aware he was a Jew, even though he knew practically nothing about Judaism – only because of his darker hair. His great-grandfather was such an ardent communist that he walked to the Soviet Union from Poland after the October Revolution, and on crossing the border he kissed the ground. In fact, the Byelorussian Soviet Socialist Republic was one of only two countries in history, along with the independent Ukrainian People's Republic, where Yiddish has ever been an official language. Dmitrij's great-grandfather became the director of the Jewish Theatre of Minsk and was shot in the Kurapaty camp in 1937 – officially as a Polish spy; in reality, most likely as a member of the Jewish intelligentsia. Dmitrij has tried, to no avail, to see his great-grandfather's KGB file.

'Haven't you had enough of my family?' he asks.

'No, tell me more,' I beg him, and I hear about his grandfather who was vice-vice-home minister of the Byelorussian SSR. He was instructed in 1951 not to prevent Jews from moving to Birobidzhan. Decoded, that was an order to relocate Jews. This is something I've read about: that year, Stalin thought he had discovered a conspiracy in which terrorist Jewish doctors were going to kill prominent communists – so for safety's sake he had them all resettled. In the last years of his life, however, Stalin's orders were no longer strictly obeyed. Before the war, he had had many of his security staff removed after the purges, blaming them for the excesses. As a result, many officials were hesitant after the war to commit excesses in the first place. In the case of Dmitrij's grandfather, there was also the fact that he was of Jewish origin himself, and that his father-in-law had been unjustly killed. Dmitrij's grandfather misfiled the order, ostensibly by mistake, where he knew it would remain out of circulation.

'Do you want to hear something about my family?' I ask.

'Don't tell me you have Belarusian ancestors?'

'Not that, but do you remember the Poles who were driven out of Eastern Poland after the Hitler–Stalin Pact? Many of them emigrated to Iran.'

Now Dmitrij remembers about the Poles who crossed the Caspian Sea in wooden boats and continued past the Elburz Mountains in buses, horse-drawn carts and sometimes on foot to reach Palestine or the West via Iran. As a child in Isfahan, my mother played with their children for some years because my grandparents invited the Polish families to their house on Fridays. More than a few settled in Isfahan; a young girl married into our family and must be almost as old as Granny Frida now. Perhaps I can find her when I get to Isfahan.

In the evening we're going to eat at the Georgian restaurant, which used to be the East's equivalent of the Italian restaurant in the West: your local Southerner. The hospitality is more rustic than hip, but the food is sensational. The philosopher Alexey Dzermant, who works at the Academy of Sciences researching the twentieth-century history of ideas, is regularly called upon to explain current politics on Belarusian and Russian television. With his pony tail and his goatee he reminds me of a hippie, while Dmitrij associates his appearance with anti-Semitism.

'Why is that?' I ask him in German.

'Because he looks like an Orthodox priest.'

But when the philosopher orders a bilious-green lemonade, Dmitrij joins him: they both grew up with the taste.

'Better than cola,' I admit after trying a sip. Both of them nod, satisfied.

'Is Belarus the last Soviet country?'

'In a way, yes,' says Dzermant, and points out that today's Russia was born with the economic liberalization of the Yeltsin years. In Belarus too there was a rupture, but it was not nearly as radical: more value is placed on public spirit, social security here.

'And what about the crimes?' I ask, mentioning the Stalinist terror under which Belarus particularly suffered.

'Of course there were crimes; no one denies that.'

'But there is no place to commemorate the victims; there is no public accounting for the events; the dark sides of the Soviet Union are not included in the school curriculum.'

'Evidently the people have no need to reflect on the Stalinist crimes. Why should the view of a few activists be imposed on the society?'

'But how could the people have a need to reflect if the mass shootings in Kurapaty, for example, are not known?'

'Who says they're not known? Anyone who wants to can read about them.'

'But they are only known because they have been uncovered by those individuals who are ostensibly imposing their view on the society. Otherwise no one would have found out about them.'

'There is no law against investigating about Kurapaty. And now there will be an official memorial. But why should the state disseminate the information itself? It would be destroying its own foundation.'

'Is the state founded on the Stalinist crimes, then?'

'No, but it continues the tradition of the Soviet Union, of which the Stalinist era is a part, with all its positive and negative aspects. That must be historically studied, there's no question about that – the mass shootings, the banishments – and that's happening in Moscow too. But here, unfortunately, we see that, when people challenge one element, the whole past is challenged. The activists have a political agenda. They want to throw out the Soviet history, and to do so they have to equate Stalinism with fascism. But Hitler waged a war of annihilation against us; that's not comparable. Hitler wanted to stamp out the Soviet peoples to populate Eastern Europe with Germans. Those were official plans, you can look them up. Just take the 1941 "guidelines", the Hunger Plan. Has that already been forgotten? Stalin was interested in preserving the Soviet system, and preserving his own power if you like. He committed horrible crimes, but not genocide. Many of Stalin's victims had been members of the *apparat*; they were dedicated communists, internationalists. It's unfair to reduce them retroactively to their ethnic background. In Ukraine we have seen what unchained nationalism leads to: everyone saw the Nazi emblems in the Maidan. Everyone is worried that the war will spread to us. We don't want any more war.'

Europe committed a severe strategic error, he adds, in supporting the illegal revolution in Ukraine without thinking about how Moscow would react. Dzermant says he is not defending that reaction, or at least not across the board; he is only pointing out that it was to be expected. And Europe repeated the same mistake in Libya and Syria, and again the results were war and extremism; only this time Europe itself is feeling the consequences in the form of refugees and terrorist attacks. For Europe in its present form to fall apart is no disaster, though, according to Dzermant.

'That means you're placing your hopes in right-wing populism, in Le Pen, Wilders, the AfD?'

'I place my hopes in the EU-critical forces, and there are some on the left as well. Melenchon in France, for example: if you count him as well as Le Pen, you almost have a majority.'

'But you were just warning us against nationalism in Belarus and Ukraine!'

'Yes, that is a paradox, I admit. If I were French, I would vote for Le Pen, but as a Belarusian, I see that Le Pen would be the end of Europe.'

'And so?'

'You have to ask how Europe got into this dilemma. And then you come to the EU establishment, which provoked the Euroscepticism in the first place. The establishment continued the Cold War instead of working together with Russia. I dream of a united Europe extending from Vladivostok to Lisbon.'

I ask Alexey Dzermant whether the European ideals mean anything to him, whether they appeal to him.

'Yes, absolutely,' he answers firmly, 'especially today, when the humanistic project of the modern era is being challenged by Islamic fundamentalism.'

'But most Muslim refugees flee to Europe. They're not fleeing to Saudi Arabia or Iran. And they're not fleeing to Russia. Evidently, the humanistic project seems to appeal more to them, too, than fundamentalism.'

'But what are they in Europe? Second-class people. And that's going to make them susceptible to fundamentalism, even if they weren't before the wars that Europe helped to encourage. And Islamic fundamentalism will in turn encourage the nationalists. Europe is creating its own problems.'

After the Georgian wine, which tastes at least as good as any Italian restaurant's house red, Dzermant orders a sweet decoction to finish with. Not for me, I say. But Dmitrij, who has been shaking his head more than at Granny Frida's, joins him.

Fifteenth Day: Into the Exclusion Zone East of Krasnapolle

To get into an exclusion zone after all, I accompany Tatiana and her son Igor, whose village no longer exists. Tatiana was thirty-two when the inhabitants were called into the cultural centre to learn that they were no longer allowed to enter the forest, drink water from the well, eat vegetables from their gardens, let their children play outdoors. And yet her village was nearly 300 kilometres northeast of Chernobyl, far enough away, initially, on 26 April 1986. Their bad luck was the wind. This time I have put on the cheap shoes, which is nonsense, it occurs to me: am I already paranoid, after just three days? If the biologist in Khoiniki is right, then I have to throw away the new pair anyway, which will leave me barefoot this evening. But, on the other hand, his reassurances sounded so dubious that perhaps I shouldn't believe his warnings either. To be sure, I have brought along a Geiger counter today.

As we drive, Tatiana recounts that, in the beginning, they only removed the soil, put a new covering on the walls of the school and tested all the villagers constantly. Her own results were almost normal; other mothers were not allowed to breast-feed their babies, though. The district supervisor always assured them there was no cause for alarm, and soon afterwards he died of leukaemia. Tatiana's husband was a teacher, like her, and his other subject besides mathematics was civil defence, so he knew a little about radioactive fallout, and he got hold of some iodine tablets. Meanwhile the farmers were soon letting their children go outdoors again. Once her father-in-law, who was the head of the school, brought home a newspaper from Czechoslovakia, which they tried to translate to get some information. Another time – Igor was two years old – the authorities wrote that his radiation dose was high and he had to be hospitalized immediately: that was the worst moment. Fortunately, Tatiana quickly realized that Igor hadn't even been tested on the date written on the form. It was another child, who happened to have the same first and last names, who was contaminated.

'It's hard to deal with something you can't see.'

Tatiana has not heard of birth defects in newborns, but she has noticed that more people die of cancer than before; whether that is connected with Chernobyl is hard for her to judge. She also noticed that an unusual number of suicides occurred. At first she had often felt tired, but apparently her body gradually adapted. The paediatrician had made it plain that she should move away as soon as possible, before the official evacuation, which didn't come until six years after the reactor accident; they decided not to wait to be assigned a flat. Instead, they went looking for a new home with a Geiger counter in hand. In Mogilov, about 130 kilometres away from their village, they found a neighbourhood where the instrument didn't blink.

In the regional capital, Krasnapolle, we make a stop to talk with the president of the regional parliament, a former colleague of Tatiana's. Our welcome is as cordial as in the countryside, and the president's home-town loyalty is touching. The population of Krasnapolle was once 26,000; today it is less than 10,000, although the schoolchildren get free lunch and the salaries, until recently, included a geographic bonus. 'We don't feel forgotten,' the president declares, and points out that the radiation levels are measured

73

regularly in all public buildings, and the children spend the summer in a sanatorium, sometimes even abroad, to recuperate. The president can't say exactly what the children need to recuperate from if they are healthy. She is eager to show off the new sports centre – not every town has something like this – and so we soon find ourselves between a whirlpool, a children's pool and an official-sized 25-metre pool.

'Look how beautiful it turned out. And you still haven't seen our sauna.'

The exclusion zone, beginning another 30 kilometres farther on, is not a continuous area like that on the southern side but looks like a patchwork quilt on the map, because the radioactivity did not diminish at the same rate everywhere. There are no barriers or fences, only signs prohibiting entry. At first, the president wants to accompany us – she is a friendly and most of all a hospitable woman, that is quite apparent – but then she realizes that she at least should respect the prohibition. We have nothing to worry about, though; the road is practically never patrolled. We want to get something to eat before we leave the city – but what? In the end we decide to buy some bananas at the market, because we can be sure they were not grown in the region.

When we're sitting in the car again, I ask Igor where he learned such good German. He answers with another question: whether I recall the expression *Tschernobylkinder*, the 'Chernobyl children'. Yes, now I remember. Like thousands of other children from Belarus and Ukraine, he spent the summers with a host family in Germany. Their youngest child once came into Igor's bedroom at night to see whether he glowed in the dark. After his third or fourth summer in Germany, his host parents called him their Russian son. He has his German skills to thank for his job with the Goethe-Institut. No, he says, Chernobyl did not rob him, at least, of his future.

We drive past young pine forests and recently ploughed fields. Only after a no-entry sign bearing the radiation symbol is the landscape left to nature, with no trace of asphalt left. But there are logs by the wayside that someone has dumped there, probably forestry workers. At a crossroads stands a weathered stone monument on which only a few names are still legible, an Ivan Saitev, a Yuri Yakimovich, 'fallen in the struggle against the German fascists'; their village had already been completely burnt down by the Germans.

Tatiana's village, too, seems to have been completely eradicated except for the war monument. But then she shows us the woods, and amidst the fir trees, which are twenty, thirty years old by now, I discern the walls of a two-storey building. This is the teachers' quarters, the house where they lived.

The last thing Igor can remember is his father cutting the cables. 'Why are you doing that?' Igor asked. 'To prevent a short circuit,' his father replied. The bulldozers usually arrived overnight so that the inhabitants wouldn't have time to take the doors, windows, floor coverings and the like, but somehow they always found out ahead of time which house was going to be torn down. Some people made good money by dismantling their house down to the last 2-by-4, loading it on a flat-bed, and selling it in Moscow as a dacha. Igor doesn't know why the teachers' house hasn't been buried – perhaps because the concrete didn't absorb as much radioactivity as the wood that the other houses were built of, or because it would have been more trouble to tear down.

We continue through the woods and come to the former grocery shop, which was also built of concrete. The roof has collapsed, heavy beams lie jumbled, but the walls still bear the tiles showing where the meat or the dairy counter was.

'There used to be a car park in front of the shop,' says Igor. 'There were cars; it wasn't some backwater.'

Again, each step is eerie, although the soil, as in Kurapaty, was removed to a metre deep. But, strangely, my Geiger counter is silent. Finally we come to the third concrete building: right next to the entrance is the headmaster's office, where Tatiana saw her bald father-in-law every morning on entering the school. On the walls are the dates of the next reunions: the class of '89 meets the first Saturday of every August. 'Vladimir, call me if you read this.' The wooden floors have been torn out, but the basketball hoops are still hanging on the walls in the sports hall. The Geiger counter still doesn't blink, neither in the building nor in the forest that was once the schoolyard. Not even the soles of my shoes are contaminated.

On the way home, another signpost along the motorway indicating the way to a death camp: at least 60,000 people were murdered in Trostinets, most of them Jews. And of the few Jews who survived the camp, many disappeared into the Gulag as 'spies' after their liberation. A group of Minsk Jews who erected a memorial stone to their brothers and sisters here in 1947 also ended up in Siberia. Since the 1960s, an obelisk at least vaguely recalls the 'peaceful civilians, partisans and prisoners of war of the Red Army' who were 'shot, buried and burnt by the German-fascist occupiers'. Of the camp itself, not even the barbed wire can be seen.

In my hotel room I Skype with Yury Bandazhevsky, the specialist in radiation medicine from Gomel who was arrested in 1999 and exiled six years later.

Today he is a researcher in Kiev. I start by asking him whether the Belarusian authorities don't collect data or whether they just don't publish it.

'I don't know. There hasn't been a serious article from Belarus in radiation medicine for the past ten, twelve years. What there are are blanket statements: everything is all right, all measurements normal, everything under control. But we have data from Ukraine. Cancer rates are clearly elevated, breast cancer for example, and, from our standpoint, the connection with Chernobyl is proven. And the situation in Ukraine is comparable with areas that are considered clean in Belarus. Now, if we extrapolate our data and apply it to Belarus, which was much more strongly affected by the radiation, we arrive at completely different results. Then we see that the problems have not diminished, but increased.'

'How so?'

'We now have the second Chernobyl generation, the people born after the disaster. I treated many of them as children back in Gomel. Because of their parents' genetic damage, they are born weaker and react to lower doses of radiation. Now, years later, many of them have died. Or they are unable to have children. Or, if they have children, they pass on their genetic damage.'

'Are the evacuated areas too small?'

'Yes, definitely; many more people would have had to be relocated – whole cities in fact, like Mogilov and Gomel. But the fact that people were allowed to go on living in the immediately contaminated areas is criminal. And that's not just my opinion.'

I tell Bandazhevsky that my Geiger counter didn't blink when I was in the exclusion zone – that means the radioactivity can't be so high any more, doesn't it? The radioactivity, Bandazhevsky teaches me, is no longer on the surface. You can stand on the soil, but you can't eat what grows in it. The radioactivity gets into the food through the roots. Forest fires, too, are very dangerous – which explains the watchtower at the checkpoint on the edge of the exclusion zone.

'The biologist who showed us around assured us that all the food is tested before it is sold.'

'Yes, they test it, and if the measurements are too high, they mix it with clean food until the norms are halfway maintained. And these foods are then distributed all over the country.'

'But are the norms themselves acceptable?'

'No, of course not; that's what I've been saying the whole time. For a generation whose genetic material is already damaged, even smaller doses of radiation are hazardous. And, apart from that, food is different from getting an X-ray. Food must contain no radioactivity at all.'

'Then that's … I won't say murder, but negligent manslaughter, negligent mass killing.'

'It's not negligent, it's going on deliberately. It is mass murder.'

'Should other countries be boycotting Belarusian food?'

'Yes. The way Belarus mixes contaminated and uncontaminated foods, they shouldn't be imported anywhere.'

'Does the biologist believe himself what he told us, or is he just lying?'

'He's lying,' Bandazhevsky is certain. 'It's not possible that he hasn't noticed any changes. If he's a biologist at all, he's lying. The scientists researching on Chernobyl in Belarus have grown up in a state based on the Chernobyl lie; they work for that state. When they see that the rector of a medical faculty can be locked away, they know the kind of harassment they can expect the minute they speak up. Getting fired is the least of what would happen to them.'

And now what do I do with my shoes? Do I have to throw away both pairs, the cheap ones and the expensive ones, even though the Geiger counter didn't blink?

On the screen of my laptop, Yury Bandazhevsky laughs. 'There won't be anything wrong with your shoes,' he assures me. 'Wash the one pair and keep them as a souvenir of Chernobyl.'

Sixteenth Day: From Minsk to Kiev

On the motorway heading towards Ukraine, I think that Valentin Akudovich was right again in counting industrialized agriculture among the apocalyptic events of the twentieth century. An earthquake couldn't have changed the landscape more drastically: 'A country that once hid shyly behind bushes, marshes and woods is now stretched out naked. Opened up flat with its ruler-straight ditches, it extends to the horizon.'[18] Akudovich writes that, in 1976 alone, 11,000 tractors, more than 3,000 excavators, almost 3,000 bulldozers and many other machines were used to transform the living earth into farmland. Land improvement in general, which went hand in hand with collectivization, urbanization and industrialization, advanced faster in Byelorussia than in any other Soviet republic. Accordingly, industrial production grew for many years at twice the national average rate. 'But the Belarusian village has paid a high price for this breakthrough. It has disappeared as a social and cultural place.' Akudovich's wording is probably too drastic. But it is strange indeed that none of the villages we pass through after leaving the motorway is still built around an old centre. At the most there is sometimes a cross-street with more houses, but never a core, never a village square; rarely enough a church; no pavements where the inhabitants might meet; only an assembly hall that is opened for special occasions, a grocery shop without windows, now and then a petrol station, and always a cemetery with a war memorial. Even the houses keep their distance from one another, as if everyone here were self-sufficient.

We drive into Svietlahorsk, a concrete prefab settlement of 70,000 inhabitants that was built along the pipeline from Russia. The 'Mound of Light', as Svietlahorsk might be translated, achieved some fame in the 1990s because it had the highest rates of AIDS, alcoholism and drug addiction in all of Belarus. The state responded by launching some development programmes, although they are not conspicuous when you drive through the city today. There is an old shopping centre and a new one, an inflatable castle and a trampoline, a bookshop with only children's comics displayed on the shelves; besides that there is – nothing. The people do not go to a pub in the evening, we learn; they do not sit in a café during the day; instead they meet to drink in the parks or in front of the residential blocks, when they're not watching television and drinking alone. The most exciting place is the petrol station, where people also meet to drink.

We have an appointment to meet a physician specializing in addiction who confirms that the rates of dependency in Svietlahorsk are still exorbitant. There are no exact figures, because only those addicts who begin in-patient treatment are registered. The hospitals' addiction wards are no worse, the rates of recidivism not significantly higher than in other countries; that's not the problem. The problem is that treatment costs money, and therefore the poor, the farmers, practically never get treatment. The doctors never see them until it's too late.

I ask whether alcoholism could have anything to do with the many historic ruptures and traumas that have been repressed.

We can only speculate on that, says the doctor; naturally the phenomenon does not have one single cause. Nonetheless, it is striking that alcohol is a problem of similar proportions in the neighbouring countries that had similar experiences in the twentieth century. 'And not just alcohol,' the doctor adds, flipping open his laptop to show me this abstract of a paper by three Austrian neuropsychiatrists:

Suicide and homicide rates are the ultimate expressions of violence. The global distributions of suicide and homicide rates are almost mirror images: rich, modern democratic countries with a functioning legal system have high suicide and low homicide rates; traditional states with a weak central government have high homicide and low suicide rates. Exceptions are some Eastern European countries, in which the rates of both homicide and suicide are very high. These states are located on the territory of the former 'Bloodlands' (Snyder, *Bloodlands: Europe between Hitler and Stalin*, 2010), where, between 1930 and 1945, fourteen million people were civilian victims of the Soviets and the National Socialists.[19]

Beyond Svietlahorsk, we see hardly any people along the road, although the fields are cultivated. There are intervals of three, four, sometimes ten minutes between the cars we see going the other way. Gradually, the illusion arises that I know only from more remote countries: that of being the first to set foot on a new continent. Something of this feeling must also have befallen the young writer Andrei Horwath, who moved to a tiny village near the border and tells about his new life in a widely read blog. He has cooked a meal of vegetables, eggs and potatoes for us on an open fire.

'Only the salt is shop-bought,' he mumbles as he sets the cast-iron pan on the table on the veranda. Although he speaks softly, almost without intonation, his pride in having grown all the other ingredients himself is evident. The bathtub is in an unroofed wooden shed and has to be filled using buckets. There is no running water, but there is electricity for the computer and the Internet router. No, Andrei doesn't often talk, you can tell; he leaves long pauses between his sentences – when he answers at all. Thin beard, earnest face, lanky body. His wife and their six-year-old daughter still live in Minsk, but he wanted to get out of the city, away from the people, to live a simple life, work on his novel. Once a month Andrei's daughter comes to visit for a few days. Otherwise he goes to Minsk to see his family, except that lately he can't stay longer than overnight, now that he has a goat. That bothers him, he says; he would like to combine the city and the country. But it doesn't work on account of the goat.

I ask him how he communicates with the people. In the local dialect, a very authentic variety of Belarusian, Andrei explains. Sometimes Russian words are mixed in, especially in reference to official matters. And then there is a word, *anihadki*, that is used very often although no one enough knows what it means: a word to fill in pauses, to express assent, praise or just about any other sentiment, depending on how it is spoken.

Such linguistic subtleties have contributed a great deal to the success of his blog, Vera says, as Andrei clears away the pan, still half full. It was delicious, but evidently a special feast for us visitors. He won't be going to such trouble every day; best if he has some benefit from it tomorrow and the next day. The Belarusian that is spoken in the cities by intellectuals, artists, more or less dissidents, always has something artificial about it, Vera continues, but Andrei writes from the source, so to speak; in his language people hear the world of their grandparents. It opens the hearts of people who are otherwise completely Russian. Especially the young people are becoming increasingly interested in Belarusian; they organize classes. Recently even the president mentioned that his son likes Belarusian. That was a sign to the functionaries, who have learned to guess what is expected of them.

The house belonged to Andrei's great-grandfather, who had been a kulak, a landowning farmer, and of course had been banished beyond the Urals. Or at least his son, Andrei's grandfather, had. Andrei's grandmother spent three years as a forced labourer in Germany, and always went on about how well she had been treated. Come again? That's right, Andrei explains: once she came late to her workplace and the German boss didn't even scold her. She made a paper flower and gave it to him to show her thanks. The farmers here knew perfectly well that the villages were burnt down because the partisans were hiding in them. Besides, the partisans just took whatever they needed; the Germans at least paid for their chickens. That doesn't mean the people liked the Germans, but it's true that the partisans were also feared, not to mention the communists. The farmers didn't hate anyone, neither the Germans nor the Russians; hate doesn't seem to have had any place in their emotional lives at all. After six decades, Andrei says, the people are still living in a kind of postwar mood in which they're glad to be still alive and not starving, regardless of who is in power.

And what are their day-to-day lives like here? The people are lazier now; they used to be obliged to work; today they get their money no matter what. Okay, Andrei continues, the only people left in the village are those who had no way to get out: the old people mainly, and the young ones who couldn't have coped in the city or who tried it and came back. And, then again, they don't need much. The village school has been closed for two years now; there aren't enough children any more. Alcohol is the biggest problem here; vodka is cheaper than anywhere else in the world; beer costs little more than water. Only the seasonal workers bring back significant amounts of money when they come back from Russia.

'Do the people vote?' I ask.

'Yes, 100 per cent of them.'

'For the government.'

'I guess so.'

The people don't talk about politics; not that Andrei has ever heard. They don't go to the polls because they like the president; they go because the local administrator tells them to. Sometimes they complain about the head of the kolkhoz, but they don't do anything to instigate change.

'Is that the Soviet mentality?'

'I think it's older than communism, a kind of mixture of Christian faith and paganism, but it goes deeper here than in Russia. And they have the same kind of relation to the president, to the priest, to the head of the kolkhoz – the same relation as they have to the gods: you complain about them sometimes, but you obey them.'

'Does Europe mean anything to them?'

'No, nothing. Europe is just a name they hear on television, but it doesn't mean anything to the people. They have no perception of Europe.'

Andrei takes us for a walk through the village, which consists of just two streets, one asphalt, the other sand.

'Where does this go?' I ask, pointing to the sand track.

'To the next village, which is even more remote.'

'And what is it like there?'

'Well, the same as here, mainly, lots of wooden houses. Only fewer of them have electricity.'

The grocery shop, which will also be closed someday, offers the bare necessities – frozen meat, dried fish, washing powder. A bottle of vodka costs the equivalent of 80 euro cents and has no screw top – once it's opened, it's always drunk up, says Andrei.

'I always wonder about the bread,' he adds.

'Why?'

'There's so much grain grown here, and then the bread is the worst and the cheapest stuff you can imagine. I don't understand it. If nothing else, the people could at least eat decent bread.'

On the sand track, we encounter first a horse-drawn cart and a short time later an old woman in an ankle-length cloak, a bright red headscarf over her long, loose hair. She is ranting at the top of her lungs, gesticulating as if she were railing at someone walking backwards in front of her. She doesn't seem to notice us. 'What is she shouting about?' I ask when we have passed her by.

'She has two grown sons. And one didn't like her cooking. That's what she's complaining about. She's the one I like best of all the villagers. Sometimes she visits me and sits on my veranda and tells me her life's story. Over and over again, her whole life.'

'And what is she on about now?' I ask, since the old woman's voice has got shriller.

'Right now she's complaining about Vera,' Andrei explains, and has to smile a little, although he is usually so serious. 'The kind of women who walk around here these days, as clean as dolls.'

This is a world on the verge of disappearing, Andrei says. The little villages are dying out; there's no need for Chernobyl to do them in – first the school, then the church, and finally the shop. Even now there are villages nearby where the bus stops only once a week, even though no one there has a car. Finally, when the last house is vacant, the bulldozer comes and covers everything with earth so that nothing is left. The people here, who are the base of Lukashenko's regime, don't want to change anything.

'And if a different regime came to power tomorrow?'

'They wouldn't even notice. To them, only the flag would be different.'

'And if the EU were to arrive tomorrow with its blue signs indicating investment projects, with a market economy, advertising, ideas of civil liberty?'

'Then they would adjust to that just the same, and inside they'd stay how they are.'

'But, for your part, what do you think?' I ask Andrei: 'Would it be a good thing if Belarus belonged to Europe? I mean, if there was a prospect of joining the European Union?'

'I'm not sure,' Andrei answers. 'The village wouldn't be ready. It wouldn't die slowly; it would be swept away at once. You know, we're at the crossroads of different worlds; that makes us special. The point of our culture is that we're both West and East. If we were to turn only towards the West, we would destroy our culture. I always imagine us with a fence on either side, to the west and to the east – but a very low fence that you can easily step over.'

I tell Andrei that people like him are necessary, people who act as a kind of translator. Without him, not even my companions from Minsk would have found a way into this rural world on the edge of Europe. Even with an interpreter along, I couldn't have simply talked with the people.

'Yes, but to understand, you have to stay longer,' he says.

'That's true,' I reply. 'But some things you understand only when you travel, not if you stay put.'

'Could be,' says Andrei Horwath, who can travel only for a day at a time on account of his goat.

We get back on the road in order to reach the Ukrainian border in daylight: a fenced-in road running several kilometres through a dense forest, with several barriers along it that open only after a thorough inspection, and, on a parking area, a solitary shop with the same brands as in every duty-free shop in the free-market economies. Men carrying heavy bags coming the other way, migrant workers, probably, on the way home – is there no direct coach line? Right after the last checkpoint, the potholes give us a jolt. Whatever else you might say about Belarus, at least I was able to take notes in the back seat and even type on my laptop. In Ukraine, it's impossible. Besides that, paradoxically, there are also significantly more Ladas to be seen on the roads: the Ukrainians buy more Russian cars. In contrast to Belarus, and in greater contrast to Ukraine's western neighbours which have joined the European Union, the average income has declined steadily since 1991 and is now 200 dollars a month. Nonetheless, when we drive into the first town in Ukraine at about seven o'clock, we encounter people on the pavements; there are shops with display windows, cafés, a kebab stand, bright, colourful lights. In Belarus, which has stayed in the Russian or perhaps even the Soviet hemisphere of Europe, people do not enliven the public spaces. I climb out of the shiny limousine with diplomatic plates that belongs to the director of the Goethe-Institut in Minsk to stow my suitcase in the boot of a decrepit Peugeot 304 whose headlights are fastened with adhesive tape. I can depend on the car, the driver assures me when he notices my uneasy glance; it's been running reliably for 400,000 kilometres. So have the plastic clogs, apparently, that my new travelling companion is wearing below his Bermuda shorts.

This evening in Kiev I am back in my own coordinate system. Perhaps because I am already accustomed to fewer sensory impressions – since Vilnius, the landscape has been nothing but flat and monotonous – the night life seems brighter, more anarchic; the restaurants and bars full to the front pavements with well-dressed, visibly hedonistic young people; a city that is booming and decaying at the same time; here picturesquely dilapidated brick buildings, there the gentrification already driving all life out of the narrow streets; the trams left over from the Cold War, whereas in Minsk everything was brand-new; dirt in the streets that was nowhere to be seen in Belarus; visible poverty and all the more ostentatiously displayed wealth. 'The people in the SUVs are all criminals, without exception,' mumbles Sashko, the driver, raised in a family of artists in Lviv, later a taxi driver and bartender in New York, now a revolutionary and ardent patriot. 'Putin understands only fists,' he says, and curses his own government with his next breath.

There are still bullet holes visible here and there in the buildings surrounding the Maidan, where photos of the martyrs are exhibited in the middle of the square. Otherwise, the gigantic square enclosed by Soviet high-rises, which gave a completely mistaken impression of the historic city centre in the TV news, has long since been reconquered by the leisure society: tourists, young people, families with children, the same street artists as in Cracow or Barcelona, all the bric-a-brac that you used to find only at funfairs. Some of the billboards show soldiers fighting in the east. The war couldn't be farther away.

Seventeenth Day: Kiev

Konstantin Batozsky guides me to breakfast in one of the coffee bars in the lower town that look straight out of East Berlin's trendy borough Prenzlauer Berg, but the 'used' look is achieved artificially: the whitewashed vintage plywood shelves, bar stools and cans, the intelligent pop music, all ingredients organically grown, the cookies home-made, the cappuccino top-notch. Konstantin is a political consultant; he once worked for Serhiy Taruta, one of the more liberal oligarchs, and, in spite of his worldliness, he is a proud Ukrainian nationalist. Yet he hasn't a drop of Ukrainian blood in his veins, he remarks ironically; born in 1980 in Donetsk, the Soviet-style industrial city in the east, where the separatists hold power today, he grew up with no ties to Ukrainian culture, barely spoke the language, and went to Moscow to study political science. When the revolution broke out, most of his acquaintances took the side of the eastward-oriented government, as if there could be no question about it. Konstantin hesitated briefly. Then he flew to Kiev and joined the marchers in the Maidan. Why? 'Because their political ideals were my own: freedom, democracy, Europe.'

'Fascist,' a friend reviled him, but Konstantin in turn does not hesitate to compare Putin with Hitler, mentioning parallels. He's now learning Ukrainian, and his children are growing up bilingual from the start.

'And what should be done with the many other people whose parents or

84

grandparents were resettled from other parts of the Soviet Union?' I ask. 'Suddenly they wake up in a state to which they have no connection at all.'

'Yes,' says Konstantin, 'that is difficult, certainly.' And he understands his family, who stayed in Donetsk: they have little sympathy for the separatists, he says, but they are old, conservative, unwilling to give up their home.

'So, what about the Russians who came to Ukraine during the Soviet period?' I probe further. 'You can't force all these people to adopt Ukrainian culture.'

'Why not?' says Konstantin; 'At least for their children, they have to decide whether they're going to be Ukrainian or Russian.'

'And what if they want to remain Russian?'

'Obviously that's going to be a problem.'

'What kind of problem? Will they be expelled?'

'No. But those who are under the influence of Russian propaganda will hardly be able to integrate in Ukraine.'

'Then it boils down to an expulsion after all.'

'No, no. But you can't enjoy all the rights of a state and at the same time reject the state. No country in the world tolerates that.'

I ask whether his Jewish origins played a role in his decision, which amounted to a break not only with many friends but also with his home town, Donetsk, where he cannot return. The most it might have to do with Judaism, he replies, is that anti-Semitism was of course rampant in the Soviet Union – as a child he was frightened, almost ashamed, when he found out his family was Jewish. Perhaps that is why the promise of equality appealed to him so strongly. But isn't Ukrainian nationalism a threat to him then, I wonder: after all, every nationalism defines some people as belonging and excludes all others from the promise of equality. No, I'm misunderstanding Ukrainian nationalism, Konstantin answers, and asks whether he should take me to meet the real bad guys, the Azov Battalion.

'Are they the ones with the fascist emblems and the straight-arm salute?'

'Yes, that's them,' Konstantin confirms, and laughs: 'the Nazis.'

'You, a Jew, want to take me to see the Nazis?'

'They're not Nazis; you can think of them more as a youth culture. These symbols – to them they're hip; they use them to be provocative. But it's not about Hitler; it's about being against Russia, more like football fans.'

'Football fans?'

'See for yourself.'

At noon I am in a little school auditorium where the Crimean Tatars of Kiev are celebrating the opening of their school – or their after-school centre, to be exact, since the exile community does not have a building of its own. Balloons, children's performances, and the cameras of Crimean television. The parents are proud, as parents are all over the world, and as the speeches drag on the children get impatient, like all children. The imam says a few words, too, but none of the women here are wearing headscarves. Besides the facial features, only the dances are clearly Eastern: floating movements over racing rhythms, disturbingly sensual in view of the dancers' age, with costumes from an exotic, altogether enchanting world. To be frank, you have only to see the children's dances, in their rare combination of innocence and awareness of their bodies, to feel what a loss it would be if the Crimean Tatars were the next European culture to vanish. The observation that his people have survived all calamities up to now is the only thing the leader of the Crimean Tatars, Refat Chubarov, can muster against the lack of any political prospect. It's not realistic to expect anyone else in the world to stand up for his little minority: not the Ukrainians, who will not wage a second war against a great power for Crimea; not Europe, which has enough other conflicts with Russia; and America ... ah! once there was a dream of America.

I visit Chubarov in an unprepossessing courtyard flat, the business offices of a people, where he recounts the calamities of the past 200 years with more melancholy than indignation: expulsion, banishments, mass murders, arrests, land grabs, discrimination, false accusations – yesterday, collaboration; today, religious extremism. Just when Ukrainian independence and the return of the Tatars from Soviet banishment had presented the outlines of a future, a secure, peaceful and free existence in which they could have gathered up the debris of their ancient culture and erected it anew, the Russian annexation of Crimea made them second-class citizens again.

In Samarkand his father always said, almost as a prayer: we will go back home; we will go back home. He went back home to Crimea and died on 13 March 2014, while Russian soldiers marched in the streets once again. Chubarov's mama – the sixty-year-old man uses that word, mama – is still living at home, only now he can no longer visit her. 'Stalin banished my parents; Putin took my parents away from me.'

Chubarov is unable to point to a realistic prospect of restoring Crimea to Ukraine. More pressure needs to be put on Russia, he says almost desperately, only to observe himself that the German foreign minister Steinmeier, quite to the contrary, wants to lift the sanctions to begin negotiations. 'You give a blackmailer everything to get him to begin negotiations with you – and what do you think you'll be able to negotiate then?'

I ask whether he is oppressed by pessimism. No, says Chubarov; no, there are so many possible solutions; you have only to look at history.

'At history?' I ask. 'The twentieth century is full of expulsions; hardly any of them have ever been reversed. On the contrary: countries like Poland, Germany, and also the Greeks and the Turks have only been able to make peace once they resigned themselves to the expulsions.'

'Yes, but Germany still had a country. The German language, the German culture weren't threatened with extinction. The leaders of the great nations have no sense of how it is for minorities. If we lose, we lose everything. We cease to exist.'

The Crimean Tatars are not so numerous; just a few million scattered throughout the world. It cannot be taken for granted that their language, their culture will survive. Hence the school opening; hence the exile television channel – will that be enough in the long term?

'There are other examples in history,' says Chubarov, seeking reasons for optimism.

'Such as?'

'Just take South Tyrol. They found a solution. You don't always have to redraw the borders. You can be a little more creative. Europe has demonstrated it.'

'Isn't that rather too optimistic?'

'No, I am an informed optimist.'

In the evening I go for a drink with the young theatre director Pavel Yurov, who interpreted for me during the day. All the day's conversations had to do with war, expulsion, the revolution; after that, we both find it hard to put up with the pleasure society that hangs out in Kiev's bars. 'Is anyone here at all interested in what's going on in the eastern part of the country?' I ask, indicating the press of young people sipping their cocktails or swigging a Heineken.

'They're exactly as interested in the war as the young people in Cologne or London,' replies Pavel, who has played in Germany with his troupe, and he explains that, where political consciousness is concerned, distance is not a matter of geography, but of sensory perception. No matter how many kilometres you are away from one of the fronts to Europe's east – whether the 3,000 kilometres from London to Aleppo or the 700 from Kiev to Donetsk – you evidently have to be shot at, menaced by terror or personally confronted with refugees to feel that there is a war on.

'And in your case?' I ask, because Pavel comes from Donbas.

'I needed the physical experience too,' he says, and tells me how he was taken prisoner in Slovyansk: at the beginning of the war, he was sitting in a café with a friend of his, an art student; they were surfing the Internet, talking; in those days nobody thought about snitches, or perhaps they were naive; in any case there were a few sarcastic remarks about the separatists, and someone must have overheard them and passed them on, because shortly afterwards some armed men were standing in front of the gabbing friends and arresting them as spies. They weren't released until three months later.

'That was traumatic,' says Pavel, 'being abandoned, the helplessness.' Now he is in the volunteer militia.

'You're fighting?' I ask, surprised, because I can't imagine a man like Pavel, a sophisticated man of the theatre with a soft voice, a gentle body, as a warrior.

'I volunteered for the reserves. If you were in the Maidan, you have to do something. After all, even if you don't notice it in Kiev, we are at war. And, besides, the militia is very interesting.'

'Why?'

'There are people from all walks of life whom I would never have had anything to do with otherwise. And it's also interesting to experience what having a weapon does to you. I'm talking about myself personally, but of course the same could be said of the country. You don't feel so vulnerable any more.'

Eighteenth Day: From Kiev to Dnipro

According to the legend that has long grown up around the Euromaidan, it was an Afghan who sparked the revolution in Ukraine: 'We will meet at 11:30 p.m. at the foot of the Monument to Independence. Dress warm, bring umbrellas, tea, coffee, good spirits and your friends.' That's nonsense of course, says Mustafa Nayyem, the Afghan in question; it was only by chance that it was his appeal to take to the streets that spread like wildfire; it could just as well have been another post, once the Ukrainian president Viktor Yanukovich had rescinded the association agreement with the European Union on 21 November 2013. Be that as it may, Nayyem can't meet me in the Maidan; too many people would accost him there. Instead, we sit in one of the side streets, 100 metres away from the scene of the revolution, on the narrow terrace of an Italian restaurant.

Nayyem came to Kiev as a child when his father married his second wife, a Ukrainian. Before the Maidan made him a hero, he was already famous as an investigative journalist for the online magazine *Ukrainska Pravda*, 'The Ukrainian Truth'. Then, two years ago, he went into politics: he won a seat in parliament on the electoral list of the governing oligarch, Petro Poroshenko. In Ukraine, almost all politicians of the old school are business-men who see politics as one of their fields of business, Nayyem explains. Anyone who doesn't own a business or a factory of his own is considered weak, not taken seriously. The new, young politicians have to prove that you don't need money to impose changes.

'As a journalist, you're automatically on the right side. But bearing respon-sibility is much harder. As a politician, you have to stand up for things that you're unsure about, that go against your instincts; you have to make com-promises. You see how it works; you see all the corruption. Then all at once you realize that the people mistrust you, that most of them are disappointed in you. I hear that often: that I've betrayed my ideals. I have a hard time dealing with the fact that many people think I'm a traitor.'

'And would you say you did the right thing when you switched to politics?'

'Yes, absolutely. It's an evolution. In the details, we've accomplished quite a bit in these two years. But of course the people aren't satisfied – I can see that – and the people are right. We're still a long way away from the democ-racy we want. But we'll never achieve it if we don't enter the institutions. It's up to us now! Our generation has to gradually take over the country.'

Does Nayyem have any particular problems as an Afghan in Ukrainian politics? No, he replies, none at all. Not even the right-wingers who criticize him for his political ideas refer to his origins.

'But the radical nationalists are a problem, aren't they?' I ask, thinking of the Azov Battalion that I'll soon be visiting with Konstantin.

'Sure, there are radicals,' Nayyem replies, 'but they have few representa-tives in parliament, and they represent maybe 7, maybe 10 per cent of the population, not more. Compare that to France, Austria. And that even though we're at war, even though we accommodate more refugees than any other country in Europe.'

Ukraine, Nayyem continues, defending the state whose citizenship he took on late in life – Ukraine embodies the European project of unity in diver-sity as no other country does; there are so many peoples here, Romanians, Georgians, Poles, Jews, Crimean Tatars, Belarusians, and so on. Mixing is the rule here; bilingualism or multilingualism is an everyday thing; I need only switch on a talk show or a football match to marvel at how the announcers switch between Russian and Ukrainian, sometimes in the same sentence. The first person who died in the suppression of the Maidan was an Armenian; the first post-Maidan government had ministers from five nations. 'Ukraine is the country where a person was most recently killed waving the European flag. We were a bit too naive perhaps, but at least we still have the passion to stand up for the European values. Yes, I like that!'

'Do you still speak Persian, by the way?' I ask, and when Mustafa says yes, a rather curious situation arises: a hundred yards from the Maidan, an Afghan who has become Ukrainian gives an Iranian who has become German the most impassioned plea imaginable for a strong Europe – in Persian.

'Europe wants to lead – okay, but then you have to lead; you have to defend your values. If Europe doesn't come to the aid of its greatest ally, its most loyal supporter, it will be leaving itself in the lurch. Look at 1938, when Hitler annexed the Sudetenland to the German Empire. Not our problem, said the elites of France and Great Britain. And what happened? Look at the NATO summit in Bucharest in April 2008: Germany rejected Ukrainian membership. What was their argument? We mustn't provoke the Russian bear. And what happened? Two months later, Russia went to war in Georgia. And six years later took Donetsk. Or look at Syria! That's what happens when you don't react to Russia's aggression: Aleppo. The Europeans think Ukraine is a buffer zone. That's a big mistake: Ukraine is the border itself. If you don't defend the border, it gets overrun. For our part, we have no choice; we have to fight regardless. But Europe has a choice. Russia wants to weaken Europe; it foments war; it supports the anti-European movements everywhere. And what is Europe doing? Allowing itself to be weakened. It's letting Russia act and not reacting.'

'But what should Europe do?'

'Let me ask you in return: what will happen if Europe does nothing? What will the next wars be?'

Of course the idea is not a direct military confrontation, he continues; no one is asking for that. The idea is to maintain the economic pressure. Yes, in the medium term it's also about giving Ukraine a prospect of NATO membership; it's about the European Union. But mainly it's about Europe's self-image. Europe is worth something; it has incredible appeal. It mustn't sell itself so cheap.

Sashko drives me from the Maidan to one of the outlying districts of Kiev that is one factory after another, many of them apparently vacant. At the address indicated, Konstantin is waiting for me with three other young people, a man with a hipster beard, another with two conspicuous earrings, and a woman in a tank top with short, punkish hair and lots of tattoos. Loud rock music is coming from the open car in front of the driveway. No, they don't exactly look like Nazis.

The site we enter was also a factory during the Soviet era, and today it serves as the headquarters and training grounds of the Azov Battalion. Because today is Sunday, I find only a few soldiers here, but also a nurse. After their origins in the Maidan movement, they were still wearing trainers when they began fighting, reports Nazar Kravchenko, the one with the beard, and the official speaker of the Battalion; now they have state recognition and are gradually getting professional equipment and training. They have 10,000 volunteer fighters, of whom 3,000 are now at the front. According to the information in my file folder, there are at most 1,500 militiamen. But whether they are 10,000 or 1,500, the Azov Battalion attained national fame in the reconquest of the city of Mariupol. On one wall hangs the portrait of Stepan Banderas, whose militias collaborated with the Nazis to drive out the Soviets. In 1941, he proclaimed the 'Independent Republic of the Ukraine', which was supposed to become part of a fascist Europe. His followers fought fiercely against Soviet partisans and Poland's underground Home Army, and later against the Germans and the Red Army at the same time; they shot tens of thousands of Polish and Jewish civilians and were ruthlessly slaughtered in turn by the Soviets. In 1946, Bandera managed to flee to Munich, where the KGB tracked him down and murdered him in 1959. After the collapse of the Soviet Union, Ukrainian nationalists glorified him as the *Providnyk*, the leader and martyr, without mentioning his collaboration with the Nazis, anti-Semitism, and attacks against civilians. In the Russian media, meanwhile, *providnyk* became a common scare word.

Are these the fascists to whom Russia always points to explain why it sprang to the aid of Ukraine's Russian-speaking population? I can't figure out how radical this militia actually is. The answers I receive sound patriotic and, most of all, staunchly anti-Russian, but they don't sound radical in the sense of a right-wing or nationalist vision of society. When I broach topics such as homosexuality or abortion, I don't get the intransigent answers that are in my file folder. Ideologically, they don't see themselves at all as allied with right-wing populist parties such as the German AfD or the French *Front national*, Kravchenko declares; they are waging a campaign only against corruption, which is endemic. You can't have an ethnic nationalism in Ukraine: the nation is much too heterogeneous for that.

'And the Nazi symbols?'

'I have no regard for the Freudian anxieties of Europeans,' interjects Alex Kovzhun, the one with the earrings. He is a friend of Konstantin's, also a Jew, and seems to be making fun, no less, of my German Nazi complex. 'Statistically, we have the fewest hate crimes in all Europe. That's what matters. And the Europeans get worked up about whatever symbols. These aren't Nazi emblems, they're our own. Look around: there are no Hitler portraits here.'

To be honest, I don't know the statistics, nor am I able for that matter to assess how well my hip interview partners represent their organization. In any case, it's well known that the leaders and many members of Azov openly belong to extreme-right organizations. And the *Wolfsangel* sign may once have been a forestry mark, but the fact is it was used by the SS and is a global token of neo-Nazi movements today. For these reasons, the US Congress prohibited all support for Azov in 2015.

In order to hear at least one voice that has not been prepared in advance for the reporter from Germany, I talk to a militiaman who is somewhat more martial in his outward appearance: crew cut, temples shaved, combat trousers and a tight-fitting black T-shirt. Serhiy is his name; he is twenty-one years old and originally wanted to study architecture, because it is nicer, he says, to build houses than to destroy them. But now the country is at war; the state institutions are corrupt, so he decided to join the militia instead of reporting for the regular army. He rejects the Minsk Protocol, obviously, and Crimea must be liberated too.

I ask Serhiy what he, as a Ukrainian nationalist, thinks of Mustafa Nayyem – perhaps he'll talk about his Afghan origins. He admired Nayyem highly as an investigative journalist, Serhiy answers. But then Nayyem became a politician, probably wanted to make a lot of money. Now he's part of the governing faction and votes against the people's interests. No, he doesn't think much of him any more.

Because an opportunity has suddenly come up to visit the front tomorrow, we drive from the Azov headquarters further out of town. I soon become acutely aware, on the passenger seat of the rattletrap Peugeot, that Ukraine is the second-largest country in Europe, and I begin to understand the first West German chancellor, significantly from Cologne, like myself, who pushed for his country's integration in the Western community: Adenauer said he closed the curtains in his train compartment on crossing the Elbe because that was where the steppes of Siberia began. But then I also remember a book by Zygmunt Haupt that I read in preparation for the journey through Poland, until I realized it was set in a Ukrainian village. In present-day Ukraine, then at the northeastern tip of the Habsburg Empire, was the place where the Polish author grew up. Ukraine, Poland, Austria – the distinction wasn't so clear during his childhood; it kept changing. When you drive across the plains that stretch from the Baltic to the Urals, from the Carpathians to the Caucasus, the borders seem all the more arbitrary since there is no visible difference between this side and that. But monotonous? Even the winter, colourless as it is, can be sensational in this landscape, 'sensational and unique, when the snow follows upon the red, violet, sepia brown and bare black, the fox-red autumn of a day'.[20] Perhaps it is no coincidence that the most beautiful description I have ever read of the onset of winter is by a writer who grew up in the endlessness that joins Europe and Asia.

In the Ukrainian part of that endlessness, there are also signs along the road, but, with 500 kilometres still to go, we do not turn off towards the ravine Babi Yar, where 100,000 people were forced to undress, then lined up beside pits and shot and buried: Jews, of course, who had not fled in time before the German invasion, 33,771 of them, meticulously counted, just between the 26th and the 29th of September 1941, plus prisoners of war, Roma and Sinti, partisans, members of the Ukrainian intelligentsia and the national movement, and mental patients from nearby institutions. Perhaps this is cynical, perhaps typical of this, the largest of the 'Bloodlands', perhaps both: because I want to visit the new war, I have no time for the previous one.

The drive into the dark is going to be long, so I look for the passage in *A Ring of Paper* where Haupt describes a December morning in the cadets' academy:

Outside, before the wide-open door leading out into some barracks yard, against the backdrop of that yard's desolation and the vermillion of other brick buildings, the first snowflakes of that winter began to whirl. And as they circled in the air and turned like flakes of soot against the background of the pale, milky sky, and like dust, powder, white down against the dark background of the yard and the muddy parade ground, it turned into a prophecy and a message from somewhere where someone holds us in favour, in esteem, and keeps us in mind, that the worst of what we have to go through is the hopelessness and the monotony, and wisely and kindly and soothingly, yet at the same time vigorously, scatters carnival confetti so recklessly over us. How changed everything was now, how auspicious and cheerful. The prefect and toady of the unit assumed a dutiful, erect posture and, since it was the first of December, he officiously reported to the captain: 'Winter has begun as expected, sir!'[21]

Nineteenth Day: To the Front in Donbas

While we are waiting for a detachment of the Kiev 1 Battalion at a petrol station somewhere along the road between Dnipro and Donetsk in eastern Ukraine, another military convoy drives up. Three dark-bearded giants who could take on a bear climb out of one of the trucks. Hand-to-hand fighters? No, it turns out they are chaplains. A small woman with pink sunglasses stuck in her blonde, permed hair, almost spherical round her middle, joins us and after five minutes gives each of the priests a big kiss on the forehead. Before I can discover whether the other hulks in the party are also clergymen, the convoy drives away again.

'I am a patriot,' the woman explains to us cheerfully, and sadly there are not enough patriots in this area, and that is why she so heartily shows the soldiers her support. The trench that the war has dug runs right through families, including her own; her mother-in-law, for example, will not hear a word of Ukrainian spoken in her house. Her classes – she works as a teacher at a grammar school – are half pro-Ukrainian and half pro-Russian; most of her colleagues, however, are positively aggressive towards her. And does she feel ill at ease because of it? Does she think about moving to western Ukraine? No, no, the woman assures me; she is doing just fine; her husband sells tyres; naturally his business is booming because of the war.

'With all the potholes,' I observe.

For twenty years, no government has done anything here in the east; the infrastructure is crumbling; naturally the people are dissatisfied, that's understandable: the same faces, the same speeches, the same bureaucracy, everything the same as in the Soviet Union. But then at every election they vote for the pro-Russian politicians again, even though everyone knows they are thieves.

'But why?' I ask.

Spreading her arms theatrically, like an opera singer, in front of the petrol pump, the little round woman closes her eyes.

Finally a detachment from the battalion arrives, several men in an Audi SUV. One of them gets into our car with us to guide us to the front. Vyacheslav is his name; I estimate he is in his early thirties, a narrow strip of beard on his face and tattoos on his forearms. He has temporarily shut down his business, supplying doors and windows, to defend his country, and he radiates enthusiasm as if he wanted to recruit me to military service as well.

'Bastards!' he curses as we pass a fleet of white Land Cruisers with OSCE observers sitting inside. 'Wherever they've just been, the shelling starts thirty minutes later. Whenever they send us a request to hold our fire, we know the other side want to move their troops. And in the evenings they hang around the bars, picking up girls, living the life of Riley on their fat foreign-mission allowance. Those Land Cruisers: they're all armoured; 110,000 euros apiece they cost – 110,000 euros! And wait till you see the junk we drive around in.'

We approach the war zone in a wide, northerly arc, passing checkpoints, abandoned houses and a demolished railway bridge, driving on side roads and sometimes right across fields, until we see from a hilltop the high-rise buildings of Donetsk, some billows of smoke among them, probably from mortar shells. We drive on through the deserted area towards the city of Avdiivka, which is divided by the front, and suddenly come to a stop in front of a chemical factory, all its chimneys steaming.

'It's still working?' I ask, surprised.

'Yes,' answers Vyacheslav, 'the oligarchs pay the separatists not to bombard the factory.'

'That means the jobs in Avdiivka help to finance the war against Avdiivka?'

'Yes, that's one way to look at it.'

In an essay as scholarly as it is sarcastic on the 'greatest redistribution of wealth since the Russian Revolution', Wolfgang Kemp calls Ukraine a 'museum of oligarchy': a museum because the big winners of the wave of privatization of the 1990s still rule largely undisturbed, whereas in Russia Vladimir Putin, in his own words, 'swings a big club that can end a debate with one blow'.[22] The purpose of the Maidan was, not least, to end the 'expropriation of the state', but the new president, far from breaking the power of the other oligarchs, didn't even honour his promise to sell his own business. Kemp mentions Rinat Akhmetov, who operates the factory in Avdiivka, as the epitome of the speculator type engendered all over Eastern Europe by the transition from communism to the market economy. He no longer deals in property or companies, but in whole industrial sectors, in national economies – which is why the first wave of primitive capitalism after

95

1991 seemed to many citizens almost like a new invasion of nomads from the steppes. Akhmetov has 300,000 people on his payroll on both sides of the front. In addition to various yachts, television stations and a private army, Kemp writes, he owns the world's most expensive home on Hyde Park: no mean Victorian townhouse, but a group of extravagant high-rises with its own entry in Wikipedia.[23] We can also read in Wikipedia how often and where in the world Akhmetov has successfully sued to suppress the assertion that he is the godfather of the Donetsk mafia. In the Ukrainian parliament, to which he had himself elected as a precaution, he has only been seen once. However, he promoted his protégé Viktor Yanukovich to governor of the Donetsk region and then prime minister. When Yanukovich plundered his way to oligarchy in his own right, Akhmetov promptly changed sides and supported the Maidan. But, in spite of his support for the new government in Kiev, he was careful of course not to get on the wrong side of the separatists who appeared on the scene in eastern Ukraine after the successful revolution. Today his palace lies 'untouched and sublime amid the war-torn landscape,' Kemp writes, and Vyacheslav confirms: 'Bastard.'

Continuing past a full factory car park, we reach Avdiivka, a typical Soviet workers' town of concrete prefabs, wide streets, a shopping centre and parks. To my amazement, it really is inhabited: cyclists, children on the pavements, mothers with prams, a football pitch where the ball is in play, washing hung outside the windows, the front gardens neatly tended.

'What do you think: how many are on your side; how many are on the separatists' side?'

'Today? Fifty–fifty, I guess. Except that a lot of people moved to Donetsk when we took back the city.'

At the far end of the town, we drive into the courtyard of a high-rise riddled with bullet holes. In the car park are a decrepit tank and some other, still older military vehicles. The building houses the battalion, a hundred fighters on several floors, every flat an all-male household. Most of them were in the Maidan and, until recently, had civilian jobs: one was a bartender, another a teacher; all of them amateur soldiers except for the captain, it seems to me; their mood is downright chipper, and very cordial towards us. It all feels a little bit like an adventure holiday. On one helmet lying around I discover the SS runes – but that's just a joke, affirms the first man who notices my shocked look; someone just drew that on a helmet because the Russians are always calling them fascists. From the rooftop, we can see the lie of the front lines a few hundred yards away.

With ten soldiers who have put on helmets and protective vests, we climb into a grey minivan, a 1960s model, called a *tabletka* in the Soviet Union because it is pill-shaped – a wonder that it still goes! No, wait: after 300 yards, the pill doesn't go. In vain we try push-starting it before setting out on foot towards the trenches. The men's Kalashnikovs date from 1972, as the engraving reveals, and are the only technical gear they have. Strange enough that there is war again in Europe in the twenty-first century – but stranger still that the equipment is almost the same as in the last war. The only one carrying a modern rifle is the bodyguard of a young member of parliament who is visiting the troops.

Through the trenches we come to a foxhole, a soldier's assault rifle sticking up out of it; the soldier looks like a weight-lifter, on his head a pirate's kerchief instead of a helmet. Three hours on duty, six hours off; that's their rhythm, adapted to the danger and the concentration of the mission. Huddled close together, we crouch against the sandbags or on the ground, far too many people for the position, but standing up in the open trench is not a good idea. We hear the impact of shots in the distance, then orders coming in over the radio: 700 yards away an exchange of fire has begun. Okay, we'd best wait here then. A suitable moment, I think, to talk about Europe.

'Who are you fighting for? For Ukraine, or for Europe?'

'Only for Ukraine,' one of the soldiers promptly answers, and another adds, 'Look at our weapons. The only thing we got from Europe was a Humvee. But they didn't deliver spare parts with it, so now the Humvee is just standing around.'

'But doesn't Europe mean anything to you?' I persist.

'Oh yes, of course,' says the weight-lifter. 'We want to see our children grow up in Europe. But we can't even rely on our own politicians.'

'As if there weren't enough money in the country to buy modern weapons,' a third puts in. 'Instead, they're selling us.'

'In other words, you reject the Minsk Protocol.'

'Of course we reject it. If the politicians had any guts, they'd cut all the lines to Europe.'

'And will you ever live alongside the people who are now on the other side of the front?'

'My own friends are over there,' says a young man who comes from Donetsk. 'They can't understand why I've chosen Ukraine, and I can't understand how they can choose to side with the separatists.'

'They won't forgive us for having killed them, nor vice versa,' says the weight-lifter. 'But, in the end, time will heal all wounds. It has to; there's no other way.'

When no more shots are heard and the all-clear comes over the radio, we walk through the trenches back to the road and then stroll back to the city. The pill is still standing by the roadside, as if the AA were on the way. The people passing us going the other way or sitting in front of their houses act as if we were the most normal passers-by in the world – there are no greetings, but no animosity either. At one point I speak to some older people who are passing a bottle in one of the front yards, but, with a squad of Ukrainian soldiers at my back, I don't find out anything in Avdiivka except that peace would be a nice thing too; cheers.

It's hot, we're wearing our helmets and bullet-proof vests, and so, when we come to a shop, I treat the squad to an ice cream. The woman from the shop has to laugh when she sees the soldiers around the freezer. As if he were playing a part in a comedy, Sashko enters the shop last, still wearing his Bermuda shorts and shower slippers along with his helmet and vest. We continue on the sandy track, each man with his ice lolly in hand, and yes, now it really looks like a – I won't say a boy scout troop on an excursion, but it does look as if the war were only a game someone thought up. And perhaps it is that: a game other people are playing, in which the men here are just figures on the board. Nonetheless, more than 10,000 people have really died so far.

Twentieth Day: Via Mariupol to the Black Sea

Seventeen kilometres away from the front line, in the town of Volnovakha, I try to strike up a conversation with people in front of a café, in a grocery store, in a flower shop. I can't. Sashko, who is usually everyone's best friend from the word go, seems reluctant today; in his translation he condenses my questions and keeps giving me translated answers that are perfectly anodyne. Finally, he tells me what's up: 'The people won't tell me what they're thinking anyway.'

'Is that the Soviet mentality?'

'No, it's my accent.'

'Your accent?'

'Yes: they can tell as soon as I open my mouth that I'm from Lviv.'

'From Lviv' implies 'from the west', and apparently that in turn implies that a person must be on the Ukrainian side. Then the people in Volnovakha and the other cities of Donbas are not? Passing through, without local contacts, there's no way to find out, at least not with an interpreter who wears his patriotism on his tongue. Hopping over to the other side of the front is out of the question; the only way to do that would be if I came via Moscow or, at the outside, if I rode along in the armoured Land Cruisers. But the separatists will mistrust the OSCE just as much as the Ukrainian army does.

At the cultural centre in Volnovakha, I meet some members of a traditional women's choir, their conductor, her two daughters, and two older ladies. All five of them have unbelievably bright eyes, an extremely light blue, and a childlike radiance seems to come from their features too, as if singing really does keep a person young. And how beautiful a headscarf can be when it is worn ornamentally, not out of shame or coercion. The office of the centre's director, where they receive me, is spirited out of the present by their costumes alone, but, when the five start to sing, then I really think I have been whisked away to the grassy steppes where a wind blows across the 5,000 miles from Asia. The voices lilt up and down in unpredictable different intervals, carry through the open windows to the city; each individual voice carries far. I imagine someone hearing this song from a long way away, perhaps from the next village, this melody like a lament, although it is a wedding song. Steppes, after all, is what this vast territory once was that we have been travelling through for days now, steppes in which one people after another settled because there was space enough for all of them, each people in their own village where the inhabitants huddled together because they were lost all alone in the solitude, so that the languages, and with the languages the dances, costumes and customs, were preserved into the twentieth century. Finally, the songs the women's choir sings in the director's office also sound like a caress.

There were once over a hundred nationalities just in this area, the choir director sighs into the silence that has filled the office and – I imagine in my emotion – the streets outside the open window. 'Over a hundred!' the director repeats, and begins to list the nationalities so fast that Sashko can't keep up. Over how many centuries, millennia, did this diversity build up? How often was it threatened? To destroy it, the modern age needed just two decades, from 1930 to 1950. Today, the choir director continues, it is hard enough to preserve Ukrainian culture, which, here in the east, survives only in the villages in the first place. Except for the Greek folk dance troupe, theirs is the only choir in all of Donbas that cultivates the old songs. And, in the city, they are not a welcome sight.

'What do you mean by that?' I ask.

'If I went out in the street in my traditional costume, people would stare at me as if I was from Mars. I can't even put our songs on the Internet; if I do I get deluged with hate comments. Most people in the city completely reject our culture.'

At midday we drive on to the coastal town of Mariupol, which is so close to the eastern Ukrainian front that you can often hear the mortar shells from the city centre. Because the separatists encountered greater resistance here than in any other city, the name of Mariupol has a mystical sound to Ukrainian patriots. Only in a few places, however, does the city face the Sea of Asov, from which the militia with the hip *Wolfsangel* emblem takes its name. The city is girdled with factory chimneys which make the ensemble of old buildings and still older trees in the city centre all the more idyllic. The municipal theatre looks disproportionately large, like those in many provincial towns of the former Soviet Empire – how long will it survive in capitalism? Up to now it is offering not musicals, but the Russian classics. To judge by the posters, which consist of portraits of the leading actors, it is not exactly a directors' playhouse; perhaps those who complain that today's productions are too rarely 'faithful to the work' can go to eastern Ukraine.

I have arranged to meet Diana Berg, a blonde, very delicate and yet resolute-looking young woman. She has German ancestors to thank for her name; she herself grew up in Donetsk, had a good job as a brand designer, was one of the leaders of the local Maidan movement there, and, when the separatists took over, they put up posters asking for her whereabouts. She fled her home town without a suitcase. Her mother later brought her her cats. Now she organizes exhibitions and other cultural programmes in Mariupol, because civil society has become more important to her than brand design. Her boyfriend opened a literary café once he was let out of prison – Ukrainian prison, note: he had gone on fighting the separatists in an illegal militia after the second Minsk Protocol. Her boyfriend was not unconditionally opposed to negotiations, Diana says; he just couldn't accept not being able to go back home, to Donetsk. 'At first you think, it's only for a week; then you say, okay, a month. It takes a while before you realize that your exile is now your home.'

Does she still have hope? In a very broad sense, yes, Diana answers; the Maidan Revolution made the people realize that the status quo is change-able, and so the country is gradually casting off its Soviet mentality – there is no issue that isn't being addressed by some group or other. And the nationalism – does it worry her? Yes, she worries about it a lot; it is toxic, she says, and she brings up the Azov Battalion, which she considers immensely dangerous. Once she took a rainbow flag along to a demonstration to mark a contrast to the nationalist symbols.

'And was that okay?'

'It was very, very not-okay.'

I confess that I have not had the impression, during my journey through Ukraine, that the whole nation is moved by the war, as it continues menacing Mariupol and swallowing up Diana's home town of Donetsk. Of course, when you get referred by one Maidan activist to the next, you can easily get the idea every Ukrainian is working for the country's freedom and integration in Europe. But is that representative? No, of course not, Diana replies; people in Kiev don't want to hear much about the people near the front; somehow it bothers them. And for that reason she can't always blame Europe, if support is lacking even from within Ukraine.

'We're on an island here,' says Diana. 'There's no airport; the main roads are cut by the front lines; the streets haven't been repaired for years, there are only two trains a day. Sometimes you hear nothing but the mortar shells for weeks, and it feels like the sea level is rising; then sometimes a famous musician from Kiev gives a solidarity concert, and our connection to the mainland is visible again.'

The Greek villages in Priazoviya, the region around Mariupol in the southern Donbas, are literally caught between the front lines, reports Oleksandra Protsenko-Pikhadzhi in the Greek community's cultural centre, which is modelled after a temple: 'Our shells often don't travel far enough, and fall on the villages. And when the other side fires, some of their shells don't go far enough either.'

Ms Protsenko is the archetypical school headmistress: bun, blouse, knee-length skirt, corpulence and a deep voice that, all by itself, makes you want to sit up straight. Her agitation in talking about the war is all the more moving. In the villages the soldiers got drunk, and then they did things – the headmistress's voice falters – some things, very horrible things. I don't find out which soldiers they were – separatists or Ukrainian militias – and so I infer that the things happen on both sides of the front. Because she brings food and clothes to the villages, and also the half-villages, that are beyond the front lines, she says, she is publicly reviled as a separatist in Mariupol and libelled on the Internet; they accuse her of selling alcohol to the upper-year students in her school – filth like that, and worse.

'If these people had a God, they would know that they'll be called to account for their lies, that sin is like a boomerang. Has our government not made enough mistakes? We should be courting every single person to keep them pro-Ukrainian, but instead we're shooting at them and calling them Russians. But what else should they do? They can't say they want to belong to Ukraine; you can't say that over there. We should be supporting them, but instead we're begrudging them even the pensions they worked their whole lives for. In my own village there has been no running water for three months, and that in summer, in this heat.'

The Greeks have always been careful to keep to themselves to maintain their identity. And yet hardly anyone speaks Greek any more, or Ukrainian, but Russian, naturally. During the Great Purge, 4,000 Greeks were arrested in Priazoviya alone, and most of them murdered. Ms Protsenko-Pikhadzhi takes out a book that contains nothing but the 4,000 names and the summary court's sentences: 'Firing squad … firing squad … firing squad,' she reads. From the seaside village of Yalta – yes, Yalta like the Crimean city, which was once Greek too – the entire male population was carted off, excepting only the old people, the children and the disabled. It was late autumn, the onset of winter, and so the 'communists', as she calls the NKVD agents, came not with the black crows, but with a ship, and forced the men to get into their own boats. The women stood on the hillside – the village is on a hill overlooking the sea – and wailed as loudly and piercingly as wolves while the men rowed out of the harbour. Then the men, to drown out their wives' wailing, began to sing a revolutionary song: 'The wide sea shall rear up, the wide sea shall swallow them.' The Greeks of Priazoviya may not speak Greek any more, but their stories could just as well be ancient myths.

We drive out of the city in the dark so that, after twenty days on the road, I can have a morning by the sea. The travel guide says something about a headland where there are a number of hotels. In spite of the late summer heat, the headland is practically deserted; the street lamps are out; there is hardly a light in the windows; all the hotels are closed. Is it because of the nearby war, or just the off-season?

Twenty-First Day: Along the Black Sea to Odessa

Because I can't find my way out of the hotel that we found in the end, I miss the sunrise that I set my alarm clock for. Not only are we the only guests, but there is no one here to serve us, either. The high fences around the building no doubt keep out intruders, but they would also be a challenge to escapees. So I look from the shady terrace at the beach shining in the early sunlight and imagine a late summer swim in the waves. When I still see no staff at 8:30, I settle for a dip in the moss-green swimming pool.

Yesterday evening Sashko already had a dispute with the three Russians who let us into the hotel, the heavily pregnant receptionist, the caretaker and the owner. Russians? Of course they may have Ukrainian passports, but a patriot like my driver doesn't need to discuss political niceties with them to assign them to the enemy camp. 'How can I live in peace with people who banished my ancestors to Siberia?' he ranted, while waiting for the vodka he had ordered four times. And when he was finally able to pour himself a glass, he returned to the topic of the Holodomor of the early 1930s: the intentional starvation of the resistant population under Stalin which claimed the lives of at least 3.3 million Ukrainians, out of the total of 6 to 7 million victims. To avoid aggravating Sashko's mood, I kept to myself the objections that Stalin was not Russian and the Soviet Union is not identical with *the* Russians, least of all those of today's generation. Nor did I ask why, with his understanding of history, he is working for a German reporter after Germany murdered 3.5 million Ukrainians during its three-year occupation, and another 3 million fell in the fight against the Germans or died as a result of the war. Meanwhile the receptionist, the caretaker and the hotel owner will have wondered why their overbearing guest should have any more right than they to live in the country where they were born, especially since their ancestors no doubt did not migrate here voluntarily. In the course of his policy of internal colonization, Stalin not only broke the Ukrainian peasants' resistance against collectivization with extreme brutality but also forced 20 million workers from other parts of the Soviet Union to settle in the new industrial centres. The receptionist, the caretaker and the hotel owner will hardly consider their parents or grandparents perpetrators. Whatever the reason, we never had a more apathetically prepared dinner in any socialist country, and breakfast is not included, we discover when the caretaker finally unlocks the gate about nine.

I go for a walk along the row of vacant hotels and villas built down onto the public beach, sometimes right into the sea – who issues the building permits? – and encounter a few people, mostly pensioners enjoying the sun on folding chairs, anglers and, every 200 yards, a man in a black wetsuit. Standing in water up to their hips, these men wear big headphones and hold a steel rod in one hand – what are they doing? They're looking for metal, jewellery and coins, I realize on seeing the third such diver. Does the dire economic situation promote ingenuity?

On my way back to the hotel, I observe from a distance a young woman jumping and dancing in the wind. What a beautiful picture, I think, and then discover as I get closer that she is only posing for her boyfriend's camera. He's not her boyfriend, he insists, as he asks me to take a souvenir photo of the two of them: he's her brand-new husband. Because I am an unusual guest, a Western European, on this beach situated so close to the war, especially in the off-season, and the young man speaks some English, we get to talking. They live in Mariupol, I learn, and as ethnic Russians they do not feel at all liberated in their city, although they were also unhappy with the separatists' rule. Some of them were not self-sacrificing defenders of the people, but criminals. And now? 'We have become strange in our own country.'

Diana's complaint turns out to be justified: the road that runs 600 kilometres from Mariupol to Odessa is in catastrophic condition even by Ukrainian standards. As we sit for hour after hour in the uncomfortable compact car – with no variation in the landscape, the same cultivated steppes since Lithuania – Sashko mentions that he bought his driving licence for 300 hryvnias, the equivalent of 10 euros.

'Was it hard?' I ask.

'To get it for 300, you have to know somebody. For 400 and up, it's no problem.'

'What, you can just buy a driving licence?'

'Yes, that's what everyone does.'

'Everyone?'

'Well, not everyone, but almost everyone buys their driving licence.'

'Was it that way in Soviet times too?' I ask.

'Oh, no, back then you couldn't do that.'

'You mean, back then there was more law and order?'

'No, back then there were fewer cars. Not so many people needed driving licences.'

Twenty-Second Day: Odessa

I was so looking forward to arriving in Odessa and walking up the big Potemkin Steps, which get narrower towards the top to make it look as if they rise all the way to the sky – and now they're closed off with a red board fence on which the crescent moon glows white: it is not the European Union, as in

104

Poland or Lithuania, not Big Brother as in Belarus, no – Odessa's prestigious project, the restoration of its most famous structure, is being financed by Turkey. The pram that rolls down step by step between the fallen civilians, shot by the tsar's soldiers, in Sergei Eisenstein's *Battleship Potemkin*, the old woman's mouth open in a silent scream, the soldiers marching down, going around the pram, the sabre slashing the eye of the onlooker – what every cinema spectator connects with the Potemkin Steps is a primal scene of human helplessness in the modern age. From the port where once the world landed in Odessa, I climb the steps along the barrier and, at the last step, walk onto a big stage: the square with the statue of the first governor, Duke de Richelieu, and behind it the wide boulevard with the sumptuous buildings all in a row, the Governor's Palace, the Stock Exchange, the Opera, and everything else a city needs to call itself a 'second St Petersburg', a 'Palmyra of the South', the 'Queen of the Black Sea', and so on.

Waiting for me by the statue is Oleg Filimonov, the actor and popular host of a satirical political television show. As he guides me around the city, he also spreads out before me his own history of Odessa, telling me about his Jewish parents, remembering the languages he heard daily as a child – Yiddish, Bessarabian, Ukrainian, Turkish and, of course, Russian – reflecting on the model of Greek antiquity which the name Odessa heralded, describing the cosmopolitan spirit that infused Odessa even in the Soviet period, listing the world-famous artists, the writers, painters, violinists and pianists, rhapsodizing about the jazz clubs that were known throughout Europe and even in America between the wars, talking about Odessa as a Jewish city too. Almost all the intellectual pioneers of Jewish emancipation spent a part of their lives here. Vilnius looks to the past, Odessa to the future, the Jews used to say: loyalty to religious tradition was not paramount here, but science, commerce and culture.

Three hundred thousand Jews lived in Odessa at the turn of the twentieth century, among them members of the educated classes in disproportionate numbers, intellectuals, teachers, artists, writers. They too shaped cosmopolitan Odessa, with rootlessness and peregrinations as part of their religious archives. Most of the better situated, socially emancipated Jews emigrated after the Russian Revolution, or under Stalin at the latest, when all religious life was prohibited. When Odessa fell under German rule for 907 days, there were still about 100,000 Jews in the city. Only 10,000 survived. Of course they were traumatized; Filimonov's parents too; every single Jew had lost most of their relatives, if not their entire family, in the camps.

They were prohibited from rebuilding any of the demolished synagogues, a further disaster for their cohesion. The Jewish presence was limited to an inconspicuous community centre. Jews were suspect because more of them wanted to emigrate. 'Apparently it didn't occur to the authorities that they wanted to emigrate because they were suspect,' Filimonov remarks in a satirical moment.

Since independence, Jewish life is flourishing again in Odessa, although on a much smaller scale than before. Most of his relatives, Filimonov reports, have moved to New York or Israel in recent years, but, for his part, although he now has the financial means to live anywhere in the world – he's in the jewellery business too, he mentions with a wink, as if acknowledging the stereotype – he is glad of every day that he wakes up in Odessa. Then he looks around and points to the flawless row of nineteenth-century buildings that could just as well line a street in St Petersburg, Vienna or Rome, the old plane trees along the pavement, the stone-paved street – what's more, we happen to be standing in front of the legendary conservatory, the National Academy of Music. 'Is this not a European city?'

And it's true: if there is one place where the universalism of the Enlightenment is manifested, it is Odessa. The city was commissioned in 1794 by a tsarina from Germany who wanted to open Russia towards the West, founded by a Spanish-Irish admiral, built mainly by Italian architects, governed in its first decades by a Frenchman, made Europe's most important marketplace for wheat by Polish magnates and Greek shipowners, and inhabited by merchants, sailors and intellectuals of many nations. Long before New York, Odessa was a melting pot of languages, religions and ethnicities. Today the governor is again a foreigner: the former Georgian president Mikheil Saakashvili. But that is not the only reason why Odessa is phenotypical of Europe – analogous to the model city Minsk, where communism is expressed in stone. What permeates Odessa is also the belief in culture, in the greatness of human creativity; the early palaces and the self-assured villas with their balconies, their high ceilings and most of all their sumptuous salons in which we can imagine the most exquisite evening entertainments, private concerts, recitations, political and philosophical debates, even if in reality the same gossip was probably discussed there as everywhere else. The parks, composed like works of art, transform themselves even today on a warm evening into open-air salons where people meet for classic partner dancing. And then the spectacular opera house, the academies, the railway station – a terminus with a distinctive cupola crowning its façade, as if an invitation to the world – and in the city centre one museum after another, without anyone feeling the need to declare a museum quarter or a museum row: museums of archaeology, of numismatics, of maritime trade, of Judaism, of Western and Eastern art; a museum just for Pushkin and one for all of Odessa's literary figures – Mickiewicz, Babel, Akhmatova, Mandelstam. Who among the great poets of Eastern Europe did not live here at some time?

Even today, the city is visited by travellers from all parts of the globe, not just the typical Easy-Jetters of Western Europe – strangely, none of the low-cost airlines flies to Odessa – rather by Americans and travellers from countries that are still more remote to Western Europeans: Turks, Arabs, Israelis, many Romanians, Bulgarians, Moldavians of course, Russians. Most of the taxi drivers come from the eastern edges of the former Soviet Union, bringing East Asia into the city. The young sailors in their snow-white navy uniforms and their blue-and-white striped shirts, peakless hats cocked on their freshly shorn heads, lend the pavements the polyglot flair of a seaport. But most of all, wonder of wonders, Odessa itself is as beautiful today as its legendary name suggests.

It is not without conflict, however. Although situated in the southwestern Ukraine, far away from the front, the city founded by Catherine the Great was Russian-speaking long before the Soviet Union, unlike Kiev or Lviv. During the most recent revolution, the conflict escalated here between Ukrainian nationalists and pro-Russian demonstrators who had set up tents in Kulikovo Polye Square, as the pro-European protesters did in the Maidan. When members of the 'right-wing sector' set fire to the tents, the demonstrators fled to the nearby trade unions building. Molotov cocktails flew through the windows, fires were started in the doorways, without police intervening or fire-fighters arriving. People standing in the windows or seeking refuge on ledges were shot at; some fell. At least forty-eight pro-Russian demonstrators died; some sources mention over a hundred.

I mention the trade unions building to Filimonov and notice immediately that, while he does not deny or relativize the massacre – there is no other word for it – he does set it in relation to the other side's actions. But mainly, he points out that only a small minority of Ukrainians are extremist. How familiar it is, from my travels, from Iran and even from Germany, that the violence committed in our side's name is perpetrated only by a few radicals, while the other side's violence is the responsibility of the whole group.

As we stroll through the book bazaar, consisting of quite a few stands on the green median of a peaceful avenue, Filimonov laughs that the books are only a pretext for every kind of commerce imaginable, or unimaginable. And, in fact, although the bazaar is full of people, no one seems to be particularly interested in the displays. People recognize the TV star, a chat here, a chat there, and the espressos we order at the coffee bar are on the house, of course. As we stir our crema, Filimonov mentions that he has read a few books about Muslims in Europe, and the topic worries him quite a bit. From the French titles he mentions, he is talking about the same best-sellers about the Islamization of the West that were held up to me on the first day of my trip in the wainscoted banquet hall of the Lindengarten restaurant. Aren't the Muslims on the rise everywhere, he asks, especially in Germany? Aren't they conquering the public sphere in every city, perpetrating attacks, harassing women, rolling out their prayer rugs on the central squares? And what about the refugees, the New Year's Eve assaults in Cologne? As a Colonian, I must have seen for myself that Europe is driving off a cliff. From my hesitant response, Filimonov seems to notice that my perception is different; then he realizes that the topic concerns me not just as a Colonian, a German, a European. The transition is interesting: as we walked through the city, we were both cosmopolitans; his enthusiasm infected me too; but suddenly he is a … a what, then? A Jew? An Eastern European? Surely not a right-wing populist, warning against Islam, and willy-nilly I become a Muslim, obliged to justify a group when I answer him. We'd better just talk about Odessa some more, otherwise the next Middle East conflict will be upon us.

Oleg Filimonov says many of his business contacts in Odessa identify more with Russia than with the Maidan. He continues to meet with them, they drink vodka together, but they don't talk about politics any more, otherwise they'd come to blows. 'I don't understand them; they don't understand me.'

The division of Ukraine runs deep in the Odessan administration. While the elected mayor, Gennadiy Trukhanov, belongs to the old, Soviet-educated establishment, Governor Mikheil Saakashvili wants to make a 'showcase of reform' out of the very city that stands for corruption and crime as no other in the country: not only do the best-known villains of Russian literature come from Odessa, but the romanticization of Odessa's culture of banditry was a commonplace of Soviet popular culture. After the collapse of the Soviet Union, a large share of Russian oil exports is said to have been negotiated in Odessa by organized crime, and the port's most flourishing industry was smuggling, to which a separate museum is now devoted. As in the movies, hired killers and shoot-outs are a part of the bandit culture of the 1990s.

Trukhanov was in the private security business in those days, and he does not deny having had contacts to the underworld, although he himself was not involved in criminal dealings, he says. Asked how business conflicts were handled in that period, he told an interviewer, 'When bandits came looking for a fight, we fought.' Later, Trukhanov represented the party of President Viktor Yanukovich in Odessa, then, after the Maidan movement brought Yanukovich down, Trukhanov called himself an 'independent'. Mikheil Saakashvili, meanwhile, who was appointed by the current president Poroshenko, prides himself on his friendship with the American neo-conservatives; during his own presidency of Georgia he was regularly portrayed in the Russian media, which most people in Odessa continue to follow, as a Western agent, a warmonger and a madman. Whether because of his tendency to polarize, or the revelations of torture in police stations, or the manipulations of his financially powerful opponents – for whatever reason, the Georgians chased him out of office in the last elections, and even out of the country, which he can no longer enter freely because of various charges against him. 'There is one thing you need to understand about me,' he announced on his arrival in Odessa: 'I hate Vladimir Putin. I am in Ukraine because this is my war. The destiny of my life is being decided here. We need to stop him.' That was not apt to calm the Russia-friendly part of the population, which has felt set upon since the bloodbath in the trade unions building, if not longer.

I visit Luba Shepovich in the provincial government offices of Odessa, housed in a typical Soviet concrete box, small windows, dark grey façade, linoleum floor, rickety furniture – the opposite of New York, where the forty-year-old Shepovich was working in a software company when the Maidan broke out. After watching one of Saakashvili's press conferences on the Internet, she found out his e-mail address and asked whether he could use her in Odessa. In the course of the ensuing correspondence, he suggested she could introduce e-government in Odessa: 'You'll get zero money here, you'll get zero staff, but you can do whatever you want.' She had never been to Odessa, but the task sounded interesting, and she had savings enough for a few months of unpaid holiday. She solicited volunteer IT specialists on Facebook and received eighteen applications in the first week alone. Besides electronic applications and forms, her department set up a direct-democracy website on which citizens could submit and discuss suggestions. After six months, Saakashvili offered her the position of director of a newly created investment agency with forty employees and a salary of 100 dollars. Luba quit her job in New York. 'In the beginning, I wanted to adapt to the mood here,' she recounts, 'but then I quickly grew depressive. The people's pessimism totally brought me down. So I decided to look at it as a kind of business training course: that made everything a little better. The people are amazed that we newcomers smile so much; they're not used to that. But we wanted to spread optimism.'

There are many people like Luba in the provincial government. Because he thought the existing *apparat* was corrupt, Saakashvili staffed a number of key positions with young expatriate Ukrainians. Luba is not sure whether they'll succeed in Odessa. By an opening fireworks display of obviously sensible measures, the governor gained such unexpected popularity that he was soon in discussion as a future prime minister. In the meantime, however, disillusionment is spreading because his new ideas are meeting with a great deal of resistance. A third of the expatriate Ukrainians have already quit. But even if Saakashvili should fail, Luba believes, her mission on the home front will have been worthwhile. The citizens' expectations and demands have already changed, she says; no matter who leads the administration in the future, it will have to see itself as a service enterprise. A few days ago, she talked to old friends who went on living their normal lives in New York. 'Work, vacation, family; the same thing day in and day out, year in and year out – sounds boring, doesn't it?'

In the evening I sit in the jam-packed opera house, where the symphony orchestra plays new Ukrainian compositions and traditional songs. The face of a peasant girl is projected on a big screen with words braided into her hair and her headscarf, including some English ones: 'Revolution'; 'Russia's War against Ukraine'. Ukrainian landscapes are visible in the background, ears of grain, folk dances, traditional costumes, villages. The rural images of the homeland seem to have nothing in common with the metropolitan, very bourgeois society that has gathered in the opera house. And yet they are anything but naive. In the course of his policy of internal colonialism, Stalin not only resettled millions of workers from other parts of the empire in the new industrial centres; he also broke the resistance of the Ukrainian peasants against collectivization by extremely brutal measures, including banishments and the Holodomor. That is why the national awakening now romanticizes rural life in cosmopolitan Odessa, why the Opera salvages the peasant songs, while Russia stands for the factories, the alienation, and the whole bloody twentieth century that began on the Potemkin Steps. They are said to be majestic, rising into the sky.

To a German, the patriotism being expressed on the screen, and still more in the faces and the speeches, in the applause for songs of the fatherland, is strange, even disconcerting. And yet, we must remember, the appeal to the nation has not always been a means of exclusion and an expression of might. There has also been, and there is, the nationalism of the weak – among peoples fighting for their independence for example, peoples whose culture is threatened with extinction. In Germany, too, the national idea once stood for emancipation. Yet it is not easy to draw the line at which the praise of one's own people becomes toxic – 'very, very not-okay'. Is it only when people die, as they did in the trade unions building?

At the end of the concert, all the listeners stand up. I stand up too, thinking they are going to close with the national anthem. But the song sounds different: not spirited and festive; more mournful or melancholy, simply beautiful. Afterwards I learn that it was a well-known Ukrainian lament for the dead.

Twenty-Third Day: Leaving Odessa by Air

Early in the morning, I attend the worship service in the orthodox synagogue. No police cars out in front; no security checks at the entrance: I can just walk in. I haven't brought an interpreter along because Oleg Filimonov claimed that many Jews speak English. That turns out to be mistaken, and so after the service I have to converse by hand gestures and facial expressions. But I understand one thing, because I remember Filimonov saying it, and now I hear it in various languages, independently of one another, once in German, once in Yiddish, two, three times in English, and I see the facial expression, the hands turned gratefully towards Heaven: in 2016, Jewish life is safe once again in Odessa. Perhaps there is no better yardstick to measure whether Europe is succeeding in the end.

Instead of climbing aboard the minibus that departs several times a day to nearby Crimea, I take a taxi to the airport. The land crossing is closed to foreigners. I could probably go with a special permit as a reporter, but I would have to apply for it in Kiev, 1,500 kilometres away, and if the permit were issued, I would be obliged to return by the same checkpoint. If I then went on from Crimea to Russia, I would be banned from entering Ukraine until further notice, since, from Kiev's point of view, I would be recognizing the dismantling of the border fences and thus legitimizing the occupation. So, although Crimea is just a stone's throw from Odessa, the only way to get there is by air, via the Russian capital, a thousand kilometres up and a thousand kilometres back. And there haven't been any direct flights from Odessa to Moscow since the war began.

Twenty-Fourth Day: Via Moscow to Simferopol

Of the conversations I have with acquaintances and colleagues during the layover in Moscow in January 2017, three remarks are strongest in my memory. A television reporter mentions that human rights stories do not sell well because the producers in Germany are tired of the reliable storm of audience protests and the complaints to the broadcasting council; the new cycle paths in central Moscow, 'soft' stories in general, sell better. A long-time newspaper correspondent remembers that no one took propaganda seriously in the Soviet Union, not even the officials themselves, who at least hinted with a wink that the reality was, well, more complicated. Today, he is constantly amazed that people actually believe what the television proclaims. An intellectual, philosophizing about Russia's historic position between Asia and Europe, gives me a startling answer when I ask him whether the polarity postulated by Dostoevsky is still relevant today: the polarity between Orthodox Slavdom – theocratic, rural and authoritarian, under a tsar by the grace of God – and Enlightened Europeanism, cosmopolitan, individualistic and decadent. Certainly, says the intellectual, that's exactly the polarity that is at work today, but unfortunately the Russian mainstream rejects Dostoevsky's political thought. Why is that? I ask; after all, Dostoevsky celebrates the Slavic, the authoritarian, Russia's eastern, non-European identity. That's exactly why Dostoevsky is rejected, he replies; the mainstream is totally oriented towards the West, Putin not least. The references to pan-Slavism, the photos with priests are just folklore; in reality, Orthodoxy has little importance except at Christmas.

'Putin is oriented towards the West?' I ask, to make sure.

'Yes, and so are 80, 85 per cent of Russians. They're just disappointed in Europe; for 200 years they've had the feeling Europe doesn't want them. And today they also think Europe is not what it used to be. But, at bottom, they still think: after all, we Russians sit on chairs like Europeans; Asians sit on the floor.'

At 20 degrees below, I can see why Putin promised, on taking office, that every broken heating system would be repaired within three hours. And has he kept that promise? The television, no doubt, says yes. I am strangely amazed, as I shiver along the streets, at the imperial splendour that this

112

Moscow radiates; the neo-classical buildings, endless boulevards and bold squares; and what a mixture of nations lives here in this capital of a colossal empire. The seven skyscrapers that Stalin had built still proclaim a unique civilization and a world power. And, today, new and still more triumphal business towers are being built. As an adolescent, I always associated Russia with the mouse-coloured suits of the party officials, the military parades, a modern, somehow depressing architecture, the huge spaces where the school atlas showed not a single city, not a single mountain. Now I understand how a person can be nostalgic for Moscow, as people in Europe's west are nostalgic for Paris.

On Red Square I walk from Café Bosco to the bridge that Boris Nemtsov, once Yeltsin's crown prince and later Putin's most prominent opponent, was walking across on 27 February 2015, when members of the Chechen security agencies shot him down. 'Those who criticize Putin are not human, they are my personal enemies,' the young Chechen president Ramzan Kadyrov boasted after doing his master's dirty work: 'As long as Putin backs me up, I can do anything. *Allahu akbar!*' Tens of thousands came to the memorial service for Nemtsov; it was the last gasp of a liberal opposition for the time being. The human rights association I visit is fighting for its survival because the government has prohibited non-governmental organizations from receiving money from abroad. Inside Russia, virtually no one offers financial support to human rights activists.

When I switch on my mobile after landing in Simferopol, I have no signal. This is what it looks like, then, when you enter a territory that the international community considers illegal: you can't make a call with a foreign SIM at any price. When I go to check into my hotel, I find that my credit card doesn't work either. With few exceptions, the number plates on the vehicles are all Russian by now; only some of them have the old Tatar name of the peninsula on the plastic frame: *Qırım*. A few cars still have Ukrainian plates, although the deadline for trading them in has, after several extensions, long since passed.

Twenty-Fifth Day: Via Bakhchisaray to Sevastopol

Except for a factory chimney in the city centre and the grey blocks dating from the Soviet Union, Simferopol looks like a Tolstoy reader's image of provincial Russia: two- and three-storey buildings from the nineteenth century, when Catherine the Great and her successors founded New Russia;

113

broad streets; the former luxury avenue with the government buildings, now a pedestrian zone; an imposing theatre, as in every self-respecting Soviet city. The statue of Lenin is still in place, of course, as it has remained since Ukrainian independence. Although it was originally Russian, Khrushchev transferred Crimea to the Ukrainian SSR on 19 February 1954, overnight so to speak, for reasons that are still the object of speculation today – better transport routes, closing ranks with the Ukrainian party organization to reinforce his own power base, decentralization, or perhaps just a whim because Khrushchev had previously been first secretary of the Communist Party in Kiev. When Ukraine became independent in 1991, Crimea became a part of the new state, although its inhabitants had voted in a referendum to remain in the Soviet Union.

After the fall of the pro-Russian government in Kiev on 22 February 2014, Russia occupied Crimea without encountering resistance. That was not in keeping with international law, although it probably was in keeping with the wish of the majority of the inhabitants, who voted for annexation as early as March, even if it was not by a 97 per cent majority: the Tatars, for example, who had ruled Crimea until the destruction of their khanate in 1783, boycotted the referendum. Russia was not only the colonial power that had made the Tatars a minority in their own country; Russia was also the Bolshevik Revolution: half of the Tatars who had been living in Crimea at the turn of the twentieth century, 150,000 people, were banished within or outside the Soviet Union, or starved out, even before Stalin. Those of their elites who remained, secular or religious, died during the Great Purge of 1937 and 1938.

One reason why the Crimean Tatars, like the Lithuanians, tended to welcome the Nazi German invasion as a liberation was that they remembered the German occupation of 1918 as a phase of relative autonomy. And, as in Lithuania and Belarus, the German occupiers allowed them to open schools and newspapers in the local language. In the case of Crimea, that was more than just a political tactic to develop local allies against the Soviet Union. It was also because Crimea had a special place in Nazi ideology: this was where the kingdom of the Goths was to be restored. Such a thing had never existed in the first place, least of all a proto-Germanic Crimea with a Teutonic, urban civilization that zealous antiquarians and archaeologists claimed to have discovered in the nineteenth century; the Goths were just one of many peoples who had migrated to Crimea. However, Crimea seems to have been in fact the last region where Gothic was spoken, even into the modern era. That was enough to motivate the Germans to rename Sevastopol Theoderichhafen and Simferopol Gotenburg. 'I will empty Crimea to make room for our own settlements,' Hitler said in announcing the *Gotenland* project in July 1941. A population to Germanize Taurica had also been found: the South Tyroleans, who had become a problem because the official policy on German minorities called for bringing them 'home to the Reich' or annexing their territories, as with the Sudetenland. As long as Mussolini was Hitler's most important ally, neither of those options was feasible in South Tyrol. So why not put the Tyroleans in Crimea? There too they would have mountains, wine, fertile valleys, all the water they could want. And a four-lane *Reichsautobahn* would make it a two-day drive from Berlin to the southern sun, where German workers on holiday could restore their *Kraft durch Freude*, 'strength through joy'. The Crimean Tatars were classed as racially 'worthless', like the Jews, but their removal was to be delayed to avoid annoying neutral Turkey, which saw itself as the protector of all Turkic peoples. The decision whether the Tatars would be exterminated, expelled or enslaved by the Aryan settlements could be postponed until later. Besides, the German Army argued that their ingrained hostility to Soviet rule could be exploited. Then the highest civil official in Crimea, Governor General Frauenfeld, who knew his Johann Gottfried Herder, developed a regular liking for the 'teeming' Tatars. He allocated funds for the promotion of the Tatar language and customs, had a Tatar theatre founded, instituted 'Muslim committees' and planned a Tatar university. Some Jews were able to survive by pretending to be circumcised Muslims. Much more numerous, however, were the circumcised Muslims who were shot as Jews. No distinction between the two was made at all towards the end of German rule, when 'Gotenland' had become as obsolete as Herder's definition of 'historic peoples'. The Germans had killed 130,000 people in Crimea: all the Roma and Sinti; all the remaining Jews; most of the Karaites, disregarding the fine distinctions that the racial bureaucracy in Berlin had decreed, and tens of thousands of Tatars.

The Goths were only one pigeonhole in the Nazi ideology, the occupation of Crimea just an episode in German history which is all but forgotten in Germany. Yet the *Gotenland* plan brought the apocalypse of the Crimean Tatars. Immediately after the Soviet reconquest of Crimea in April 1944, whole villages were executed, and dead Tatars hung from the street lamps of Simferopol. Although far more Crimean Tatars had fought in the Red Army, with the partisans or in their own resistance groups, than had collaborated with the occupation, Stalin had them all banished, and they were not allowed to return when Nikita Khrushchev, at the twentieth Party Congress in 1956, declared Stalinism abolished and explicitly condemned the expulsion of the Crimean Tatars. Not until perestroika and the end of the Soviet Union, more than a generation later, did the Crimean Tatars gradually begin returning to Crimea. Glad of the cultural autonomy that Ukraine granted them, they were afraid the Russian annexation would make them second-class citizens once more.

I ask our driver Ernes, who is a Crimean Tatar himself, what practical changes have taken place since Russia has taken over Crimea. Not many, Ernes says; not in the city's appearance at any rate, apart from the new number plates and flags. The people were already watching Russian television before the annexation. The local government has also stayed the same: the mayor, the police, the civil servants. No, says Ernes, everything has basically stayed the same. And for the Crimean Tatars? Ernes takes a moment to think. If he doesn't get home in the evening at the expected time, he says, his wife calls him within minutes: too much has happened since the annexation – arrests, kidnapping, harassment.

In a Tatar café-cum-souvenir shop on the high street – hospitality and folklore are permitted, apparently – I have arranged to meet Nariman Dzhelyal, the acting chairman of the Mejlis, the council of Crimean Tatars, in the absence of the exiled leader Refat Chubarov. The council has been prohibited as an extremist organization and many of its members have been arrested, but it is still possible to meet with Nariman Dzhelyal, a middle-aged man in jeans and a long-sleeved T-shirt, a trimmed, light beard, horn-rimmed glasses. The council still meets, Dzhelyal reports, but in private homes, and then the police are often waiting for them outside, take down names, impose fines, 500 to 1,000 roubles – less than 20 euros. The authorities aren't interested in the punishment; the intention is to demonstrate that they could crack down at any time. After all, Dzhelyal notes, everyone who continues to respect the internationally recognized legal status of Crimea has suddenly become a separatist.

I ask whether the Mejlis really advocates reintegration with Ukraine. Not necessarily, Dzhelyal answers; the Tatars will remain a minority one way or the other; they could live just as well in a European Russia. The problem is *this* Russia. The Tatars have been Europeans for centuries, have always had their faces to the West, fought on the side of England and France during the Crimean War of the nineteenth century. Europe's treatment of Ukraine will decide, he says, whether Europe remains true to its values today.

'And if not?' I ask.

'Then Europe will continue to dissolve at its borders.'

I strike up a conversation with a young woman who used to head the Crimean Tatars' radio station and also hosted a music show on television. I had best not mention her name, she says – my God, she never would have thought she would be afraid again, but she feels alone even in her fear: the majority are going along with the new state of affairs and so don't miss their freedom of speech. Because only Russian-language media are permitted since the annexation, she now teaches journalism at a private college of the Crimean Tatars, which is also not permitted but nonetheless exists; half of her students are compatriots and half are Russians. The resentment against her people is a legacy of the Soviet Union, she says, and is less pronounced among the younger Russians. When she returned from Central Asia with her parents, the other schoolchildren still thought Tatars were monsters, real monsters with horns on their heads. And the teacher asked her on her first day of school whether she knew how to read and write – and up to then she had attended an elite school in Uzbekistan; she was the only one in her new class who had learned German.

I wonder what might make the woman recognizable as a Tatar: she has reddish hair, a pale complexion, a short dress, black tights, elegant shoes. Of course she's recognizable, she says; everyone in Crimea has an eye for ethnic origins. I ask about her hopes. She too mentions Europe first – equality, democracy, freedom of religion, pluralism, human rights. But then she remembers the real EU, and she knows how remote Crimea is to Europeans. And here?

'Here, we used to be 90 per cent; now we're only 12. Not even democracy would help us much.'

In Simferopol's Historical Museum, no display recalls the original inhabitants of the peninsula, to say nothing of their expulsion. Yet the Crimean War, in which the Great Powers of the nineteenth century met on the little peninsula, is re-created in period uniforms. At least 750,000 soldiers died in the space of three years, two thirds of them Russian, 100,000 French, 20,000 British. It was the first war of the modern age inasmuch as brand-new, industrially manufactured weapons systems were deployed, and the war machinery included steamships, telegraphs, railways. It was also the first time the global public observed the battles quasi live – through photographers and embedded journalists. At the same time, the Crimean War is considered the first 'total war', since the civilian population was purposely

117

included in the military operations, and humanitarian distress was a strategic tool.

Many exhibits are also devoted to the Second World War – the 'Second Defence', as it is called in Crimea's official history. The annexation by Russia, which posters in the city celebrate as the 'Third Defence', is not yet exhibited in the museum. The elderly guards slumbering, meditating or doing crossword puzzles in the twilight are nonetheless glad of the opportunity I bring them to switch on the lights in one room after another.

On the way to the Memorial for the Victims of German Fascism, we pass some of the illegal settlements that were built all over Crimea in the 1990s, the streets unpaved, many of the houses still without electricity and running water. When they returned to Crimea, the Tatars found their houses inhabited by Russians. And other houses or apartments were hard to find, because Asians were not welcomed in the neighbourhood. Jobs too were found only rarely, in the bigger companies and in the public sector, so that most Tatars today are self-employed. Ernes, for example, owns a little bed and breakfast by the sea. A Ukrainian friend from Cologne recommended him to me as a guide since he speaks English well, knows the country, and is a nice guy generally. And he is that – a soft-spoken, very polite man of about thirty; the only thing is, as I noticed yesterday evening, I will meet no one but Crimean Tatars through him, which is interesting without a doubt, but not representative. Russians and Tatars have always lived more separately than together on the peninsula, Ernes says in his defence, and since the annexation the mistrust has become greater, friendship rarer. I'll have to think of something else for tomorrow if I want to find out how the 88 per cent see things.

The memorial was opened last year at the site of the trench where the German occupiers shot 15,000 people. Ernes admits that our visit makes him slightly nervous, because in school the Crimean Tatars were always listed among the perpetrators, not the victims. He is all the more surprised to find compatriots among the names engraved on a big wall. Still, there is no mention of the fact that the victims of fascism were mostly Jews. In Crimea too, as everywhere in Russia, the Germans killed only 'Soviet patriots', as they are called on the memorial plaque.

The museum director, who comes out of his office when he sees me talking to a staff member, explains that they did not want to highlight specific ethnicities; after all, the mass shootings were a crime against humanity, and it would not have been morally right to set up a hierarchy of victims. 'We would have been reproducing the ideology on the basis of which they were killed. But no one prohibits commemorating individual groups of victims.'

To my question whether affiliation with Russia affected the conception of the exhibition, the museum director prefers not to answer; he makes it a rule not to comment on politics. His employee just gave me exactly the same answer, and I received the same information this morning in the Museum of the History of Simferopol. People in Crimea seem to be cautious when talking to foreigners about politics. All I can learn offhand is that they are Russian and of course glad about the reunification. The museum employee nods.

We drive on towards the coast, and after an hour we suddenly arrive in the Middle East: the historic centre of Bakhchisaray, a little town that was once the capital of the Tatar khanate, still consists of stone buildings with traditional wooden roofs, narrow streets running up the mountainside, domes, minarets, iwans and the khan's palace, which looks like something from the Thousand and One Nights. But don't be fooled: the palace was built in the early sixteenth century by an Italian. The Russian colonists were not the first to bring their architects from the West. Sadly, the palace is closed, and when we hint at baksheesh to visit it anyway, the guard points regretfully at the video camera which has recently been installed to combat corruption.

In one of the narrow streets, I see a cat behind a window, and behind the cat a man with a friendly wave. 'Fuck Putin,' he laughs after opening the window and learning that I am from Germany. His name is Alex, and he worked abroad until an accident cost him his leg. Now he is glad to be able to exchange a few words of English again; it's been a long time. Because he seems to have no problem with talking about politics, I ask without beating around the bush whether he would rather see Crimea united with Ukraine or with Russia.

'Preferably with America,' Alex laughs, adding, 'and if that's not possible, then with Lukashenko.' In Belarus there is at least work and sufficient pensions; he has seen that with his own eyes. Although almost everyone who lives here is Russian, the annexation was not greeted with any rejoicing. At bottom, the people don't care which state they live in, as long as it works. And can I spare him a little change so that he can buy something to eat? I am puzzled, because Alex seems to own his own house, and a well-fed cat, and, to judge by the kitchen table, he has house-mates, most likely a family. Are the people in Bakhchisaray so poor that they have to beg for spare change, or is this one just a drinker?

A few steps further on, we enter a small museum displaying handicrafts – pitchers, bowls, plates. It belongs to Rustem Dervish, a stocky, tall Tatar with a finely embroidered cap on his grey hair, who makes the exhibits himself and offers workshops. His students include both Tatars and Russians; that's all one to him, as long as their bowls turn out well. He asks whether we'd like to drink a real coffee and brings out a tall, slender grinder made of silver into which he pours the beans very carefully, as if each one were precious. Remembering Alex's curses, I ask whether many people here are dissatisfied with the new conditions.

'Ah, people are always dissatisfied with something,' Rustem replies, 'before the annexation or after the annexation. I'm one of the other kind of people: I was content before and I still am now.'

It was hard for him too to buy a house when he came back from exile, but then he pretended to be a Greek, and, since the owner was overcharging, he didn't investigate. That was during perestroika, when the government agencies were in chaos. Rustem waited to register the deed until later, and then they could hardly take the house away from him. It had to be a house in the historic centre, a traditional house with a courtyard, so that he could make it into a museum; that was his plan from the beginning. He used to work on pipelines, applying synthetic insulation. 'There are jobs you do because you have to, and jobs that are fun. What I'm doing now is fun.'

Rustem's gratitude is so boundless that he finds something good even in the expulsion: the deprivations and the longing only made his people stronger, more independent and more demanding. Does he feel comfortable in a neighbourhood where only Russians live? Someone always has something against somebody, wherever you go in the world, Rustem says, and, besides, he has to be careful what he says, because he can't talk about politics.

'Because that's dangerous?' I ask.

'No, because I lack the expertise. If you have a question about your appendix, after all, you go a doctor, not a cobbler.'

His job is to revive the old culture of their people, he says, to make proper copper vessels, grind coffee, and teach younger people the trade. Then Rustem stops cranking the mill – the little room is full by now with the aroma of the beans – and he takes down two long-handled copper coffee pots, one quite simple and uneven, the other ornamented and perfectly regular.

'This pot we made ten years ago, and this one is what we make today – you see the progress? Not even our ancestors had such good coffee pots!' As evidence, Rustem takes a third pot off the shelf.

Without having tasted the genuine Tatar coffee, which apparently needs a few more hours' grinding, we follow Rustem on a tour of the museum. A Russian flag is waving over the courtyard, jutting over the wall from the neighbour's house. Rustem pre-empts my question, repeating that only doctors should talk about appendices. His political agitation is limited to getting the stone pavement in front of his house restored. We climb a narrow staircase from the courtyard and take our shoes off in front of a door. Rustem has furnished the upper storey as his ancestors would have done. Hence there are no chairs.

On the way to the seashore, we come by Chufut-Kale, the city of 170 caves and 400 stone houses once inhabited by the Karaites, whose compatriots, few as they are in the world, I have already encountered in Lithuania. Like many other tiny religious groups, such as the Albigensians in southern France, they lived in remote, fortress-like places for safety from persecution and, most of all, to be able to live by their own strict rules. Before the Karaites, the caves and houses were inhabited by Alans, an equestrian people from the Caucasus, and Theodoro or Mangup is nearby, where the Germanic Goths retreated after their defeat at the hands of the Khazars; their rule of Crimea had been ended before that by the Huns. Huns, Goths, Khazars, Karaites, Alans – all within a few square kilometres. Will visitors one day walk through our cities and wonder who we all were, Germans, Italians, Turks, Greeks, Jews, Serbs, Iranians?

Back in Simferopol in the evening, searching once more for something edible and hospitality – in vain. Today the pizzeria is what the Agrarian Production Co-operative once was in Eastern Europe: everywhere, identical everywhere, and identically callous everywhere. In the big cities, you can ask for regional cuisines and always find at least a Georgian restaurant, but in the provinces you can count on ending up with Margherita, Funghi, Salami, Prosciutto and Hawaii. Even the interiors all seem to come from the same catalogue: brown floor tiles, beige leatherette seats, dark wooden tables, strangely all sized for six guests, antiqued picture frames with black-and-white photographs, Marilyn Monroe, the Brooklyn Bridge and occasionally Muhammad Ali. Naturally there are no actual Italians to be found. But, after all, actual Muslims are not necessary for people to feel threatened by Islamization. Cultures can abolish themselves with no outside help.

And then here I am in classical antiquity. In 421 BC, the Greeks founded the city-state of Chersonesus in the bay where Sevastopol is now. What remains of it are the amphitheatre, the columns, and the foundations of the houses. What also remains of that time is the name of the peninsula, Taurica, where Goethe's Iphigenia found refuge from her father. We are still vaguely aware that the Greek Empire expanded this far towards Asia, much farther than it did westwards. But not even all of Goethe's readers will know that that native soil of Europe – which is also one of the wellsprings of Arabic-Islamic culture – extends northwards too, as far as the territory of the Soviet Union. If we then also remember where the Tatars came from, namely Mongolia; remember where the Russians came from who dominate Crimea today, most of them as blond as Scandinavians in these southern climes; remember that the tsarina herself, the colonizer, was a German and brought many Germans here; remember the innumerable other peoples who settled on the wild, fertile coast, Scythians, Sarmatians and Romans, as well as those mentioned yesterday, Ostrogoths, Huns, Alans and Khazars, and the famed Cimmerians, whoever they are; later the Byzantines, Mongols, Genoese, Venetians and most of all the Ottomans, who consisted in turn of many separate peoples; remember the British and French who did not return from the Crimean War in the nineteenth century – if we remember all that, then Crimea almost looks like a navel of the world. The only thing Crimea doesn't have is indigenous peoples. But wait – excavations on Taurica have brought to light the 100,000-year-old skeleton of a Neanderthal.

How can a nation assert its claim to be autochthonous, a status considered so important since the nineteenth century, and again today? Between 1930 and 1934, 85 per cent of the professional archaeologists in the Soviet Union were fired, and a majority of them banished to Siberian labour camps – 85 per cent! The whole concept of mass migration in late antiquity was prohibited under Stalin, I learn from Neal Ascherson's great cultural history of the Black Sea. It was replaced by the doctrine that the entire territory of modern Russia, Ukraine, Eastern and Central Europe had been settled by proto-Slavic peoples at least since the Iron Age. The Crimean Goths were no longer Germanic invaders but developed out of existing tribes. The Khazars were no longer Turkic-speaking nomads but descended from mixed marriages along the Don. The Tatars were discovered to be the original inhabitants of the Volga region. The Scythians too had allegedly migrated from there to Crimea, never mind how Iranian their language was. Most of all, the Varangians, who had founded the first 'Rus' state centred on Kiev, were no longer Vikings, but Slavs. Archaeology has long since returned to the universities, and Byzantine studies in particular have flourished since the end of the Soviet Union. Russia may be politically and economically 'totally Western-oriented', as I heard said the day before yesterday in Moscow, but its identity politics have returned to the imperial era, and thus to the Black Sea, whence it once more looks westward towards Constantinople.

In Sevastopol itself, over 1,000 monuments, memorials and museums recall the two great sieges, that of the Allies in the Crimean War, which lasted 349 days, and that of the Germans in the Second World War, lasting 250 days. Literature has captured the horrors more impressively than all the monuments and plaques, and especially Tolstoy, who in 1854, as a young soldier in Sevastopol, experienced 'war, not from its conventional, beautiful, and brilliant side, with music and drum-beat, with fluttering flags and galloping generals'. Tolstoy recorded, for example, how 'the repulsive, but beneficent work of amputation' was carried out in the military hospital:

You see the sharp, curved knife enter the healthy, white body, you see the wounded man suddenly regain consciousness with a piercing cry and curses, you see the army surgeon fling the amputated arm into a corner, you see another wounded man, lying in a litter in the same apartment, shrink convulsively and groan as he gazes at the operation upon his comrade, not so much from physical pain as from the moral torture of anticipation.[24]

Day after day, an average of 800 people died in Sevastopol near the end of the first siege; the city was like one big sickbed, the civilians were so starved, the soldiers in their trenches so exhausted and overwrought – lack of sleep caused by the constant bombardment was only the first of their torments. At the end of the second siege, Sevastopol lay in ruins a second time. Of the 112,000 inhabitants, only a few thousand had survived; 99 per cent of the buildings had been destroyed. The Soviet Union awarded Sevastopol the title of 'Hero City' and rebuilt the nineteenth-century architecture with astounding fidelity. The city retained its special status as the home port of the Black Sea fleet after Ukrainian independence and remained closed to visitors until 1994. Sevastopol is the most Soviet of all cities, in a way – in the collective memory, as a military base, and with its population, reconstituted after the Second World War. No other place in Crimea is hung with more Russian flags today.

Driving further along the coast from Sevastopol, you understand why the Greeks felt at home in Crimea: it looks like Greece, broad hills with sparse Mediterranean vegetation, continually interspersed with vineyards, subtropical trees left by southern peoples in the vicinity of the settlements, idyllic bays, cliffs jutting into the sea, and inland the tall mountains, now covered with winter snow. On the coast is a row of hotels and former hotels, sanatoriums remodelled as hotels, and hotels repurposed as sanatoriums, one after another. In the Soviet Union, most of these hotels were associated with factories, and they were typical holiday accommodation for the workers, with morning gymnastics for everyone and folklore in the evenings. 'Crimea was one of the few places of happiness that not even Stalin's Soviet Union could do without,' writes the historian Karl Schlögel.

Red Army soldiers seized the opportunity to take off their badges of rank; their wives, to put on their jewellery. And it is as a scene suffused with the golden glow of better days that Crimea was recorded in the family albums of generations of Soviet citizens: the beach in the background, the flight of white marble stairs lined with palm trees, the park in which peaches and oranges grew.[25]

Whether by chance or otherwise, the Soviet Union found its end precisely at the place of its happiness: from the southernmost point of Crimea at Cape Sarych, only 264 kilometres away from the Turkish coast as the crow flies, we look at the roofs of the 125-acre dacha where Mikhail Gorbachev was surprised by the coup attempt in Moscow in August 1991. For three days, the conspirators held him captive here with his family, the phone lines cut. After that, the coup collapsed and, a short time later, so did the Soviet Union.

Every 5 kilometres, by my estimation, a big billboard pops up beside the road with the face of Vladimir Putin, sometimes in a suit and tie, sometimes sporty with dark sunglasses, sometimes smiling obligingly, then looking fierce again, each time with a quotation promising a golden future for Crimea, tourism, industry, security. A sign in German, on the other hand, evokes the past: 60,000 Germans fell in Crimea, and their remains are progressively being reburied in a cemetery near the town of Honcharne. Sixty thousand makes a very broad field, picturesquely rising towards a hill. Scattered across the well-tended lawn are groups of three stone crosses, each middle one taller, as if it were standing on a winner's podium. Closely spaced along the footpath are granite steles engraved on both sides with names and dates. I don't know why this should happen in a graveyard, but it suddenly strikes me how beautiful German names really are: Heinrich, Johann, Albert, Nikolaus, Bruno, August, Fritz, Max, Georg, Matthias, Andreas, Berthold, August, Ernst, Valentin. Perhaps a melting pot like Crimea makes a person aware of the wealth that there is in the fact that every people has its own names. And it is perhaps fitting that in a cemetery, a simple soldiers' cemetery, there is no more need to speak of guilt. Instead, the inscription is a general appeal for peace and a commemoration of the dead regardless of which side of the front they stood on. On the door handle of the little cemetery building, the Russian and German flags are intertwined. Who knows, perhaps Stalin invited the Allied heads of government to Crimea in February of 1945 not only because of its pleasant climate, but also because it had been, as few other spots on earth, a setting of war 'in its real phase – in blood, in suffering, in death,' as Tolstoy wrote.

The street names in Yalta still sound pacific more than seventy years after the conference at which Germany was divided into four zones of occupation and lost the lands east of the River Oder. The seafront promenade, named after Lenin, merges into Roosevelt Street, and the main thoroughfare along the river is called Moskovskaya on one bank and Kievskaya on the other, as if Russia and Ukraine were fraternally united by the waterside. Furthermore, a remarkable number of streets bear the names of poets who came to Yalta for recreation, amusements and meetings: Pushkinskaya, Gogolya, Chekhova, and so on. At one time, Yalta was Russia's heaven to the south. Now that it belongs to Russia again, however, the fashionable side of the city has the character of a museum: the cruise ships, once the most important source of revenue, no longer call. At least that has stopped the 'Mallorcaization' of Yalta after the end of the Soviet Union which Karl Schlögel summarizes in a time-lapse description: 'Animators have supplanted agitators; physical culture at daybreak has been replaced by gym classes. The patriotic songs have fallen silent, and everyone plays their own favourite music, usually at maximum volume.'[26]

Natalya Dobrynskaya is the editor-in-chief of Crimea's only travel magazine, and she is so overwhelmingly cordial by disposition that it is no wonder she has made hospitality her profession. 'Yes, tourism has fallen off, sadly,' she concedes, only to bubble one sentence later about the euphoria of 17 March 2014, when the peninsula voted on its annexation by Russia. She tells of the daffodils that she and others distributed to first-time voters, of the general feeling that their destiny was being rewritten, now or never.

Were there pragmatic reasons to leave Ukraine, then? I ask. Certainly, Natalya replies, and mentions the fish factories, renowned throughout the Soviet Union, that had been ruined by privatization, and the decay generally, the streets, schools, public buildings. Perhaps the government in Kiev neglected other regions as well, she doesn't know exactly, but here people always looked and compared the situation to Russia. And then the parliament's rejection of Russian as a second official language in February 2014, even though hardly anyone in Crimea knew Ukrainian – that felt like being shown the door.

On the day of the referendum, Natalya recalls, it was so stormy that her neighbour, an old woman who has worked for six decades as a guard in the Chekhov museum – hired by Chekhov's sister personally! – was blown off her feet by the wind and knocked against a wall. In the hospital, Chekhov's oldest guard still cast her vote for Russia. The day was very emotional everywhere, Natalya says, although admittedly bitter for the opponents of annexation. Her own brother, who has lived in Kiev for the past thirty years, has declared he will not return home again as long as the peninsula is occupied by Russia. Of course he is still her brother; they talk often on the telephone, and argue about politics every time. Deep down, she can understand him, not only because of his Ukrainian wife but because he supported the Maidan from the start; likewise she can understand the Crimean Tatars, who suffered so much in the Soviet Union; but she herself, like the vast majority of Crimea's inhabitants, is Russian, and she can't help being happy about the reunification. The house she lives in was built by her Russian great-grandparents in 1850.

I ask Natalya about Europe.

'Why should we belong to Europe?' she asks in return: 'Just to make it easier to get visas?'

'Your brother would say, because of the values; that is, democracy, human rights, freedom.'

'Maybe I have different values. Maybe I think too much freedom isn't such a good thing. The liberties *Charlie Hebdo* takes, for example. Or the freedom to own weapons, as in the USA. Maybe I don't think homosexuals need to marry. I know gay people; I have nothing against them, but still I like the way Russia does it better: that is, tolerating homosexuality, but not abandoning the traditional family on that account. Maybe I'm religious, too, and believe in what it says in the Bible.'

'What makes Europe different from … hm, from what? … from Russia?'

'Hard to say,' says Natalya, and thinks a while. 'In Europe they stick to the law,' she says finally. 'That makes Europe rational and predictable. In the East, you always have to expect the unexpected. If you obey the law here, you can't survive.'

'But is obeying the law so bad in itself?'

'No, and here in Crimea we obeyed the law when the Maidan broke out. The revolution was the violation, the chaos, the anarchy.'

'Then you, a Russian, are actually more European than your brother who marched in the Maidan.'

'Yes, if you look at it that way, I am.'

'And the Russian Revolution – was it Eastern too?'

'Yes, a violation too, chaos and anarchy.'

Because I have another appointment in a village outside Yalta, I ask what the most Russian place in Yalta is. The Chekhov museum! Natalya bursts out, and offers to take me there. The city centre that I see along the way was aptly described by Chekhov himself as 'a mixture of something European that reminds one of the views of Nice, with something cheap and shoddy'. Part of what he meant by something cheap and shoddy were the many 'box-like hotels' that have only multiplied since then. A hundred years later, however, I meet no 'unhappy consumptives' pining away, nor

> the impudent Tatar faces, the ladies' bustles with their very undisguised expression of something very abominable, the faces of the idle rich, longing for cheap adventures, the smell of perfumery instead of the scent of the cedars and the sea, the miserable dirty pier, the melancholy lights far out at sea, the prattle of young ladies and gentlemen who have crowded here in order to admire nature of which they have no idea.[27]

The good old days that Chekhov stands for in Yalta were over even in his time.

As we pass the German-Russian Association, Natalya asks whether I would like to say hello to my countrymen. My countrymen? And then I think, yes, why not? In a way, an Iranian whose parents moved to Germany sixty years ago belongs to the same nation as the Germans whose ancestors emigrated to Russia in the nineteenth century – or the reverse: they're Russians, I'm German – as if it made any great difference. Regardless of my background, the director of the association is glad to hear our language, which she herself speaks with a delightful accent. The association's meetings are held in Russian because not all of the members understand German any more.

Like the Crimean Tatars, the Germans were resettled under Stalin, but they were allowed to return twenty-five years earlier, in the mid-1960s. Now their culture is disappearing again since most of them have emigrated to Germany. That is sad, says the director, who is also called Natalya and is every bit as cordial as the editor of the travel magazine; the Germans contributed so much to Crimea's development under Catherine the Great and even today have a good reputation, ambitious and industrious as we are. I believe Natalya is including me in her 'we'. The association works to keep the 200 remaining Germans in Yalta, she says, and does a great deal for their German culture. And, yes, some Crimean Germans have already returned, if only to seaside holiday homes, so far.

As we drive on to the museum, I think there is another remarkable thing besides the dissolution of the centuries-old hotchpotch of nations and languages which took place between 1930 and 1950 – in several phases, but on the whole very rapidly and brutally – everywhere in Eastern Europe. It suddenly strikes me as no less remarkable that the multiculturalism has persisted longer and runs deeper than on the Western side of the continent, for example, and especially compared with the New World, where ethnic origins are often reduced to popular folklore, and the mother tongue lost forever, within one or two generations. Even today – after colonization by the Russian Empire, after genocide, banishment, discrimination and Russification during the Soviet Union – even today, Crimean Tatars, Russian Germans, Greeks and the rest, although they have dwindled to tiny minorities, still cling almost desperately to their languages and their traditions. Do they cling to them because they were persecuted? No one talks about 'American Germans' trying to preserve what remains of their German culture and language over generations, although far more Germans have emigrated westwards than eastwards. Stalin did not simply annihilate the ethnic diversity: he wanted – like today's nationalists who claim they have nothing against other cultures, saying Turks, Syrians, Mexicans, Armenians, Rohingya, or whoever, should be happy and self-determined in their own countries – Stalin wanted to break up the diversity into its component parts. Like Lenin before him, he had a Herderian conception of each people needing its own territory, even if it was somewhere out beyond Siberia – in fact, that was where he created an autonomous district for the Jews, the first Jewish state in the modern age.

Spontaneously, Natalya – the Russian Natalya, not the Crimean German one – interjects into my train of thought that, deep down, she is still a Soviet citizen. She knows about the crimes under Stalin, the banishments, the Gulag, and she certainly doesn't want to turn back the clock. But it is good, she says, to belong to a real family of nations, this security of knowing, everywhere in the gigantic empire, how to behave to be met with respect. And the Crimean Tatars? I ask. Are they respected too? Certainly there were tensions when the Tatars returned; they wanted their old houses back; they claimed them, often enough they simply squatted them. Naturally many Russians were afraid of being driven out of their homes, of feeling like strangers in their own neighbourhood. The Crimean Tatars refused the land the state offered them, Natalya says, because they wanted to live near the sea as their ancestors had; she finds that understandable. But the seaside land happens to be the most expensive and the most densely populated. That was in the early 1990s, and it was just a huge upheaval in which everyone looked only to their own survival.

'So, in your view, it was a mistake for the Crimean Tatars to come back?' I ask.

'No!' Natalya exclaims, almost shocked. 'They wanted to return to their country; you can't argue with that. It's their country, after all.'

In a quiet street on a hillside where the view of the sea has remained unobstructed, we get out of the car: a century has passed since Anton Chekhov planted his garden on a barren patch of land near a Tatar cemetery; they say he planted more than half the trees, bushes and grapevines himself. And gardens run through the plays and stories he wrote in the last years of his life in Crimea, not least as the places where people declare their love. But Chekhov also sets the most awful events in man-made natural surroundings, such as the felling of the trees at the end of *The Cherry Orchard*, which anticipated the downfall of a world, his world, at the turn of the twentieth century. What kind of world was it?

I walk into the house, and from the first step I feel transported into one of his plays, yes, as if Chekhov had been his own dramatic character; the hall where he hung his hat, the kitchen where he occasionally made himself a pot of tea, the salon where no less a person than the venerable Tolstoy often sat, the bedrooms and the guest rooms, the portraits of his beautiful wife, the dining room table with the chairs that are still the originals; all the seats, for that matter: armchairs, sofas, benches; and also the beds – almost nothing in the interior is specifically Russian. What Natalya calls the most Russian place in Yalta is a genteel European house the like of which could be found in France, Germany or northern Italy, or in a nineteenth-century neighbourhood in Beirut or Alexandria for that matter, but it is a world apart from Bakhchisaray, where the houses had courtyards inside instead of gardens outside, you took your shoes off at the door and sat on the carpet to eat. Just a few kilometres and a whole continent away.

The Tatars too have blessed Crimea with a rich culture – but how strange that, today, that culture, the Asian one, is dependent on Europe for its survival. In the evening we take off our shoes once again to enter a house. Cordially friendly, perhaps grateful for the foreign visitor, the singer Elvira Sarykhalil greets us in her grandparents' village some 50 kilometres east of Yalta along the coast, where she has returned with her parents to live. After many applications, and because the mayor took a great deal of trouble, her father was allowed to build a house, although only on a hillside above the village where the ground is actually much too steep. Fortunately, he was an engineer, and in his mind's eye he saw the terrace with the most beautiful sea view for miles around. By now the house is inhabited by the next generation: Elvira's two sons, who are learning four languages, Crimean Tatar, Russian, Ukrainian and a little Arabic, because education will be critical for their future. That is what Elvira's parents learned in exile, and why they made sure she was able to study at one of the best conservatories in Ukraine. Today she is known both for modern jazz vocals and for her traditional songs, and she is most famous for connecting the two. In her house, you take your shoes off at the door, and yet you sit on chairs.

After the dinner, which transports me to the Far East, her proud father projects YouTube videos of her concerts on the living room wall, Kiev, Berlin, Amsterdam. It is a long time since Elvira has given a concert in Crimea, I learn, and if she were too critical abroad – that is, too pro-European – she would have problems on her return, as many other artists have, or would not be allowed to return at all. 'Haven't you ever thought about moving away,' I ask, 'to Kiev, Berlin or Amsterdam, where you can sing?'

'No,' answers Elvira, 'the countryside here permeates my singing. We all spend as much time as we can on the terrace.' Then she sings an old folk song in which the loved one's brow is like the waves upon the sea, uneasily rising and softly sinking again.

Twenty-Seventh Day: From Crimea to the Russian Mainland

Pushing back the curtains in my hotel room, I see the sea. Up to now it has been raining since I've been in Crimea; I haven't mentioned that because I wanted to record the beauty of the landscape, not write that Crimea in the rain looks much the same as the countryside around Siegen in Westphalia, where I was born – the coast was barely discernible in the thick clouds. Now, though, the sun is shining and, because it snowed in the night, not only the faraway mountains but also the hills huddling in a semicircle around the little bay look sprinkled with powdered sugar. The shingle beach was no doubt perfect too at one time. Now it must put up with one abandoned snack stall after another, some made of weathered boards, a few of corrugated steel. The somewhat elevated promenade, and also the stairs leading down to the beach, are bare concrete, and, between the stairs, jetties of various lengths and kinds jut into the water, as if each angler had built one out of the contents of his shed. The stacked-up paddleboats look discarded, as does the rubbish, which is really rubbish. But then I walk to the end of the bay and hop from rock to rock, so as not to get wet, around the cliff. Suddenly I am standing all alone on another beach with nothing built on it. Like Elvira, I look at the sea and forget for the moment the world I am in.

The same thing will have happened during the war, during the world wars that were fought on Crimea in the middle of both the last two centuries; a British, Russian, French, Turkish or German soldier will have walked out from his camp on a quiet day, perhaps because the sun was shining again at last after long, cold rains mixed with snow. Then he looked at the sea and thought of his dearest at home, of the children, of his daily cares and wants, or he sank into the landscape for a moment, breathing the salt, hearing the waves, closed his eyes and felt the warm light. He forgot everything around him. Is there another catastrophe looming today, of which the tensions in Crimea, the wars nearby in Donbas and on the other side of the Black Sea are only portents? In eastern Turkey, in northern Iraq, in the southern Caucasus and all over Syria, even in Yemen, in Libya and further off – or is it all one big war by now? Since Donald Trump's election as president of the US, which delighted many autocrats, Moscow has been talking about a 'new Yalta', a revised division of the world into spheres of influence, which would probably be preceded by a few more wars to facilitate the acceptance of a cold peace. Maybe that's why the urge is so strong to stay on this beach unmarred by human beings.

We drive on along the coast towards Russia. The Greeks, Ernes says, have not just left myths, grapevines and countless ruins; they also gave Crimea many place names, which remained when Catherine the Great had the Greeks carted away northwards to the steppes in order to put Russians in their villages. So that means, I realize only now, that the Greek villages I passed through in eastern Ukraine were themselves a result of the tsars' colonial policy; we unthinkingly assume everything Greek is ancient. But, in Crimea, the Greek place names were two thousand years old when they were rubbed out by the Soviet Union.

So many peoples turning up where, according to the school atlas, they don't belong; migrating or expelled or getting along together, or side by side; rarely making friends, and when they do, then usually after first bashing each other's heads in, Greeks, Russians, Cossacks, Tatars, Germans, Jews, Armenians, Italians, Poles too, and dozens of other peoples, in Crimea alone. Ultimately, every people, if they haven't been wiped out, have inherited from their ancestors their claims, grudges, traditions, songs, or just a piece of land, to which others also had hereditary claims, so that the seed is already planted for new conflicts. But exactly that, precisely this mishmash and nothing else, which often enough has taken the form of war in Crimea, and of world war – this mishmash is what history consists of: of people who are attributed, sometimes against their will, to nations; yet not only history, but culture too, which always forms in contradistinction to other cultures; this mishmash is what the richness consists of that we call civilization. There are no monocultures anywhere. There are only peaceful and non-peaceful ways of coexisting, assuming neither is willing to exterminate the other.

The country grows progressively more craggy, the vegetation more sparse, the villages that pop up along the roadside littler. The smartphone that is plotting our course towards Russia sounds the alarm at all five prayer times, without Ernes stopping once. But this time it is calling us to Friday prayers, and since a big mosque turns up almost at the same time, its façade shining white, we turn off the coast road. I am curious because there is also a church in the little village which is just as new and looks just as faceless.

All around the mosque, the streets are unpaved and the power lines are do-it-yourself; the houses, on the other hand, are new; almost all of them have a car parked in front. This is where the Crimean Tatars live who have returned from exile to their ancestral village. But, although it is prayer time, we find the mosque closed, and the men are marching in various bunches to the other half of the village, towards the church, which did not exist during the Soviet Union either. Has everyone here converted to Christianity?

We follow the Tatars to the older part of the village, which is where their parents or grandparents lived, walk past the church, which is also locked up – as I was saying, it's Friday morning – past the present inhabitants, who are neither friendly nor unfriendly, and through an inconspicuous passage between two walls we come to an iron door, behind which a stairway leads up to the prayer hall of the old mosque, which was a storeroom during the Soviet Union. Another building was built onto the façade. The men tell us that they broke open the door a few years ago and cleared out the warehouse. No one needed the junk any more: painted signs for Soviet holidays, worn-out school equipment, and what not. Even the head of the village looked the other way. They just feel more comfortable in the old prayer hall, they say. Besides, the new mosque, which was built with Turkish money, is much too big for the few Tatars who haven't been rubbed out over the centuries.

Not far from the mosque, an old woman stops us and asks whether we have news from Ukraine. Apparently we are recognizable as travellers, foreigners. Why from Ukraine? we ask. The woman is from Donbas, from Lugansk to be exact, and came to this village three years ago to care for her son, who had been beaten up by bandits; then the war broke out unexpectedly and her son didn't let her go back. And now he won't let her turn on the news. He tells her nothing has changed, her house is undamaged, but she doesn't believe him. Do we know, she asks, how it looks in Lugansk now, when the war will be over? How do you answer an old woman?

On the way back to the coast road, we see a man with a cigarette in his mouth pruning the grapevines. I ask him whether the wine was better before or is better now.

'Before,' the man replies, and by that he doesn't mean before the annexation by Russia; he means the Soviet Union: 'They gave us more fertilizer then.'

He doesn't know, he says, why there's not enough fertilizer today; he is only an employee of the sovkhoz, has to prune 140 vines to get his wages, which doesn't leave him time even for a cigarette break. At least since the Russian annexation the wages are paid regularly; they didn't use to be before. This time, before means Ukraine.

A few villages further on, Ernes takes us to the house where his grandparents lived until they were banished: a truck pulled up in front of the house, half an hour to pack up the family's most important belongings, documents, and the Quran, then up on the truck, where the neighbours were already gathered, and from there to an overfilled freight car that rolled for seven days to far-off Asia, without anyone being allowed to get out, without anything being passed in, no food, news or hope, only water from time to time. Since their return, Ernes's father comes out here once a year to visit his parents' house.

'And there's no problem about that?' I ask.

'No, no,' Ernes assures me, 'the present occupants are friendly and always invite us in for tea.'

Beside the Soviet-era town sign stands a stone pillar with the Tatar name Ay Serez, which comes from the Greek. The column has been destroyed five times so far, says Ernes; we'll see how long the sixth one lasts.

We drive through the village, which, like most villages along the coast, runs up the hillside, and park the car in one of the highest streets. The little houses have two storeys, the bottom one of stone, the top one of wood, and they are divided into flats. Ernes carefully knocks on a door, and a woman appears with a blue knit cap on her blonde hair. She is wearing a bright red ski jacket over her sweaters. Unintentionally no doubt, the blue-blonde-red of her upper body looks almost like the Russian flag. More businesslike than enthusiastic, the woman invites us into her living room, where she also eats and sleeps. The only object that does not seem useful in the cluttered room is a little aquarium.

Tatiana has lived since she was born in the house from which Ernes's family was banished. Her father, who came from central Russia, was assigned the house in 1957.

'Did he have a choice?' I ask.

'No, he had grown up in an orphanage.'

Growing up in an orphanage, for the generation to which Tatiana's father must have belonged, could have meant that his parents had been shot or banished, or that they belonged to a people whose culture and language were undesirable, so that the NKVD abducted their children. Was that the case with her father? He never spoke about her grandparents, says Tatiana. She knew as a child that the house had once belonged to Crimean Tatars, but in a family of six they had too many cares of their own to worry about that. Now she is fifty-six years old and has worked for thirty-five of them, most of that period as caretaker in one of the sanatoriums on the coast. She is divorced; her children live elsewhere and have children of their own. Her pension is 7,000 roubles, worth a little over 100 euros. Whatever grows, she grows herself in her front yard. The money isn't enough to pay for heating, though.

I ask whether she was worried about being driven out during perestroika when the Crimean Tatars returned. No, says Tatiana; a few Tatars had already made their way back to their old village in the 1970s: they were nice people; their children had played with her children. And when Ernes's father turned up on her doorstep the first time?

'That was in the summer of 1989,' Tatiana immediately recalls. 'He was crying like a little boy; naturally that touched me. I made him tea.'

'And you still weren't afraid?'

'No; why should I be? He offered to buy the flat, but we didn't want to sell it, and he accepted that. Where else could we have gone? You see, we don't have a conflict with the Tatars; we have other kinds of problems.'

'What problems do you have, then?'

'After so many years we still don't have running water, for example. We have to carry water into the house in canisters. That's really a problem, especially in winter.'

'Hasn't anything changed since the annexation, then?'

'Nothing at all.'

'And are you glad nonetheless that Crimea belongs to Russia again?'

'I'm glad there's no war. That's what I'm glad of.'

The mountains to our left ebb away like waves, and after one last hillock we are back in the great plain, which must look like a trench from the sky. Towards evening we reach the easternmost town in Crimea: to see Kerch, you wouldn't think it is all of 2,600 years old – and no wonder, since it was destroyed by the Huns in the fourth century AD, and by other people since then: by the British and French in 1855 and by the Germans not a hundred years later. But the church, one of the oldest extant Byzantine churches anywhere, built in the eighth century, still stands – and that even though the ground is seismically active, the priest proudly points out. As if by a miracle, he adds, the church even survived the rule of the Tatars, who made it into a mosque. He was about to lock up, but he is so happy about the rare foreign visitor that he turns on the light once more and shows us every nook and cranny. He just held the worship service in the second, larger nave, which was added in the nineteenth century, when the city was in Christian hands once more, although the little church from the early Middle Ages would have been ample for the few churchgoers who attended the evening Mass. And yet by the Julian calendar, still used by the Orthodox Church, the new year begins tomorrow. It's only because the holiday falls on a working day, the priest says apologetically, adding that the Russians remained devout even under the Soviet Union. Since the end of the USSR, religion has been booming.

'And the younger people,' I ask, 'are they active in the church as well?'

135

'Yes,' the priest assures me, 'only not on working days.' The priest himself is not old; under forty, I estimate. With the dark grey pin-striped suit that he wears over a black shirt, his hair tied in a ponytail at the back and his neatly trimmed beard, he could be an American movie godfather. In his hand he holds a smartphone, an electronic car key, and a rosary wrapped around his fingers. 'Russia and faith are practically synonyms,' the priest continues.

Is it true, I ask, that Crimea is as holy to Russia as the Temple Mount to Jews and Muslims, as President Putin declared in his agenda-setting speech on the state of the nation? There is no question about it, the priest replies, citing Grand Prince Vladimir, who ushered in the Christianization of Russia with his own baptism in Crimea in the tenth century. Catherine the Great too had appealed to Vladimir to give her claim to Crimea a religious justification. But the priest also mentions a footprint left by John the Baptist. Unfortunately, it is already too dark, otherwise I could see it in the courtyard of the church. I heard about wonders like that in Jerusalem, too.

The priest puts out the light, locks up the church, takes his leave with friendly words, and presses the electronic key of his SUV, which, for whatever reason, has a Ukrainian number plate. This is surprising because the deadline to trade in number plates is long past, says Ernes, for whom Crimea will always belong to Europe.

Because the sea is unpredictable, we make the crossing to the mainland the same evening. It can happen, especially in winter, that the ferry stops running for hours, if not days. Even before the First World War, the British planned a railway line across the straits which would provide a connection all the way to India. Construction was begun by the Germans in May 1943, during the occupation. A third of the bridge was done when they blew it up because the Red Army was approaching. The Soviets nonetheless finished the bridge, having found plenty of material on the site, only to have it collapse again in the first ice storm. President Putin promised a bridge across the Kerch Strait after the annexation; it is supposed to be finished in two years. Even Russian newspapers raise the criticism that the number of travellers and the volume of freight are too low to warrant the cost of such a spectacular structure. Furthermore, the Kerch Strait lies in an earthquake region, as the village priest confirmed.

Although there are no customs inspections any more, it takes forever before the ferry casts off. And, in spite of the wait, there are only a few passengers aboard. It was somewhere around here, on one side or the other of the Kerch Strait, that once 'were born a pair of Siamese twins called "civilization" and "barbarism",' writes Neal Ascherson.

This is where Greek colonists met the Scythians. A settled culture of small, maritime city-states encountered a mobile culture of steppe nomads. People who had lived in one place for uncounted generations, planting crops and fishing the coastal sea, now met people who lived in wagons and tents and wandered about infinite horizons of grassy prairie behind herds of cattle and horses. It was not the first time in human history that farmers had met pastoralists: since the Neolithic Revolution, the beginning of settled agriculture, there must have been countless intersections of these two ways of life. Nor was it the first witnessing of nomadism by people from an urban culture: that was an experience already familiar to the Chinese on the western borders of the Han dominions. But in this particular encounter began the idea of 'Europe' with all its arrogance, its implications of superiority, all its assumptions of priority and antiquity, all its pretensions to a natural right to dominate.[28]

As our car rolls onto the mainland, it has grown too late to drive on to the next city. Over the Internet we book a hotel in the middle of nowhere. It turns out to be somewhere after all: there is a dance hall made of logs next door with many cars parked outside it. 'Who are you?' asks the broad-shouldered bouncer at the door with amusement when we appear before him, not exactly dressed for a night out.

'People,' answers Dmitrij, the Belarusian, Jew and photographer.

'Oh, I see,' the bouncer grins. 'And here I thought you were Turks.'

Inside the dance hall, I feel as though I have been transported to a carica-ture of Russia: the women uniformly have long, straight hair parted in the middle, overextended eye shadow, and revealing long dresses like the wife and daughter of Mr Trump. And the men look like – no, not the head of the presidential household; more like his bodyguards. The model seems to be replicated all over the world: the same hair and clothes were worn at my daughter's school leaving ball; the only question is who is copying whom. The music, at any rate, to which, strangely, only the women dance, is 100 per cent that of the former class enemy. The men prefer to pull at their hookahs, as if they were – the bouncer is not reading this, fortunately – Turks.

I think back to the study that looked as if Chekhov had just left it yesterday, the desk still strewn with papers, the telephone as big as a personal computer today, the tray for his visitors' calling cards. There, in that chair, Chekhov wrote his great dramas in which everyone is constantly longing for Moscow. 'And when just a bit more time goes by,' he writes in *Three Sisters*, 'say two or three hundred years, people will look at our life today both with alarm and with mockery, everything we have now will seem clumsy and burdensome and very inconvenient and strange. Ah, what a life that will surely be, what a life!' No doubt the optimism that Chekhov put into the mouth of the officer Vershinin was deceptive – the early modern era's optimism that 'people will be born who will be better than you.'[29] Rustem, easy-going Rustem in Bakhchisaray, would say that the two or three hundred years are not yet past. That we still have time.

Twenty-Eighth Day: To Krasnodar

The first thing that is really different in Russia is the speed traps. The flat countryside, with no trace of a hill or tree, the faces, the Cyrillic letters and lighted signs, the war memorials, flags and uniforms, the automobile makes, number plates, and patriotic bumper stickers – 'Thank you, Grandpa, for the victory!' – all that has remained the same since we crossed over to the mainland. But suddenly Ernes is respecting the speed limits, which are posted at frequent intervals. In Crimea, he had no qualms about speeding. After the annexation, the main roads in Crimea were repaired, but no radar cameras were installed, he explains; fortunately, the state doesn't work that efficiently.

'And in Russia it does?' I ask.

'Better than in Ukraine, anyway.'

He has hardly said this when a policeman waves us down, his uniform as thick as an astronaut's, with a fur hat, ear muffs, and a fluorescent yellow vest. In the Russian winter, you sympathize with anyone who has to work outdoors. I only wonder how the weatherproofed police officer fits behind the wheel of his official Lada, which is parked behind him.

'You weren't speeding,' I say as our car rolls onto the shoulder, guessing that an injustice is about to be committed.

'I crossed a solid line while passing.' Ernes pleads his guilt as if in a show trial. 'That's going to be expensive.'

When he gets back in the car, Ernes has paid 3,000 roubles, the equivalent of 50 euros, a fifth of his monthly income. He is nonetheless relieved because the police officer at first wanted to suspend his driving licence – on the spot, so that our trip would have ended, for the time being, here in the frozen steppes. But that was only a threat to get the negotiations rolling, Ernes says.

'How could you tell?' I ask.

'Because he took his time looking through my papers while he was talking to me: first my driving licence, then the vehicle registration, and finally my ID. That's a sure sign that you need to ask whether there isn't some other way. If he pulls out his report form right away, then there's nothing you can do.'

'I thought that only happened in Ukraine.'

'In Ukraine you can dicker about the amount; that's the difference. In Russia you just have to accept it: the state is too strong.'

About noon we reach the city of Krasnodar, the administrative centre of Russia's breadbasket. On the ruler-straight highway into town, we spend a long time driving past prefab concrete blocks and high-rise housing estates. Closer to the centre, the buildings get smaller and humbler; apparently they were built before mankind's dream of socialism. The main square has been remodelled with a colossal monument to Catherine the Great and a reconstruction of the cathedral that was demolished somewhere else during mankind's dream. Tsardom and Orthodoxy, the square apparently signifies, are the cornerstones of Russia's new, old world.

Russia has actually benefited from the sanctions, says Tatiana, who sells agricultural refrigeration equipment for a German company. The products she offers are now made in Russia, she says, because otherwise no one could afford them, and the same is true of foods, only more so. Parmesan cheese from Parma is not really essential, and the Russian cheese is just as good – and requires a lot of new cold storage; as a result, Tatiana's business is booming. The people don't blame their own government for the rising prices; they blame the government that has declared an economic war on Russia – their country will withstand the current attacks, just as it has withstood earlier ones. The war in nearby Donbas, according to Tatiana, is a Ukrainian aggression against the Russian-speaking population, whom Russia must support; the intervention in Syria is a humanitarian operation; and Crimea is an integral part of Russia. Europe, meanwhile, is drowning in refugees.

I hear the same thing throughout the rest of the day. I talk to a German teacher, the owner of a bakery chain, a law student and a taxi driver: chance acquaintances, true, and yet it seems to me more than a coincidence that all of them see the world today pretty much the way their president does. Accordingly, they don't miss any freedom, because in all freedom the Russians would elect Vladimir Putin anyway. And if it's true what they say – and I have no reason to doubt it – then their friends, acquaintances, business contacts and fellow students more or less share their opinion. That's why people don't discuss politics much.

'No, not at university either,' says Alexandra, the student, who is surprised that students in other countries or in other periods are rebellious; in Russia today they're certainly not. As a law student, she has a relatively secure future – that's important to her, and certainly not to be taken for granted when she hears from her parents about the chaos that reigned under Yeltsin. Not to mention Gorbachev – a criminal. Putin restored order; that makes up for his drawbacks, of which there are some, naturally. Economics, for example, says Tatiana, is not the president's strong suit; his successor will have to see to it that Russia overcomes its dependency on raw materials. Putin's mission is different, namely Russia's greatness and stability. What we experienced with the traffic police is typical, sadly, admits Viktor, the bakery owner: corruption is a festering sore in business too, and in the bureaucracy, and especially in the highest levels of society. Still, you have to give the government credit for the measures that have been undertaken, such as the many court trials, from which not even the oligarchs are safe any more. And recently they have installed little video cameras in the police cars so that no dirty dealing remains secret. Ah, so that's why the police officer did his business in the open air, in spite of the cold.

The people are not angry citizens rebelling against a system or the fake news media; they are not marginalized; they seem neither agitated nor radical; they have friendly smiles for the foreign visitor, even if he belongs to a religion that is, to put it mildly, 'problematic'. Chechnya, my next destination, is one to which Tatiana and Alexandra would never travel because they could not move freely as women in a Muslim country. The attitude that the right-wing populists propagate in the West towards the primacy of the nation and Western identity, towards authoritarian democracy and Islam, towards homosexuality and gender nonsense, towards America's world domination and Brussels's dictatorship, seems to be mainstream at least in the Russian middle class. If their views seem to me to be rehearsed, predictable down to the subordinate clauses, Tatiana, Alexandra, Viktor and Mariana would say the same thing about my views – when I call the siege of Aleppo a war crime or claim that, wherever a refugee shelter is set up in Germany, a citizens' initiative forms – for the refugees, not against them. The only explanation the people I talk to have for the fact that most Germans are, by and large, content, indeed thankful for the conditions they live in today, including the cultural diversity, is propaganda by controlled media.

'People here are for Putin,' confirms the taxi driver, who is the only one of my chance acquaintances who belongs to a different class, and he adds that people are not this satisfied everywhere with the state of affairs. The Krasnodar region is comparatively well off, with its strong agricultural sector, many foreign investors and the oil pipeline to the Black Sea. But Tatiana, Alexandra, Viktor and Mariana also have quite different assessments of the social reality and find much that is exemplary in Europe's West, where they have travelled – the health care system, for example, the better infrastructure in general. As he warns against Islam, Viktor assures me that he doesn't mean me, of course. He is only angry about those who don't assimilate.

'But do the Russians taking their holidays in Egypt or Antalya assimilate much?' I ask, 'Or those buying up the City of London?'

'No,' Viktor concedes; 'sometimes I've been ashamed of my compatriots.'

Their view of the world is not so closed that everything that clashes with it has to be a lie. Tatiana has never heard that Donald Trump boasted of grabbing women between the legs, although she stays informed through Russian media daily. Actually she thinks Trump is a good man who speaks a clear language and understands economics, otherwise he wouldn't have ended up with so much money. But sexism like that, no, that would be disgusting, obviously, if it's not fake news. Alexandra, who doesn't think about politics much, considers Trump 'a clown' anyway. Only where Syria is concerned is she, and all those I talk to, firm: Russians would never bombard civilians. This is too much for Dmitrij, who has to talk about the crimes of the Russian princes and later the Soviets in Belarus. Tatiana finds that believable. No one wants to go back; if there is a kind of nostalgia for the Soviet Union, then only among the older people; the younger generation's orientation is European.

'European?' I ask, surprised.

'Well, modern, I mean,' replies Mariana, the German teacher; she thinks that Russia is on a good course.

Twenty-Ninth Day: From Krasnodar to Grozny

On the way to Grozny, I am amazed at all the heroes whom every child in Chechnya knows. The greatest of them is Sheikh Kunta-haji, who in the

141

nineteenth century preached love for all creatures, friend and foe, animal and plant. The sheikh was a regular environmentalist: he exhorted people not to leave rubbish anywhere, always to plant more trees than they cut down, and to have special regard for those that bear fruit or give shade to travellers. Domesticated animals should be treated no differently from friends; every bush and every blade of grass should be treated as a housemate. 'Cows, sheep, horses, dogs and cats have no language to communicate their needs,' he said, and inferred from that: 'so we must understand their needs ourselves.' Sheikh Kunta-haji advocated the rights of women and the separation of state and religion: 'Do not contend with those in power; do not try to replace them with yourselves,' he said to the religious scholars; 'All power is God's.' As a mystic and the founder of the Qadiriyyah order, which is still one of the most important religious organizations in Chechnya today, he railed against a piety that defined itself by outward forms and practices: 'Do not rush to wrap your turban – wrap up your heart first.' But, most of all, the sheikh was a radical pacifist, and his pacifism deeply impressed Leo Tolstoy, who came to the Caucasus as a soldier in his youth and became an opponent of war and a conservationist in his old age. 'Let your weapons be your cheeks, not guns and daggers,' Kunta-haji exhorted the faithful. 'To die in combat with an enemy who is much stronger is the same as suicide, and suicide is the greatest of all sins.'

Is it possible? I wonder in the back seat as Russia's snow-covered breadbasket rushes past outside the windows. Chechnya's most famous religious scholar was an early ecologist and a pacifist? After all, the Chechens today are known more as fighters, if not terrorists. Yes, it is possible, I am assured by Akhmet and Magomet, who picked us up in Krasnodar, and they go on to the next hero: in the eighteenth century, the itinerant preacher Mansur Ushurma taught that all people are equal, condemned blood vengeance and called on the faithful to support the sick, the orphans and the needy. The Russians sent soldiers to stop the 'false prophet', burnt down his village with 400 farms and killed his brother. Then Sheikh Ushurma called his followers to arms and beat the Russian troops in a legendary battle in 1785. Prince Pyotr Bagration, who would later become a hero of the war against Napoleon, was wounded and captured. The sheikh ordered the fighters to care for the prince and carry him to the Russian camp. Moved by the magnanimity of the enemy, the officers wanted to show the bearers their gratitude. But they refused all payment: treating guests well was self-evident to Chechens. After other victorious battles, Sheikh Ushurma was finally defeated by superior forces in 1791. He was locked in a cage like a wild animal and transported to St Petersburg, then thrown into a dungeon in Shlisselburg Fortress, which he never left again until his death. His guards knew no hospitality.

Akhmet and Magomet chose their pseudonyms themselves. No Chechen, they announced before we left Krasnodar, would speak freely to me if he had to fear that his real name would be published. I would have to think up many more pseudonyms, they said, and fictitious circumstances, occupations, places, and dates, if I wanted to write the truth about Chechnya. After all, they live in a country where the president personally lays hands on prisoners. Is that true? It has been written over and over again in reports on Chechnya that the young Ramzan Kadyrov, the head of government since his father's assassination in 2007, takes part personally in torture. Akhmet and Magomet say they know people who were themselves imprisoned in the president's jail: Chechnya is so small, they say, and the trust within families so great, in spite of the secret police, that word of such things gets around quickly. And that is also the reason – so that word doesn't get around – why so many people disappear without a trace. In fact, human rights organizations have documented nearly 10,000 cases in the past fifteen years. Officially, all Chechens love their president, says Magomet; unofficially, everyone knows he is just Russia's lackey.

Russia's, of all countries: there is the massacre of Dadi-Yurt on 15 September 1819, to take just the next story I note from the back seat: one of the most terrible punitive operations of the tsar's army. Having seen that the Chechens defended their villages especially fiercely when there were still women and children in them, the Russian commander, General Alexey Yermolov, ordered an example made: all 200 houses in Dadi-Yurt were levelled and all the inhabitants killed except for 140 young girls. To escape a life in servitude, and probably rape too, forty-six of those girls jumped from a high bridge into the foaming River Terek, pulling their guards after them. Nonetheless, the general was content: 'The example of Dadi-Yurt has spread terror everywhere,' he noted in his diary, 'and no doubt we will not find women or families anywhere in future.'

The other stories are also about resistance against foreign rulers, formerly Khazars, Huns, Arabs, Persians and Mongols; then, from the eighteenth century on, Russians or Soviets. Chechnya is the only country in the Caucasus which never had feudal structures or serfdom, neither princes nor kings, no taxes, no central authority. Chechens defined themselves by their quality as free peasants on their own soil, with no obligations to any ruler, only to their own family. Thus I understand, on another leg of the long drive, why the one rebel celebrated in world literature, Tolstoy's Hadji Murat, is not a hero at all from the Chechen point of view: because he was not only a liberator but at the same time a usurper. 'I hear that the Russians show favours to you and call for your submission,' Imam Shamil implores the Caucasians in Tolstoy's novel. 'Believe them not, do not submit, but be patient. It is better to die at war with the Russians than to live with the infidels. Be patient, and I will come with the Koran and the sword to lead you against the Russians.'[30] Imam Shamil and his followers prevailed in spite of the Russian superiority and established a theocracy which expanded in 1845 to form a North Caucasian emirate. But more and more families rebelled against Shamil's brutal regime and made a separate peace with the Russians. Shamil retreated to the fortress of Gunib with his last 400 stalwarts. At first he wanted to fight to the death, but his love for his family, who were with him in the fortress, softened his heart. He became an honoured prisoner of the tsar and died in 1871 in Medina, after having been permitted to undertake the hajj.

'It's no wonder he surrendered,' mutters Akhmet contemptuously, pointing out that the imam was not a true Chechen but born in Dagestan. Nevertheless, Chechen history is replete not only with heroes but also with traitors. Again and again, tribes offered the tsars their services when it seemed advantageous, and such pragmatism has not become rarer in recent times: when the battalion commander Sulim Yamadayev fell out of grace with the current president, his soldiers did not hesitate to abandon him. And since they had dissociated themselves from their commander, they also testified against him – Yamadayev himself showed understanding for their lack of loyalty, saying that, after all, they had to feed their families.

And not only have heroes become traitors, but sometimes traitors have been the true heroes. Hadji Murat, for example, a historic figure who is portrayed positively not only by Tolstoy, was also a defector, committed a betrayal in other words, but only because he wanted to free his wife and his children whom his former companion Imam Shamil held hostage – every Chechen understands that; even today, blood relations are the only alliance that can be counted on beyond all doubt. Akhmet and Magomet admit that blood vengeance is still a reality in Chechen society and, although they find the custom archaic, I perceive in other contexts a subtle note of pride in the great cohesion of their families. On that account, they ought to take a somewhat milder view of Imam Shamil, who decided against death and for his family. But, then, Shamil was born in Dagestan; to Chechens that's a problem in itself.

His closest comrade in arms, Beisungur, is said to have been of different blood: in their victories over the Russians, he lost first his left arm, then his left eye and, in another battle, his left leg. His wounds barely healed, the one-armed, one-legged and one-eyed Beisungur had himself tied onto his horse and led his men into the next battle. As the troops were arrayed face to face, a giant of a Cossack proposed a single combat. Beisungur took up the challenge and rode forward to face the Cossack. When he came back to his camp with a wound in his chest, Shamil asked him furiously, 'Why do you bring shame upon us? You are wounded, and the Cossack is still in the saddle.'

'Wait until his horse moves,' Beisungur replied.

When the horse took a step, the Cossack's head fell to the ground.

Beisungur fought on after Imam Shamil traded his freedom for his life. He succeeded yet again in organizing a rebellion, but then, on 17 February 1861, Beisungur was ambushed, taken prisoner, and sentenced to death by hanging. To humiliate him, the Russians offered a reward for the one who would carry out the sentence. No one among the crowd gathered in front of the church in Khazavyurt volunteered, until finally – what else? – a Dagestani stepped forward. At that, Beisungur kicked away the stool under his foot and hanged himself.

There is no danger in mentioning that Akhmet and Magomet are of rustic mien, broad-shouldered, bearded, with big hands, because their physiognomy is fairly typical of middle-aged Chechens; the president looks like a wrestler too. I may also mention that one of them makes his living by commerce while the other lives from hand to mouth. He has the necessary family connections, says Magomet, to be a teacher or a clerk. But he doesn't know how to curry favour, act friendly and negotiate the bribe that is necessary in Chechnya to get any job at all, even with connections. And, once he had a job, he would have to 'donate' 10 or 20 per cent of every month's salary to the Kadyrov Foundation to finance the ruling family's pretentious lifestyle, up to and including their private zoo with lions and tigers. As if that were not enough, he would also be expected to follow the president on Instagram – having to read Ramzan's heroic deeds every day, that's really going too far. Ramzan Kadyrov has 2.4 million followers: twice as many as he has subjects. Rather than typing enthusiastic comments under pictures in which the president greets high-priced pop and sports stars brought in from the West, fearlessly holds up a python or holds Vladimir Putin in a beaming embrace, Magomet prefers to remain a free peasant on his own soil, barren though it may be. Or, in more sober terms: Magomet gets by from one job to the next. Now he's accompanying his cousin Akhmet, who doesn't like to drive long distances alone.

'Because the landscape is so monotonous?' I ask Akhmet.

'No, because of the crime.'

The landscape is monotonous, though, flat all the way to the horizon, so we go on with the history that Chechnya wrote in the twentieth century. There's Hazukha Magomadov, the last *abrek*, as the Caucasians call a certain mixture of Robin Hood and Che Guevara. He fought against the secret police during the Stalinist terror, stayed on underground in 1944 when his people were banished to Kazakhstan and Siberia, scouring the deserted villages. He was the first to enter the village of Khaibakh after all 700 inhabitants had been burnt alive in a horse shed. He escaped from an ambush by stabbing a lieutenant colonel and quickly putting on his uniform before being seen. Another time, the Soviets recruited one of his comrades in arms to kill him in his sleep. But Hazukha suspected the danger, crawled out of his coat and waited against the wall. The assassin stood up in the dark and shot at the coat before being shot himself by Hazukha. Afterwards, the newspapers claimed the *abrek* had murdered his most loyal comrade. Aged seventy-one years and exhausted from a lone wolf's life, Hazukha was caught on 28 March 1976, after a bitterly cold winter, and was riddled with bullets on the spot. No one dared approach the body until the evening of the next day, so great was the fear of the dead *abrek*, who weighed only 36 kilos.

'And the last two wars?' I ask, 'did they produce heroes too?' Magomet fought for Chechnya in the first war. But Akhmet was against the war, and against independence too for that matter, because he thought it was foolhardy to revolt against big Russia. Both of them, nonetheless, consider Dzhokhar Dudayev the last Chechen hero. As a general in the Soviet air force in 1990, Dudayev refused the order to attack demonstrators in Estonia, left the service and returned to Chechnya to lead his own country to independence. 'My entire conscious life was preparation for that,' he later said about his mission,

the injustice, the violence, the pressure that weighed upon my soul, on the soul of my people – and not only mine – I became aware of it as I was growing up in a clay hut, in Siberian conditions, with hunger, poverty and repression. Nothing could scare me – not hunger, not cold, not poverty. The most terrible thing was the feeling of complete lawlessness, the fact that the law, the state, offered you no defence. Quite the contrary – its explicit goal was to annihilate you as a human being, as a personality.

When a democratic constitution took effect in 1992, developed with the help of the grateful Baltic states, Dudayev was swept into the presidential palace with 85 per cent of the vote. He did not give up his independent spirit. Not only did he go on living in his village outside Grozny and drive to state receptions in his private car; he also discerned the danger of Islamic fundamentalism earlier than others: 'If the negative external factors are reinforced, Islam will continue getting stronger,' he predicted in 1992. 'But if there is the possibility of an independent choice, an independent development, then an independent, secular state will become established.' All of Moscow's attempts to bring the Dudayev government to its knees by economic and transport blockades failed. Finally, on 12 December 1994, 'the final solution to the Chechen problem' followed, to use President Boris Yeltsin's phrase for the war. With no consideration for the civilian population, Russia strewed the country with vacuum bombs, fragmentation bombs and defoliating poisons. Dudayev showed extraordinary military skill, and yet he died through carelessness. On 21 April 1996, when he had to make a telephone call during a cross-country drive, he first sent his wife a safe distance away because the Russians were able to locate his satellite telephone. But he made the call and was hit by a cruise missile before he could ring off. As Yeltsin proclaimed victory in Grozny, the Chechens reorganized in the mountains, marched on the capital and triumphed over one of the most modern armies in the world. The peace agreement of 1997 marked Russia's *de facto* recognition of Chechen sovereignty. The war had killed 100,000 civilians and made cripples, widows or orphans of at least twice that number. Almost half of the population, 460,000 people, had fled to the neighbouring republics, and most of them returned to destroyed houses. 'Nobody spoke a word of hatred for the Russians,' Leo Tolstoy wrote in *Hadji Murat* about the Chechens' reaction to murder, looting, destruction and the desecration of their mosque:

The emotion felt by every Chechen, old and young alike, was stronger than hatred. It was not hatred, it was a refusal to recognize these Russian dogs as men at all, and a feeling of such disgust, revulsion and bewilderment at the senseless cruelty of these creatures that the urge to destroy them – like the urge to destroy rats, venomous spiders or wolves – was an instinct as natural as that of self-preservation.[31]

The second Chechen war did not write any heroic history. Instead of contributing to the reconstruction, as agreed in the peace treaty, Russia sabotaged the new, still secular government, not least by supporting the religious opposition in which Wahhabis from the Arabian region increasingly held sway. The invasion of Dagestan by the radical Chechen field commander Shamil Basayev in August 1999 provided the pretext for a military operation. For the rebirth of the Russian Army and national feeling, the disgrace of the previous defeat had to be expiated, the new prime minister Vladimir Putin demanded. At the same time, the war against terror practically allowed the secret service to seize power and the former FSB officer to take the throne as the new president. 'The Chechens must be destroyed like vermin,' Putin declared then, and announced, 'We will hunt them down in every corner of the globe and drown them in toilets.'

In the evening, we drive into Grozny, 'the world's most thoroughly destroyed city' at the end of the second Chechen war, according to a United Nations report. In 2001, Grozny had practically ceased to exist. Other cities had been levelled too; all the factories in the country had been bombed; the entire infrastructure had been destroyed, another 200,000 civilians killed; this time 570,000 Chechens had fled. The independence movement had dissolved into its component parts: secularists, traditionalists, defectors, many criminals and growing numbers of jihadists.

In 1999 at the latest, it became clear that the resistance had been broken when another traitor went down in history: the Mufti of Grozny, Akhmat Kadyrov, who in the first war had proclaimed a 'jihad' against Russia. But was he really a traitor? After all, even the case of Hadji Murat is not so clear. 'He honestly believed he was saving the Chechens from certain death,' acknowledged Ilyas Akhmadov, the foreign minister of the separatist government. Kadyrov had made a pact with the Russians, not for personal advantage, but because he considered Wahhabi Islam the more dangerous enemy. He ensured the bloodless surrender of the second-largest city, Gudermes, and Putin thanked him by making him president of the autonomous republic in 2003. A year later, he died in a bomb attack in a football stadium. Although Kadyrov had gone over to the enemy, Akhmadov called him, in an interview he gave to the *New Yorker*, 'an energetic and brave man, with a great deal of personal courage.'

Today, no trace of the war can be seen in Grozny. Russia is trying to prove, with tremendous transfers of funds, that its federation is the best of all possible worlds for Chechnya: skyscrapers blinking with lighting designs in every colour, neo-classical fantasy architecture, the theatre a mixture of Taj Mahal and St Peter's Basilica, the presidential palace with more columns than ancient Rome, the great mosque, built with tons of gold and marble and with chandeliers so heavy that it was a feat of engineering just to install them. The eight-lane thoroughfares are lined with residential and commercial buildings with stucco ornamentation in imitation of the European nineteenth century. Every second corner is hung with photos of Vladimir Putin and the Kadyrovs, father and son.

After a thorough security check, we are admitted to the grounds where the skyscrapers stand, fenced off from the rest of the city. The slim doorman of the five-star hotel which occupies one of the towers wears a peaked cap that is much too big for him and trainers below a red coat that was tailored for a wrestler. Idle employees sit scattered about the lobby, in front of the boutiques and at the bar, all of them following the fashions of their president: the close-fitting suit with hip-length jacket, the narrow tie worn demonstratively loose, hair combed down over the forehead, the cheeks shaved but an inch-long beard under the chin. We do not encounter any guests in the hotel.

'We defeated ourselves,' says Magomet, who has come up to my room to see Grozny from the eighteenth floor, and he tells the story of the family in the village of Alkhan-Kala, which was also reported in the Western press at the time. When the third daughter came of marriageable age, the son demanded that she should marry him. Their father asked the son if he had lost his mind. But the son appealed to an alleged word of God which said a good Muslim must marry his third sister; his emir had explained it to him. For that reason he would not permit his sister to leave the house.

'We had never heard of a son contradicting his father,' Akhmet says. 'That never happened in our culture.'

The father took his son by the collar, dragged him out to the shed and shot him. No one in the village condemned the father. Order had been restored, and yet was irreparably broken.

Before bed, I go to stretch my legs along the new prestige boulevard, which of course is called Putin Prospekt. I am the only pedestrian; only occasionally does a car go by. I don't need to worry, Akhmet and Magomet assured me, conceding to their president that Chechnya today is at least safe. The buildings are brightly lit from outside, but there is no light in the windows anywhere. The skyscrapers too seem to be mostly uninhabited. Does anyone live here at all, or is all Grozny just a big Potemkin village? The last story Akhmet told was about an old woman: when he returned with his family after the second war, they found her sitting in front of the ruins of his house.

'What are you doing here?' Akhmet's mother asked her.

'Surviving,' said the woman.

'You're surviving?'

'Yes, I'm surviving,' the woman repeated, and pointed to a rubble heap across the street where a high-rise block had once stood. 'That's where I lived.' When Grozny was bombarded, the woman had wanted to take shelter in the basement. She beat with her fists on the steel door, only to be told time after time by voices shouting through the door that there were already a hundred people jammed together inside and there was barely enough air for all of them. In vain the woman begged to be the one hundred and first. Finally she went out to the street to look for shelter somewhere else. She had hardly gone a few steps when a bomb hit the building. All one hundred people in the cellar were dead. Since then, the old woman had been surviving.

Thirtieth Day: Grozny

No, says the young woman, who for her safety shall remain nameless, as she guides me through the newly built city centre – no, hardly anyone lives here. The apartments are not affordable to normal people, and the rich prefer to live in a villa they have commissioned themselves rather than deal with the shoddy work of a developer who can do whatever he wants because he's also the ruler of the country. The water pressure in the luxury flats, for example, is so low that the spa showers barely work even on the first floor, the electric wiring has already set several buildings on fire, and the opulent stucco on the imitation nineteenth-century façades that line Putin Prospekt is crumbling like blackboard chalk. Only no one is supposed to notice, so every owner is obligated to renovate the façade regularly and to bear the costs for the bright outside lighting at night that makes the rooms as bright as day. And then the skyscrapers: in an earthquake region, who would voluntarily move into a tower built by Chechnya's young president? One high-rise is completely vacant; another is occupied by a hotel, although the few guests could be housed in a single floor; in the other buildings, almost nothing is used but the lower floors, for offices, restaurants or gyms. The apartments that face the president's palace are reserved anyway for members of his security organization. But the rebuilding of Grozny was worthwhile in spite of the high vacancy: to buy real estate from Ramzan Kadyrov, you don't have to want to use it. You buy it to demonstrate your loyalty.

And maybe the luxury boutiques, cafés and Italian shoe shops are open only for show; I see no shoppers anywhere – it's part of the pretence that Grozny is a metropolis. When I walk into the tourist information office, which looks from outside like those in Florence and Madrid, the staff, taken completely by surprise, are unable to tell me about any sights to be seen in the city. And yet the sumptuous new buildings would be a credit to Disneyland, Legoland or any other theme park: they imitate every architectural style, from the Blue Mosque of Istanbul to the White House in Washington. And, to top it all off, another skyscraper is being built that is supposed to be the tallest building in Europe. 'Thank you, Ramzan, for Grozny,' is the legend on huge posters, as if no such city had existed before.

In fact it didn't exist in 2004 when Akhmat Kadyrov, Moscow's freshly appointed governor, died in a bomb attack and his 27-year-old son was appointed his successor. In the few pictures of the destruction of the second Chechen war that were published abroad in spite of the information black-out, Grozny looks like Dresden after the firebombing. Instead of rebuilding the city, Kadyrov has created a Caucasian metropolis that makes Berlin's new city centre around Potsdamer Platz look positively organic in comparison. A Russian peace in Syria, I think, could look similar, and would probably be better in fact than the continuation of the war: well-ordered, pristine and free of any past. Only the planners who rebuild Aleppo, say, should at least plant trees along the streets, not forget playgrounds for the families, and build parks that consist of something more than prestigious lawns.

Grozny is supposed to have been the greenest city in the Caucasus at one time but, in its reconstruction, no one has given any thought to shade for the hot summer days or to any kind of liveable urban environment. Instead there are gigantic squares of concrete where further vacancy was undesired and pictures on every corner of Chechnya's new Trinity: Kadyrov the Father and Kadyrov the Son, with Putin as the Holy Spirit. Accordingly, the central Kadyrov Square, overshadowed by the brand-new Kadyrov mosque, is where Kadyrov Prospekt and Putin Prospekt cross. Anyone who thinks it is impossible to break a nation's backbone has not seen Grozny. Not even the National Museum recalls the two wars with Russia which cost the lives of a quarter of the population and drove more than half from their homes –

a higher proportion than in Belarus during the Second World War, and there at least there are monuments commemorating some of the victims. In Chechnya, not even the banishment of the entire people under Stalin is worth a display panel in the official history. And the National Library is hardly able to preserve a collective remembrance, since almost all Chechen books and manuscripts, and thus the cultural memory of the Chechens, were destroyed in the course of the Soviet writing reforms.

And what about the present – is it possible to talk about that? Yes, but only under the conspiratorial conditions of a spy film: the civil servant is sitting in the appointed car in the car park of the government agency. His superior, whom he has taken into his confidence, did not want us to enter the building because of the cameras at the entrance. The official's cousin is one of 10,000 Chechens who are supposed to have disappeared since the end of the war. The first thing I ask is whether he can confirm this figure, which turns up in human rights reports again and again. Yes, says the official; about 10,000 cases is realistic; a critical remark at work, a joke about the president overheard by the wrong person, or a Salafist beard is enough to get a person kidnapped. They are living in a totalitarian system again, he says, as they once did under Stalin, except that today the Chechens are being gagged by their own compatriots. That is the 'Chechenization' of the conflict that Vladimir Putin always talked about: delegating the repression to local allies.

'But there really is a problem with religious extremism, isn't that the case?'

'Yes, there is,' says the civil servant, 'especially among the young people. And when they or their friends get kidnapped, then they really turn radical.'

In the past year or two, the oppression has once again been massively increased, and hence the relatives of the missing persons no longer report them, human rights organizations no longer collect data, and law enforcement no longer even pretends to investigate. Instead there is a new wave of flight from Chechnya, as we in Germany may have noticed. In the best case, the missing relatives turn up in a prison cell, but most often only as corpses by the roadside, if at all.

'What had your cousin done?' I ask.

'We don't know,' the official replies. 'But he always was an impulsive person, and we assume he just couldn't keep his mouth shut. You see, he was a professor, and when I imagine him lecturing in an auditorium ... and things happen fast, and he knew it.'

When the civil servant's cousin disappeared two years ago, his superior addressed an inquiry to the minister. The professor had been arrested, was the reply, no cause for alarm, he would soon be released. But then his body was returned to his family, his torso dotted with bruises and wounds. Officially, the cousin, who was survived by three children, had had a car accident. Nevertheless, the family was not allowed to hold a funeral, much less have an autopsy performed.

I ask whether it's true that political prisoners are held in the basement of the presidential palace. You often hear that said, the civil servant confirms; his office often deals with people from palace circles; besides, in Chechnya everyone is ultimately related to everyone else; his superior found out that Ramzan hit his cousin in the face for talking back to him. At that point, if not before, there was no help for him.

'And yet you work for this state,' I say, puzzled.

'What else should I do?' the official returns. 'Should we all quit working? We concentrate on the apolitical cases; there's quite a bit we can accomplish in labour law, in civil law. All the laws are there; that's not the problem; they're just not applied. And human rights cases are taboo for the courts.'

'And yet you have the courage to come and sit in our car.'

'Yes,' says the civil servant almost tonelessly, and takes a deep breath: 'Have you seen *Grozny Blues*?'

'The film?'

'Yes, the film.'

Yes, I saw the film, which ran in European cinemas some time ago, a documentary about three friends, three women, who talk candidly about their life in Chechnya. Six months ago, two of them were kidnapped, the official reports. They are free again now, thank God, but only after severe maltreatment. The third woman was able to flee just in time; no one knows where to. That's what happens, he says, when someone recognizes you speaking out in Chechnya.

The sociologist I visit at the university a short time later has no objection to her name being mentioned. I express my surprise that there are so many women students on campus. Yes, Lida Kurbanova confirms, not only the majority of the students but also 60 per cent of the professors are female. That says little about the state of emancipation, however, which is her field of empirical research. The answers to her questionnaires – 'How has your personal situation changed in the past ten years? Have you personally experienced violence in your family?' and so on – are so disastrous that she has been able to report her findings only in Berlin or at Columbia University, not on Chechen television, where she is invited to appear on talk shows often enough.

In the Soviet Union, women were present everywhere in the public sphere. During the two wars, too, the men needed them. But now there are no longer enough jobs, she says, and the threat of Wahhabism is being countered with such a conservative, cold version of Islam that there is almost no difference any more between the two. Not only the headscarf, but polygamy too is being publicly advocated again, although it is actually prohibited in the Russian Federation: 16.8 per cent of Chechen women between the ages of eighteen and forty live in polygamous marriages, her studies have found; the practice was practically unknown among older women.

I ask how her findings fit with the fact that the proportion of women in the university is higher than in Europe. The university is the last avenue of escape from the traditional role, Lida Kurbanova explains. Just having a diploma already makes a woman somewhat more independent from her husband. Those who really want to live their emancipation, however, often have to decide against having a family. Among her colleagues, at least half of the female professors are single.

When noon has struck, I ask my guide, who is risking her life for the truth, like the civil servant and the three protagonists of *Grozny Blues*, where in Grozny we can get a Chechen meal. Up to now, we have seen only foreign cuisines, pizzerias, fast food, Uzbek, and so on. So we drive to one of the outlying districts of Grozny that were not carpet-bombed: little, poor houses with front yards along straight streets with little traffic that are as broad as boulevards out to the last unpaved turnoffs. There has always been space enough in the steppes of Eurasia, and Grozny, moreover, lost half its population in the two wars with Russia: the city that will soon be home to the tallest skyscraper in Europe already looks like a shirt that's too big. The Russian state offered every homeowner 300,000 roubles, the equivalent of 5,000 euros, to rebuild or repair the war damage. That was not much, and it was less still after the Chechen authorities withheld half of it. But it was better than nothing, especially since the local government threatened to tear down all damaged houses so that no trace of the war would remain. Consequently, we see practically no ruins, but many vacant lots where people must have once lived.

We enter a log house that is identified as a restaurant only by its hearty aroma: although most Chechens live in the plain, they have remained a mountain people in their traditions, their songs and their cuisine; the menu conjures up an image of a small farm with livestock, not much ploughed land, difficult trails, potatoes as the staple. The dried meat which makes up

154

the national speciality keeps for a whole winter and still tastes fresh with the hearty sauce.

After lunch, I strike up a conversation with the four cooks, whose head-scarves are tied at the back of the neck in the old style. As long as I ask about the recipes and where they come from, they cheerfully answer my questions. And they happily recount that the restaurant is doing well because it is one of the few that still offer Chechen cooking. But when I want to know whether they are content with the conditions, since their business is booming, the cooks self-consciously stir their big pots, go back to peeling potatoes, chopping vegetables for the sauces. Only the oldest, who evidently takes pleasure in eating as well as cooking, goes on talking: of course they're happy; after all, they're finally living in peace after so many years of war. Without my having to ask, she goes on with almost motherly pride to praise young Ramzan, who so energetically rebuilt Chechnya and personally attends to every complaint.

When we are back in the car, my guide confirms that many Chechens are grateful to the president because he has brought about a kind of normality, security and a regular day-to-day life. Besides, what with the funding from Moscow and the construction boom, there is a great deal of money in circulation in Chechnya, and some of it trickles down, into restaurant kitchens, for example. And Ramzan's boyish charm is a hit with older women in particular. Nonetheless, the other three cooks stared into their pots or at their vegetables.

The farther we go from the centre, the more Soviet the city looks. Chechnya was once the industrial heart of the Caucasus; Grozny was a modern city early in the twentieth century. But, unlike the houses, the factories have not been rebuilt, so that, although there are working-class neighbourhoods, the workers are no longer there. The façades are covered with corrugated steel to hide the bullet holes. We drive through the mud, which is what the side streets consist of in winter, stop in front of one of the concrete prefabs, and ask in the bare concrete lobby whether we can have a look around. The building is inhabited by refugees, we learn, although they are no longer called refugees because the word is a reminder of the war. Now they are 'people with housing needs'. The director of the shelter tells us about the income situation: unemployed adults receive 800 roubles, plus 130 roubles for each child. Thus a family of five receives the equivalent of about 30 euros if both parents are unemployed. There are few surviving fathers here, though; otherwise the families wouldn't be in the shelter. We meet a former soldier who is somewhat better off; he was once stationed in Wittenberg and still speaks a few words of German, *Guten Tag* and *Wie geht's?* His pension is 8,400 roubles, 130 euros, which he shares with others in the shelter because he has no one else. In return, the neighbours take care of him as if he was their grandfather. Thank you, Grandpa, for the victory.

We go into one of the apartments, which consists of bedroom, kitchen, bath: four women, one adolescent girl, three children, no husbands, and fortunately a grandma drawing a pension. In spite of that, the children go to bed hungry every night, say the mothers. School is compulsory, although the mothers often can't afford the exercise books. An organization used to help out but, since NGOs are no longer allowed to accept funding from abroad, the helpers have no money either. Still, once in a while good people come by and open up the boot of their car. Otherwise, the only pleasant thing about their lives is the togetherness: eight people in 35 square metres can be great fun.

'Has any of you been to the city centre lately?' I ask the semicircle that has formed around us. Yes, they've all seen the new skyscrapers and shopping malls, from the outside, and of course the expensive SUVs that drive up and down Putin Prospekt.

'And what did you think?'

No one answers.

'That's not such a good question,' the director of the shelter hopes I'll understand, as she leads me back out into the corridor, where there is a smell of chemicals.

Outside Grozny, in a village where old trees lining the streets make for an idyllic atmosphere, I visit Asya Umarova. She is one of the few prominent artists who still live in Chechnya. She is only thirty-one years old but constantly draws pictures of the war. Yet Asya has kept such a clear, contagious laugh that I find it hard to connect her with the grim motifs of her works. One picture shows an old man and a horse running away. Is this a drawing of the war too? Yes, says Asya, and tells us about her grandfather: when his wife died in the first Chechen war, he announced that he didn't want to go anywhere any more and set his only horse free. In those days Asya lived with her grandparents in the mountains to escape the bombs. Her uncle brought her back to Grozny; they walked for three days with seven other children, everywhere bombed buildings, burning cars, checkpoints where no one knew who was behind the machine guns. In the second war, their village was surrounded by the Russian Army for six months; military operations, they said; no one was allowed out even for the most urgent supplies. Fortunately they had provisions, enough water and a garden to grow vegetables. When the blockade was lifted, what she and her girlfriend looked forward to most was music. As they were on their way to class with their instruments, a young soldier carrying a Kalashnikov on his back blocked their way and shouted, 'Stop!' A terrible fright pulsed through the girls. But the Russian only laid a daffodil at the two girls' feet, looked at them briefly, and ran away, as if he were frightened himself. No wonder that all Asya's drawings are about the war. And all the more beautiful that she has kept her laugh.

In the evening, Salamat Gayev welcomes us, a former history teacher who has made researching the Khaibakh massacre his life's work. In the course of the 1944 resettlement, all 700 inhabitants of the mountain village were driven into a stable and burnt alive. 'In view of the impossibility of transport, and the objective of fulfilling the operation in a timely manner,' the responsible commander telegraphed to Lavrenty Beria, the head of the Soviet secret service, he was forced to liquidate the people. 'For resolute action in the course of the resettlement of the Chechens in the Khaibakh area, you have been recommended for a state distinction and promotion,' Beria wired back.

Do people in Chechnya like to remember the story? I ask at the dinner table, while Gayev's wife in the living room learns on the news where Vladimir Putin has been today. 'Like' is too strong, says Gayev, a clean-shaven gentleman of seventy-six with a few white hairs at his temples, horn-rimmed glasses and tired eyes, wearing black pleated trousers and a black turtleneck sweater. In 2004 he was able to present his findings to the European Parliament, including historic photos and photocopies of the decrees issued by Stalin and Beria. Back in Grozny, he says, he was arrested by the Russian Army and told to sign a statement that he had forged the documents if he didn't want to be killed. Then he would be the seven hundred and first victim of Khaibakh, he answered. The crucial documents were already known anyway; it wouldn't have helped the Russians a bit if he had retracted his book. The investigators apparently realized that and released him the next day.

Today Gayev is unafraid to talk about the resettlement. Not only has his book been published in a second edition, but he was allowed to present it in the Kadyrov museum. There is still no mention of the massacre in the National Museum, however, although the director said he would have a display made. But last year, for the first time, Gayev was finally able to visit Khaibakh which, over seventy years later, still lies in a large prohibited area. Gayev brings out an album with photos: bricks scattered across a mountain meadow, the base of the watchtower that was dynamited in 2007, long after the war was over. He put up a signpost pointing to the site of the stable, but with nothing written on it, he says, and shows us the photo; no other commemoration of the victims was permitted him. Next summer he wants to go back with friends to rebuild the tower.

Thirty-First Day: In the Chechen Mountains

Perhaps a people cling to their stories all the more strongly when so many attempts have been made to erase their memory. We drive to the mountains to visit the grave of the mother of Kunta-haji, Gandhi's precursor in Chechnya. In 1864, when Kunta-haji was arrested, thousands of his followers took to the streets in protest. Although they were waving white flags, the Russian troops opened fire. Hundreds of Sufis died. Kunta-haji himself remained in prison until his death. The saint's followers have only his mother's grave in the village of Ilaskhan-Yurt, where he grew up, as a shrine to pray for him. At first glance, the mountains here don't look nearly as wild as I imagined them from my reading: deciduous forests, gentle slopes and the cosy covering of snow on even the ugliest of the kolkhozes. If you come here, as Tolstoy did, by travelling through the steppes for days and weeks, perhaps even the foothills look wild.

When we take the turnoff for Ilaskhan-Yurt, which lies on one of the mountains, a woman of perhaps thirty-five, forty, waves us down. Hitchhiking is part of the public transport system here. She has no distinct memory of the first war, which didn't reach her in the mountains, but she remembers the second one all the more clearly. The Russians bombed them from above; the rebels prowled the woods.

'Were they good people, the rebels?' I ask.

'How can I call someone good who did us no good?'

'And the Russians?'

'The Russians came to the village and said we were hiding rebels. We had never seen the rebels. The Russians took the men anyway and beat them. And then they sprayed poison to defoliate the trees. No, the Russians weren't good either.'

'And now?'

'Now it's quiet, thank God. Except that the children still get sick if they go in the woods; that's a real problem.'

'Do you have enough to live on?'

'Not more, but not less either. God gives enough.'

In front of the cemetery of Ilaskhan-Yurt, we ask Malkan, the caretaker of the saint's mother's mausoleum, why she is still working at seventy-seven.

'Yes, I could stay home,' she explains, 'but I'm afraid then I would die.'

She was five years old when the inhabitants of her village were herded onto trucks like animals. They didn't even have time to put on shoes, much less pack warm clothes. Because the men were separated from their families, Malkan thought she would never see her father again. Fortunately, he found his way to them at the Grozny railway station. Other fathers were not able to find their families before the train left. Although they had a small stove on which they could barely cook what other families had brought along, her brother froze to death on the way, as did other children and old people, so that more and more bodies lay in the waggon. When they got out, after seven days, Malkan, who had never known anything but green mountains, saw only steppes. The night outdoors was colder than in the train, so that her second brother died too. For the second night, they built a little village of plywood huts. Fortunately, Malkan's father was a stove builder; their hut was soon heated, and he found work, too. But he still had no shoes, and it was a long way to the factory where he worked, and when he came down with a fever and didn't go to work for three days, he was arrested and spent four months in prison. Then there were only the three of them, Malkan, her mother and her older sister, with no food, no money. They spread their skirts in front of the windows of the houses for the scraps people would throw them. They washed them, ate them and survived until her mother found her cousin who had met a Russian, an agronomist with an apartment and a salary. The agronomist, who would later marry the cousin, saw the three of them through. Others starved to death, says Malkan, standing in front of the cemetery of Ilaskhan-Yurt, weeping through most of her story. 'I can see all of it as if it was yesterday.'

Her mother bore two more sons, so that they were complete again, two brothers, two sisters. Now she herself has forty-five grandchildren.

'And do you tell them all about the banishment?'

'Yes, all our grandchildren know the story.'

I ask Malkan whether she could ever forgive the Russians.

'No,' she says in a firm voice.

'And other Chechens – that is, the older people here in the village – can there ever be any kind of forgiving or forgetting?'

'No, I don't think so. No one who lived through that can get over it. Russians are people too; some are good and some are bad. One saved our lives; I'll never forget that either. But I will not forgive Russia.'

159

'And what do you think when you see the Putin pictures all over Chechnya today?'

'What are we supposed to do?' Malkan asks in return. 'We had two wars; we tried everything. We belong to Russia. But forgive? With no explanation, no apology? No, that is too much to ask. I'm glad we have peace now, that's all. But I will not forgive.'

I ask her what she thinks of a Chechen president who calls himself 'Putin's footsoldier' and sends Chechens to Ukraine and Syria to fight for Russia. Ramzan's father brought peace to Chechnya, says Malkan with the same ardour with which she refused to forgive Russia one sentence before. And Ramzan himself is a good boy who built roads and a new mausoleum for Kunta-haji's mother. As she walks away, Malkan mutters to our driver that he knows what she means by that.

'Just don't show my photos to any granddads in Germany,' she calls after Dmitrij, giggling like a young girl. 'Otherwise one will come around wanting to marry me.'

In the newly built mausoleum, a surprisingly simple, elegant domed building in comparison with the kitsch in Grozny, two men are sitting, one in his mid-forties, I estimate, the other well over sixty. The younger man, wearing a youthful hooded sweatshirt, has a ringtone by Deep Purple and introduces himself as the scion of a noble line of mystics. He has only contempt for the official Islam. Those in charge refer to Kunta-haji, he says, only because he exhorted people to inner purification rather than political struggle. They manage to preach passiveness, but they need to work on their inner qualities. Hardly anyone in Chechnya still knows the sources of Sufism, the writings of Saadi, Rumi or al-Hallaj; the schools teach nothing but obscurantism. The state suddenly only pretends to be religious. But a new mosque or an obligatory headscarf does not constitute piety.

'And Ramzan himself,' I ask, because the president likes to show himself in prayer poses on Instagram: 'Is he only pretending too, or is he really religious?'

'I have the impression that he would like to be religious,' says the mystic sardonically. 'He just doesn't know how.'

He knows many influential people today, he says; he has served on one commission and another; somehow people respect him for his family's sake. In such contexts, he speaks his mind, but it doesn't seem to him that anyone pays attention. The people in charge consider democracy a dangerous concept.

160

'And do they have a realistic view of society?'

'No, they think everybody's happy. They really believe that; they're not just pretending.'

He has always been against independence, which is why he went to study in Europe when the war broke out. His classmate, however – the mystic indicates the older gentleman sitting beside him on the rug – was in the other camp in the early 1990s, in the pro-war camp.

'Your classmate?' I ask, because the gentleman looks fifteen, twenty years older.

'Yes, we've known each other since we were children.'

The classmate, who wears a grey beard, an old-fashioned suit with a knit sweater over his shirt and the traditional green cap, fought under Dzhokhar Dudayev, the first president of independent Chechnya. He was one of the last eight soldiers who held the presidential palace in 1995, he mentions with visible pride. When he was following Dudayev to the mountains, his car exploded. All six of his comrades died; he himself woke up from a coma thirty-seven days later. With the help of his friend's family, he was moved to Germany, but the doctors there had no hope for him. Three operations later, he seemed to have survived miraculously. The scar on his neck where his breathing tube went in is recognizable at a glance. His movements are now slow and he can speak only quietly, almost soundlessly, but he thanks God and Germany that life was breathed into him a second time. At the hands of the Germans he experienced nothing but humanity and compassion, he says; although Christians, they are better Muslims than most people here. More painful than the cruelty of the Russians is the betrayal of his own people who allowed themselves to be bought by Russia. He looks away, he says, when he sees a picture of Putin by the road; it is hard enough for him just to speak the name of the Russian president.

I ask whether he would have fought in the second war too if he had not been wounded. He doesn't think so, the old gentleman says; the second war was doomed to failure from the beginning, as Dudayev predicted before his assassination.

'Dudayev predicted the second war?'

'Dudayev always said he feared Russia less than the fanatical, false Islam. The Russians only break our bones with their weapons, Dudayev used to say, but the Wahhabis corrupt our spirit. And that's what happened.'

Would Dudayev have changed sides, then? The older gentleman would probably reject the thought indignantly, so I don't ask him. But apparently the 'hero' Dzhokhar Dudayev was driven by the same worry as the 'traitor' Akhmat Kadyrov. Only in stories are good and evil easily distinguishable.

Once, shortly before his death, they asked Dudayev how much longer the war would go on, the older gentleman continues, without waiting for me to ask. This war will not simply end, Dudayev answered; it will go on, with interruptions, for at least another fifty years.

The younger of the two men – who are actually the same age – doesn't want to translate the question whether it was a mistake, looking back, to have fought for independence. The answer would be too painful for his friend.

We stop in the village of Kharachoy at the monument to the *abrek* Zelimkhan, whose resistance against Russia is the source of many of the Chechens' stories. When a price of 5,000 roubles was placed on his head, he mocked the tsarist police with the announcement that he would rob the bank in Kizliyar on 9 April 1910, at 12 o'clock sharp. The Chechens are still laughing today about Zelimkhan's prank.

'You mean these stories are not forgotten?' I ask a sturdy man with very bright eyes who is carrying two well-filled plastic bags past the monument.

'Some wanted people to forget,' says the man, putting down his plastic bags to tell another story. Once Zelimkhan purposely left his whip behind in the bank he had robbed. He asked a comrade whose courage he wanted to test to go and get the whip for him; it was one he liked. His comrade asked if he was crazy, since the bank was full of police by this time. Then Zelimkhan jumped on his horse, and in a while came back, unhurt, with the whip. Zelimkhan never kept a rouble for himself, the man insists; the booty was all distributed among the poor and needy. We are about to get back in the car when the next cops-and-robbers story begins, one that is too good to be left in Kharachoy. Once the Russians had surrounded Zelimkhan's hideout in the mountains. Zelimkhan undressed and tied his trousers, shirt, jacket and cap onto a log as big as a man. Then he shod his horse with the horseshoes backwards. He rolled the log down the mountain, and while the Russians were shooting at the wooden Zelimkhan, the real Zelimkhan rode away uphill. The Russians found his tracks, but they read them backwards. Like so many stories of Chechnya, however, this one too ends in betrayal: a comrade who had been paid by the Russians shot Zelimkhan in the back on 27 September 1913. The *abrek* was able to drag himself into a house, but it was surrounded, and he never got away again.

The man does not want to be on his way before he has personally shown us the monument: Zelimkhan, with a long moustache and with pistols in his belt, resting by a campfire, and his horse grazing. Beside him flows water that bubbles out of a spring above the hillside.

'Does the spring have a story too?' I ask.

'Of course,' says the man, 'only it's not about the war. Do you want to hear it anyway?' Two lovers here, as everywhere in the world, could not marry because of enmity between their families. The lovers wanted to elope, but the girl's father heard the horse's hoofbeats, ran outside and threw a dagger in his daughter's back as she sat behind her beloved. 'That wasn't such a good ending, either,' the man admits.

'If their love had come to a good ending, it would have been forgotten long ago,' I say, as if there were some consolation in that.

'That's true too,' the man concedes to my surprise, and then he tells us that the spring arose on the spot where the girl's blood flowed on the ground. The water still flows today, past the *abrek* Zelimkhan into the village.

We drive on into the mountains, which gradually grow as wild as they are in literature. The stone houses with their smoking chimneys, the children riding sledges, the sun which has driven the clouds away, an old car driving along in the distance: this really looks like peace, now, although the war is not supposed to end for fifty years. Everyone we ask for directions, without exception, invites us to tea and, as noon approaches, to lunch. There are no inns in the area, not even pizzerias; only a little grocery shop here and there; and so we are glad to enter a house where the packed meat is hanging from the eaves. The living room, soon filled with the aroma of the sauce, attests to a certain prosperity: a big flat-screen TV, a satellite receiver, stereo, gas heating, a new sofa suite. Our host, a tall, slender man, was a policeman and has a metal splint in his arm since a certain robbery. He draws the highest disability pension there is, 45 roubles a month. First he talks about ordinary robbers who set a bomb when he was on patrol, but then about rebels who started shooting to boot.

'Rebels?' I ask. 'Just now you said bandits.'

'Bandits, rebels, it's a question of your point of view. They were no Che Guevaras in any case.'

In a country like Chechnya, you can only be one of two things: either a perpetrator or a victim. In Europe, you don't have to choose; that's why he would like to move there.

'And why not to Russia?' I ask. 'After all, you lost the use of your arm and almost your life for Russia.'

'I served not Russia but the Russian Federation, to which Chechnya belongs – there is a difference.'

'And are you content that Chechnya remained in the federation?'

'There are people here who say they are content. And there are others who say nothing because they don't want to lie. If people in Russia are afraid to express their opinion, the people in Chechnya are terrified.'

'But you decided in favour of this state.'

'I told you, I had to choose. That was in 2004: the war was officially over; I had studied law and had to make a living somehow. I was faced with the question whether I was rational or patriotic. And I pictured where that patriotism would lead. In the first war, I was still able to choose the middle ground and just didn't fight. But the second war was just complete chaos; there was no more middle.'

On the way back to Grozny we come past the barracks from which a Chechen battalion was deployed to Syria. The driver mentions that he knows someone who came back from there.

'And what did he have to say?'

'Not much,' the driver replies. 'He said they sat around and waited the whole time. Said it was boring.'

'That's all he said?'

'No, he also said that there are weapons everywhere, and the Syrians are even more afraid than we are. When someone from the secret police turned up, everyone stared at the ground.'

Perhaps the war will last fifty years after all, and all that lies between Chechnya and Syria is the interruption that Dzhokhar Dudayev mentioned.

Thirty-Second Day: From Grozny to Tbilisi

The Caucasus is probably the only region in the world where you can drive through three different wars in two hours. All right, they're not real wars any more: assassinations, occasional skirmishes and state terror aside, the weapons are currently silent. Besides, there are more than fifty ethnic groups here, each with its own language, in a territory little bigger than Germany: the density of the conflicts has to be put into perspective. With regard to Chechnya, Europeans know more or less what the conflict is about; with regard to Ingushetia and Ossetia, a typical European knows only that something was going on there, if that. If I had set out eastwards for an hour, I would have come to Dagestan, another country where war has stopped but peace hasn't started. And a few hours further west is Abkhazia; a day's journey south, Nagorno-Karabakh. What we generally don't know is that all of these fronts run through Europe. Our perspective, then, is very Western European.

We leave Grozny early in the morning and, on a perfectly straight motorway, we reach the checkpoint with soldiers and machine guns that marks the end of Chechnya. Beyond the checkpoint, the minarets remain the same. Just like the Chechens, the Ingush fought the Russians bitterly in the nineteenth century, and under Stalin were – for that reason? – banished. When they were allowed to return, they had lost most of the territory they had inhabited to the predominantly Christian Ossetians. The strip to the east that was left for the Ingush is so narrow that we see church spires after a half hour, but not only church spires: hammers and sickles too, and billboards for the heroes of the Second World War, as if we were back in the Soviet Union. Unlike the other peoples of the Caucasus, most Ossetians had a friendly attitude towards Russia, which offered them protection against the Muslim neighbours and conquerors. Hence it was no coincidence that Catherine the Great chose Ossetia to build the city from which her army conquered one people after another. Vladikavkaz is its name even today: 'Rule the Caucasus'. Russia lost a million soldiers before the mid-nineteenth century, when it succeeded in pushing back the Persians and Ottomans, breaking local resistance and extending its rule far along the shores of the two southern seas, the Caspian and the Black. 'If we were to depict for our French readers the details of an expedition in the mountains, they would be amazed at the privations which the Russian soldier can bear,' remarked Alexandre Dumas, who travelled this route in the opposite direction in 1858. The French had waged a similarly bitter war in Algeria, he found, but not on such difficult terrain. Besides, the French soldiers were well paid and fed and enjoyed shelter and at least the theoretical prospect of advancement. And their fight had lasted only three years, while the Russians in the Caucasus had been at it for forty. The Russian soldier often had nothing to eat but moist black bread. 'He sleeps on snow, carries himself, his artillery, his baggage and ammunition by paths where no man ever trod, where only the eagle soars above the snow and granite. And what a war he is fighting! A war without mercy, without prisoners, where every wounded man is counted dead, where the bitterest enemy cuts off any Russian's head, and the gentlest, his hand.'[32]

Like the Western European advances into Africa, Asia and America, the Russian expansion to the south was a colonial project that was long in yielding economic advantages: the European culture and Orthodox Christianity were to supplant the 'Caucasian barbarism'. Catherine the Great went so far as to proclaim the goal of overthrowing the Ottoman Empire, rebuilding Byzantium and thus achieving 'eternal peace in the East'. The project was a spectacular failure because the European coalition she had hoped to lead against the Sublime Porte did not come about. And, in the Caucasus, Russian sovereignty remained fragile, and after the end of the Soviet Union the conflicts broke out along the colonial fault lines: in Chechnya, in Ingushetia, in the war between Georgia and Ossetia, dominance in the Caucasus is once more the object of contention and struggle. And, like the Ottomans in the past, the peoples who would prevail against Russia today place their hope in Europe, not in the Islamic world.

Vladikavkaz marks the beginning of the Caucasian Military Road, by which the Russians crossed the rugged mountain range. One of the world's boldest engineering projects in the nineteenth century, the road carries few cars and still fewer trucks over the pass today, since Georgia is once again in conflict with Russia. The road climbs at first along the Terek, the river into which the Chechen women threw themselves on 15 September 1819 to avoid falling into the hands of Russian soldiers. General Alexey Yermolov, who declared he would not rest 'as long as a single Chechen is alive', is demonstratively honoured with a great monument at the border crossing. Russians need a visa to be let through, while we need only our Schengen Area passports – it is always strange to arrive from so far away and still be favoured over the locals. When we approach the gate right after the border opens at nine o'clock, we are glad to have a whole day for the many spectacular natural sights and historic landmarks along the way, places often celebrated by authors from Pushkin to Lermontov, from Alexandre Dumas to Knut Hamsun. But then we are asked to get out of the car, and we spend the next few hours in a Russian office that is completely filled by a desk, a few chairs and a filing cabinet.

Politely, the officer tries to get out of us what we were up to in Chechnya; he takes our driver aside, asks trick questions, and jumps on apparent contradictions in our statements. Fortunately, we have all the necessary papers, including our press accreditation; the claims about our identity can be verified on the Internet; and there is no law against having visited Chechnya, since relations are officially normal again. Still, the officer, who is typing our answers into the computer himself, finds our route 'peculiar'.

'What for?' he asks again and again.

'My God!' I cry, exasperated at the fifth repetition. 'So many writers have travelled this road, now there's just one more.'

Again and again, the interrogation is interrupted by other officials opening the door with a smart card to throw in a question. Some of them join our group and listen for a while before leaving again without a word. One young official in plain clothes watches music videos on his smartphone for over an hour. Evidently there's not much to do at the border between Russia and Georgia. Only the officer complains that he has to take care of everything and everyone at once – 'and now you too!' At best, he thinks I'm one of these eccentric Westerners who waste the time of people like him who have work to do. What kind of a crackpot idea is that: from Germany via the Baltic countries to Belarus; from Ukraine via Crimea to Russia; from Chechnya via the Caucasus to Isfahan, wherever that is? From time to time one or the other of the two telephones on the desk rings. The officer answers the black one only when he feels like it, but he always answers the old-fashioned, chunky beige one on the first ring. What headquarters is on the line?

When the officer has taken down all our answers several times, he asks us to wait outside. From the corridor, we hear him explaining our project to someone – on the beige telephone, no doubt. The officer sighs repeatedly that he doesn't understand it either. Finally he calls us back into the room to ask a few additional questions. Among others, he wants to know whether I will be writing about Russia positively or negatively. He finds it 'peculiar' that I cannot reduce my impressions to such categories. Be that as it may, he suggests that I do not report on my impression of today. When he goes to send us out again – to talk on the beige telephone again, probably – he suddenly can't find the smart card needed to open the door, even from the inside. The officer turns over every piece of paper, opens every drawer, and rifles his pockets – all in vain. So we wait in silence for someone to open the door from the outside. But now of course none of the other officials has a question to throw in. We should all be laughing, but apparently that is not done in a Russian government office.

It is past noon by the time the officer, with a sigh, pronounces his investigations complete. All that is left is for us to take the batteries out of our mobile phones, please, so that he can note the serial numbers – will Russia be eavesdropping on us from now on? The driver grumbles audibly that now he has to buy a new smartphone. While accompanying us to our car, the officer apologizes for the long interrogation: for the authorities to know who is crossing the border and why is necessary in the struggle against terrorism and is ultimately for the sake of our own safety. He hopes that we have nonetheless enjoyed our stay in the Russian Federation. Have we visited the monument to General Yermolov?

A hundred yards further on, the Cyrillic lettering has disappeared. The language with which the older half of the population grew up no longer exists in the public sphere. For my part, I already feel a bit more at home because I can now read the road signs again, which are written in the Latin alphabet in addition to the Georgian. Furthermore, the Georgian passport check is as cursory as those familiar to citizens of the European Union from most borders: a glance at the papers and the face, a rubber stamp, and we are waved on into Georgia. Just a hundred yards, and terrorism is apparently no great danger any more.

The road leads in switchbacks up the mountainside. Soon our view is filled with snow, except for the strip of asphalt. Only by twisting my neck can I see out of the window a little piece of sky and, under the sky, the bare rock face. Somewhere out there is the cradle of humanity: one of these cliffs is supposed to be the one to which Prometheus was chained. 'That was the Caucasus,' wrote Alexandre Dumas in 1858 about the panorama with the 5,000-metre peak of Kazbek, 'unlike the Alps or the Pyrenees, and for that matter unlike anything else we have ever seen or imagined. The Himalaya and the Chimborazo are higher, but they are just mountains, without myths. The Caucasus is the stage on which the first dramatic poet of antiquity set his first drama, its hero a Titan and its actors the gods.'[33] The portable toilets stationed by the roadside, left and right in alternation, at intervals of 500 metres, are all the more comical.

The pass is so narrow that just a few soldiers can stop a whole army, as the Roman travel writer Pliny noted 2,000 years ago, and beyond it the gorge opens out into a gently descending plateau. The fact that most conquerors, before the Russians, came from the south, not the north, is perhaps explained by the topography: only the north side of the Caucasus is so rugged, so forbidding. At the first sight of houses, villages, people, I think I am in a different climate: suddenly in the south. The physiognomies, foods and customs of continental Europe seem to have spread with the Russian colonization only as far as Vladikavkaz or Crimea, but not beyond the Caucasus. The darker faces and black hair, the energetic gestures of the street merchants selling wine, pomegranate juice or exotic delights, the avid haggling if you're willing to buy the buttery-soft candied walnuts on a stick by the dozen, and the old women's headscarves and black clothes – it's as if I had just taken the direct route from Germany to southern Italy. But it's not just southern: the boutiques and supermarkets of the ski resort Gudauri offer the whole world of Western consumer goods. Georgia's upper class don't need to fly to the Alps or the Rockies to go heli-skiing and to enjoy the après-ski. And to think the West only came to Georgia after the 'Rose Revolution': thirteen years are practically nothing to a cradle of humanity. The signs along the road to Tbilisi betray the country's previous orientation: Tehran 1,240 kilometres. At the fortress of Ananuri, which was rebuilt during the Persian occupation in the seventeenth century, we make the only stop that our remaining time permits. In the church, besides the nuns veiled and wimpled to the chin, there are only young people in Western dress praying. The arabesques on the portal bear witness to the Safavid influence in Christian architecture.

'Surely love is the same in Georgia as in Iran,' we read in *Ali and Nino*, Kurban Said's novel about a love between an Azeri and a Georgian in the early twentieth century. 'Here on this spot, a thousand years ago, your Rustaveli was singing of his love to Queen Tamar. And the songs of this greatest of poets are exactly like Persian rubaiyats. Georgia is nothing without Rustaveli, and Rustaveli is nothing without Persia.'

'We are no Asiatics. We are the furthest eastern country of Europe,' Nino contradicts her beloved:

It is because we have defied Timur, and Genghis, Shah Abbas, Shah Tahmasp and Shah Ismail, because of that it is that I exist, your Nino. And now you come along, without a sword, without trampling elephants, without warriors, and yet you are the heir of the blood-covered Shahs. My daughters will wear the veil, and when Iran's sword is sharpened again my sons and grandsons will destroy Tiflis for the hundredth time. Oh, Ali Khan, we should belong to the world of the West.[34]

Past an endless string of European stores we push on into Tbilisi, which is jammed with traffic, as every evening. There was room to spare in the Eurasian steppes, but now the driver fights for every centimetre. Although the waiting is annoying, it quickly makes the city familiar, simply because it is a city, in the ordinary sense of a metropolis: too many people in not enough space. The hotel is full of Iranians taking a brief holiday from the Islamic Republic. And not only the hotel, as I find to my amazement on my first walk around: the historic city centre looks like Tehran in photos from the nineteenth and the early twentieth centuries, elegant, even delicate-looking buildings of reddish brick, their façades adorned with slender-columned wooden balconies and decoratively carved bay windows protruding over the alleys. My own great-great-grandfather, it crosses my mind for the first time in years, was born in Tbilisi and emigrated, or possibly fled, to Isfahan at the turn of the nineteenth century when the city fell under Russian rule. What was once only an abstract item of information, probably comparable with a German child of today learning that his forebears came from Silesia or East Prussia, congeals in the alleyways of Tbilisi to a concrete and somehow plausible image: this is the place, then; this is one of the places where I come from. There is no city anywhere in Iran where the Iranian early modern period has been preserved with its original fusion of Middle Eastern architectural traditions and European influences. Tehran, the capital of this new departure, where the Constitutional Revolution of 1906 seemed to mark the breakthrough to democracy earlier than in Germany – Tehran is today a faceless behemoth which has spared nothing from its own heyday but a palace here and there.

Nonetheless, the Iranians from my hotel seem to be more interested in gastronomy than in architectural landmarks: no other cuisine is as close to Iranian as the Georgian, with its walnuts and pomegranates, symphonies of herbs and sweet-and-sour aromas, except that with your Georgian dinner you can also order wine, which is not to be understood merely metaphorically where we find it in Hafiz and Omar Khayyam. The central square of the historic centre, which, like its counterpart in Kiev, bears the Persian name Meidan, must once have been the beginning of the labyrinthine bazaar into which Nino led her Ali in a symbolic plea for forgiveness for her outbreak of anger, grief and fear:

Forgive me, Ali Khan. I love you, just simply you, as you are. But I'm afraid of your world. I'm mad, Ali Khan. Here I am, standing on the street with you, my betrothed, behaving as if all Genghis Khan's wars were your fault. Forgive your Nino. It is stupid of me to make you responsible for every Mohammedan who ever killed a Georgian. I'll never do it again.[35]

At the sight of the gay confusion of the bazaar, Nino is already half reconciled with the Orient: a Kurdish girl with light grey eyes telling fortunes, looking surprised at her own prescience, framed between fat carpet merchants from Armenia; a few paces from Persian cooks and Ossetian priests;

here Russians, there Arabs or Ingush, Indians too, nearly all the peoples of Asia in fact, peacefully or not so peacefully united in commerce: 'There is an uproar in one of the booths. The merchants are standing in a circle: an Assyrian is quarrelling with a Jew. We just hear: "When my ancestors were taking your ancestors as prisoners to Babylon ..." The crowd is hooting with laughter. Nino laughs too – at the Jew, at the Assyrian, at the bazaar, at the tears she shed.' Now the Meidan is populated by young people, night owls, tourists who dress and move no differently than in any other European city. The cupolas and wooden balconies on the houses seem to be no more than a backdrop for the bar scene, which caters for every need, up to and including the 'Irish Pub' and the 'Quality Hamburger'. I am all the more amazed to find that, 200 years after the Persian occupation, the two literary Georgians with whom I have a date in a jazz café still greet each other with the Persian *salām*. Surprised in turn, Ana Kordzaia-Samadashvili and Lasha Bakradze – she a writer, he the director of the Tbilisi Museum of Literature – say they weren't at all thinking that it's the ordinary Persian greeting, but now that I mention it: that's true. They have followed the signposts to Tehran, but more often they fly to Europe, by which they mean Western Europe. From Chechnya, on the other hand, and from the world north of the Caucasus for that matter, to which Georgia still belonged in their youth, little news reaches them. It is a long time since anyone has travelled by the Caucasian Military Road, they say.

Thirty-Third Day: Tbilisi

Because Mikheil Saakashvili, carried into office in Georgia by the Rose Revolution, was so impressed by the Reichstag building in Berlin, the Georgian presidential palace now has a glass cupola on its roof too. Saakashvili is already history by now, not simply voted out but in exile to evade the reach of law enforcement, but the domes are still in vogue. Many of the severe, hermetic-looking concrete blocks from the Stalinist period now wear transparent hats. And now there is a real skyscraper, too, the most recent addition, placed right in the middle of the wonderful ensemble of neo-classical architecture north of the old centre. In Western Europe, no developer would get away with such a monstrosity. Meanwhile the efforts to save the historic centre from deterioration have got bogged down halfway, in the truest sense of the word: while the lower half is being gentrified into a Walt Disney kind of Near East for tourists, the houses in the upper half

171

look as if they could collapse at any moment. 'Sometimes the developers help them along,' says Ana Kordzaia-Samadashvili, who has devoted her morning to showing me Tbilisi.

Ana, who teaches literature at the university in addition to writing, has lived in Germany for several years and has an eye for the curious aspects of Westernization under the former President Saakashvili: the glass cupolas, or the fact that the thoroughfare to the airport is named after George W. Bush, who is not thought of as a hero today even in Texas. She also sees the dark side of a free-market economy that, as everywhere after the end of the Soviet Union, is almost unregulated and therefore dominated by oligarchs. Nevertheless, she thinks Georgia made progress under Saakashvili. In 1992, returning on one of the first flights from abroad after the wars in Abkhazia and Ossetia, she saw nothing but blackness below on the approach to Tbilisi. Only the runway was marked by oil lamps. Until 2004, power cuts were common, and the district heating system ceased operations at the same time as the Soviet Union. And then the corruption: no cross-country drive without being stopped multiple times and squeezed, politely or firmly, by police. That's not all past now, but it's incomparably better than before the Rose Revolution, which was portrayed by the pro-Russian media and by the clergy as the work of Western agents. And yet, nevertheless, in 2012 Georgia performed the first parliamentary change of government in a post-Soviet republic outside the Baltics.

I ask whether there is a place that commemorates the revolution. Yes, there is, says Ana, but it's constantly being moved. Initially it was the central square of Tbilisi, where people had demonstrated in November 2003 against electoral fraud under President Shevardnadze; now, only an ugly street junction is named after the Rose Revolution. Even Stalin is being rehabilitated now – not in Tbilisi, but in the countryside and in his home region, Gori. People are not fond of remembering nights in complete darkness. Among the younger people, among her own students, she is worried about another, more radical ignorance of history: some of them don't even know any more who Stalin was.

We have stopped in at a café that's really cool, as was the jazz bar where we were yesterday evening. As early as Vilnius I noticed – there was such a moment in central Berlin too, after the opening of the Wall – how aesthetically stimulating it can be when the free market, with its cult of individualism, ploughs into socialism. In London or Berlin, people invest a lot of money to get the kind of patina that was available naturally in the cheaply remodelled warehouses, workshops and storefronts of the Soviet Union, the cross between modern design and working-class art, although inevitably the bare brickwork, the worn planks and the Russian film posters end up as interchangeable as an Ikea kitchen suite. Perhaps the reason why nostalgia for the Soviet Union is still so strong, I remark over a caffè latte, which I prefer to the local brew that passed for coffee under socialism – perhaps nostalgia for the Soviet Union is so strong in Georgia because Stalin himself was Georgian. No, says Ana firmly, raising her eyebrows. Every family in Georgia experienced the terror first-hand, the fear of being arrested for no reason, the disappearance of relatives, and not being able to ask after them, the paralysing insecurity. The only reason why the starvation genocide against the rural population who opposed collectivization did not cost 3 million lives in Georgia was because the soil was more fertile. And for writers, in Georgia as elsewhere, there were only two paths open under Stalin: be an informer or be dead. No, Ana repeats, she has no interest in a competition among Soviet nations over who mourns the most victims.

'But didn't some peoples in fact suffer more than others?' I ask. 'At least, I haven't heard of any particular nostalgia among the Crimean Tatars, the Chechens or the Ingush, nor among the Jews or the Russian Germans.'

'That's true, banishment was a different experience altogether,' Ana agrees. Some time ago, she saw in the newspaper a large photo of Refat Chubarov, the exiled leader of the Crimean Tatars, in which he seemed to be raising his hand in a Nazi salute. In fact, as she later found out from an Internet site, he was standing on a dais and waving to his supporters who were assembled below him. That is how propaganda is used today against the same peoples who were bullied worst under the tsars.

'But, if we're making distinctions, we must also remember the peoples who have been completely exterminated,' Ana continues. 'There's nothing left of the Circassians or the Meskhetian Turks, for example, except the names. And then there are peoples of whom not even the names remain.'

The Swabians who came to Tbilisi in the nineteenth century are recalled at least by a strip of tourist bars. The neighbourhood where they settled is so tarted up that hardly anyone lives there any more. Which is too bad, really, since they are pretty little two-storey houses, looking as though they were beamed to Georgia from a southern German town. The reputation of industriousness that the Swabian immigrants continued to enjoy did not save them from being banished to Kazakhstan in 1941. A person who could afford to live in their houses today would not want to hear the din of revellers every night.

One block further on, Tbilisi returns to melancholy decay. The cast-iron balustrades on the balconies of the old buildings are the result of a decree by the Russian governor Vorontsov, known to Tolstoy readers from the novella *Hadji Murat*. The imperial authorities wanted Tbilisi transformed into a modern European city, and the wooden ornamentation of the buildings was undesirable. But the Tbilisians didn't like the iron. They couldn't do much about the decree, so they moved their wooden balconies and bay windows to the back of the house. Thus in many streets we see European façades, while in the courtyards we are surrounded by Middle Eastern forms. A typical Persian miniature painting with lovers courting to music and wine turns out to be a Christian work when a closer look reveals a pig roasting over the fire. Green as their courtyards are, and lovingly furnished with sofas, chairs and tables, the Tbilisians also seem to have retained their love of gardens from Persian times. As in the traditional Iranian city, life seems absent in the street but flourishes behind the walls. My Iranian soul moved by so much familiarity, I ask how my compatriots are viewed in Georgia – at least as well as the Swabians, I hope.

'To be honest, not so well,' Ana replies, recalling the 800,000 Georgians who were carried off to Iran by Shah Abbas II. And Shah Agha Mohammad Khan – yes, now I remember – sacked Tbilisi mercilessly in 1795, desecrated the churches, burnt down almost every house, and kidnapped 22,000 inhabitants into slavery. As if to console me for my ancestors' bloody history, Ana declares that she personally likes Iran very much: the people, the cuisine and the architecture were marvellous; only the Islamic Republic was horrible. In the Feridan region, where the largest Georgian minority lives today, tears came to her eyes when she heard her compatriots speak – in an eighteenth-century Georgian almost untouched by Russian influences.

'And?' I ask, hopeful once more, 'did the Georgians feel at home in Iran?'

But Ana's answer disappoints me once again. In Georgia they say that, if you go through a rainbow, all your wishes come true. But, in Iran, the Georgians say that beyond the rainbow lies Georgestan – which is the Persian name of their lost homeland.

Because I haven't much time left before my flight leaves for Cologne, I ask Ana to show me the mosque and at least one church, her favourite one. Ana is not much on religion, so she has to think for a moment. The famous Sioni Cathedral is too touristy, so she takes me to the Anchiskhati Basilica, the oldest church in the city. Because she is in trousers, she waits for me outside; she doesn't feel like being admonished by a pope.

Inside the church, which is as pristine as Ana promised, they are celebrating the Feast of the Baptism of the Lord. There is nothing solemn about the atmosphere, however. Most of the faithful are standing together in small groups and talking, laughing, looking around. Others are in silent prayer, chanting from a book, or in earnest conversation with a priest. Two strong priests with their sleeves rolled up are filling holy water into plastic bottles that the faithful have brought with them. An older priest is talking on a mobile phone while making sure they do not spill a drop. It is a different form of piety, probably an older form, than we know from post-Reformation Europe, not solemn, but rather busy, like the rabbis at the Wailing Wall who talked on the phone and recited the Torah simultaneously. The inner state of the believer is not so important; the main thing is that his holy work gets done. For the ritual is a service, not to man for his purification, but to God. Whether it looks nice is secondary; hence a plastic bottle is sufficient to carry holy water home.

Ana does not have to wait outside the Jumah Mosque. Trousers are fine, we are assured by the men in the antechamber, who speak Turkish among themselves; no, a headscarf is not necessary. In our stockinged feet we enter the prayer hall, filled with natural light from big windows – a white, modern-looking work of sacred architecture, given colour only by the red carpet and the sky-blue miniatures.

Ana is briefly startled when an older woman takes her by the hand, but the woman has merely seen that Ana is shivering and wants to show her where the heater is. And, in general, the atmosphere is relaxed; while some are talking, other mosquegoers are having a little nap or performing their ritual prayers. In this mosque there is no partitioned area for women. But the hall is divided by columns into two halves, each with its own prayer niche indicating the direction of Mecca – I have never seen a mosque with two mihrabs side by side. And, while one long wall is painted with Sunni sayings, the opposite wall praises the Shiite imams. In the nineteenth century, there was only one mosque; the Russian authorities would not allow a second one. So the Sunnis and the Shiites agreed to share and share alike. Each group has its own mihrab; all have a common roof.

I strike up a conversation with an Iranian family sitting on the Shiite half of the carpet. 'Have you ever seen such a thing?' I ask, 'a Sunni mihrab and a Shiite mihrab?'

'No,' says the father, who, unlike Ana or the Iranians in my hotel, still seems to be big on religion. 'Sunnis and Shiites everywhere beat each other's heads in, in Iraq, in Syria, in Saudi Arabia and in Yemen. And here we pray side by side.'

'That's good, is it not?'

'Yes, it is. But maybe they're not really aware of the differences here.'

'Or they don't attach so much importance to them.'

'Yes, maybe they don't attach so much importance to them.'

There are more than fifty peoples living in the Caucasus in an area not much bigger than Germany. Tbilisi alone has experienced almost every form of hostility: desecrated churches, demolished mosques, terror, war, genocide and banishment, all of them calamities that can follow from the doctrines of salvation, Christian or Muslim, religious or secular. But, at the same time, Tbilisi, the whole Caucasus, has an experience of the coexistence of peoples as few other regions have. Just as the mosque stands alongside many churches, inside the mosque itself no distinction is drawn between the faithful, or between men and women.

'That's a slight exaggeration,' Ana teases again.

Maybe so, I think, and refrain from recalling the three wars I drove through yesterday in the space of two hours. A traveller who comes to Tbilisi by the Caucasian Military Road soon grows sentimental on finding something like peace.

Thirty-Fourth Day: Tbilisi

The hotel I check into upon my return early one morning in June 2017 is full of Jewish extended families, emigrants to Israel visiting their old home I assume, the men in leisure attire and yarmulkes, the women in knee-length dresses, all with the same brawny physiognomy, including the children, as if they were members not just of the same people but of the same clan, loudly and expansively babbling, as Easterners often are. Are they Easterners? Ever since people have given thought to such questions, the boundary between Europe and Asia has run somewhere along the small strip of land between the Black Sea and the Caspian. In Herodotus, who probably never set foot in the territory of present-day Georgia, although he wrote exhaustively about his visit, the border follows the River Rioni: in that case, Tbilisi would lie in Asia, which would probably not please the Tbilisians, or in any case not their state, which hoists the ring of gold stars on a blue ground beside nearly every national flag. Yes, there are so many flags of Europe flying in Tbilisi that the EU has protested, they say; but surely not because they've been reading Herodotus in Brussels – rather, because they don't want to let in any more have-nots. Besides, the Russian Bear might be roused.

When one of the Israelis, waiting for the lift, speaks to me in Russian, I can only shrug my shoulders. We communicate with our hands that we both want to go up. When the lift door has closed, the Israeli points his finger at me questioningly; apparently he wants to know where I come from. I ponder for a second which answer will evoke the more interesting reaction, and I decide on the country to which my great-great-grandfather emigrated.

'Iran?!' the man almost screams, and looks at me with, no, not just dismay, but shock. What memories, threats, fears may have come into his mind at the word 'Iran'?

'Iran,' I repeat, and smile very peaceably to relax the tension in his face.

'Iran?!' He still seems to hope he heard wrong.

'Yes, Iran,' I confirm, and for safety's sake I add a 'shalom' to make it plain that I'm not about to cut his throat.

'Shalom, shalom,' he mutters, relieved, as the door of the lift opens again.

In the sumptuous yet charmingly run-down Museum of Literature, which seems to be a standard feature of any major city in the former territory of the Soviet Union, and in this case still retains an air of the old days and of the older, pre-revolutionary days, Georgia's poets are honoured by outsized busts, their death masks conserved like icons, their manuscripts and possessions displayed to visitors like relics. How different the relation to literature is in this part of the world straddling the border with Asia! Whereas Marbach, Germany's only museum of literature, comparably imposing to see, is dedicated to historical and critical research, that in Tbilisi also serves a devotional purpose. Reverently, the curator lifts out of the shrine the two rifles with which Hadji Murat fought to his last breath against the Russian soldiers outnumbering him. Afterwards, his head was skewered on a lance and displayed in Tbilisi on Freedom Square. We are a civilized country, protested Governor Vorontsov, whom Tolstoy, for all his sympathy with the Caucasian freedom fighters, portrays as a relatively enlightened politician. Vorontsov had the head taken down and sent it, preserved in alcohol, to St Petersburg, where it is still kept. Dagestani representatives have demanded time after time that the skull be repatriated, but there is great concern that it would become an object of pilgrimage – not for literary devotees, but for Islamists.

177

The cosy decayed courtyard of the museum is the terrace of a café where the smart set are typing in their notebooks, the committed citizens are holding a meeting, and the non-conformists are ostentatiously sprawling on the chairs. Without concentrating, I can distinguish four languages being spoken, sometimes several in the same conversation, and even in the same sentence, which may start out Georgian and end up Russian or may shift from English to Turkish: the last time Tbilisi was this multilingual must have been before the First World War. I get to talking with two of the committed citizens, Irakli, an urban planner, and Natalya, who introduces herself as a member of the Georgian Greens, whoever they are. They are both members of a big, constantly growing group of activists opposing the destruction of the historic buildings. In communism, they complain in excellent English, it's true that the old buildings were neglected, thoroughfares were ploughed through the city, the riverbanks were cast in concrete, ugly commuter towns were built – but only the free market has brought irreparable destruction to the centre, with its organic structure as a residential district, as a breathing, permeable organism surrounding the people. Without regard for the residents or the historic landmarks, the buildings are being revamped or replaced with tasteless swank, cheap imitation historic stuccowork or Dubai futurism. The quiet squares, the streets too narrow for traffic, the countless little stairways and green courtyards of the old town, all the features that make up the quality of life here because they constitute places for neighbourly encounters, are falling prey bit by bit to an economistic thinking, say Irakli and Natalya, which sees streets exclusively as paths for cars, sees a few architectural landmarks as touristic highlights or luxury suites, but most of the old buildings only as ruins to be pulled down, sees the lots only as numbers of apartments that can be built and sold.

Strange that young Georgians are defending the city's architectural traditions, and still more its Middle Eastern character, and often physically protecting them by sit-down blockades, even while those young Georgians' whole bearing, their language skills, their cosmopolitanism would seem to identify them as protagonists of the same globalization they are fighting. Their European orientation goes without saying, but to them Europe is something else besides the subsidies that the state would like to get its hands on; to them it is more a world of ideas whose essence is not at all this uniform levelling but, rather, the peaceful coexistence, side by side, over and under, within and without, of differences and uniquenesses. Anyone can belong to a world of ideas, no matter which side of the river you live on.

Socialist architecture has its beauty too, say Natalya and Irakli, and they take me to the former Institute of History, which was built in the 1930s. Unfortunately, it has been surrounded by a fence of plywood sheets and covered with tarpaulins since a few activists chained themselves to the building. And there are blue-uniformed guards posted every few metres along the pavement. Natalya raves about the generous balconies, the high ceilings, the early communist formalism. Where one of the tarpaulins has fallen down, I can see that the windows and balconies have already been torn out of the greyish-brown walls. The tarpaulins look like rags, full of holes, hanging down loosely from an exhausted, wrinkled body now dotted with wounds. Soon the gleaming new Ramada Inn will jut into the sky here. A guard requests that we move along for our own safety, as chunks of masonry could fall on our heads.

In the garden of the House of Writers, the second grandiose institution of literary Tbilisi after the museum, I am again beguiled by the symbiosis of pre-revolutionary splendour, Soviet formalism, Middle Eastern melancholy and a few select dabs of what is intended as Western or global taste, topped off by the hedonism manifested in the menu and the wine list. What is the attraction of this synchronicity of the diachronic that is currently so typical of Tbilisi? It is what forms the heart of the European project as it evolved in opposition to nationalism in the nineteenth century, and perhaps the heart of every civilization: that a place does not repudiate its history, that which went before; does not tear down or paint over what has grown up but lets it persist side by side with the present, thus relativizing the present as passing. Only ideologies wipe the slate clean of the past.

In the great salon of the nineteenth-century villa, which is packed to the walls today because a poet is presenting her first book – what happens when a famous poet reads, then? Do they rent a stadium? – the head of the Georgian writers' association, Paolo Iashvili, jumped up in the middle of a meeting in the summer of 1937 because he would not denounce his friend Titsian Tabidze, as he was instructed to do during the ritual of 'criticism and self-criticism' that had become customary in communist organizations. As every evening, the NKVD's black crow was already waiting outside to carry off the accused to the torture chamber or directly to their executions. Iashvili ran down the wide staircase to the first floor and shot himself between two stuffed hunting trophies, the front halves of a tiger and a lion. When his body was discovered, his colleagues tried to escape collective punishment by hastily condemning his suicide as an 'act of provocation' which must arouse 'revulsion and outrage in every self-respecting assembly of Soviet writers'. Titsian Tabidze also voted for the resolution but was killed nonetheless a short time later. Purged of the blood stains, the lion and the tiger still half stand in the first floor of the House of Writers, mutely opening their mouths.

'You can't skip over history,' says the writer Giwi Margwelaschwili, who lived under two totalitarian regimes, resisted both of them, and survived both of them. He was born in Berlin in 1927, the son of the well-known intellectual Titus von Margwelaschwili, who had fled the Bolsheviks in 1921; having lost his mother at the age of six, the son built out of books a German world of his own within his father's Georgian exile society.

'Did you suffer discrimination as a Georgian in Nazi Germany?'

'No, not exactly,' Margwelaschwili replies, 'but my name naturally stuck out, and my looks, and as a child you're naturally ashamed if you're different from the others.'

Later he fell in with a youth culture, the *Swingjugend*, who were not partisans, nor even especially political, but who, in the Nazi period in Germany and during the war, were naturally subversive and were arrested again and again; still, Margwelaschwili does not care to say they were 'persecuted'. 'Persecution' in those days meant something else, he says, something much worse. Many Nazis liked the '*Negermusik*' themselves and turned a blind eye. After the war, an old acquaintance from university lured Titus von Margwelaschwili to East Berlin, where the NKVD were waiting for him, and seized the opportunity to take his son into custody as well. While his father was carted off to Tbilisi and executed there, Giwi was held in Special Camp No. 7, the former concentration camp at Sachsenhausen which the Soviets had taken over from the Nazis. He was released only in early 1947 but not allowed to return to Berlin: he was deported to Georgia, where he looked like everyone else but hardly spoke the language – he knew little Georgian and no Russian. 'I was even more foreign there than in Berlin.'

He studied German language and literature, was inducted into the Academy of Sciences, and rebuilt his world of German books, which he got in Moscow if he could not find them in Tbilisi. In 1968, Heinrich Böll visited him and wanted to take his autobiographical cycle of novels *Captain Vakush* back to Cologne with him to publish it. Remembering his father's fate, Margwelaschwili flinched at the last moment – if he hadn't, he would have reached his readers decades earlier. In 1969 he returned for the first time to East Berlin, but because one of the people he visited there was the dissident songwriter Wolf Biermann, Giwi was afterwards prohibited from leaving Georgia again. After the collapse of the Soviet Union, he moved back to Berlin, together with his novels, which were finally published there; he was honoured with the Italo Svevo Award and an honorary presidential stipend; he went on reading tours and frequented colleagues who understood his language. 'I felt at home then.'

What was it like to have readers, finally, after so many decades?

'The reception of my books was positive, but not enthusiastic. That was a damper in itself. I am self-critical enough to see that part of the reason is the books themselves.'

That is probably true, I think, although it does not diminish their literary quality: Margwelaschwili's narration of his life story is as cumbersome as the story is suspenseful. The two volumes of *Captain Vakush* are more a philosophical reflection on a biography than a biography in the strict sense. Most of all, though, Margwelaschwili alludes so often to things he has read that you wonder whether life to him is anything else but the interpretation, or a consequence, of literature. He himself described the plan of one of his stories as 'a good reversal of text and reality'.

'You could have written a best-seller if you had written a simple autobiography,' I say, 'with the life you have lived.'

'To be honest, I expected my books would become best-sellers. But apparently the inside of my head is too rambling.'

Margwelaschwili lives in Tbilisi again now, because at his age he can't get by without help: bowed, brittle, his white hair down to his shoulders, but his mind fully alert.

'You have to see history through,' he says with his Berlin accent when I visit him in the little flat, filled to the ceiling with German books, where his daughter looks after him. 'If you skip over a chapter, it catches up with you, forcefully.'

I ask him about Georgia today. Margwelaschwili finds the developments are not so bad. 'Why?' I ask, surprised because I have heard so many complaints in the course of the day.

'Everyone here talks like a waterfall these days. People come out with an incredible number of banalities, sheer nonsense, true. But the people are talking, they're speaking for themselves. That didn't use to be the case. You know, Stalin was fond of reading Rustaveli, the great Georgian poet, or at least he claimed to be. And he had internalized half a line of Rustaveli: Out of fear love arises. That is exactly what happened. The people loved Stalin not because he was friendly but because he was terrible, because the terror could strike anyone. That's why everyone was paralysed, petrified with love if you will, or with terror; you couldn't tell the difference. But, now, the people blather away with no inhibitions. This is better.'

When our talk touches on the dispute among German historians as to whether there is a connection between Nazism and Stalinism, I ask Margwelaschwili whether he thinks the two ideologies he lived under are comparable.

'They are equally despicable,' answers Margwelaschwili.

'But are they similar?'

'The similarity is their militarism. Both of them rescinded the commandment "Thou shalt not kill". What is evil is the legitimation of death.'

'Could Hitler have been overcome without war?'

'He should have been.'

'But how?'

'By reading him. In Landsberg prison he wrote down exactly what he intended, including his plan for the Jews. It was all there from the beginning in *Mein Kampf*. If people had read him, they would have stopped him earlier. By that I mean to say that the fundamental mistake in dealing with Hitler happened much earlier on. The fundamental mistake was ignorance, looking away, not wanting to believe it. By the time the war came, it was already too late.'

'Then books are not the result of events, but, rather, events can be read from the books?'

'Yes, that's exactly what my novels are about: how reality is derived from books, and not the other way around.'

In his view of literature as nothing less than a prophetic medium, the German writer Giwi Margwelaschwili is very Georgian after all.

Thirty-Fifth Day: To Gori and the Georgian–Ossetian Ceasefire Line

The sign on the motorway that connects Tbilisi with the western half of the country says 'Istanbul 1,715 km'. The first part of the route runs close to the border with South Ossetia, or, rather, close to the line reached by the advancing Russian troops in 2008. In no state that became independent with the collapse of the Soviet Union was the population congruent with the new nation. Georgia, for example, was inhabited by Abkhazians, Ossetians, Russians, no fewer than 6.5 per cent Azerbaijanis, 5.7 per cent

Armenians, plus Adjarians, Mingrelians, Svans, Kists, Imeretians, Jews, Yazidis, Meskhetians, Greeks, Chechens, and so on – at least twenty-six ethnic groups in a territory the size of Bavaria, with various religions, and most of them with their own language. In 1991 they all found themselves in a state named after a single people, under a flag bearing five copies of the symbol of a single church. Some minorities had suffered so much in the Soviet Union that they were glad enough to see it gone. Abkhazians and Ossetians, on the other hand, had been Russified since the time of the tsars, and hence had stronger connections to far-off Moscow than to nearby Tbilisi. And because in the early 1990s a Russian nationalism also flared up which held that all those who speak Russian belong to Russia, two wars broke out simultaneously which Georgia, much smaller and barely consolidated, could only lose. Since then, one fifth of the country has belonged, for all practical purposes, to Russia. Mikheil Saakashvili's 2008 attempt to regain at least South Ossetia ended within days with the Russian troops' advance almost to the motorway. We can see out of the car window the settlements of the internal refugees: ranks and files of cheap prefab houses in the middle of the fields. Their villages have long since been razed by the separatists. Georgia's new government, which strives to be on good terms with Russia, prefers not to raise hopes of return. And Saakashvili himself is no longer a figure of hope either: by now he has resigned as governor of Odessa, and after his flight from Georgia he has now fled Ukraine too. At least there are no uniformed highwaymen lurking along the motorway: the leader of the Rose Revolution was more successful in fighting corruption than in fighting the foreign enemy.

After just under an hour we reach Gori, where the heaviest Russian bombardment fell in 2008, although the city is the birthplace of none other than Ioseb Jughashvili, whose *nom de guerre* Joseph Stalin evokes the former greatness of the Soviet Union. Not until 2010 did the city fathers have the confidence to remove his statue from the central square, and even then only under cover of darkness and with police protection. No one dared touch the house where Stalin was born, which is at the head of the central boulevard – the old city centre having been moved after Stalin's death to permit this arrangement. The Soviet Union enclosed the simple cottage in a Greek-looking temple, as if to hallow the spot where a demigod had come into the world. The imposing museum, which is full of youth groups during our visit, displays room after room of Stalin devotionals, including jubilee portraits, marble busts and poets' homages, illustrating the stations of his life as a three-dimensional hagiography. Visitors can sit in the train car in which the dictator rode around his gigantic empire, look into the bathroom where he bathed and the little kitchen where his meals were cooked during his journeys. Joseph Stalin did not travel in great luxury.

Forty-five per cent of the people in Georgia have a positive image of Stalin, a survey has found – a far higher proportion than in Russia. Nonetheless, Lasha Bakradze, the director of the literature museum, who is accompanying me today, assures me that few Georgians would want the Soviet Union back, and they are proud of Stalin more as a Georgian than as a Soviet leader. That sounds nonsensical, he realizes, since after all it was Stalin who – perhaps in order to prove that he was not attached to any native soil, any mother tongue – Russified the Soviet Union and suppressed the national cultures, including Georgian culture. But Lasha calls to mind the mass demonstrations of 1956, after Nikita Khrushchev had criticized his predecessor's political leadership at the twentieth Party Congress. What began as a protest against reform in the Soviet Union metamorphosed within days into a call for Georgian independence. When the demonstrators tried to enter the radio station and the telegraph office, the Red Army opened fire. At least eighty people, or as many as 150 or 800 according to other sources, died for – for what, exactly? For Stalin's Soviet Union, and at the same time for Georgia's independence.

The museum of course makes no mention of the nationalistic hero-worship, celebrating Stalin only as the leader of the Soviet Union who made an agrarian country into a leading industrial nation and defeated German fascism; as a young daredevil, a down-to-earth comrade, a respected statesman, a friend to children and a lover of literature. Only two tiny rooms in the basement have been revised with a general reminder that there were also victims – without names, figures, or further explanations. A brochure that is free for the taking gathers testimonials to Stalin by historic personalities such as Roosevelt, de Gaulle, Churchill, Hitler, Picasso. 'The ancient philosophers,' the last page reads, 'ended their works with the words: I have done what I could; improve on it if you can.'

From Gori we drive for three quarters of an hour in the direction of South Ossetia and reach the village of Nikosi, where a sandstone church has stood out among the farm cottages since the fifth century. By Georgian standards it is not even particularly old – after all, the country has the second-oldest national church in the world, after Armenia's. The cassock the bishop is wearing looks as though he's been working; there is still plenty of renovation work to be done. Before the church was reconsecrated, it was used for decades as a granary. The monastery was also restored, but destroyed in 2008 by – Bishop Isaiah counted – twenty-eight Russian bombs. The balcony of his modest palace overlooks the part of Georgia that Georgians can no longer so much as set foot in: a forest, some ruins, a lane between the fields leading nowhere, and beyond the fields, which haven't been planted for a long time now, the concrete housing blocks of the town of Tskhinvali, which is now a capital.

To Ana and Lasha, and to everyone I talked to in Tbilisi for that matter, the Church has a terrible reputation: homophobic, misogynistic, reactionary in every respect. And, on YouTube, priests can almost always be seen leading the mobs that beat down every incipient Gay Pride parade. But this priest, Bishop Isaiah, is so winningly friendly and has such a cheeky smile under his long, hippyishly wild beard that, I can't help myself, I am suddenly tempted to see those judgements as prejudices. He is especially glad to hear that my forebears are Iranian. 'Why?' I ask.

'Because we have so many martyrs in Iran,' replies the bishop cheerfully, and he takes me to the picture of St Razhden, an Iranian convert in the service of the Georgian king, until he was killed in a Sassanian campaign.

After the war, Bishop Isaiah held out on the other side of the front, where half of his parish live, for fear he wouldn't be able to return if he left. He didn't even dare visit his brother on his deathbed or attend his funeral. Only after more than two and a half years did the separatists allow him to commute between the two halves of his parish, but not a step further into South Ossetia. He has not been to Tskhinvali, near though it is, since then.

Before the war, many people didn't know if they were this or that, says Bishop Isaiah, as so many others have said after many civil wars. Georgians and Ossetians often married one another; they feasted together, prayed together, were buried side by side. Only the war forced them to choose. There are not many who chose Georgia and yet remained in their houses. The bishop who ministers to them cannot say exactly how they are getting on because he is afraid he would no longer be allowed to enter South Ossetia if he were to get involved in politics. So he prefers to show us the community centre, which he has transformed into an art and music school. He himself studied film animation as a young man before he got interested in religion.

'How did that interest arise?' I ask.

'How it arose?' The bishop answers with a question: 'Have you got all day?'

Briefly, the story of his faith begins as he is watching a Soviet film that makes fun of monks and priests: the malice rubs him up the wrong way – although he is not even baptized; it's more a matter of instinctive empathy. A short time later, he meets an old woman in his native village who needs twenty signatures to lodge a request to reopen the church. But all the neighbours are afraid. He helps the woman collect signatures, and although his intention is to help her, not the church, it turns out to boost his faith. His curiosity aroused, he is trying out monastery life in Abkhazia when the war breaks out. He witnesses how peaceful coexistence turns into hatred, how neighbours who raised a glass together one day fight each other the next, how they die in a hail of bullets or from exhaustion while fleeing. He can see that spiritual guidance is more urgently needed than animated films.

I note that Bishop Isaiah has remained an artist at heart in the community centre, where an army of children are rehearsing shadow plays and folk dances, practising songs and musical instruments. I recall the performance at the exiled Crimean Tatars' school in Kiev, the bright, exotic costumes, the flowing movements, the whirling hips – how different the Georgian tradition looks: the children wear black, close-fitting costumes and demonstratively severe faces, stretch their spine straight when they dance and whirl only their legs and feet, their arms and fingers; once in a while their heads may suddenly swing to the side. And how different the traditions sound: in Kiev, the quivering, fragile sound of the lutes brought far-off Asia into the auditorium, whereas here the dull beats of the drums and the shrill brasses sound almost like what we know in Germany as Balkan beat. I couldn't say which I like better, the supple or the jagged movements, the bright or the deep tones; they are two different worlds, even though both are from the Black Sea coast. The peoples do well to preserve their respective traditions. 'Anyone, no matter who, given the opportunity to choose from among all the nations in the world the beliefs he thought best,' wrote Herodotus, 'would inevitably choose those of his own country.' Herodotus was taking issue with the arrogance of his fellow Athenians. But the sentence need not necessarily be read as criticism: the pride in children's eyes after a performance is the same everywhere in the world.

The Georgian tradition I read about most often – the ritual feast at which the participants take turns making toasts, reciting poems and singing songs, and occasionally dance between courses – would probably not have a counterpart among the Muslim Tatars, however. We are about to say our good-byes when the bishop leads us back to his palace, where a long table

186

full of food has been conjured up, fresh herbs and unimaginable dishes of vegetables, fried potatoes and aromatic sauces, walnuts and pomegranates, cheese and bread. 'Guests are a gift of God,' says the bishop, sweeping aside our objections that we are not staying long and don't want to be any trouble. I can't pull my plate away as fast as it gets refilled whenever a part of it is free. The wine does its part to turn the interview into a feast, with toasts to friendship, our loved ones at home, peace, and everything else imaginable. Being as I am a reporter, I still want to bring up the criticism of the Church that I have heard. But to ask about homophobia, Russia and gender relations in such an atmosphere, with such hospitality, is somehow out of the question. So I try Europe for a start: 'Some Georgians don't seem to be so happy with Georgia's orientation towards Europe. What do you think?'

'Why wouldn't they be happy?' Bishop Isaiah returns the question.

'Perhaps because they're afraid of decaying morals, or of losing Georgia's identity. Don't you see such dangers?'

'No, not at all.'

'But, then, how do you explain the fear?'

'It is easier to live as a slave than in freedom. Freedom requires us to do something, to take responsibility.'

'Isn't the fear especially widespread in the Church?'

'There is fear, that's true, but it is not as deep-seated as you might think. It's just expressed very loudly. For my part, I enjoy seeing our country opening up. It does my heart good when I see an Iranian film.'

'But the Persians killed so many of your saints.'

'That in itself shows how closely we are connected. Georgia was always oriented towards the south, towards Persia in the East, later towards the West as well: towards Constantinople, towards Europe. The northward roads are relatively new, a hundred, two hundred years old perhaps; that's not long for a country as old as ours. I think it's wonderful that the borders are opening. Now you come and visit us from Germany, from Iran, wherever – but you come and visit us. That is a blessing.'

Later, as we are taking turns singing, my doom comes closer, chair by chair. Because the bishop would smile away any excuse about not being able to sing, I think feverishly what song I could present. As a good West German, I know by heart at most a couple of American songs, which are not at all appropriate here. And the interest in Germany is not so great either here beyond the Caucasus, where the *Wehrmacht* left behind so many mass graves. While Dmitrij makes a good showing with a Belarusian tune, I take his smartphone and google up the text of a classic song that I often heard as a child in my parents' car: 'Marā Bebus'. An Iranian communist wrote it for his beloved the night before his execution, it was always said: 'Kiss me, kiss me for the last time'; and, although I know of course that that's only a legend, I repeat it to the monks in introducing the song. They are not much on communism, but they certainly appreciate martyrdom, and love too. Finally I begin to sing for the first time since primary school, only to stop after the first verse because the bishop's smile now looks all too forced, and I reach for the phone again. Holding my hand up high, I play them 'Marā Bebus' from YouTube. It isn't really loud enough, but the monks are so attentive, and the singer's voice reverberates in the big hall still more wistfully, and the violin weeps so bitterly that the sound alone communicates the distress of the lover going to his death. I am thinking this is a bit ridiculous, but then I witness how the monks' heads gradually begin to sway to the Persian song: 'Kiss me, kiss me for the last time, and then may God protect you.'

After the meal we walk the few yards to the cemetery beyond which the border runs these days. These days? Yes, the border moves, say the soldiers, who are officially police officers, because officially the border is not a border; sometimes they advance two fields overnight, two more fields that lie fallow from then on; sometimes they retreat a few lines of trees further back. Border violations are also a regular occurrence, and in fact a regular source of income for the separatists: a peasant gets kidnapped and taken to the other side of the front and released only on payment of a ransom. In front of the cemetery are high defensive positions made of car tyres covered with nets, easy to relocate. The border defenders are not wearing bullet-proof vests, although they have lined up in front of the black walls, which look more like art than war; evidently they are not expecting a firefight. Between the graves are tables and benches, because in Georgia the dead are often invited to join in the feasts. Most of the tombstones are engraved with the faces of the departed; some of them also depict, strangely, the cars they drove. Or are those the cars they crashed in? On the other side of the meadow, perhaps 800 metres away, two flags fly in front of a dilapidated building, probably the Ossetian and the Russian flag; a few people are also visible. Borrowing a pair of binoculars, I spy a soldier with a pair of binoculars looking at me.

On the way back, we stop at the cave city of Uplistsikhe, 10 kilometres east of Gori. From the sixth century BC, this was the political and religious centre of the Iberians, whom Herodotus praised, unseen, as a peaceful, civilized people: a population of 20,000 once lived on this mountain, worshipping the sun. In the first century BC, the Romans arrived; in the seventh century AD, the Arabs; in the thirteenth century the Mongols – to name only a few of the less peaceful conquerors. Each time, the inhabitants took refuge in their caves and were able to sustain long sieges because a tunnel through the mountain led to the Mtkvari, the largest river in the Caucasus, known outside Georgia as the Kura, or Kyros in Greek: there they drew water without being seen. Visitors can still descend the tunnel, although the Mtkvari has changed its course and now runs several hundred yards away from the exit. The caves would not be safe against the next invaders.

In the evening in Tbilisi, Lasha tells me about an older friend, a writer, who constantly dreamt while he was in the Gulag that Stalin had died. Then for a few days there were no orders and addresses, and the prisoners suspected something was happening. Finally the commander of the camp had the prisoners assembled and announced Stalin's death. Everyone fell to their knees weeping, including Lasha's friend. He wept and at the same time wondered why he was weeping, after having longed for nothing so fervently as for 'that swine' to finally die.

Thirty-Sixth Day: From Tbilisi to Kakheti

There is another tradition in Georgia that has been rapturously praised by travellers in every century: the public baths. Ana recommended one that has not been spruced up for tourists and that has a higher sulphur content, almost unpleasant to the nose: the former soldiers' bath, once the cheapest in the city. After the attendant, disregarding my cries of pain, has scrubbed the dirt out of my skin, covered me with soap suds from head to toe like a baby, and rinsed the soap even out of my nostrils, I splash dazedly in the pleasantly warm, rotten-smelling water, feeling as if relieved of a half-inch layer of skin. How must this deep cleanliness have felt in earlier times, 200 or 2,000 years ago, when people lay as if reborn after sweaty toil, after a hard week's work in the fields or in a workshop, after travelling hundreds of leagues across deserts and mountains? Suddenly I think of that border which Herodotus assumed, sight unseen, to be the Rioni River, and which Kurban Said held to run between Georgia and Azerbaijan: the border between Europe and Asia. The Greeks were not the only people who thought themselves the protectors of civilization against the barbarians; the Roman and the Byzantine empires likewise justified their wars as the defence of a highly developed order against a rude, even a bestial primitivism, as did the Holy Roman Empire and all of

189

the modern colonial powers. Neal Ascherson continues the list of Western powers in his cultural history of the Black Sea:

> By the middle twentieth century, few European nation-states had not at one time or another figured themselves as 'the outpost of Western Christian civilization': France, imperial Germany, the Habsburg Reich, Poland with its self-image as *przedmurze* (bastion), even tsarist Russia. Each of these nation-state myths identified 'barbarism' as the condition or ethic of their immediate eastward neighbour: for the French, the Germans were barbarous, for the Germans it was the Slavs, for the Poles the Russians, for the Russians the Mongol and Turkic peoples of Central Asia and eventually the Chinese.[36]

Is that true? Colonialism, to begin with, expanded towards all points of the compass instead of respecting the topography of classical literature, according to which barbarism begins with the eastern neighbour – the Scythians in Herodotus, the Persians in Aeschylus, the Tauri in Euripides; in Colchis in present-day Georgia, whither the same poet moves the birthplace of murdering Medea; in Thrace, where Sophocles sees the exiled hero Tereus transform into a rapist, a cannibal, a tyrant – the empire of the tsars, with its opera houses and its libraries, expanded southwards; and now, as I lie in a hamam that looks like a mosque with its cupola, it occurs to me that the Middle East situated barbarism not further east, in China or India for example, but in Europe, which, after the fall of the Romans, no longer had baths. That the Franks stink is a motif that permeates the Arabic travel writing of the Middle Ages, and the upturned noses were always figurative as well as literal: while the rise of Europe is accompanied by a renaissance of the cult of purity, the decline of the Islamic world is manifested in its rubbish-filled streets and the state of its public sanitation systems. In Tbilisi, turned towards Europe, dirt is still scrubbed out of the skin in the Middle Eastern way.

As I step out of the bath, the air embraces me like a cold pool, vitalizing the senses, like a final shower. I avoid the renovated corners of the old city centre and walk through streets in which the rows of houses on either side are joined by high scaffolding to keep them from collapsing onto each other. Cars can't get through here; the asphalt is worn away; the façades are like a huge multicoloured *Neue Wilde* canvas. The finger-thick and even hand-thick dark lines are no ingenious brush-strokes, however, but cracks in the walls. The houses seem to be inhabited nonetheless; that is indicated by the washing hung out, by the flowers visible inside the cracked and taped windows in their decaying frames; by the old people leaning out here and there; by the children in the courtyards. In the middle of Gudiashvili Square, where Irakli and Natalya have blockaded investors, stands a sculpture of a mushroom or an umbrella under which two lovers intertwine to form a single body. The town houses, still erect, barely; the trees, placed in no order or pattern, likewise bent over like old men or grown aslant and askew; the square itself, half of paving stones and half of dark earth; two rusty structures of climbing bars for children which could well date from the Soviet Union, and park benches from a still earlier time. On one of them sits a black-clad woman telling a story to her two grandchildren. 'Oblivion, in Captain Vakush's view, is a Black Sea breaking against the shore of our present consciousness in which we are wont to have a swim,' we read near the end of Giwi Margwelaschwili's autobiographical novel, 'but actually the Black Sea of oblivion is for diving, for sinking down into the lower shelves of temporal consciousness and biding a while with bygones. Then we remember and locate a fault on a low temporal level of our existence, something past which is lacking in our present life, which we see with melancholy or longing and perhaps with new eyes.'[37]

Lasha has proposed that we stop on the way to Azerbaijan at the birthplace of the writer Giorgi Leonidze, just under an hour east of Tbilisi, to experience a real Georgian feast. The lunch at the monastery, he says, for all its hospitality, was rather Protestant. If that was Protestant, I think, the real thing must be orgiastic.

Leonidze, who was director of the Museum of Literature for almost twenty years in the 1960s and 1970s, was born in December but, because winter is not good for celebrations, his annual commemoration has been moved to June. When we arrive in the village, shortly after noon, the literary programme is already over – so quickly, Lasha says, surprised – and the company has already sat down at six long rows of tables laid in two layers: on the bottom, more substantial foods such as potatoes, beans and olives; on top, smaller bowls containing sauces, spinach, creamed aubergines, hummus, and the like. Squeezed in between the platters are large pitchers of water, lemonade for the children, and wine. Every few minutes, one of the men stands up – toasts are apparently the last male preserve in Georgia – and with a flourish recites his poem or makes a speech, sings solo or in chorus with the other friends of literature, or invites one of the boys to sing.

Some of the guests, with scarves, in spite of the warmth, tossed nonchalantly over one shoulder, or with shoulder-length white hair and dandyish light-coloured suits over shirts open to the fourth button, look the poet from a mile away. One of them sets a theme – love, freedom or the natural beauty of Georgia – on which the others take turns improvising in their toasts. For lack of language skills, I am spared at least this ordeal. One after another, instruments are brought out, a drum or an accordion, and, in between, more big platters are brought with meat, sausages and fish and served as a third stratum, skilfully balanced on top of the half-empty bowls. The brandies to stimulate the digestion have been going around since the starters. And after every recitation, every toast, every song or poem, we all stand up and drink, spine straight and with crisp movements, to something, which Lasha has given up translating for me in detail because, in the end, everything boils down to a celebration of poetry, life or home, the place where we happen to live. And anyway the verse in particular is of rather dubious quality, the director of the literature museum intimates with a wink; some Georgian poets look best from a mile away.

Later than planned, and much too cheerfully, we set out for Azerbaijan. I had best not ask whether Maka drank every toast. She is our driver, has been plying this profession for twenty-five years, and is of the strong, almost intimidatingly dominant, and incidentally hard-drinking type of woman that I have encountered more often in Georgia than anywhere else. She no longer has a husband, but she has four children, who are with their grandmother now, and – right – she also works as a teacher. With only one income, you can't raise four children in Georgia in such a way that they'll be better off someday. Through a mountain range that looks gentle in comparison to the rugged Caucasus, the road takes us deeper into Kakheti, famous for its wine and its old churches. We have had enough wine for the time being, but the churches are a sight you can't get enough of. They fit so harmoniously in the landscape, as if they had grown up out of the ground – this is not only because of the sandstone, or their human proportions, the domes barely taller than the tallest trees; it is also because of their condition since they have been reconsecrated. Critics may hold the Church's wealth against it, but no riches are visible in the restoration works, which have done no more than repair, uncover, replaster, stabilize what is absolutely necessary. And this, the fragility, the imperfection, the quarter-renovated state, is precisely what makes up their aura. Every single fresco in which the figures are barely discernible, every one of the stones which show the traces of humidity and smoke, the hammer strokes and nail cavities of the shepherds and sheltering wanderers, revolutionaries and invaders, the stucco that has probably been peeling off the bricks for how many centuries now, every tile missing in the floor – all of this together tells of life that is past, but not ended.

No, the state does little for the preservation of the churches, and the parishes hardly have any money, says Sister Mariani, who talks with us in front of the Alaverdi Cathedral. Without private patrons and the work of volunteers, she says, not even the absolutely necessary repairs could have been done. The nun tells us about the foreigners who attacked this church over the centuries: the Persians who used the convent as their barracks, allowing the faithful to pray in the church only on holy days; the Soviets who stored grain or raised pigs in the cathedral. Who was worse? The Persians fought with bows and arrows, but the Soviets attacked the people's minds and souls. Besides, the Persians left behind something beautiful, Sister Mariani adds, pointing to a garden pavilion whose latticework turns out to be Safavid. What is now the bishop's palace was also built by Shah Abbas's governor.

I ask her how she knows so much about Persian architecture. She studied Middle Eastern cultures in Tbilisi, Sister Mariani replies, and it was in part through the encounter with a foreign culture that she found her own religion. That was towards the end of the Soviet Union, and, no, it was not unusual; after all, Ferdowsi, Hafiz and the other great Persians were part of the Georgian canon, at least in her generation. Communism had placed value on education, if nothing else. She still knows a few words of Persian, which she happily recites, and she has set herself the task of writing a history of her convent, which she also intends to have published in Iran. Then she quotes – go ahead and picture it: a nun, wimpled down past the eyebrows and up over the chin, in a remote convent south of the Caucasus – quotes Goethe, who said East and West are inseparable, which is true of all compass points, and of literature most of all. At some point the bishop wanders over and kisses first Sister Mariani, then us on the head, smiling mutely like a yogi. I can see I won't get far at this church either with questions about homophobia, Russia and gender relations. Where love is, there is no room for violence, answers Sister Mariani in very general terms when I ask about the attacks on homosexuals. When Dmitrij asks whether he may take photographs in the church in spite of the sign prohibiting it – after all, he doesn't use a flash, which could burn the frescoes – she shakes her head, sympathetically but firmly: 'What burns the frescoes is not the flash, it's the haste.'

Thirty-Seventh Day: From Kakheti to Azerbaijan

On getting up it occurs to me that yesterday was the first day of my journey on which I didn't talk about politics, and very little about current events, for that matter, and only about history several centuries past. Did I even mention the sitting president? In Kakheti, where there are more cows than people on the roads and communism has apparently disappeared without anything else taking its place – no billboards, no glass office buildings, nowhere gold stars on a blue ground; neither new housing estates nor industrial zones, no Lidl and no Carrefour, few Western cars, but also no checkpoints, soldiers or gangs that are a law unto themselves – in Kakheti, the question where the river flows that marks the beginning of Europe doesn't come up constantly. Here the people are on a continent of their own anyway. And even the twentieth century, which seems so violent to us, although history has consisted of wars, massacres and expulsions since Cain and Abel – at last, I am no longer confronted with the twentieth century everywhere I look. No signposts jump out at me pointing to sites of death camps, mass graveyards, ghettos, battlefields; the abandoned industrial sites, the concrete estates and the kolkhoz farms that the leap into the modern era seems to have left in its wake elsewhere in the east are seen only rarely in this Georgian hinterland. We are travelling in an older time.

We set out early in the morning to arrive in time for Sunday Mass at the monastery of Nekresi. The Georgian rite is one of the earliest Christian rites in existence. Replaced with the Russian Orthodox rite by the tsar in 1802, written down beginning in 1894 to preserve the cultural heritage, painstakingly reconstructed after Georgian independence in 1917, it was prohibited again under Stalin (strange that people blame religion for all kinds of calamities that have taken place in its name, but never godlessness). I am all the more curious to see, over 200 years after the abolition of Georgian autocephaly and after seventy years of state atheism, how the rite has been preserved, for actually, as I learned in Serbia, the Orthodox liturgy is not something that can be easily relearned from books once the tradition has been interrupted – the procedures are too complex: not just the recitations, but the correct modulation; not just the steps, but the genuflections at the exact places prescribed; not just the solo chant, but the responses of the choir; not just what words are accompanied by incense wafting through the church, from what spot, with which rattling sounds, but also the lighting and snuffing of the candles, carried from one place to another with such great determination that we understand only one way can be the right way. The reason for precisely these steps or that gesture has been known since time out of mind. The Orthodox liturgy is not taught in seminaries but is passed on from generation to generation, especially in the monasteries, where the worship service is practised every day for hours. In the Soviet Union there were churches here and there, but there were no longer the monastic orders that had ensured the preservation of the liturgy over the centuries. Sister Mariani said yesterday that the tradition was preserved only by individual priests and small communities that met in private premises. Under Stalin, she said, more members of the Church were shot than intellectuals.

We cannot understand the power of Orthodoxy in the countries of the former Soviet Union if we look only at its secular role or its leaders, most of whom were appointed by the state, at the sinecures, the political interventions, the anti-Semitism, which is said to be virulent, the rigid moral ideas, the nationalism for which the clergy often stands today, against the innermost teaching of Jesus. This Church has gone through seventy years of oppression; seventy years in which it was anything but advantageous to identify oneself as faithful; seventy years of secrecy, caution, perseverance, poverty, pastoral care without reward or recognition, inner resistance; seventy years in which everyone was beset by the present, by life as it was in that place at that time, and yet a few reckoned in a different time, in celestial time. And what are seventy years? The Georgian Church has prevailed for 200 years against Russification and for 1,400 years against Islam. It is not only the age of the buildings still being used, that is, not turned into museums, an age unknown in the West – fifth-, sixth-, even fourth-century buildings – it is something about the faces that I associate, rightly or wrongly, with early Christianity, an altogether metaphysical concentration, a detachment from the world, and at the same time that serenity that may arise when all earthly things seem transient. I admit the priests do not look enraptured, unworldly, serene, when they lead the mobs on YouTube. And yet anyone who talks with Sister Mariani or Bishop Isaiah will not be able to dismiss the word 'love'.

Shortly after eight, when we arrive at the monastery that has stood alone high on a mountain above the fertile plain of Kakheti since the sixth century, the warden gruffly turns us away because we are not baptised Orthodox. How would he look at us if we told him he is dealing with a Jew and a Muslim, and our driver is waiting in the car because she has trousers on? Fortunately, Sister Mariani has written down the abbot's number for us, and he steps out of the church immediately when we call. Apparently, people at Mass here have no more qualms about answering the phone than the rabbis I have observed at the Wailing Wall. We are welcome to attend Mass, the abbot cordially assures us, although he cannot stay with us long because the prayers have already begun; only for the Eucharist itself, he begs us to understand, we must leave the church; someone will give us a sign. Yes, I can well understand that, after the seventy years, they take the rules all the more seriously. The performance of voice, light, smell, vestments, movements, mime and architecture seems to me to be less complex and artistic, not nearly as elaborate, as what I know from the Serbian monasteries. Is it because the Georgian liturgy developed earlier and is therefore simpler? Or because the rite could only be revived in a simplified form? None of the eight monks is old enough to have been a bearer of the tradition during the Soviet Union; the generation from which they could have learned the tradition is missing. Some of the monks make mistakes in the recitation, more than just fine details, and are quietly corrected by the abbot, and an acolyte holds a programme, or perhaps a crib sheet, laminated in plastic. The fragility that I perceive in the proceedings is strangely highlighted by the fragility of the space, every stone of which speaks of its age, by the delicacy of the frescoes, moreover, precisely because they are not lustrous, but shimmer wanly in the candlelight, webbed with cracks like an ancient face for which seventy years are little more than a flash, although one that nearly burnt them.

Dmitrij, who did not grow up with the religion in Belarus, is at least as strongly impressed as I am. 'It was a concert,' he mumbles as we walk down the mountain to the car, 'a symphony – crazy.'

'Told you so,' I reply, quietly gloating because Dmitrij hadn't believed me when I told him how beautiful, really – beautiful in the everyday sense, artistically good, and also simply overwhelming – worship services can be: 'You can toss the whole Documenta in the dustbin,' I say, giving contemporary art a reactionary diss while I'm at it.

'But it doesn't beat a rock concert,' Dmitrij replies, loyal to his music.

Towards noon, Maka lets us out at the border. She doesn't even think of taking us to the next city. Although the countries in this part of the world are smaller than German states – North Rhine-Westphalia or Hesse – and have fewer inhabitants, and although they belonged to the same union for many decades, the people do not just pop over to the neighbours. Did they before? Only four lorries with Turkish number plates are waiting to be processed;

not a single passenger car. Maka asks us to call her from Azerbaijan; she'll wait until we do before she drives away.

'Why?' we ask.

'You never know.'

But we do get across the border; that's a start. To Dagestan – which we had originally chosen as our next destination on the way eastwards, because it adjoins Georgia for many centimetres on the map – to Dagestan there is not a single border crossing. Ossetia and Abkhazia are also closed, as is the border between Azerbaijan and Armenia or Nagorno-Karabakh, of course. Furthermore, you can't go from Armenia to Turkey, nor to the Nakhchivan Autonomous Republic. Two seas left and right leave few opportunities for travel. The only country in the region from which you can go in any direction is the one that is called a 'rogue state', the Islamic Republic of Iran. We roll our suitcases through a roofed walkway that follows the multi-lane road with the abandoned inspection stations for about 500 metres. From time to time there are other pedestrians with heavy baggage coming the other way. The last international border I crossed on foot was the one between Syria and Lebanon, I recall, and that was in wartime; the one before that was probably the border between East and West Berlin.

There are many taxis waiting on the other side of the border, but only one of the drivers speaks Russian, so that Dmitrij can communicate with him. His limp has to do with the war, he tells us before we ask; he stepped on a mine in Nagorno-Karabakh in 1993. But we mustn't worry; he can press the clutch pedal with his prosthetic leg just as well.

'Was the war against Armenia necessary?' I ask, starting right in with the political questions in Azerbaijan.

'Nonsense,' says the driver. 'The people in power made war. We only contributed our dead, our homes and our limbs.'

'But there was hatred too, wasn't there?'

'The war didn't break out because of the hatred; the hatred broke out because of the war.'

The landscape, for the moment, is the same as in Georgia: the wooded mountains on the left; the broad plain, still fertile here, on the right. Turkish was spoken before the border too; the cows and sheep are also unchanged, and there are mosques and churches on this side as well as that. So what is different, then, besides the flags, to warrant making such a big deal about the border? The tea houses, I realize: they line up one next to another in the villages and cities, as if all the male inhabitants had to be accommodated at once. That is not a small difference from Georgia, when you consider everything the tea house stands for: for time, of which there is enough; then no doubt for work, of which there isn't; for the conviviality, which is not that of wine, of pleasure, of the embrace that is already forgotten the next day, but which consists of sober conversations and at most card and board games; in former times, for the culture, which was more that of the epic and less of lyric poetry and mysticism; for the public space, which the tea house creates only for men, it is true, and for the segregation of the sexes for that matter, although none of the women in the streets are wearing headscarves.

'But isn't Ramadan observed anywhere?' I ask, because I had been expecting to fast.

'Oh yes,' the driver assures me, 'no alcohol is served during Ramadan.'

In the evening we walk through the old caravan city of Shaki, now done up for tourism. There is nothing Persian about the architecture here: neither delicate columns for wooden balconies to rest on, nor ornate balustrades; the local style is more robust: blocky stone houses with tiled roofs and unornamented windows; even the palaces rather functional. The khanate of Shaki was always Turkish in character, both under the shahs and under the tsars, and the city centre is therefore more reminiscent of Mostar than of its neighbour Tbilisi. The restaurants too, which are well filled in spite of Ramadan, offer dishes similar to those of Istanbul or the Turkish restaurants in Cologne: no more pomegranates and walnuts, no compositions of herbs and spices, but shish kebab, chicken skewers, lamb chops and similar savouries, served with bread and yoghurt. Strange that the world gets more Western as we travel east.

A music dealer happily shows us his instruments. Interest in tradition has grown, he explains, especially among young people. His father could only play at weddings, but now there are proper concerts, there are academies and private music schools. It is true that the religious roots of maqam music dried up in the Soviet Union; the communists sank whole carloads of books in Arabic script in the Caspian Sea, dissolved all the Sufi orders, murdered or banished thousands of mystics under Stalin. There is no mysticism left in Azerbaijan. Today the young people go to Prague or Istanbul and return as Salafists – even though they are actually Shiites; they don't even notice the contradiction. Nevertheless, the music dealer is content with the new nation, which buys his lutes and drums.

Thirty-Eighth Day: Along the Azeri–Armenian Ceasefire Line

Towards noon we drive to another border, but we can't find it. No matter who we ask, no one knows which way to go to Armenia. And why should they? A border that is closed off creates a special kind of space: people live before it and probably beyond it as well, but no one has to visit it any more, no one has to cross it, it is not on anyone's way. Gradually the people themselves move away, so that only the old people are left, and no one who is interested in their recollections. When they are dead there is no one who might ask what has become of the neighbours, because no neighbours have ever lived on the other side. That's how it is at the exclusion zone around Chernobyl and at the wall that Israel uses to keep Palestine away, how it used to be at the German–German border. In Germany too there used to be areas on the map, *Zonenrandgebiete* they were called, areas along the boundary of the Soviet zone of occupation, that were far from any route and remote from all interest.

Now we are in Tartar, because it is closest place to the ceasefire line on the map. We can't get to the line, we are told, time after time. Okay, we say, but it must be possible to drive to the place beyond which we can't go: a checkpoint, a prohibiting sign, a roadblock – the roads must end somewhere. Theoretically, that's true but, practically, no one we ask has ever driven out of town westwards. At the town hall, an official leads me into a meeting room instead of receiving me at her desk and looks at me incredulously for a long time before she even understands what I am asking. Then she mutters something about permits – no, he doesn't want a permit, the interpreter interjects in vain, he wants to go to the farthest point you can go to *without* a permit – telephones her superior, leaves the meeting room and comes back in. We are welcome to submit an application, she says, but processing it will take ... Come on, I whisper to the interpreter, get out your phone again.

On Google Maps, which shows even the lanes between the fields, we find the village of Tap Qaragoyunlu, which lies right on the ceasefire line. It is only a centimetre away on the screen, but we have to drive a long way around to the north, because in between lies a dogleg of – depending on your point of view – Armenian or occupied territory. Not counting Chechnya, the conflict over Nagorno-Karabakh is the most severe legacy of the union of Soviet peoples. Fifty thousand dead, pogroms on both sides, far more than a million expelled from their homes, two peoples that isolate themselves completely from each other although just thirty years ago they were joined, indeed almost intertwined, by their most important transport routes and supply lines, by jointly inhabited territories, a mostly shared history, the same rulers, a joint rebellion against Russia as late as the early twentieth century, and family ties going back to time immemorial. And, unlike the Chechen wars, the war between Armenia and Azerbaijan still goes on: severe fighting last broke out in April 2016, with well over a hundred dead. Soon the dying will enter its fourth decade. All this for a territory as big as Somerset, with 140,000 inhabitants who have remained or moved there from Armenia.

Before we set out, we have a look around Tartar. In the streets, which are straight as a ruler, nothing is visible of the oil boom that is supposed to have made Azerbaijan rich overnight in the 1990s: little traffic, vacant businesses, and even the shops seem to have been passed over by the brave new consumer world. The river is dried up – because Armenia has cut off the water, we are told. In Thomas de Waal, whose *Black Garden* is the standard text on the war, I read that anyone who travels a few days through Azerbaijan ends up thinking Armenia is the aggressor, and anyone who travels through Armenia thinks it is Azerbaijan, because so many irrefutable arguments can be heard in either country as to who started the war and why Nagorno-Karabakh historically belongs to one country or the other. De Waal himself, having researched the matter so thoroughly that his book has been published, and praised, in both countries, does not adjudicate the question.

We are already on our way out of Tartar when I see something like an oil bonanza after all: at the petrol station, a man is loading his Lada with large plastic containers of petrol on the back seat, on the front passenger seat, in the boot and on the roof. Far from the cities, he explains to us, the petrol is mixed with water, so he gets a good price for his jerrycans. We hope he will turn out to be the first Azerbaijani we've seen who doesn't smoke in the car.

In the covered market of the neighbouring town of Barda, I discover where the women are while the men are drinking tea: they're at work. Simple farmers, I think, to judge by their clothes and their furrowed faces – only to learn that one used to be a teacher, another a forewoman in a factory, a third a housekeeper in a sanatorium. You earned a proper salary in those days! they sigh; in the Soviet Union they had health insurance too. All they have left is the little piece of land behind their houses, where they plant fruit trees or keep a goat, at most a cow. Some women have nothing more than a little kitchen or even just a worktop: there they make canned goods, spreads, jams or sauces, and with luck they can sell two or three jars in a day. Others have husbands who work as drivers or have full-time jobs, so they get by somehow. Do they vote? Only when someone asks them to. And the children? They move away, to Russia or Turkey. Not to Baku? No, the oil has driven the cost of living too high there.

When I try to buy apricots and cherries, a bag of nuts, some sheep cheese and a jar of jam, I have to call the market attendant over, the only man present, to get the women to accept my money; after all I am a guest, they say. I write so often about oppression, war, the bloody parts of history, on many days of this journey, as on others. Too seldom do I mention the friendliness in the world. Hospitality in particular is more natural the poorer the people are. Any explanation I might offer would probably come out too kitschy, socially romanticized or ethno-psychological. Or perhaps I have simply grown used to the embarrassment.

We spend the afternoon stuck at a road construction site. One or the other of the two flagmen, young workers in yellow safety vests who are supposed to be directing traffic, didn't pay attention, and they let cars enter the narrow single lane from both directions at once. Now the two columns of traffic are inseparably wedged together. While both of the boys disclaim all responsibility, the bulldozers cover every driver who gets out to complain or to suggest a solution to the chaos with a layer of dust.

It is early evening by the time we arrive in Tap Qaragoyunlu. It was probably a silly idea to drive north for two hours and then in an eastward curve back to the west just to see the front. Maybe the front doesn't even exist! Indeed, maybe the war takes place only on television, as in Hollywood satires. As it happens, even Tap Qaragoyunlu, which on Google Maps is only millimetres away from the ceasefire line, looks peaceful at first glance: chickens in the unpaved street, a tea house that consists only of a garden with a corrugated steel hut, clattering mopeds, simple bungalows with back yards, probably growing marketable produce. But at the end of the village we come to a wall 2 to 3 metres high running along the cross-street. Several women have spread out cloths under a tree in front of it, and children are swinging from the branches to shake the mulberries loose. The villagers are sitting in front of their houses and watching the day draw to a close. The scenery still looks relaxed but, when we stop the car on the other side of the street, a man shouts at us that we had better not get out there.

'Why not?' we ask.

'Because the wall doesn't shield you there.'

Now I realize that all the life is going on only on one side of the street. There are shots fired almost every day, the man says, and adds – dutifully or truthfully? – that it is always the Armenians who start the fighting. They have snipers posted over there too; just last week a resident was wounded.

'Can we see the Armenians from here?' I ask.

'Come with me,' says a woman with her hair pinned up, her eyelids conspicuously made up, and leads us into the courtyard where her husband is working on a tractor. A strange country, or a strange time: in the city, farm women sitting behind market tables are really teachers, factory workers or cleaning women; and here, in the village, the women are dressed up like city-dwellers. There is a place where a piece of concrete has broken out of the wall, and we can look through the hole. Perhaps a thousand, perhaps two thousand metres away I can see a defensive position, but I don't see the soldiers. Tap Qaragoyunlu has always been Azeri, the husband explains; the Armenians lived in the neighbouring village of Talesh, which is now in no man's land. Before the war, relations between the villages were normal, the woman adds; friendly, actually. Would she visit Talesh again when the wall is gone?

'You mean, if peace comes?' the woman asks.

'Yes, if Talesh were inhabited again.'

'No, I wouldn't go there any more. It would be inhabited by our enemies.'

The couple don't care to give any more information; they don't want their names written down, nor do they want to talk about what happened in Tap Qaragoyunlu during the war. We try to strike up a conversation with one person and another out in the village street, but without success. The people are not unfriendly, they just don't answer much. Only one man complains that in Shusha, the old capital of Nagorno-Karabakh, pigs are now kept in the great mosque – how is he supposed to live together again with such people, who expelled, massacred and insulted his people?

'Do you know that for certain about the mosque?' I ask.

'Yes, it was in all the newspapers; I saw the pictures of the pigs.'

Such pictures are easy to pose or to forge, I want to object, but the interpreter points out a man who is watching us from some distance while talking into his mobile phone. We should leave quickly, the interpreter adds, since I don't understand right away; this is a security zone, and apparently someone is being informed about our visit, if we haven't been observed the whole time.

'Will we be in trouble if we don't leave?'

'You won't, but I will.'

Because we wasted so much time in the town hall and in the road construction zone, and aren't making any progress at the front – either we can't find it, or when we do find it we don't learn much as foreigners – we decide to catch the night train in Ganja. But it's not just a matter of gaining a day. It's also the idea itself that fascinates me: the night train to Baku.

There is time for one last detour: we visit Göygöl, 20 kilometres south of Ganja, a city that was not destroyed by Germans, for a change, but built. Refugees from poverty were assigned by the tsar to cultivate this remote part of his huge empire in 1830. They named their settlement Helenendorf, planted grapes, and built front-gabled houses of such quality that they are jewels even today. As if the settlers had been nostalgic for America, every house has a wooden veranda worthy of Hollywood. No, the veranda was probably typically German at one time and was exported towards both sides of the compass. From Germany the church brings with it a gabled roof, tall windows, reddish tiles, a sharp spire, and even the clock in the bell tower. And, unlike the Swabian quarter in Tbilisi, Helenendorf still has vitality. In its tree-lined streets, which are unusually wide for a little Caucasian town, and its charming, likewise shady square, the inhabitants sit in front of their houses or stroll about in small groups. There is hardly any traffic; the evening is just warm enough to be outdoors in shirtsleeves and, if I didn't know that we are near the Caspian Sea, I might think I was walking through a northern German town – although one where the proportion of immigrants among the population is 100 per cent. As chance would have it, two cars are being washed in front of their owners' houses, as if these immigrants were fully integrated in German culture.

The very first person we talk to, a middle-aged gentleman with an unpretentious full beard and warm eyes, Imran Isaev by name, chauffeur by profession, tells us that his wife's grandfather's first wife was a German who was banished to Kazakhstan, along with her two children.

'Did her grandfather talk about his first wife?'

'No, not much. He only said that he loved the German woman and that the separation was not voluntary. And that his missed his first two children.'

'Did they ever have any contact again?'

'Not that I know of. Maybe that would have been a problem for his second wife. You see, my wife's granddad was one of those men who love women. If his first wife had turned up again ...'

'Then, in a way, you have benefited from the banishments?'

'Why do you say that?'

'Well, otherwise your wife's grandfather wouldn't have remarried. And then he wouldn't have had the granddaughter who became your wife.'

'If you look at it that way, yes. But Granddad never spoke ill of his German wife, never, and he always longed for his first two children as long as he lived. My wife sometimes wonders too how her half-cousins might look, whether they have blond hair, or black hair like ours. It would be moving for all of us if someday the descendants were to meet. After so many years.'

I ask two women sitting on the steps of their veranda whether I might have a look at their house; I come from Germany, I add, and before I can say another word the older of the two is already inviting me in. Gülbahar is her name, and she is especially proud of the stove, as big as a wardrobe, that dates from my compatriots: you can even roast shashlik in it, and if you let the fire go out the house is still cosy and warm for hours. She herself only came back from Russia with her husband and their two daughters in 2004, and when they were looking for a home she immediately fell in love with the German houses. The wood floors, the high ceilings, the solid walls, the veranda: 200 years old, but still in perfect shape. To say nothing of the cellar: practically a walk-in refrigerator. Sadly, her husband died shortly after they moved in; her older daughter is married, and now she lives with just her younger daughter in the house that has grown much too big for them. What will happen if Lamia moves out too? Hopefully, her son-in-law will also fall in love with the German house.

We're already back outside in the street when I ask whether she knows who owned the house before. No, she says; she knows only that an Armenian family lived here after the Germans were banished to Kazakhstan. How long?

'Until 1988; after that they couldn't.'

'And how was it when the Armenians moved away? They must have liked the house too.'

'I don't know; we lived in Moscow then.'

'We got on well with Armenians here,' interjects Imran Isaev, who waited for us on the pavement. There were often mixed marriages in Göygöl, he says: among the Armenians, women were allowed to marry outside their religion, and among the Azeris, men; in that way the traditions were complementary. And even at weddings that weren't mixed, the people sang first an Azeri song, then an Armenian one, or vice versa. Some Armenian women still live in Göygöl with their Azeri husbands, although they generally don't talk about it.

'And do you remember how it was when the Armenians were driven out of Göygöl?'

'It was just the times. The Azerbaijanis had to leave Armenia; the Armenians had to leave Azerbaijan. It all hit us like a flood, or an earthquake.'

'Wasn't there any hostility, then?'

'Apparently there was, but I personally never saw it. In retrospect, I think we should have said something.'

'To whom?'

'To the Armenians. I mean, they were good neighbours; there were no problems at all. We didn't even say good-bye. And now everyone says they don't remember.'

But everyone in Göygöl remembers Viktor, the last German, says Imran Isaev: he was such a unique, lovable old gentleman, thin as a whip and a head taller than the Azeris, a bachelor who lived with his mother until her death and always wore a Panama hat in summer. He must have spoken a little German; he was proud of his German roots but spoke better Russian and Azerbaijani. He died four or five years ago.

'Four or five years ago?' I ask, amazed that any Germans lived in Göygöl after the world war.

'Certainly Germans still lived here. When I was a child, we had at least fifteen families with blond hair.'

Mr Isaev doesn't know whether they escaped banishment or returned afterwards: he was too little. Many people in Göygöl want Viktor's house to be conserved as a museum, so it hasn't been sold yet. From the veranda, we shine a light from a smartphone into the front rooms, Viktor's bedroom and the living room, where a big bookcase and a piano are visible. It would be good for more than just Göygöl if this German reminder of Helenendorf were preserved.

Half an hour later, we are in Ganja, but we see practically nothing of the city. Although it is the second largest and historically the most important city in Azerbaijan, the capital of the short-lived Democratic Republic of 1918, Ganja lies in darkness. It is always ghostly, a feeling almost as if during a war, an uprising or some other state of emergency, to drive through a major city at night with no street lighting. There are lights on in the windows and some of the shops, so it can't be a power cut. An austerity measure? A technical fault? It doesn't look as though Ganja is a boom town. The street lanterns are lit only when we get to the city centre: the squares are as if on display, the broad streets, the modern railway station as big as an airport terminal, although there are only five trains a day, two of them at night. The night train to Baku! Our children don't even know what night trains are, and yet

205

the rolling hotels once represented every promise of the modern age: mobility, convenience, comfort. More than electricity or the internal combustion engine, and long before the first aeroplanes, they were like magic: go to sleep in one country and wake up in another. In Ganja the night train is not the return of a sensation, however. No one rushes when the venerable locomotive arrives from Tbilisi, probably in need of a night's rest itself. A conductor fetches us from the station hall and leads us at a leisurely pace to the platform. There he has time for a tea and a shmooze with his colleagues getting off the train. We are awaited at the sleeping car by a tired steward with holes in his uniform who takes our luggage. Later he brings us sheets and towels in our wood-panelled compartment. The carriage in which Stalin rode around the Soviet Union looked much like this one.

Thirty-Ninth Day: By Night Train to Baku

It is not just sleep that makes me rub my eyes when I look out of the window: desert! This far north? Yesterday morning, in the southern foothills of the Caucasus, all was green; there were forests, springs, rivers, mountains. In my inner atlas, the desert began in Iran and continued south to Arabia and Baluchistan; and yet Kurban Said, whose novel I finished reading during the night, develops whole theories about the difference between forest people and desert people, which is at the same time the difference between Georgia and Azerbaijan, between West and East, indeed the key difference between the civilizations:

> The Orient's dry intoxication comes from the desert, where hot wind and hot sand make men drunk, where the world is simple and without problems. The woods are full of questions. Only the desert does not ask, does not give, and does not promise anything. But the fire of the soul comes from the wood. The desert man – I can see him – has but one face, and knows but one truth …. The woodman has many faces. The fanatic comes from the desert, the creator from the woods.[38]

That reads like pure Orientalism: the image, or the self-image, of an East shaped by the exotic expectations of the West. Does that make it completely false? As I look now through the dust, the sand, the scratches, the smears and the fingerprints marked on the window of the train, I think it is the desert – nothing else – that has made the difference, over all the aeons, between

206

the Middle East and Europe. Obviously there are all kinds of climate zones between Morocco, Yemen, India; there are fertile plains, deep-green river deltas like that of the Nile, steppes, seacoasts and lakes, mountains with meadows, flower-strewn slopes and eternal snow, in northern Iran even primeval forests. But the desert, if my inner atlas is not wrong again, is never more than two, three days' march away, and that is what makes the East what it is: its rugs like gardens, its art like a picture of a world without objects, its ornament a formula for the infinite horizon, its hospitality a necessity – life insurance for the host. The desert could even explain some of the difficulties that democracy has in the Middle East, since it intensifies the contrast between town and country – no major oasis was ever safe from robbers, conquerors, vandals. The development of a bourgeois society was already limited by the topography to a few centres whose cohesion was constantly thwarted by migration from the countryside. Hence the desert society remains segregated by clans and tribes well into the cities. The mythic antagonism between nomads and settlers continues today in the slums that envelop the metropolitan centres like cocoons. All cities, and even the gardens – no, especially the gardens – are shaped, as refuges and paradisiacal anti-worlds, by the void all around them, something possible in Europe only in inaccessible glacial regions. It can't be a coincidence that the prophets of biblical stature, those moralists, misfits, poets, visionaries, fanatics to their contemporaries, came, if not from the desert itself, then from the edges of the desert, went into the desert, survived the desert, preached from the desert, after the paradigm of Isaiah 40, 'The voice of him that crieth in the wilderness ...', quoted often in the Bible itself. Nowhere else perhaps is a person so immediately subjected to a higher power, to be called upon in adversity, in supplication or in complaint, as there where human need grows with each day's march, every shift in the weather, every mirage. And nowhere does a person feel life more strongly to be Creation, and hence a gift, as where it is surrounded by the void. 'The desert is the gate to a mysterious and unfathomable world.'[39]

Dmitrij, who remembers the routine from the Soviet Union, tears me away from my reverie: we queue up in front of the toilet to brush our teeth, then we drink the tea made with tea bags in paper cups that the steward has brought into our compartment, while his look casts an accusation at each of us that he is the only person working in this carriage (although his snoring was audible from the other end of the passageway). Then it is time to fold our sheets and towels, fold the bunks upward to get at our suitcases, and roll into Baku. The social inequalities at the turn of the twentieth century, when oil was already making a few magnates extremely rich and the workers in their barracks were too exhausted in the evening to scrub the dirt out of their skin, can hardly have been greater than the contrast between the mournful concrete silos on the outskirts and the skyscrapers in the centre. Decades later than Tbilisi, but drunk on black gold, Baku came storming into the modern age: villas, concert halls, industrial plants, class struggles, and on the boulevards not just Asia any more, but half the world.

Kurban Said himself, with his fantastic biography, was almost a typical child of the city at that time: born Lev Abramovich Nussimbaum in 1905, his parents Jews, his father from Russia, his mother from Georgia, he received a German education, something not uncommon in the better circles. As Giwi Margwelaschwili fled Tbilisi, Lev fled before the Bolsheviks with his father and arrived in Berlin in 1921, after an odyssey through the entire Middle East and half of Europe. He read Islamic studies at university and soon converted, became a star author of *Literarische Welt* under the pseudonym Essad Bey and wrote flagrantly Orientalist best-sellers that were nonetheless more readable, and more engagingly written, than most books on Islam today. After the Nazis banned him from publishing, an Austrian aristocrat supplied him with another pseudonym, and he landed his last success as Kurban Said with *Ali and Nino* before dying in Italy in 1942 during his second flight from persecution. The novel later appeared both in Georgia and in Azerbaijan with no indication that it had been translated from the German. And, really, it is easy to understand why both countries claimed the author as their own: *Ali and Nino* is not just a colourful story masterfully told; for all its stereotypes, the novel captures as no other the atmosphere of the Caucasus in the early twentieth century, with its cosmopolitan cities and archaic villages, its wars and rebellions, dying traditions and beginning industrialization. In the process, it draws characters in brief strokes that I have found again a century later. I am thinking of Bishop Isaiah, cheerfully telling of the martyrs, of the driver at the border contemptuously pressing his prosthetic leg on the clutch pedal, and also of the Chechen Magomet, who prefers to remain a free peasant on his own land, no matter how barren: so many wars and so few winners; such little countries and such rich cultures, the days arduous and the feasts all the longer.

'Arslan Agha, what on earth will become of you?' Ali cries to his drunken friend, a proper ne'er-do-well.

'I'll become a king.'

'You will what?'

'I want to become a king of a beautiful country with lots of cavalry.'

'Anything else?'

'Die.'

'What for?'

'When I'm conquering my kingdom.'[40]

As I take my first steps through Baku in June 2017, however, I encounter neither the original desert people nor the newly arrived forest people – the two population groups distinguished by Kurban Said – but members of a whole different species, if not life forms from another planet: they are wearing orange or light brown overalls of wrinkled synthetics or shorts and polo shirts that are either turquoise or sunny yellow, but in either case printed solid with advertising, and all of them have red baseball caps on their heads, plugs in their ears and a plastic cord around their necks identifying them as members of the same crew: this weekend, Formula 1 racing comes to town. Not only has the race route been built up for days with high barriers, concrete blocks and plastic sheeting, so that no non-paying gaze may fall on the gladiators' chariots; many other streets are also closed to traffic too, so that an eerie or, after all, perhaps a desert-like silence reigns.

I try to get to the Caspian Sea, which according to the map is just one street away. After zig-zagging for an hour, I finally find the underpass through an underground station that leads me under the home straight. On the wide embankment, the occupying forces have pitched their camp: media centre, VIP lounge, child care, Red Crescent; separate areas for the drivers, their crews and the mechanics; in addition to pizza and pasta, hot dogs and hamburgers, a tent with local cuisine. A whole armada of golf carts awaits to provide transport; some are already driving back and forth; and in many corners the young teams are being briefed by their instructors – service, security, transport, statistics, race supervision, ticketing, first aid. The only old people I can see anywhere are pointlessly sweeping the asphalt. It is not too late to walk along the promenade, which is almost reminiscent of Florida, with its lawns, fountains and palm trees; from the first practice laps on, only paying spectators will be admitted to this area. Ninety euros is the minimum just to see a Ferrari or a Silver Arrow; the qualifying session and the actual race are priced accordingly. Tickets are still available in all categories; interest seems to be limited, with the average wage at 400 euros a month. There's no reason that should bother the extraterrestrials: the guaranteed fee for their landing is supposed to be 60 million dollars; in addition, all costs must be borne by the host planet, which demonstrates to the universe its progressiveness by hosting other gladiator battles as well, such as the Eurovision Song Contest, art biennials and the first European Games.

A cylindrical metal building lying in the middle of the boulevard could easily pass for a spaceship. In fact, it turns out to be a carpet museum, built in the shape of a rolled-up carpet. Because it has no straight walls inside, the traditional textile art hangs on a slant in the futuristic space. No matter; the historic carpets have such beauty and perfect craftsmanship, and such modernism in their abstraction, that my reactionary streak comes through: what has happened to our artistic sense since the early twentieth century? All the carpets knotted later – since the story of Ali and Nino, which would then be not the prelude but the coda of a culture – show a striking tendency towards kitsch, towards imitation of Western art, and towards a representationalism which is already dated today. The same seems to be even more true of architecture as I look out of the rolled carpet at the city: while the silhouettes of the Middle Eastern and the early European city are coherent, fit together harmoniously for all their difference, the 'Flame Towers', built as Baku's new landmark, look monstrous: three skyscrapers modelled after oil lamp flames and lit up at night like fires. On the other hand, the blazing glass towers, Baku's answer to Dubai and Abu Dhabi, do go with the orange overalls and the red baseball caps. 'Land of Fire' is also the slogan of the tourism board, because, besides oil, it is also able to list a Zoroastrian temple among the tourist attractions. There are volcanoes too, although no glowing lava; only brown mud wells up from them.

I go back through the underpass into the city, which looks as lustrous as ever: the villas, theatres, academies and squares are all decked out, as are the narrow alleys of the old Middle Eastern city centre. On a closer look, however, I notice that the nineteenth-century buildings are often brand-new, with luxurious furnishings to fit: instead of going to the effort of reconstruction, or taking on the registry of historic landmarks, some owners have replaced their old buildings with imitations. So this is how sterile Berlin's historic centre will look once the palace of the Prussian kings, and next no doubt Schinkel's Academy of Architecture, have been reconstructed. After that, they could start replacing the old buildings that the war failed to destroy. Baku is leading the way.

There is a 'zone of fortune' in every Azerbaijani city, says Khadija Ismayilova. In the other cities, development is concentrated in a few streets, shopping centres and parks, just enough so that the president will see his country flourishing when he visits. In Baku, however, where the wealth, the business world and the tourism are concentrated, the 'zone of fortune' is especially long: it runs from the airport, 13 kilometres north of the city, to the flagpole in the south, the second tallest in the world, where the flag of Azerbaijan waves 162 metres up. It was supposed to be the world's tallest but, eight months after it was erected, the Tajik flagpole in Dushanbe topped it. It is hard to become a self-confident society, says Khadija, when the state is founded on a sham victory: the war with Armenia, which is supposed to have been a triumph, although 20 per cent of the country has been lost.

Khadija is an investigative journalist and has exposed numerous cases of corruption, as well as – long before the Panama Papers – the assets of the Aliyev family, who are now second-generation rulers; she has been threatened, slandered and arrested, and in 2014 was sentenced to seven and a half years in prison. After international organizations and celebrities spoke out in her support, up to and including Amal Clooney, she was released last year on probation. In Azerbaijan, dozens of colleagues joined together in a 'Khadija Project' to carry on her investigations.

'The government has noticed that, when they arrest a critic, two new ones pop up,' says Khadija, 'plus the damage to its image internationally – the price for my imprisonment was more than they wanted to pay.'

I meet Khadija in a street café, with good visibility, in front of a fountain in one of the many beautiful squares in the pedestrian zone. Everyone should see whom she meets with, she says. Her lawyer is with us too. Khadija is not allowed to work since her release from prison; she is not allowed to leave the country; she has to report to the police regularly; she is under surveillance and her Internet access is disrupted; her siblings too lost their jobs; one sister has moved to Ankara for that reason – and yet she is more than just unbowed; she is more determined than ever, a woman so young, barely forty, that her biographical sketch makes you wonder whether her first exposés appeared in her school newspaper. Almost with amusement, Khadija recounts how they tried to silence her before her conviction using sex tapes. She was accused of having pressured a lover to the point that he tried to kill himself, and then a video appeared on the Internet that was shot in her bedroom. 'An unmarried woman having sex – they thought that would finish me in our conservative society.'

It didn't work that way: Khadija deduced from the perspective of the video where in her bedroom the camera must have been mounted. She broke open the wall at that spot and found a cavity with a loose cable in it. She called the telephone company and reported an ordinary technical fault. When she showed the technician the cable, he told her straight away he had installed it himself. He was shocked to learn of the video and the libel; like every Azerbaijani, he had to deal with the corruption day in and day out; he swore he had no idea that the cable was to be used to connect a surveillance camera. He had been surprised himself that the company had instructed him to do the job off the clock so that it wouldn't appear in the records.

'Where did you get the idea of calling the phone company?' I ask.

'I'm an investigative journalist,' answers Khadija. 'I knew that each district is covered by only three technicians, so I just tried my luck.'

The telephone technician testified, as did the lover, who had neither felt pressured by Khadija nor attempted suicide, and when a number of Friday preachers and even the Islamist party took Khadija's part, she had succeeded in exposing another scandal. Secret police officers were fired, and a short time later a minister resigned. Khadija meanwhile was soon convicted of something else: a tax evasion charge works in any dictatorship.

I ask why the Friday preachers and the Islamists supported her.

She wondered that herself, Khadija replies. She is an admitted atheist and has criticized the clergy many times. 'I think there were two reasons: first, they recognized – I'm sorry, this will sound immodest – my courage. And, second, they were dissatisfied with the government themselves and they knew this wasn't only happening to me. My case followed a pattern; there had been the same kind of slander and also a series of sex tapes anonymously posted on the Internet. I was just the first person with whom the threats didn't work. I said, put whatever you want on the Internet; I am not backing down. And the result has been that the practice has stopped. And that earns me some recognition from those who might also have been targeted, even if their opinions are otherwise quite different from mine.'

'Is that a step forward?'

'Yes, of course. In the old days, a woman would have been stoned for something like that.'

Nevertheless, Khadija does not see any new democratic wind blowing in her country. Too many people are too dependent on the state to rebel, she says. An example, one of many: in Baku alone, some 500,000 apartments are not registered with the land office as a result of the chaotic circumstances of the 1989 privatization wave and the unregulated building during the oil boom. Multiply by four, and that makes 2 million inhabitants who have to keep their mouths shut if they don't want to lose their homes. Or take the many teachers who intentionally neglect their work so that the students have to take private lessons from them: that works only as long as the head and the school board look the other way. Conversely, the teachers look the other way in the election committees, to which they are the preferred appointees. 'It's not simply a dictatorship. It's a system of complicity.'

Khadija breaks off. I have already noticed her laywer, who is still younger than she is, typing agitatedly on her phone. Now the lawyer explains to me that she hasn't heard from her husband, who is also involved in human rights work, in three hours. He visited one client, then missed his next appointment, which is not at all his habit. Three hours – there's sure to be a harmless reason. Khadija promises to text me as soon as the lawyer has news of her husband.

In the evening I attend an opening. The gallery occupies three storeys of a palace in the old city centre and is filled with elegant, edgy people, many of them beautiful, most of them young. Some Westerners too feel right at home here. They know each other; they clink glasses of white wine or Campari on the terrace. Only the exhibits, I find, are terribly banal: video art that no one looks at for longer than two minutes, and sticker slogans brushed onto finely finished walls. Perhaps I just lack the sense for new things, I think, as I compare the contemporary art with the Georgian Mass or with the carpets that I found inspiring this morning in the museum; perhaps I am just too attuned to deterioration. Perhaps writers in general are always the ones standing on the rear platform of the last train car. While everyone else is looking forward to arriving, we write down what the train is leaving behind – nostalgia, then, is an occupational hazard. Other people are qualified to observe the new: the researchers, the business executives, the conquerors, inventors and leaders, and in general the younger people, not the old, who prefer the past not least so that they can die consoled. But from the rear platform even I can see this much: the new is not what's on display in the chic gallery in Baku's old city centre.

'The best exhibit is still the view from the terrace,' says Sabina Shikhlinskaya, a video artist herself, rolling her eyes. She offers to show me an exhibition of current Kazakh art tomorrow that is actually worthwhile. Yes, why not Kazakhstan too? I think, although I am mostly curious what Sabina has to say. She belongs to the first generation of video artists, and her work deals with the recent history of her country; she is a warm-hearted, spirited lady who is so successful internationally that she can pick and choose whom she works with in Azerbaijan. Without identifying as an activist, she keeps her distance from the state, which has discovered art as a way to present itself to the world. 'I can't advertise for the "Land of Fire" while young people are immolating themselves in desperation.'

Happily, Khadija's lawyer's husband has turned up unscathed.

Fortieth Day: Baku

When I set out to go running on the promenade I can't find the underpass any more. I'm not the only jogger looking for a path between the barricades. The Grand Prix seems to have brought a lot of jocks to Baku who want to start their day with a morning run by the seashore. Now we are running up and down in our neon colours past the camouflage-green soldiers who have started guarding the racecourse today. There are thousands of them, posted at intervals of 10 or at most 15 metres along the barriers, and they are rather bored because behind them not even engine noises can be heard, and in front of them there is only us. Counting the relief that there must be for the watch, the Grand Prix is being guarded by a whole army. And if the enemy were to invade the country this weekend? What would be worth more: the racing cars, or villages like Tap Qaragoyunlu?

On the way to Yarat, Baku's new centre for contemporary art, Sabina points out to me the modern façades that are covering up the Soviet archi-tecture in central places. In the state's commemorative policy, she says, the history of modern Azerbaijan begins neither with the democracy of 1918 nor with the Socialist Soviet Republic in 1920, nor with the second independence in 1991, but in 1993 with the election of Heydar Aliyev as president. After having served for decades as first secretary of the Central Committee of the Communist Party of Azerbaijan, he was initially sidelined after the end of the Soviet Union, but then, in the chaos of the founding of a new state and the war with Armenia, he finally came out on top as the father of independent Azerbaijan. Fourteen years after his death, his large portrait hangs everywhere in the country, as if he were still in office. His son Ilham, who since 2003 has won the elections with Soviet-style percentages, is significantly less photogenic, with his chubby cheeks and double chin. Almost all the Soviet war monuments have been demolished, and no new monuments have been built to commemorate the 1920 war against the Red Army, but the memorial of the war against Armenia is so vast that one might think it honours every dead soldier individually: several broad avenues lined with graves, born 1973, 1970, 1969, 1974, and all died 1992, as far as I walk.

And yet one of Heydar Aliyev's most important achievements was that he ended at least the daily dying with the ceasefire line of 1994, thus granting his country a kind of normality: an ordinary, everyday autocracy.

From the hill where the memorial stands we can see the island Nargin, which, under the tsars and in the Soviet Union, was a prison, like Alcatraz or the Château d'If. When the Democratic Republic collapsed, 2,000 Azerbaijani and Turkish soldiers fled to the island but soon wondered whether it wouldn't have been better to die in the hail of bullets. Since the collapse of the Soviet Union in its turn, the island has been vacant. Sabina knows its history so well because she secretly lived there for a week in 2004 for an art project. Now her photography is historic, because three years ago all the buildings were demolished and the remains of the prison removed in order to make the island into an amusement park. But then the Disneyland wasn't built after all: Turkey was outraged because 'our' soldiers lay buried there who died for 'your' independence. Thus Nargin is still deserted, and now not even ruins remain.

There are countless places like that in Azerbaijan, says Sabina: places where remembrance is systematically prevented. Where else? We drive out of the city in a southerly curve and come past the battlefield, colloquially called the 'Lake of Blood', Qanli Göl, where the Red Army defeated the national forces in 1920, a sloping, arid plain between two ranges of hills. It was undeveloped land in the Soviet Union and is now a commercial zone with warehouses and duty-free goods.

We have hardly left the battlefield behind us – indicated by no sign – when Sabina points to the wall along the motorway. A noise barrier, I think at first, but actually the wall is too low for that. Furthermore, I discern through the gap between two sections of the wall that there are no houses behind it, but the beginning of the desert. There are walls like that all over the country, says Sabina, and she turns off the motorway to drive through a narrow street enclosed between corrugated steel barriers left and right. Ordinarily, such walls hide the poor neighbourhoods and informal settlements, along the motorway to the airport, for example; there the logic is understandable. But many roadside walls, Sabina continues, hide industrial zones or cemeteries – what is so embarrassing about them? And others hide nothing at all, that is, only the desert, or a mountain – are they an end in themselves, then? That could be, considering many of the walls are decorated almost artistically, with marble slabs or ornamental bands that you can see through. That is indeed strange, I agree, when we have merged back onto the motorway:

driving on a multi-lane highway with walls along both sides – but nothing at all behind the walls. 'Perhaps they already know what they're going to build behind the walls,' I suggest, 'and they have put them up in advance.'

'My theory is rather that we're not supposed to look at the horizon.'

At the seaside once more, we see in the distance the tremendous platforms that have been built in recent years, but on shore the little oil pumps from the early industrial era, when Azerbaijan exported half of the world's oil consumption – you can imagine the struggles, coercions, interventions to which the world powers subjected the little country. The oil pumps, which really belong in a museum, seem to be still in use; in any case the head with the thick tube at its point, looking like the beak of a prehistoric bird, still rises and sinks towards the ground. Somewhere around here, in the oil fields south of Baku, is where the huts of the workmen must have stood who were unimpressed with the liberal ideas of the independence movement, and who put their hopes in communism to make a more just world one day. Baku was not only a bastion of Bolshevism, one where a young leader named Joseph Stalin ingeniously agitated; Baku was also, with more than 100,000 Iranian workers, a centre and later a refuge of Iran's communist movement, which thought itself close to seizing power many times. When Reza Shah tightened the repression, the leadership of the communist Tudeh party went into exile in the Soviet Union, most of them in Azerbaijan. There Stalin completed his neighbouring dictator's work by having almost all the Iranian cadres executed. The Great Terror is thus one of the darkest chapters of Iranian communism as well, which has barely had a word to say about the murder and banishment of its own leaders. But the Tudeh party was definitively annihilated, exterminated, in the early 1980s by Ayatollah Khomeini, whose rage was on a par with the Stalinist frenzy. Shortly before, during the Islamic Revolution in which they too marched, the Iranian communists had once more thought themselves close to taking power. The oil pumps really look like birds, glistening black birds, dripping with grease, on thin legs and with long necks, unstintingly filling their beaks from the bounty buried in the earth.

The World Is Not Enough, the 1999 James Bond film, was shot in this apocalyptic setting, and soon Baku's traffic-free promenade is supposed to be extended out to here, replete with palm trees, beaches and cafés, so that Baku can pretend to be Miami for a few kilometres more.

We drive along the coast back towards the city until we come to the former navy base that has been transformed into a cultural complex. What with the nightclub that occupies one of the big halls, Sabina counts it among the best that the new Baku has to offer. Even if her records aren't played there, but rather electronic music, she realizes how important the club has become to many young Azerbaijanis. I could say much the same thing about the exhibition through which the director of Yarat leads me, the Belgian Björn Geldhof: even if videos and installations don't hit my aesthetic nerve, I can still perceive how earnest the exhibited works are. Almost all of them deal with the recent history of Kazakhstan, which, like that of most former Soviet republics, seems to be subject to numerous taboos. Alaksandr Ugay has stood a big wooden boat on its end and filled it with drawers like an old office cabinet: when you open the drawers, you find letters, photos and other documents of the Koreans who were banished to Kazakhstan by Stalin in 1938. Nurahmet Nurbol has painted three faces with closed eyes or empty eye sockets, in an aesthetic similar to that of Christian icons, on a canvas 3 by 3.5 metres hung in a corner, creating an oppressive image of fear, repression, speechlessness. Baxit Bubinakova imitates heroic poses of Soviet historical painting with her naked, emaciated-looking body in her little flat. No matter how you find the exhibition, says the very enthusiastic museum director Björn Geldhof, it definitely provokes questions, discussion, even if in disagreement, and that is exactly what it is intended to do. It has reached 7,000 visitors a month, in addition to 2,000 schoolchildren, and young, alert staff are always on hand to answer questions or to ask some themselves. In the neighbouring districts, which are suffering from gentrification, the staff go round to communicate to the inhabitants that Yarat is their centre, a place for encounters and neighbourly communication, with nothing insular about it, in spite of its aesthetic aspirations. Although I know little about museum education, I notice at once that there is something contagious about Geldhof's enthusiasm.

'Could you imagine an exhibition,' I ask, 'that confronts Azerbaijani history in a similar way to the Kazakh show?'

'Probably not in all its aspects. But, on the other hand, much of what is in this exhibition is applicable to Azerbaijan.'

'Do you mean, then, that an exhibition could not address the war in Nagorno-Karabakh? Or the pogroms against Armenians?'

'There are boundaries within which we can act as a museum, certainly. I could say I don't accept that: then I'd go back and work in Europe again, or in some other part of the world. But you can also contribute to gradually moving those boundaries. Which option does more for freedom? We're critical, but we're not partisans. That's not our role.'

We are already back in the car when Sabina says that so much money is blown on megaprojects: stadiums for sports events that are held only once and never again, a concert hall just for a stupid pop-song contest, and the annual remodelling of central Baku into a racetrack for a race hardly a single Azerbaijani gets to see. But Yarat, and the whole cultural centre south of the flagpole, are some of the places in Baku that will remain from this time after the current rulers have become history.

'Are there more?'

'Yes,' says Sabina emphatically, and drives us to a monument that the world will retain from this regime: a gleaming white building that seems to be put together out of individual sheets of paper, rising in curves to a towering height, while at the same time the concrete layers merge into the ground, so that, going around to look at it, you are practically walking on the walls. It is the Heydar Aliyev Cultural Centre, designed by the Iraqi-British architect Zaha Hadid in 2012, a breathtakingly elegant palace that even a reactionary like me would count among the great buildings of architectural history. In the middle of Baku, maybe it looks like an unidentified flying object. But unlike the rolled-up carpet, and definitely unlike the Grand Prix, Zaha Hadid's edifice comes from a beautiful planet.

The interior of the cultural centre is all the more disillusioning. Not only does Zaha Hadid seem to have run out of inspiration, so that the halls look quite run-of-the-mill – high ceilings and wide stairs, the coffee lounge with a semicircular bar, and everything white, as museum architecture just is today. But, most of all, the exhibitions themselves are grotesquely unimaginative. We walk past blinking display cases and technically sophisticated projections that reinterpret Azerbaijan's sorrowful past into a triumphal parade. The exhibition omits the defeat of the first independent republic as well as the Great Purge; in exchange, the 1992 massacre by the Armenian army in Khojaly in which, by various accounts, 200 to 600 Azerbaijanis died is declared a genocide in a separate 'memorial complex', and Heydar Aliyev is celebrated as the telos of the nation's history. His memorabilia can be seen on several floors, from his evening suit to his desk to his official car and the silly gifts that presidents receive from state visitors. In another exhibition, the landmarks of Baku are reproduced as scale models, and the museum shop offers scarves and iPhone cases that were designed by the presidential daughter personally. The young woman is not likely to become another Zaha Hadid.

'All that can be replaced,' says Sabina Shikhlinskaya, thinking of a future

218

when the museum will exhibit art. 'The building is there; that's the main thing.'

I have a dinner appointment with the writer Akram Aylisli, whose 2012 novel *Stone Dreams* broke the taboo that no museum dares touch: he told the story of the Armenians who, in the late 1980s, after the territorial and party organs of Nagorno-Karabakh resolved to join Armenia, were expelled from or beaten to death in Azerbaijan. When the hero of the novel, the actor Sadai Sadygly, tries to stop a deadly beating, he is beaten senseless himself. In the intensive care unit, Sadai dreams of his childhood in Aylis, Akram Aylisli's own home village, where Christians and Muslims once lived together in friendship. After the novel was published in Moscow, President Aliyev revoked the author's state medals of honour and cancelled his honorary pension. Politicians called for him to be prosecuted; the television rained insults on him; he was prohibited from travelling and expelled from the writers' union; his books were not only banned but removed from all the libraries and publicly burnt; his plays were banned from the theatres. Aylisli's wife and son also lost their jobs. And yet the novel's most provocative scene is neither the pogrom itself nor the recollection of the genocide after 1915: 'If a single candle were lit for every Armenian killed, the radiance of those candles would be brighter than the light of the moon.' It is a kind of conversion: Sadai dreams, in the intensive care unit, that he understands the prayer of old Aikanush, who was one of the few Armenians in the village to survive the invasion of the Turkish soldiers – and, unconsciously, he makes the sign of the cross.

> Never again did Sadai Sadygly see the earth so lit up with unimaginably bright light, but he never stopped believing that in Aylis there exists some other light that belongs only to Aylis. Sadai was deeply convinced that it really must be so – you see, in both length and breadth Upper Aylis probably encompassed no more than three or four miles. And if the people who at some time raised twelve churches on that tiny scrap of earth and created a heavenly corner near each of them had not left just a little of their light after themselves, then for what reason does a person need God?[41]

Aylisli, who has paid such a high price for his literature, is a generous man in his personal life too. Instead of giving me his address, he insisted on picking me up in the city centre himself, where we would get nothing decent

219

to eat, only some newfangled stuff. And when I am three quarters of an hour late getting to the corner where we have agreed to meet, because I have got lost time after time in the Grand Prix barricades, Aylisli is not a bit put out: a small gentleman with narrow, deep, dark eyes and his white hair parted on the side, pleated trousers and a short-sleeved shirt who speaks every sentence with a smile. What German writer would have such patience with a foreign reporter who made him wait three quarters of an hour in the summer heat? I certainly wouldn't.

We get into one of the Baku taxis that, for whatever reason, look like London cabs, leave the city centre by side streets and drive past concrete prefabs that have not been given new façades. And even now, as he tells how he went from being the country's most respected poet to a pariah overnight, Akram Aylisli doesn't stop smiling. What hit him the hardest was the reaction of his colleagues and the writers' union, which proclaimed him an 'enemy of the nation' and took down his photo in the association's building. 'The writers, the association – that was my family.' Only a few younger authors sided with him, he says, and in general the young people are much more courageous than his generation. The protests abroad probably saved him from worse reprisals.

'Did you expect those reactions when you published the novel?'

'I knew I was in for quite a bit, of course, but that it would go so far – no, I couldn't have imagined it. To be honest, I thought my celebrity would protect me; my medal, and my age. They might do that to a younger author, but not to me. And for that reason, I thought, I have to lead.' Aylisli looks out the window, as if reflecting whether he nonetheless did the right thing. 'Well,' he sighs, more in disbelief than outrage, 'when all is said and done, for a writer it is a greater honour than any medal if you get treated the way they treated a Pasternak.'

As we are getting out of the taxi, the driver addresses Akram Aylisli by name.

'You know him?' I ask the driver.

'Everyone knows Mr Aylisli,' the driver replies with ardent pride, whereupon Aylisli's smile becomes a joyful laugh.

In the restaurant – an outdoor dining space offering an unexpected idyll between Soviet residential towers – the writer invites the waiters with a sweeping gesture to fill the table with all the specialities on hand. He briefly considers my suggestion that we order a domestic wine and then decides we should drink well rather than patriotically. The food in Baku, with sweet or slightly tart rice dishes, is almost identical with Iranian cuisine. No, it's the other way round, the many Azerbaijanis in Iran would say: the Persians adopted our dishes.

I ask Akram Aylisli whether the Aylis he describes in his novel is the real one or one that exists only in his imagination.

'It's the real village, stone for stone. It's the Aylis I saw as a child, the Aylis my mother told me about.'

'Did she tell you about the December day in 1919 when Turkish soldiers drowned the Armenians of Aylis in a "lake of blood"?' The expression is from the novel itself.

'Yes, of course; everyone remembered that. She never spoke unkindly about the Armenians; on the contrary, my mother missed the Armenians.'

'Would you describe the events from 1915 on as a "genocide"?'

'Yes, I think I would. Nazim Hikmet used the word; so did Orhan Pamuk. The wisest people in Turkey called it genocide. Only in Azerbaijan, no one. And that was an existing problem in 1988: no Armenian had forgotten what happened between 1915 and 1919. That explains their behaviour: they didn't want history to repeat itself.'

Aylisli reminds me that the Armenian population in the Nakhchivan Autonomous Republic, which lies southwest of Armenia but belongs to Azerbaijan, was almost completely forgotten for decades. 'The Azeris had absolutely no awareness of what the Armenians had suffered. And so they didn't understand the reaction. Yes, the Armenians started the conflict by claiming Nagorno-Karabakh. But the truth also includes the fact that our people attacked them first, not the other way round.'

'And did you see that with your own eyes too?'

'I can't write about something I haven't experienced personally. Everything that's written in the book I saw with my own eyes. Everyone saw it.'

'How do you explain the outbreak of hatred?'

'That was like a collective madness, a psychosis. Nobody understood what they were doing. Everybody suddenly ran in the same direction, like a herd blindly following its lead animal. It was during the Gorbachev years; we mustn't forget that; everything had got more expensive; only people no longer had any value. Anyone could buy them, and a few were enough to unleash violence. I don't understand why they revere Gorbachev in Germany. For me, every day between 1988 and 1990 was a personal tragedy. Every single day.'

'A personal tragedy? In what way? Were you attacked too?'

'So many of my friends had to leave. My friendships with Armenians are worth more to me than independence.'

'You said everyone saw what happened. What happens to a society when it sees terrible things, when some even commit terrible things – and no one talks about it?'

'It becomes lethargic. It becomes apathetic. Like my generation. Like my colleagues.' He didn't mean to accuse or judge his society, Aylis continues; he wanted to open up an opportunity to find words. That's why the hero of the book is not an Armenian, but an Azerbaijani who behaves humanely. Anyone can identify with him. And that's why the novel also addresses the suffering of all the Azerbaijanis who were driven out of Armenia and Nagorno-Karabakh.

Yes, that is another great scene in *Stone Dreams*: Sadai himself, who has embraced even the victims' language and their religion, doesn't want to hear about it, but his wife reminds him that hatred and violence exist on both sides, that the Armenians 'don't care about us because, according to their thinking, we're also Turks – if the Turks slaughtered your people, go ahead, fight it out with them, why are we Azerbaijanis even involved? In what way are those Armenian screamers better than our homegrown ones? Why don't you think about that, my dear? Since all this began, you haven't been yourself.'

Certainty Sadai is traumatized, and his view of the events is subjective. He accuses only one side: his own. But isn't that literature's job, to criticize one's own, not the other, especially if the other has already been declared an enemy, a threat, a barbarian? And, at the same time, literature creates a space in which a variety of voices are heard, including the voice of Sadai's wife, who is equally right to contradict him.

'Yes, there are many truths,' says Akram Aylisli when our table has long been covered with sweets – but the smile has disappeared from his face after all. 'Everyone saw something different. And, at the same time, everyone knows what happened. Everyone knows it. I didn't want to die without having finally said it out loud.'

'Do you think the border with Armenia will ever be opened again?'

'Yes, but I can't give you a date. First we have to change ourselves. As long as we have a state in which 10 per cent of the population are thieves ruling over the rest, nothing will change at all.'

'Is it different in Armenia?'

'No, there it's exactly the same,' says Aylisli, laughing again. 'We're very similar that way.'

'Will you live to see the opening of the border?'

'I hope so,' the writer answers, and pauses while his face becomes serious again. 'I think I would have died long ago if I didn't believe that.'

'To your health, then,' I say, raising the glass of Georgian wine, which as a good German I insisted on over the French, to optimize at least the carbon footprint, if not the domestic sales.

At that Akram Aylisli smiles again: 'My books were burnt, my wife and my son lost their jobs, I was threatened and reviled, my colleagues and friends turned away from me. But do I look like a sad person?'

'No, you certainly don't. Although it amazes me. How do you do it?'

'I've already won: the book is published; no one can reverse that. It's even been translated into many languages. In the end, the attacks on the author were probably good for the book. I won: what happened has finally been said. That's all I was after.'

And I think Akram Aylisli is right to speak every – almost every – sentence with a smile. And also that his *Stone Dreams* is one of the books that people will still read in a hundred years, when no one in the world remembers the president.

Forty-First Day: Baku and Qobustan

In front of the Museum of Literature, the poet Nizami gazes grimly over the barriers at the racetrack. Although he wrote his epic poems in Persian, he came into the world in Ganja in 1141 and hence is revered in Azerbaijan as a national poet. A number of the nineteenth- and early twentieth-century authors who are immortalized in busts and pictures on the outside of the museum are also associated with Persian literature. Nevertheless, Azerbaijan has every reason to celebrate them: not only did they live in the territory of the present-day country, but they created the basis for the nation in the first place. Like Germany and Belarus, Azerbaijan too originated as a very literary idea. The poets, novelists and dramatists who wanted to lead their people into the modern era considered themselves nationalists, yes, and yet the word was meant in a different sense than the one that has become usual in the course of two world wars; even the word 'nation' had a different sound, an emancipatory one, before it mutated into something ethnic, meaning an exclusive community of one race, language and religion. Mirza Fathali Akhundov, for example, for whom the National Library is named today, not only invented the Latin alphabet for Turkic languages and founded the Azeri prose genre in the mid-nineteenth century with his novels. At the same time he was a leading proponent of Persian national romanticism and is honoured even today by secular forces in Iran as Mirza Akhundzadeh, an advocate of enlightenment and a critic of religion. His admiration of European philosophy and literature was typical of Middle Eastern nationalists in the nineteenth century. The intellectuals in Baku, who read Russian, spoke Turkish and wrote Persian, devoured everything that was written or translated in St Petersburg or Moscow. Nationalism, then, did not mean a commitment to a single nation, putting one's own nation above others, or allying only with members of one's own ethnic, language or religious group; once it was an affirmation of a humanity that drew on many cultures and opposed all forms of oppression, whether colonial or indigenous.

The ideas of the modern age reached Iran not only from Paris and Istanbul but also from Baku, Ganja and Tbilisi, places where Persian culture had put down deep roots, yet out of reach of the Shah's censorship. Thus it was not the capital Tehran, but Tabriz, which is in the Azerbaijani part of Iran, that became the hub of the Enlightenment in Iran and, in 1906, the centre of the Constitutional Revolution. Baku's Persian newspapers, exhibited in the display cases, advocate freedom, secularization and women's rights with a radicalism that is almost incredible today and was rare even in Europe at the time. The magazine *Molla Nasreddin*, named after the wise fool of folk literature, published the Islamic world's first satires and cartoons criticizing religion. Another visitor notices that I am reading the Persian script in the display case, and he tells me the editor of *Molla Nasreddin*, Mirza Jalil, fled to Iran with his wife to escape the Russians. But there he was so displeased with the backwardness of the country that he refused to speak Persian. As soon as he crossed the border, he was shocked to see that the women were heavily veiled and walked behind the men. To make matters worse, it was Ramadan, and the whole country was fasting. Mirza Jalil returned to Baku and founded *Molla Nasreddin* to poke fun at the mullahs – a century before Salman Rushdie and *Charlie Hebdo*.

Are the people still aware of how closely intertwined Azerbaijan and Iran once were? No, says the knowledgeable visitor, a professor of history at the university; today there is little communication between the two countries; even the films of the great Iranian cinema are only rarely shown in Baku. Azerbaijanis know more about Nizami's time or about European auteur cinema than about contemporary Iranian culture.

That is not only because of the Soviet Union, which Russified Azerbaijan more thoroughly than the tsars' hundred years of imperial rule; there is also a current political reason: although both countries are Shiite, and although Azeris are the second largest ethnic group in Iran after Persians, the Islamic Republic took the side of Christian Armenia from the very beginning of the Nagorno-Karabakh conflict. The fact that Iran recognized the genocide against the Armenians long before the German Bundestag did, and officially commemorates it on 24 April with marches by the Armenian communities, not only expresses respect for Iran's own Armenian minority, which has always been held in esteem; it is at the same time *realpolitik*, a slight against Azerbaijan, which Iran accuses of promoting separatism among the Iranian Azeris (just as Azerbaijan in turn accuses Iran of exporting its political Islam). In the story by Kurban Said, alias Lev Abramovich Nussimbaum, alias Essad Bey, on the other hand, the same Ali who loves the Georgian Nino fights against Russian colonial rule in Azerbaijan and becomes part of the rebel movement in Iran against the reactionary regime of the Qajars: 'Persia is like the outstretched hand of an old beggar. I want it to be the clenched fist of a young man.' Both movements fail, the movement for Azerbaijan independence and the parliamentary democracy in Iran: while Baku was subsumed into the Soviet Union – after the brief interlude of the Democratic Republic, which had a secular constitution and introduced women's suffrage before many European countries – the Persian Cossack officer Reza Pahlavi transformed Iran's constitutional monarchy back into a dictatorship in 1925. 'Father, Asia is dead, our friends are dead and we are exiles,' Ali laments shortly before he dies on the battlefield and the love story ends tragically, as a novel should. 'You are a brave man, Ali Khan,' his father consoles him.

But what is bravery? Europeans are brave too. You and all the men who fought with you – you are not Asiatics any more. I do not hate Europe. I am indifferent to it. You hate it, because there is something European in you. You went to a Russian school, you have learnt Latin, you have a European wife. How can you still be an Asiatic? If you had won, you yourself would have introduced Europe in Baku ....[42]

Not far from the statue of Nizami, in the marionette theatre that lies on the other side – the inside – of the old city wall, his verse epic *Layla and Majnun* is being rehearsed; in 1908 Üzeyir Hacıbəyov composed the first Azeri opera ever around the Arabian legend of a woman like the night, *'layla'*, who belongs to an enemy tribe, and a prince who is driven mad, *'majnūn'*, with love. The instrumental passages weave the Middle Eastern intervals and string instruments into the European orchestral form with surprising coherence, and between them lie the vocal improvisations on Nizami's verses, which are heartrending to anyone who loves maqam music. Naturally the opera conserves the gestures of the nineteenth century, which often seem false or even ridiculous in 'faithful' performances today, but because the marionettes, lifting a hand to their wooden chests or falling to their rattling knees before their beloved, are as fragile as they are beautiful – in other words, the estrangement from reality (the puppeteers are visible on stage throughout) allows the feelings to remain as great as those of young love and of Persian mysticism; they do not have to be toned down to the level of TV drama, as often happens in modern productions, to avoid pathos. In the dark, empty stalls of the Baku Marionette Theatre, I imagine a Wagner festival in which Tristan and Isolde, young and uncompromising, are played by marionettes instead of aging singers in business suits, ashamed to be dying a lover's death behind their desks.

Still enchanted by the singing and the puppets, we take a taxi to go farther back in time than we have been on this journey so far: the petroglyphs of Qobustan, some 30 kilometres south of Baku, are up to 15,000 years old. On the motorway our view is obstructed by only a few stretches of wall, so we can see the sea to the left, the desert to the right; oil platforms to the left, tall gas flares to the right. Very few countries, I think, can offer such a panorama of nature and industry. The rock paintings, which a workman discovered by chance in the late 1930s, just when archaeologists throughout the Soviet Union were being shot or disappearing in the Gulag, are in a craggy range that rises above the coast. Until then, there had been practically no archaeology in Azerbaijan, says the director of the museum, Fikrat Abdullayev, explaining why the state tolerated the excavations at that time; the commissars in Baku probably didn't know that archaeology was counter-revolutionary. After all, the newspapers didn't say who the black crows were hauling away.

After Abdullayev has guided me to the dancers, mothers, hunters, mourners and worshippers painted on the huge rocks, I ask him whether it changes a person's sense of time to walk every day among these 8,000-, 10,000-, or even 15,000-year-old documents. Nothing is left of the people who danced, bore their children, buried their parents, made their living and worshipped their gods – no settlements, no languages, no history; their names are not known, nor even the names of their people: only the few drawings they left behind, and these so inconspicuous that a hiker would walk right by them if there were no signs pointing them out.

'Yes, of course,' Abdullayev replies, 'you get the feeling that everything has just always existed.'

'But so much has happened in the twentieth century, especially in this part of the world: revolutions, wars, regime changes, expulsions, and whatever else.'

'That's what I mean: from here, all that looks like just a brief moment. And I'm sure all of it has happened before, revolutions, wars, regime changes, expulsions.'

'That would mean the world is not getting better or worse.'

'Well, for 15,000 years people have believed that things used to be better than they are now.'

'But at the turn of the twentieth century, people saw salvation in the future.'

'As I said, a century is just a tiny moment; it doesn't even count.'

'And what do you believe?'

'What do you mean?'

'Do you believe things used to be better?'

'I am old now; I used to be young. Therefore I too believe things used to be better. It's as simple as that.'

In the evening, I take a last walk through Baku's new quarter, barely a hundred years old. By now I know where the racecourse runs, and how to get from one place to another, and where the Grand Prix doesn't intrude. And, yes, the squares and boulevards do win me over after all, although they are still too dressed up for my sentimental nature. After the anarchic capitalism of Tbilisi, where something seems to be shooting up out of the ground on every corner, I would almost be ready to recognize the advantages of authoritarian urban planning, if only it devoted as much attention to preserving historic monuments as it does to memorializing the president's father. Certainly, at prices of 3 euros for a beer and 8 euros for a hookah, I suspect it is not the common people who are sitting in the cafés and restaurants – but was that any different when Baku entered the modern age? And the tables on the count-less terraces are all occupied; the promenades are full every evening. Where the tourism is concentrated, at least, the city looks almost as cosmopolitan as it was in its heyday: Iranians, Russians, Turks, Israelis, Arabs, Western Europeans, and this week the Grand Prix visitors, who constitute a national-ity all their own: well-heeled enough to fly around the Formula 1 circuit, but the very opposite of glamorous; both the men and the women, even those of advanced age, in sleeveless shirts and Bermuda shorts and sporting tattoos. The locals don't care, especially the young people, who can afford only an ice cream perhaps, or who get their drinks from the supermarket and listen to the guitar that one of them is playing on a park bench; whatever they may think about this time and its rulers, they are visibly enjoying the splendour that is once again Baku, or at least the city centre, the promenade along the Caspian Sea and the road to the airport, where it doesn't run between walls.

Forty-Second Day: Leaving Baku by Air

I am visiting another synagogue before my departure. Apart from everything the artist Sabina Shikhlinskaya finds to criticize in Azerbaijan, she finds Jewish life is more than just tolerated: it is safe and relaxed. And her own parents, like many Jews, fled helter-skelter from Baku when nationalism flared up in the late 1980s, but that was less on account of their religion, Sabina says – her father's religion to be exact; her mother is Muslim – than because of their Russian language, which was suddenly dangerous to speak. Sabina decided to stay, and doesn't regret it. She likes her country, and she likes today's Baku very much; that's why she feels it is important to show me more than just the shadow hanging over Azerbaijan's history. After having heard Yiddish as a living language in Odessa, I wrote, with a certain pathos, that there is perhaps no better indicator than Jewish life to judge whether Europe will succeed. But perhaps it is not as simple as that, I concede now in Azerbaijan, where the citizens have no freedom, but the Jews nonetheless have a safe home. The government not only supported the building of the new synagogue but also maintains excellent relations with Israel while fighting the Islamists with an iron fist. The synagogue has already had a visit from Benjamin Netanyahu, as a large photo in the vestibule attests. The Azeri and Israeli flags are hoisted harmoniously side by side – in what other Islamic country would you find that?

'All Jews here have two passports,' says Milikh Yevdayev cheerfully, who is both the rabbi and the chairman of the Community of Mountain Jews in Baku, 'all of them.'

Unlike the Ashkenazi community, whom Yevdayev seems to look down upon somewhat, the Mountain Jews value their traditions, their language and their home villages; for that reason even those who now live in Israel return regularly. Because the Mountain Jews have always been rather prosperous, most of them can afford to do so. Then Yevdayev proudly guides me through all the rooms, showing me even the kitchen, where Muslim and Jewish staff are chatting as they wash up the breakfast dishes. Although I have seen few headscarves in Azerbaijan – fewer than on a single afternoon in my neighbourhood of Eigelstein in Cologne – during interfaith washing-up, everyone's hair is covered.

'And what language are you speaking?' I ask naively when Yevdayev introduces me to a few men who are drinking tea while the women work (apparently the division of gender roles is the same as among the Muslims).

The Mountain Jews immigrated from Iran around the seventeenth century, Yevdayev explains, and so they speak a Persian dialect which is not mixed with Arabic as Modern Persian is.

'Persian?'

'Yes, Persian, but the Jewish Persian, very different from what is spoken in Iran today.'

The rabbi and chairman of the community speaks to me in his, our, language, and I understand no more than I did of the Yiddish in Odessa.

'A stick has two ends,' says the first-person narrator Ali about his external transformations since he began to love Nino, and perhaps Lev Abramovich Nussimbaum alias Essad Bey alias Kurban Said was also writing about himself, the son of a Russian and a Georgian who received a German upbringing in Azerbaijan, the Jew converted to Islam who remained bound to the Jewish world all his life, the Muslim maligned by his brothers in faith as a 'Jewish falsifier of history' although he honoured and lived Islam until death, the Orientalist who rose in Berlin to become the star author of the *Literarische Welt*, the European hounded to his death as a Jew in 1942 and buried as a Muslim in Positano, Italy, mourned by John Steinbeck, Gerhart Hauptmann and most of the population of the village, who had concealed the stateless exile's Jewish origins from the authorities in a conspiracy worthy of *The Good Soldier Švejk* – 'A stick has two ends: an upper and a lower one. Turn the stick upside down, and the upper end is down, while the lower end is now up. But the stick itself has not changed at all. Thus it is with me.'[43]

Forty-Third Day: Yerevan

Not only are border crossings an exceptional matter in this little patch of land between the Black Sea and the Caspian, in which so many states, rebellious territories and autonomous republics lie. In addition, you can't always choose the order in which you cross the borders. From Georgia it would seem logical to go first to Armenia and Nagorno-Karabakh if you're on your way to Isfahan, but then you would be turned away from Azerbaijan, which considers Nagorno-Karabakh an occupied territory. So from Tbilisi you have to go first eastwards to Baku before you visit Armenia further west, and then continue your route eastwards from there to Iran via Nagorno-Karabakh. Because the border between Azerbaijan and Armenia is closed, to go back westwards you must either swing north through Georgia, where I have already been, or swing south through Iran, where I don't want to go until last. That is why I took a plane from Baku, and eventually – there are no direct flights any more – landed in Yerevan on an early July morning in 2017. Having been conquered by Romans, Parthians, Byzantines, Sassanids, Arabs, Seljuks, Mongols, Tatars, Mamluks, Safavids, Turks and Russians, the Armenians don't let foreigners tell them what to do, as the Austrians found out during our stop in Vienna: the Austrian Air flight attendants had their hands full persuading the Armenian matrons, who were still walking up and down the aisles as the plane taxied onto the runway, to sit down and buckle up. One had to tell her relatives in the last row something that couldn't wait until we'd reached cruising altitude, another had to find room in the overhead bin for her fourth piece of hand luggage, and a third wanted a closer look at the commotion the first two were causing. '*Elle est débile*' was the friendliest of the comments directed at the head of the cabin crew.

Hayk Demoyan probably thought it was not such a good idea on my part, having barely arrived, to make the drive, the pilgrimage almost, to the Armenian genocide memorial, which stands like a temple atop a hill outside the city, where the view of Mount Ararat must remain a promise today because of the haze. The diaspora tends to define Armenia by the genocide, says the director of the genocide museum that was built into the hilltop in 1995. In Armenia itself, however, there are other paradigms for national identity: independence, of course; Nagorno-Karabakh, Christianity, and Armenia's ancient written culture; and also Stalinism, which claimed 30,000 Armenian victims, and the Second World War, with 300,000 fallen, one half of the 600,000 Armenian soldiers. For the diaspora, every day is a 24th of April 1915, because the fact that they live far away from the original settlement areas dates back to the beginning of the genocide, when 250 representatives of the Armenian community of Istanbul were arrested within hours – writers, politicians, composers, clerics, officers; the Armenians in Armenia, on the other hand, lived in their nation on the 23rd and the 25th of

April as well, and every other day. Moreover, the diaspora can afford eternal hostilities, but Armenia itself must get along with its neighbours, sooner or later.

I ask Demoyan about differences between Armenian and Israeli memorial politics. The Armenians, he replies, had lived in this country continuously for thousands of years before 1915 and founded their first independent republic as early as 1918 – in response not to the genocide but to the revolution in Moscow and the withdrawal of the tsarist troops.

'And what did that mean for your work in creating the exhibition?'

'Naturally we studied all the comparable exhibitions, and not least Yad Vashem. One aspect emerged as central to us: not just to recall the loss but to safeguard what has survived.'

As we leave the office, I think back to the museum of Jewish history in Warsaw, recalling Michael Leiserowitz's words: that it would be important for the Israeli youth groups touring Eastern Europe to seek out not just the Holocaust but the Jewish life that existed before it. The exhibition here surprises me by its objectivity, which does away with Soviet-style pomp, yet without Americanizing the commemorative culture as the Schindler museum in Cracow and the tower of silence in the Jewish Museum in Berlin do: neither propaganda nor empathy is at work here, but information. There are moments nonetheless when the visitor is overcome with feelings, but those very feelings are aroused by nothing but the documented reality, blurred though it must be at such a historical distance: black-and-white photographs on which often only outlines are discernible of the crucified, hanged, starved and humiliated victims or their dumbfounded children. Only our imagination is able to see the unimaginable, that is, the absolute evil that would take away a person's individuality, and thus their soul – our imagination opens up a gateway through which the blurred, yellowed, sometimes wrinkled old photographs, often enlarged and backlit for the exhibition, penetrate deep into our spirits.

A person who has been to Yad Vashem, where Israel remembers the Holocaust, cannot help making comparisons. A crucial difference in Yerevan: the exhibition's purpose is not solely national self-reassurance; to a greater degree, it invites us to accept the crime as a fact. Not only does it list the evidence, item by item – population figures, the numbers of churches, the locations of Armenian villages, quotations, documents, photographs, personal accounts, eyewitness statements – as if it was aimed at eliminating doubts which an Armenian doesn't have in the first place, but it also resolutely avoids positioning nations in confrontation against each other by including the voices of the 'righteous' who saved Armenians from death, as well as those of the Turks and other Muslims who showed sympathy for the Armenians or accused the perpetrators. Hayk Demoyan points out that the museum has more Turkish visitors than the bad political relations might lead one to think: not just tourists, but also a regular stream of journalists, academics, writers. The pointedly nuanced tone of the exhibition indicates that they are more than welcome. In Jerusalem, on the other hand, during my visit in 2002 – I am told the entrance area has since been redesigned – I found the Grand Mufti of Jerusalem, who had sympathized with the Nazis, prominently placed at the beginning of the tour. By placing the Arab cleric's complicity with Adolf Hitler at the entrance to its official memorial Yad Vashem, the state indicated the succession in which it sees its Arab citizens and the present-day conflict with the Islamic world. The comparison high-lights the Yerevan genocide museum's efforts to enter into dialogue about the historical events rather than presenting them as a reason why dialogue seems impossible.

Like the differences, the similarities are also conspicuous: just as Yad Vashem emphasizes the uprising in the Warsaw Ghetto to show the Jews not merely as victims, the museum in Yerevan too emphasizes the heroic struggle, for the history of suffering alone is not enough, neither in Israel nor in Armenia, to evoke a willingness to defend the young state against new threats. Franz Werfel, who erected the greatest monument to the Armenian resistance, is given special importance in the museum – and in Armenia in general, where schools and squares are named after him and he has posthu-mously been given citizenship. In a display case lies the 1934 first edition of Werfel's *The Forty Days of Musa Dagh*, which was passed from hand to hand nine years later – another connection to Yad Vashem – in the Warsaw Ghetto as the inhabitants braced themselves for the uprising, which was similarly hopeless: 'Whenever the Turks began to attack, his men aimed with what only could be called bored certitude, as though they were equally at home in life or death, and it really made no difference which of the two they inhabited in the immediate future.'[44] And just as Werfel places the genocide against the Armenians in the context of nationalistic ideologies, instead of Orientalizing it as an archaic conflict of ethnic groups or religions, so too the exhibition traces the forces emerging from the downfall of Ottoman imperialism, the zealous modernism of the young Turks and Europe's interest-driven politics. The 24th of April 1915 stands not for a holy war but, to a greater degree than the assassination in Sarajevo on 28 June 1914, for the beginning of the twentieth century as an age of genocides. 'Who today remembers the annihilation of the Armenians?' the exhibition asks, quoting a sentence spoken by Adolf Hitler in 1939, which confirms Franz Werfel in his early conception of the Armenians' fate as a handwriting on the wall for the Jews. 'Germany, luckily, has few, or no, internal enemies,' says the mastermind of the genocide, the minister of war Enver Pasha, in his conversation with the German pastor Johannes Lepsius, which the novel reproduces after the historical record. 'But let's suppose that, in other circumstances, she found herself with traitors in her midst – Alsace-Lorrainers, shall we say, or Poles, or Social Democrats, or Jews – and in far greater numbers than at present. Would you, Herr Lepsius, not endorse any and every means of freeing your country, which is fighting for its life against a whole world of enemies without, from those within?'[45]

It is impossible to read the sentences, spoken in German by Enver Pasha in 1915, without recognizing the crude rationality that also guided the German extermination of the Jews. Franz Werfel himself recognized in the Ottoman politician a type he had first encountered in 1914, when Franz Kafka read to him the unpublished story *In the Penal Colony*. The officer supervising the torture machine doesn't seem so cruel or brutal; on the contrary, he is exceptionally civilized in his manners and his words. Something else stands out about him: he knows no morality in the traditional sense of values to be upheld regardless of their pragmatic usefulness; his argumentation is mercilessly functional. 'If only the man were malicious,' Werfel writes about Enver Pasha, 'if he were Satan! But he had no malice, he was not Satan; this quietly implacable mass murderer made you like him the way a child would.' To Werfel, both the Turkish minister of war and Kafka's officer are examples of a 'breathtaking species' which is 'beyond guilt and all its qualms,' having 'overcome all sentimentality'. In the genocidal ideology of Enver Pasha there can be no place in the body politic, because of a regrettable but 'necessary *raison d'état*', for a 'plague germ' such as the Armenians.[46] Their expulsion and destruction was not an end in itself, nor was it born of sheer blood lust; it was the means of a 'modern' demographic policy intended to create a homogeneous Turkish nation-state. And, just as Enver looked to the nation-states that had been created by ethnic cleansing during the Balkan wars, Adolf Hitler, on trial before the Munich People's Court in 1924, cited as a model for a German 'awakening' not only Mussolini but also Enver Pasha, who, he said, had managed to purge the Gomorrah of Constantinople.

When I crossed the Caucasus, I thought for a moment I had left behind me the history that Germany wrote in the twentieth century. But now I realize that the Yerevan museum is also a German memorial, and not just because of the silent acquiescence in the genocide by the Kaiser's government in Berlin and the active participation of many German officers who served in key positions in the Ottoman Army. This museum also documents the demographic politics and the bureaucratically managed mass murder that preceded the Holocaust. At the same time, it is moving, especially for a German who has just been in Georgia and Azerbaijan, to see that, in each of the three Transcaucasian countries, a novel of the modern nation, so to speak, was written by a writer whose language was German and whose origins were Jewish. Werfel's emphasis on the modernism of genocide, of racism, that the Young Turks had learned in Europe, their 'fanaticism of religious hatred' and their attitude of 'frantic Westernization, boundless reverence of Western progress in all its forms,' could also be a bridge that allows Turkish readers to conceive *The Forty Days of Musa Dagh* as their own novel – and not to go on dismissing the murder and expulsion of the Armenians as the continuation of a Western strategy of humiliation and subordination that had already been used against the Ottoman Empire. Such a bridge would be all the more inviting to the social milieu from which the ruling AKP has arisen. For it seems almost romanticized today when we read what Werfel wrote about 'the simple Turk, peasant or town proletarian', and also about the traditional scholars of Islam, especially the Sufis, who found their country infected with ethnic hatred, the 'most dangerous pestilence' of modern times. 'It is the worst of doctrines, to bid us seek our own faults in our neighbours,' laments Agha Rifaat Bereket, prophesying the downfall not only of the Armenians, but also of the Turkish people, if victory should fall to 'that absurd pack of imitators at Istanbul' and 'the imitators of those imitators,' the 'apes in frock coats and dinner jackets,' traitors and atheists 'who would annihilate God's universe itself, merely in order to get money and power.'[47]

The imams too fulminated against the Armenians; they were beaten, murdered and robbed by their neighbours in the villages, as the exhibition shows and the novel describes, and describes quite drastically. Nonetheless, Werfel reminds the reader time after time that it was mainly the European-oriented, laicist middle class that 'stood to a man behind Enver Pasha's Armenian policy'.

Often, as he rode about his district, a surprised müdir would pull up in the village street where he had just read out his decree of banishment, to watch Turks and Armenians mingle their tears. He would marvel as, before an Armenian house, its Turkish neighbours stood and wailed, calling after its dazed and tearless inhabitants, who without looking back were leaving the doors of their old home, 'May God pity you!' And more, loading them with provisions for the road, with costly presents, a goat, or even a mule. The amazed müdir might even have to see these Turks accompany their wretched neighbours for several leagues. He might even behold his own compatriots casting themselves down before his feet, to beseech him, 'Let them stay with us. They haven't the true faith, but they are good. They are our brothers. Let them stay with us.'[48]

That was written by the Jew Franz Werfel, to whom the genocide museum in Yerevan accords a special place among all the righteous; it was written in Vienna while Adolf Hitler was seizing power in Germany; and yet it could be an appeal for reconciliation today.

We walk a hundred yards through a corridor whose walls are engraved with the names of the exterminated villages. Then we step out onto the area where the genocide memorial was built in 1965 – a sensation at the time in the Soviet Union, which had never before permitted its republics any commemoration of their own. 'Under Stalin, speaking publicly about the genocide would have been a ticket to Siberia,' says Hayk Demoyan, noting that about 100,000 refugees, barely arrived from western Armenia, were banished to Siberia as Turkish spies, and their memories went with them. To preserve the evidence for future generations, Demoyan continues, many Armenians built metal boxes full of documents into the walls of their houses. It is a strange situation for a historian if a house in which people are living has to be torn down to get at their history. After Khrushchev's removal from power, the right to remembrance could no longer be suppressed: on 24 April 1965, hundreds of thousands of Armenians demonstrated in front of the opera house for an official memorial. Before that, nationalist demonstrations in Georgia had been brutally put down. Why not in Armenia? The Armenians had managed to preserve their language, religion and culture comparatively well, Demoyan says, whether because the Soviet Union presented itself to the outside world as a home for all Armenians or because, conversely, communism had always had many supporters among Armenians. Perhaps it also counted for something that the Armenian Soviet Socialist

Republic was by far the most homogeneous in the union, with 96 per cent ethnic Armenians, so that Moscow did not fear tensions between different groups. One way or the other, the demonstrators were surprised themselves when first the Church, then the Armenian Communist Party adopted their demand, and soon the approval arrived from Moscow to build a memorial which would be called *Medz Yeghern*, the 'Great Crime' or 'Great Atrocity'. Striking while the iron was hot, the authorities in Yerevan announced an architecture competition the same week.

Photos show how volunteers worked on the building site – and how they stood in amazement before the finished monument. The sculptural ensemble itself, designed by the young architect Arthur Tarkhanyan, was sensational for the Soviet Union at that time in its abstraction and its stillness: twelve pylons arranged in a circle, arcing inwards over an eternal flame; beside them an obelisk jutting 44 metres skywards, symbolizing the self-assertion of the Armenians and also, with its splintered point, their division between homeland and diaspora. Not a single word, not one picture, not even an ornament or decoration; only straight lines and the grey, uniform stone – but soft background music too: a choir, rather martial after all, singing of war, resistance and 'our blood'. The design is the sort of avant-garde that is not made obsolete by the passing decades, and every year on 24 April hundreds of thousands make the pilgrimage to the monument. If the air is clear, they can see their national mountain, Ararat, which lies beyond the closed Turkish border. Then they go home, and on 25 April life continues, which the director of the genocide museum finds equally important.

A generation lies between the two largest genocides of the twentieth century, and also between those who are able to bear witness. In a suburb of Yerevan I experience what will happen in Israel, in Germany, in Eastern Europe when memory dies out: it doesn't happen suddenly; it takes a long time until the very last have died, and it doesn't necessarily end with their death but can gradually fade into vagueness even before that. Hovhannes Balabanyan was two years old when he was driven into the desert with his mother. Today he is 104 and one of the last survivors of the genocide, possibly the very last. Not only was he too young to remember the march himself – his memory goes back only to Hama in Syria, to working with his mother in a carpet factory to pay the rent, to worrying about his father, who had gone to Musa Dagh with half of the male inhabitants of their village to fight, to the loss of their home that dominated the conversations of the adults, and to the blackness that seemed to envelop – everything to come.

Today, the images dart back and forth in Balabanyan's head, and, listening to him, it is often hard to tell whether he is recounting something he experienced himself, something he heard as a child, or something he read later.

'He wants to know what you saw with your own eyes, Pappi,' his granddaughter shouts, since she is better able to make herself understood than the interpreter accompanying me, but Balabanyan is already back on Musa Dagh, where he can't really have fought himself at the age of two. It is as if the whole history of his people has become indivisibly his own. There is the port of Alexandretta and a French ship; there are calls, shouts; help, we are in danger; help, we are Armenians, we are Christians; there are younger people diving into the sea to get to the ship, and now boats being launched to pick up the older ones; there are mothers with children – of whom perhaps he was one after all? No, he was in Hama, he remembers then, where his mother worked in the carpet factory.

'Was your father evacuated on the *Jeanne d'Arc* too?' I ask, to indicate that I'm aware of the French Navy's action from the literature.

'I'm coming to that,' Hovhannes Balabanyan answers his granddaughter. 'I want to tell him the whole story.' But he is 104 years old, and so he gets bogged down in details, because each one is equally important, and after a while it seems to be all the same whether he experienced them, heard them told, or read them. 'Only oppressed and persecuted peoples are such good pain conductors,' writes Franz Werfel. 'What has befallen one has been done to all.'[49]

'What is his earliest memory?' I ask his granddaughter to ask him, hoping to find out something that is not already written in *The Forty Days of Musa Dagh*, but first – 'I'm coming to that' – Balabanyan has to tell about a pact that the Armenians made with the French.

'Pappi, that's all from books,' his granddaughter now gently chastises him; 'The man is here because you're one of the last survivors. He wants to hear your story.'

'Yes, I'm coming to that,' says Balabanyan undaunted, and continues with the French. I do learn this much, however – although more from his granddaughter than from Balabanyan himself, who is still holding out on Musa Dagh – that he returned, after four years in Hama, with his mother and the other refugees, to their old village of Bithias, which Franz Werfel also mentions. The Turks had renamed the village, Balabanyan interjects during his granddaughter's account; other than that, everything was normal.

'Including coexistence with the Turks?' I ask, surprised.

'Yes, yes, everything was normal,' Hovhannes Balabanyan declares, and returns to Alexandretta, now called Iskenderun, where his father seems to have been rescued by the French. Then in 1939 the Turkish Army came again, he says, suddenly jumping to his own biography, and the Armenian inhabitants of the village had to flee to Hama again. In 1939? There's nothing in my books about this second expulsion, and Balabanyan gives no further explanation, in spite of my questions. From Syria they moved on to Lebanon, lived in tents in the Beqaa Valley for six years before the Armenians from Bithias were finally scattered to the four winds. Balabanyan was a teacher by this time, although he had been to school only for four years himself, if his previous recollection is not mistaken, and moved to Armenia in 1949, where they were assigned a flat together with three other families. That's how it was in the Soviet Union, which broke all its other promises too.

'What do you think about Turkey today?' I ask, and to everyone's surprise I get a direct answer.

'Turkey will never recognize the genocide. Never.'

'And what do you think about the Turks?'

'They are not human,' says Balabanyan, with still greater determination, and adds in Turkish: 'The Turks are born to kill, to burn, to steal and to destroy.'

'And if a Turk was sitting in front of you now?'

Hovhannes Balabanyan looks at me carefully, and seems anything but absent-minded: not on Musa Dagh, not in Alexandretta; only on his granddaughter's sofa, where he usually naps.

'If a Turk were sitting in front of me now? I would not show him my hatred. I would receive him politely and speak Turkish with him.'

We drive back to the city, where Tigran Mansurian is expecting me in a private booth at a very old-fashioned café: an older gentleman with rectangular metal-rimmed glasses and a narrow face in which his snow-white hair falls every time he turns his head. He is a composer, the most famous one in his country, whose name appears on the programmes of philharmonic orchestras and New Music festivals. And yet his quartets, sonatas, concertos and choruses sound quite different from what a Western audience expects of New Music: emotional, often tragic, no less, yet without being melodramatic, as a simple melody or a children's song can sound tragic, but with the full, powerful sound of a symphony orchestra pulling out all the stops. Is it harmonic, perhaps? Yes, often it is harmonic too, without exposing melodies over long passages; more in the way a carpet is harmonic that is composed of individual ornamental elements, possibly even representational miniatures, yet abstract in its overall effect.

With his CDs still resonating in my mind, I want to ask whether the musical heritage of the Middle East provides a natural link to New Music inasmuch as it does not set the tones of a scale in a hierarchy. But I have hardly sat down when talk turns to the *aghet* again, the 'catastrophe', as the genocide is called in Armenia, simply because I mentioned the word 'heritage'. Mansurian's mother was just a few months old when Turkish soldiers locked his grandfather, along with the other men of her village of Marash, in a shed and set it on fire. His grandmother and aunt died on the march to Syria. Only his mother survived, just a few months old, and grew up in an American orphanage in Beirut. So much for the heritage of an Armenian of his generation.

Did his mother talk about it? I ask, meaning her childhood in the orphanage. Yes, of course, Mansurian replies; he grew up with her stories of the death march. But she was just a baby herself, I say, surprised. Mansurian's uncle also survived; he was a few years older than his mother and later emigrated to Brazil; he remembered everything as if it had happened just yesterday. Mansurian was born in Beirut and moved to Armenia with his parents in 1947, when he was eight. What is his strongest memory of Beirut? I ask.

'The sea!' replies Mansurian, who was prohibited from leaving the Soviet Union. 'Sadly, we don't have the sea in Armenia.'

And why did his parents leave Beirut? They felt safe, Mansurian explains; the city was under French administration and very cosmopolitan. Yes, everything was good, including their standard of living. Only his father wanted to live in a country of his own, and he believed the promises of the Soviet Union – completely false promises, Mansurian adds, to work in a joke every Armenian knows: an Armenian who wants to resettle in the Soviet Republic arranges with his friends and relatives in the diaspora that he will send them a photo after his arrival; if the photo shows him standing, that means everything is fine and his friends and relatives should follow him; if he is sitting down, they should stay away. When his friends and relatives open the envelope and see the photo, it shows the man lying on the ground.

'Nevertheless, I am grateful that things happened as they did,' says Mansurian amid the sad smiles.

'In spite of all the suffering?'

'If we acknowledge that life is a succession of losses, then coming to Armenia as a child refugee was the best thing that could have happened to me under the circumstances. It was the best loss. I would never have had the foundations I had as a composer if I had grown up in a different country.'

The foundations Mansurian means are more than sixteen hundred years old. Yes, on reading the dates of Armenian composers, you think you've overlooked a '1' until you check and see that this one and that one actually died in the fifth century.

'And they really existed?' I ask. 'I mean, are those verified names and compositions that were written down that long ago and have been preserved since then?'

'Of course they existed,' replies Mansurian, amused, and begins to sing in his throaty voice so loud that the guests in the next room must hear the melody written down by Mesrop Mashtots in the fifth century. And in the chant, which sounds monotonous and at the same time mournful in its constantly repeated rising and falling, I believe I do recognize structures my ear remembers from Mansurian's CDs. The tonal system that the European avant-garde dismantled, he patiently continues, never existed in the East; that made his point of departure a completely different one.

'Is that true of all Middle Eastern music?' I ask.

'Yes, but if an Arab composer stops thinking in his musical system, he also stops making Arabic music. It may still sound good, just not Arabic. For an Armenian composer, it's different.'

'How so?'

'Because Armenian music appropriated the West much earlier and assimilated it. Long before my time. That is, what characterizes Armenian music is precisely that it works with both systems.'

Mansurian, who initially gave the impression of a quiet, contemplative man, now grows more and more animated, gesticulating with his hands and singing more examples.

'You have to take your own tradition seriously,' he cries; 'it contains everything that is specifically yours, everything you have to contribute to music today. The richness of the world lies in diversity, not in monotony. And this diversity doesn't come from ourselves; it comes from the past.'

'And can music transcend the boundaries of its own tradition?'

'Yes, absolutely,' Mansurian believes, and points to the performance of his works in Istanbul. 'We have so many borders in our part of the world, so many new borders that didn't use to exist. But just as you don't have to

240

be French to understand Debussy, it's not necessary to be an Armenian for Armenian music, a Turk for Turkish music, an Iranian for Iranian music. Music doesn't even need to be translated, as literature does. That is its utopian element.'

I look at Mansurian, whose hair has fallen in his face again, and imagine that his great requiem about the genocide, which was first performed in Berlin in 2011, will someday be understood in Istanbul. If we admit that life consists of losses, then the best thing under the circumstances, the best loss, in Mansurian's words, would be for something bonding to arise out of the catastrophe.

In the evening, I finally get to stroll through Yerevan, which is not beautiful in the sense of picturesque, but a pleasant city nevertheless. When Armenia became a republic in 1918 and a Soviet Socialist Republic in 1922, there was a country, and there was a population, but there was no capital, strictly speaking, because the urban settlements of the Armenians lay on the other side of the border, the Turkish side. Yerevan meanwhile was just another Middle Eastern barracks town of 14,000 inhabitants on the long border with Iran, a town that the tsar had won from the shah in 1828, and it was populated for the most part with Muslims and had far more mosques than churches. The Soviet Union tore down the clay houses, caravanserais and bazaars to build a model city, twenty years before Minsk, but one that had nothing yet of Stalinist bombast and neo-historicism. But buildings are not so important on a summer evening, and all the Yerevantsi seem to be outdoors anyway – the city centre is like one big café terrace with every table occupied. The squares and the promenades too are full of people, young, old, children – and among the tourists there are many who look like Armenians but speak broad American English: the diaspora. Apart from them, the Iranians have reconquered Yerevan, if only as paying guests this time. The poster pillars, which in other cities would advertise cars or toothpaste, are pasted with photos of famous poets and singers, of whom the only one still living, to my knowledge, is Charles Aznavour.

A gallery owner rails against the unbridled power of the developers, who are as blind to the old urban fabric as those in Baku or Tbilisi. Yes, the little parks that were placed all over the city when Yerevan was rebuilt are beautiful – but not for long; soon every last one will be covered by a mall. But there are so many cultured Armenians, I interject, thinking of my Armenian acquaintances in Germany and Iran, who are all old-school. Nonsense, there is no intelligentsia, or, if there is, they're at the flea markets selling used books or their own furniture to make ends meet. The greatest Soviet stronghold in all Armenia, she says, is the art academies, where even Picasso is still too modern.

I meet an Armenian-Iranian who immigrated ten years ago – no, not for political reasons, nor as a refugee from persecution, he explains, but because of a more personal dispute with the country after President Mohammad Khatami failed to enact reforms. He was angry when he walked through the streets, the immigrant says; angry at Tehran, at his fellow citizens, at every taxi driver. He couldn't even enjoy the mountains any more. Then he said to himself he had better move away before he had an irreversible falling-out with the land of his birth. Europe or America would have been logical places to go, but Armenia struck him as somehow more adventurous. Now he visits Tehran as a resident of Yerevan and is a successful translator of Persian contemporary poetry. Does he regret his decision? No, not at all. Why not? I ask. Because, since he has been in Armenia, he has begun to like Iran again. He would have emigrated sooner or later anyway; there is no future for the Armenians in Iran. Of the 500,000 that there were before the revolution, only 50,000 remain, and those who are left, he says, will soon die out or move away. Because they are second-class citizens? No, he says: because all young Iranians want to leave, but the Armenians among them have more opportunities to do so.

An intellectual, a typical member of the intelligentsia, I would say, is the first person I talk to on my entire trip to eulogize the Gorbachev years. People don't remember how it really was; they remember only the chaos when the Soviet Union collapsed, the power cuts, no heat in winter, highwaymen along the main roads and every government agency a pool of sharks; and then the violence that broke out at the drop of a hat, the hatred of the others, whoever the others were. But before that! the intellectual cries, before the chaos, but after the paralysis had been broken – that precise moment was the glorious time, when people began first talking, then smiling, art and literature flourished, and all things seemed possible.

Such are the thoughts I hear in the evening, whether or not they are representative. Yet I remain unmoved, after a day that took me back 104 years. Hayk Demoyan is right: it is not fair to Armenia to think only of the 'catastrophe'. So, before I go to sleep, a word about food, which is also flour-ishing in Yerevan: the people eat Lebanese, Persian, Turkish, *steak-frites* or hamburgers, but the sign outside always says it's original Armenian – it's a great thing for the cuisine, at least, when three quarters of the people are scattered all over the world. Even Azeri cuisine is Armenian in Yerevan.

Forty-Fourth Day: Yerevan

The reading I have along is not Franz Werfel's *Forty Days of Musa Dagh*, which I have already read years ago, but Osip Mandelstam's *Journey to Armenia*. Writing at about the same time as Werfel, in 1931 and 1932, Mandelstam sets Armenia, the 'younger sister of the Judaic earth', in relation to his own Jewish nation. But it is not so much an evil presentiment that permeates his book as a retrospection, a mythification, an escape from a reality already saturated with terror. Armenia becomes for Mandelstam a 'promised land':

> But by that time in any case I had seen
> Rich Ararat like a Biblical tablecloth,
> And two hundred days I spent in the land of sabbaths
> That they call Armenia.[50]

The journey was a last respite before the poet was arrested again; he spent the last years of his life in poverty and banishment, persecution and drudgery, and finally died in 1938 under the miserable conditions of a Siberian labour camp. In Armenia he was given 'one additional day', as the final sentence of his second-to-last note in his last published book has it, a day 'full of hearing, taste, and smell, as it was before'.[51]

The note consists of the retelling of a fifth-century legend and was an essential factor contributing to the scandal that the *Journey to Armenia* provoked in the Soviet Union. The Armenian king Arshak referred to in the legend is imprisoned by the Sassanid ruler Shapur II in the dungeons of Anyush, the 'Fortress of Oblivion'.

1. The body of Arshak is unwashed, and his beard has run wild.
2. The king's fingernails are broken, and the wood lice crawl over his face.
3. His ears have grown dull with silence, but once they listened to Greek music.
4. His tongue is scabby from jailers' food, but there was a time when it pressed grapes against the roof of his mouth and was adroit as the tip of a flutist's tongue.
5. The seed of Arshak has withered in his scrotum and his voice is as sparse

as the bleating of a sheep.

6. King Shapukh – thinks Arshak – has got the better of me, and, worse than that, he has taken my air for himself.

7. The Assyrian grips my heart.[52]

As early as 1923, Mandelstam had associated totalitarianism, which he foresaw earlier than others, with Assyria. By making Shapur II an Assyrian in his retelling of the legend, he hints that the cruel king stands for Stalin; the Armenian's heart stands for Mandelstam's own. With his own ostracism in mind, the poet identifies with the Armenians as an aboriginal people which prevailed, in spite of occupation, expulsion and mass murder, up to the genocide of 1915 to 1919.

My morning walk confirms the impression that Yerevan is a unique city, one worth seeing for that reason alone. Fortunately, there is not much traffic during the day on the broad streets, many of which have a shady promenade in the middle with benches or cafés. As uniform as the buildings are, built in the 1920s after the same design by the Armenian architect Alexander Tamanian, of the same brownish-red stone blotched with natural textures, the passage of barely a century has drawn a separate history on each façade. And the proportions were still human when the Soviet Union began – it created a city then for its inhabitants, not inhabitants for the realization of an idea – the size of the squares and the buildings, the warm colour of the façades, the many parks and green areas, the trees lining the streets. Yerevan is not the Middle Ages or the Renaissance, nor even the Industrial Revolution; Yerevan is the interwar period, which I encountered for the first time in the form of an architectural ensemble in Kaunas, although there it was northern, more severe, forbidding, and largely restored by now. Like everything else in Armenia, its modernism too is the oldest anywhere. The ochre colour of the playground equipment must have been yellow once; the moss-green must have been the colour of grass; the pale pink, red. Does the hand-cranked roundabout still work? What was once a primordial form of our bumper cars is piled full of garden implements. When might the last ride have been in these little mechanical cars, still parked in a row? In the Matenadaran, the manuscripts museum perched on a hilltop in the middle of the city like another temple, texts from the fifth, sixth century are on display that are signed with the authors' names and are still easily readable. The Germans and the French have difficulty understanding their own late Middle Ages, and in Iran the linguistic continuum goes back only to the ninth century. Naturally the Armenian Church is also the world's oldest state church. Would Armenia exist at all without it?

'Certainly not,' says Bishop Anushavan Andranik Zhamkochyan, who receives me in his big office at the Faculty of Theology. 'There has only rarely been an Armenian state, but the Armenian Church has always existed.' He is a friendly and evidently optimistic person who praises his Church's good relations with the Armenian government, with Iran, with Europe, with the Vatican, with the Muslims, and even underscores the positive aspects of the Soviet Union, whose treatment of the Armenian Church was comparatively lenient. Although he says of Azerbaijan that, after all, it is not a historic nation like Armenia or Iran but only an artificial construct, it sounds more pitying than aggressive. However, there also happens to be a professor of archaeology in the room who strikes a different tone. Not a single Turk – there are no Azerbaijanis in his diction – was driven out of Armenia; not one civilian killed, not one mosque destroyed. And the Khojaly massacre? Was no massacre; it was self-defence. And the hundreds of thousands of Azeris who lived in Armenia and Nagorno-Karabakh before the war? All got into their cars voluntarily and drove home. Vice versa, of course, everything was massacre, ethnic cleansing and torture, as might be expected of Turks: 'If Turkey enters the EU, they'll destroy Europe as well. Then nothing will be left of Christianity.'

Where I grew up, my West German generation, to say nothing of the younger generation, never learned how hostility is expressed in conversation. We know of resentment against this or that bigger or lesser group, and we know about hate, violence; but hostility, enmity, in the sense of two groups facing each other as enemies, has been relegated to the field of sport, where people burn the opposing team's flag or thrash their supporters. In Yerevan, I experience how it is when the mere name of the other evokes wrath, disgust, spite. And perhaps that is what is unequal, insoluble, about this war over little Nagorno-Karabakh: on one side, the front is not thirty years old; on the other side, it is more than a hundred. One side bemoans 20,000 dead; the other side 1.5 million; on one side, hundreds of thousands have been exiled; on the other, three quarters of the nation are scattered across the globe. Azerbaijanis today hardly know the history, to say nothing of feeling responsible for it – the history that will burn forever in every Armenian's soul. Right or wrong, Armenia is still at war against the Turks. Perhaps that is also why the Armenian army proved the stronger in the war against Azerbaijan: because, like everything else in Armenia, its enmity is older too.

'It's the my-grandmother-Araksi war, the my-grandmother-Hriopsime war; it's the Deir az-Zor war,' says the film director Sarkis Hatspanian, who took part in the peace marches in Germany in the early 1980s, only to volunteer for military duty in Armenia a few years later. He knows his family tree back to 1792, and knows of eighty-six relatives who were alive in 1915. Only three survived the genocide: his grandfather and two great-aunts. Today his family once more number eighty-nine; Sarkis Hatspanian always has the number in mind: three more than before the genocide.

I already learned yesterday how dramatic family stories are in Armenia between 1915 and today: grief, expulsion, hunger, emigration, war, Gulag, regime change, one new start after another. But there are a few more twists to the biography that Hatspanian, in a black Armenian-agitprop T-shirt and jeans, relates almost breathlessly in one of the many garden cafés in the city centre. Indeed, he seems amazed himself at how much fits into a single life; he shakes his white hair again and again, and sometimes he betrays by a mischievous grin that the story is about to get even crazier. He was born in 1962 in southeastern Turkey, where his grandfather had gone back with his two sisters in 1919. Gone back? I wondered yesterday too why Hovhannes Balabanyan and his mother went back in 1919. Although by then the expulsion and murder of the Armenians in the years between the defeat of the Ottoman Empire and Atatürk's rise to power had been declared a 'crime against humanity' by the parliament and in the newspapers, and the principal persons responsible sentenced to death, including Enver Pasha *in absentia* – still, I wonder where the villagers got the courage to live among Turks again so soon after the genocide. Now I learn that the area around Alexandretta was part of the French Mandate, and the survivors had been told they could feel safe again in their villages; in the meantime the houses had new inhabitants, however, who swore they would not move out. Thus the three siblings started over again from zero. In 1939 the French handed over the territory to Turkey to stop it from making a pact with Germany. That, I now understand, is why Turkish soldiers were standing in Hovhannes Balabanyan's village too in 1939.

Although he went to an Armenian school, Sarkis had mostly Turkish friends, was politically active and was arrested three times after the military coup of 1980 – as a dissident, he emphasizes, not as an Armenian. He was able to flee to Cologne, where he was the only Armenian member of the committee against the Turkish military coup. For Günter Wallraff's best-selling exposé *Ganz unten*, Hatspanian pretended to be a Turkish migrant labourer doing the Germans' dirty work. He made the acquaintance of Heinrich Böll, was active in the Spartacus League at university, whose members were mostly Iranians, and, considering how quickly he made himself at home among the leftists of Cologne, sooner or later he would have ended up in German politics. But then, in 1982, Germany's political police, the *Verfassungsschutz*, rang his doorbell and suggested he leave Cologne because the Grey Wolves, a Turkish right-wing extremist group, had put him on their list. The officers gave him a month to find a new country of exile, saying he would be deported if he stayed longer.

Hatspanian applied to the authorities in Armenia, where he wanted to emigrate, but the Armenian SSR, which he had thought of as a home, didn't even answer him. The BND, Germany's foreign intelligence agency, advised him sympathetically to go to France; there are 500,000 Armenians living in France, they said; you can go underground there. Unfortunately, he didn't know a word of French; he had to learn it as fast as he had learned German. Two policemen escorted him via Saarbrücken to Paris, where he was given a travel document after a month and a half. The first thing he did with it was to go back to Cologne to say good-bye to his German, Turkish and Iranian friends, all of them comrades; besides, it was New Year's Eve, one reason more to raise a glass.

In Paris he worked for Yilmaz Güney, who had won the Golden Palm in Cannes with the film *Yol*. Through the Turk Güney, he met the Soviet-Armenian director and dissident Sergei Parajanov, whose 1968 film *The Colour of Pomegranates* is one of the avant-garde classics of the twentieth century. Parajanov offered to hire Hatspanian as an assistant for his film *The Confession*, and so Hatspanian finally flew to Yerevan after all on 26 March 1990. He had bought a one-way ticket, without asking whether a return might have been cheaper, because he didn't want to become French; he wanted to be Armenian at last. But Hatspanian had barely landed when Parajanov fell ill with cancer. Jean-Luc Godard organized a government aircraft to fetch the director for treatment, and so his assistant too was suddenly on his way back to Paris.

There above the clouds they were just four passengers, Parajanov, Hatspanian, an Armenian director and a Turkish director, while on the ground the Armenians and Azeris were driving each other from their homes. 'Fly back,' Parajanov advised him when his health failed to improve under treatment. 'Try again; it's your country; you can be useful there.'

'All right, master,' Hatspanian replied, 'I'll fly back to Armenia and try my luck, but only if you tell me three wishes.'

Parajanov wished to visit Andrei Tarkovsky's grave in Paris before he died, to see the Eiffel Tower, and to meet the writer Françoise Sagan.

After he had fulfilled Parajanov's three wishes, Hatspanian took a second one-way flight to Yerevan, but this time no one was waiting for him there. He knew no one; he stood out with his West Armenian accent; he had nothing in common with people in the film scene who were making conformist Soviet cinema. Soon he saw the neighbours gathering in the street outside his little flat. 'Come with us, we're going to Nagorno-Karabakh,' the men cried, and Hatspanian went along without even stopping to change his T-shirt. No one knew exactly what had happened; the rumour was simply that the Turks had attacked, and they were the fourth generation after the genocide. Hatspanian describes the mood by paraphrasing a slogan that still rings in the ears of every Bonn peace marcher: 'What if they had a war and everyone came?'

Hatspanian too affirms that the Armenians used no violence against civilians. Because he spoke Turkish, he was the contact officer for the inhabitants who had been asked to leave their houses, he says, so he had an overview of the events. In just five days, 60,000 Azeris were deported without even a voice being raised; on the contrary, many Azeris expressed gratitude for the politeness of the Armenians, to whom their soldiers had not shown such consideration. In four years, his unit liberated twenty-seven Azerbaijani villages without a single civilian death. Hatspanian – who still speaks excellent German with the soft accent of the Rhineland – Hatspanian really says 'liberated', *befreit*. I am startled. Liberated? Then I realize that, of course, they can't have freed Azerbaijani villages; they freed the villages of Azerbaijanis.

And Armenia today?

'Oh, I'm not the one to ask about that; I'm part of the radical opposition here.'

He already knew Turkish prisons, and he made the acquaintance of the Armenian ones in 2008. Together with thousands of others, he had demonstrated in front of the opera house for days against the 'KGB coup', as he calls the presidential election of Serge Sarkisian. He was not the only one sentenced to prison, but he was the only foreigner, and he was imprisoned for three and a half years. After his release Hatspanian was supposed to be immediately deported, but he took refuge in the French embassy and didn't step outside again until the diplomats had negotiated a residence permit for him. Since 2013 he has been an Armenian citizen at last, but he is barred from all political activity until 2023.

'And then?'

'Then I'll found a party. We need a government that wants peace.'

'Peace?'

'Yes, peace; we have to make peace with the Turks; there's no other way.'

'And how is that supposed to happen?'

'I don't know. I only know what the prerequisite is: democracy. Because the ten, twelve oligarchs who have got their claws on the country are profiting from the current situation. They don't feel how badly off the people are; 2023, that will be the year, and then I'll found a party.'

'And what will the party do?'

'We'll march to Baku.'

'To Baku?'

'Yes, we'll organize a peace march. A peace march to Baku.'

That sounds a bit – how shall I say? – audacious in view of the enmity between the peoples, the nationalism of both governments and the failure of all diplomatic efforts. But I would not put it past Sarkis Hatspanian's life to send him on a peace march again in 2023, as it did in Bonn in 1981.

He has more to tell, he says, about Paris, about Cologne, about the struggle against the dictatorship – and if he gets started on his relatives, his parents who still live in Turkey, his five siblings – only I have to be on my way, I interject as he stops for breath, or else I'll miss my appointment with the government against which Sarkis Hatspanian demonstrated in vain in 2008.

The politician is an adept diplomat, and I don't get far with questions about corruption, oligarchy and political prisoners. So we are soon talking about today's wars of religion, the expulsion of Christians from the Middle East and the role of Iran, which is on Armenia's side, although, like Azerbaijan, it is a Shiite country. I can't write the politician's name, however, because before authorizing his quotations he would rewrite each one into a press release. So I prefer to leave him anonymous and stick with what he actually says in conversation.

'The Azerbaijanis would like to make the conflict over Nagorno-Karabakh into a war of religion to gain the support of the Islamic world, including the Sunni extremists, but it is not one, and it is dangerous to claim it is.'

'Dangerous to Armenia?'

'Yes, to us. We Armenians have been a minority in the East for as long as Islam has been in existence. We have always had to prove that we are good neighbours, good citizens. And look around: everywhere we live, in

Lebanon, in Iran, in Syria – we are accepted everywhere.'

'In Iran you are more than accepted: Armenians are highly respected.'

'That doesn't come naturally. It is because we have no other choice but to be on good terms with the majority. We are too few to wage a war against Islam or the Muslims; we would be overrun.'

'In the West there are many who say Armenia is the last bastion of Christianity in the Middle East.'

'But that doesn't help us.'

'And now there's the renationalization wave in Europe; there's Trump; there is jihadism; there are people who see the West at war with Islam.'

'As I said, that is a very dangerous kind of thinking.'

'Are you afraid of being co-opted?'

'I said before, we Armenians have a long memory. We remember the crusades. We were supposed to be freed from Islam once before, and the result was that we got slaughtered along with the Muslims.'

Some cities have so much history that the present, no matter how hard it tries, always looks less interesting. And yet Yerevan is not a historic metropolis like Rome, Cairo or Tbilisi. It is mentioned only in passing in old chronicles, and hardly any of the present-day buildings is more than a lifetime old. Nevertheless, when I walk through Yerevan, and especially when I talk with the inhabitants – even the worldly diplomat – nevertheless I can't shake the feeling of being more in the past than in the present. Perhaps that's how it is in a country whose culture, language, writing, religion and music have hardly changed, for all the dramatic changes and revolutions, or in any case less than we would expect coming from Europe or the Middle East – perhaps the past doesn't need to have a physical form but can be something more ethereal. Osip Mandelstam felt that, and in his day Yerevan was a brand-new city: 'As a result of my incorrect subjective orientation, I have fallen into the habit of regarding every Armenian as a philologist.'[53] Rather than praising revolutionary progress, as was expected of him, he found everywhere the continuity of a people who had descended Mount Ararat after the landing of Noah's Ark, as even Persian legends acknowledge:

I love this hard-living people –
counting years like centuries –
giving birth, sleeping, screaming,
nailed to the earth.[54]

To see something of the present at last – more precisely, to see those recent developments that people have linked to Europe again and again during my travels – I have invited myself to visit PINK Armenia, a non-governmental organization working to promote the rights of lesbian, gay, bisexual and transgender persons. Just in the past few days, a film series scheduled as part of the International Film Festival has had to be cancelled because the programme included a documentary about Armenian homosexuals. Now PINK Armenia is hastily organizing a screening outside the festival, so my appointment has been pushed back half an hour. Because this gives me some extra time – only chance could have arranged such a fall-back programme! – I make a quick visit to the only mosque left since the expulsion of the Azerbaijanis. The sky-blue cupola is a reminder that Yerevan was once a Persian provincial town. The Islamic Republic financed its restoration, and hence the mosque is also the fitting seat of the Armenian-Iranian Friendship Association.

In no other country in the world have I heard so many good things about – no, not just about Iran, although that is unusual enough for an Iranian abroad – but about the government in Tehran. Just today, the bishop praised the Islamic Republic for renovating the Armenians' churches; the politician expressed his gratitude for the fraternal relations with Tehran; and even Sarkis Hatspanian, the leftist with a background in the Cologne Spartacus League, said Armenia would have lost the war for Nagorno-Karabakh without the support of Iran. And, in the Matenadaran, the entrance hall is devoted to manuscripts from Iran, with the shah's tolerance edicts prominently displayed. The strong religiousness of the Armenians and the outstanding role of the Church in public life are no doubt conducive to the country's good relations with the Islamic Republic: a mullah would feel more at home in Christian, but devout, Armenia than in Shiite, but more secular, Azerbaijan. The Iranian tourists, meanwhile, do not seem to be much interested in matters of faith: I am the only visitor in the mosque on this early afternoon. Fortunately, the funding did not cover gardening, so the courtyard looks delightfully bewitched. The sky-blue of the cupola, the green of the trees and bushes, with flowers strewn among them as in a miniature painting, far away the noise of the street and the only sound that of the water splashing in the fountain, the gates open and no one in sight – a mosque, of all places, radiates an almost celestial peace in Armenia. Unfortunately, I cannot linger, or lie down for a nap, otherwise I'll miss my appointment with PINK Armenia, where, I suspect, religion is not associated with peace.

251

An ordinary apartment in a multi-storey building, with no name plate by the front door – this is the only roof under which homosexuals in Armenia can embrace one another outside their own four walls. Public activities are out of the question, says Mamikon Hovsepyan, who at thirty-five is one of the oldest in these three or four sparsely furnished rooms. According to surveys, he continues, 90 per cent of Armenians are homophobic. The war has further exacerbated the nationalism and chauvinism that are deeply rooted in tradition. The government? The publisher of the newspaper that rails the loudest against homosexuals is a member of parliament for the government party. The police? They don't even take down hate crimes. The Church? Always the same priests on the talk shows mixing everything up together: decaying values, poverty, materialism, and on top of it all spreading the idea that homosexuality is the ultimate sign of Western decadence. As often as they talk about the biblical punishments, always with the disclaimer that of course no one wants to apply them literally today, there's no call to be surprised that some spectators nonetheless take action. And himself? Since he appeared on one of those talk shows, he avoids being seen in the street, and by now too many people know where he lives. It looks as though he's going to have to move soon and leave the country sooner or later, or, at the very least, withdraw from activism. You wouldn't want to be gay and out in Armenia in the long term, he says.

PINK Armenia's funding comes mainly from Europe. Mamikon knows that this feeds a homophobic prejudice, but without the funds from Holland or Sweden this office, which provides counselling or even just a safe space for homosexuals, wouldn't exist. Moreover, many Europeans are in fact only interested in this one issue, as another stereotype holds. At conferences abroad, he always explains that, while he is gay, his life is not limited to being gay and that Armenia has other problems – political and social problems – that are at least as important. But it's hard to find an ear in Europe, he says, for the issues of social distortion, oligarchy, nationalism or the never-ending war. Instead he always gets asked about same-sex marriage. As if same-sex marriage were the only indicator of development! Introducing same-sex marriage in countries like Armenia would be like building a roof where there's no house. Educating the society, working to raise consciousness, is more urgent. Adolescents who attract attention as being gay, or perhaps openly admit it, are commonly 'brought to their senses' by physical violence or sent to a therapist to be 'cured'. It's worse for adolescent lesbians: they are often raped to make them 'normal again'. When PINK Armenia finds out

252

about such cases, the activists talk to the parents directly and are surprisingly often successful. Politicians or activists in Berlin or Brussels may get a good feeling out of taking an uncompromising stance and making recognition or funding conditional on this or that regulation, but here in Armenia the homosexuals suffer from the aggression that always follows such demands.

We take a taxi to get to the screening of the film that couldn't be shown at the festival. I ask the driver, who has wedged her ample girth between the steering wheel and the seat of the compact Opel, whether men here are shocked when they see a woman at the wheel.

'And how!' she cries, and laughs so hard that the car goes off the edge of the road for a moment. 'Do you want to get out?'

Before I can answer, she assures me she was just joking. No one wants to get out; the men are a little uneasy at most; they'll be all right, they say. She is forty-five, married early, didn't get pregnant for nine years, and the second time she did her husband died shortly thereafter. So she started driving a taxi so that her children will have a better life someday. Not before? No, her husband had forbidden her to work.

'And if he could see you now?'

'He would still forbid it.'

'And what would you do?'

'I would obey him.'

'Why? Such a self-assured woman as you!'

'Because my husband was always good to me. Because he bore with me through the nine years I didn't get pregnant.'

Emancipated or not, our driver has spirit: gesticulating constantly, slamming both hands on the steering wheel when the other drivers – men of course – make her mad. Is she content with life in Armenia?

'I'm content with my two children.'

In the overfilled 'media centre' that several non-governmental organizations share for their events and conferences, the mood is tensely defiant. Rumour has it that opposing activists have found out about the screening; someone claims to have seen some vicious-looking characters outside. The doors are locked from the inside for safety. The audience is young, hardly anyone over thirty, and in Western attire, as the saying goes: the haircuts, the jeans, the tattoos no different than in Berlin or Brussels, in other words, also the physicality of people's interaction and the women's self-assurance. Everyone I talk to understands English, which is not something you can take for granted in Armenia. And, as far as I can find out in this short time, all the participating NGOs are funded at least in part by European institutions, including the association for the normalization of Turkish–Armenian relations. Little wonder, then, if the vicious-looking characters in the street think this is a rendezvous of European cultural imperialism. But is that any reason for Europe to withdraw its support for these young Armenians who are standing up to homophobia? In the film, a middle-aged man, clean-shaven, wearing creased trousers and a short-sleeved shirt, casually remarks that he is grateful when someone is not unpleasant to him. Why grateful? he asks himself. Pleasantness in human interactions should be the least we can expect of one another. If he can't expect it – is he then not human?

On exiting the building, I see no vicious-looking characters; across the street is a lanky young fellow, under thirty I estimate, as old as the visitors of the media centre, whom he is photographing. At first, I turn my back to him, as do all the others – not frightened, but with the feeling of being helplessly exposed to his camera lens. Then I turn around again and cross the street. When the man realizes I am walking over to him, he seems to consider whether to run away, so I walk faster. Now he is the one who is scared – or perhaps not scared, but uneasy and nervous. To his surprise, I strike a pleasant tone so that, after some initial hesitation, he answers my questions willingly. Haik Ayvazian is his name, and he says Armenia is a Christian country; that's why he's here. The Bible leaves no doubt that homosexuality is a sin, a sin worthy of death. Then, I ask, does he want the young people across the street to suffer the biblical punishment?

'No, we have nothing against these people. We only have something against recruiting for homosexuality.'

'Who do you mean by "we"?'

'We Armenians: 98 per cent of us reject it.'

They – Haik continues to speak for 'them', the Armenians – don't want to outlaw homosexuality, that's not what they're after, and they certainly don't want violence. They only want to stop the foreign propaganda, which the government tolerates, and against which not even the Church takes a clear enough position. That's why he has joined an organization, Luus ('light'), in which young people defend Armenia's Christian identity.

'And why are you taking photos?' I ask.

'I want to know who watches a film like that.'

'Then stand by the door and look at the people. Why do you have to take photos?'

'They're just for me.'

'But what for?'

'Why do you want to know?'

'I'm as curious as you are.'

'Maybe I want to know whether anyone from the government is here.'

'So that you can denounce them?'

'Don't I have a right to know what the government is supporting?'

To Haik, the people his age on the other side of the street are not the ones at fault; they are merely victims of the European Union, before which the government is abjectly capitulating. Where does he get that idea? I ask; the audience seemed very autonomous to me.

'Because the EU is constantly talking about the rights of homosexuals. Constantly. Why? How many people does that involve here? Why is the issue so important to the EU? What is the purpose behind it?'

'What do you think?'

'It's because they want to alienate us from our own culture and provoke opposition against our religion.'

'Wasn't it rather the Soviet Union that did that?'

'The Soviet Union conquered us by force of arms, but Europe wants to mess with our heads.'

'But where do you get that idea? You must have some evidence for your claim.'

'Look, in Germany children get taken away from their parents if the parents criticize sex education, if they say homosexuality is a bad thing.'

'I come from Germany; I've never heard of children being separated from their parents for something like that.'

'But it's documented!'

'And how do you know your documentation is true?'

'I can show you the reports, with photos and everything; they're all documented cases,' Haik assures me, and he writes down my e-mail address.

In the evening I go to a party where the guests are few enough that the whole thing seems spontaneous. Apart from a few doing-nothings – people who do a little of this, a little of that, and by preference nothing at all – a few literary types are here, including the translator of Orhan Pamuk, and a group of lesbian activists from Istanbul, whose visit is probably the reason for the party. Characteristically, dialogue with Turkey is advocated in the same circles that are working for the rights of homosexuals, as if the one issue had some connection with the other. Perhaps there is a connection: I don't know if women are less nationalistic than men, but LGBT people certainly are;

they know that any nation's 'others' can always refer to them. I ask about Akram Aylisli, whom all the Armenians in the group know; his *Stone Dreams* is available in several translations. What happened to him after it was published is not really imaginable in Armenia, they say; the conditions here are still liberal in comparison. But, on the other hand, someone like Aylisli, who wrote a great novel about the suffering of the others, the enemies – there isn't anyone like that in Armenia.

In bed I click through the links that Sarkis Hatspanian and Haik Ayvazian have e-mailed me with best wishes. In a press photo published in 1993 in *Libération*, Sarkis squats, his hair still full and black, with an assault rifle, next to an old woman hugging him. A caption introduces her as an Azeri villager and quotes her as saying she loves this Armenian officer more than her own son, who abandoned her. The day after the photo appeared in *Libération*, the Turkish newspaper *Milliyet* reprinted it, but there the caption claimed that an old Azeri woman was kissing her grandson and telling him to take revenge on the Armenians who had massacred the rest of her family. Sarkis writes that he sent both publications to the European Union as an example of Turkish propaganda. I have no reason to doubt that he and his unit treated the civilians with respect. But he's unable to grasp that the bad guys in this war can't have been all on one side of the front, and the heroes all the other side; that's counter to his experience – and that will probably be a problem in 2023 if he marches to Baku, because there he will meet people who believe their own memories.

Haik, surprisingly, doesn't flood me with propaganda but sends me links to *Deutsche Welle* and *The Guardian*. The articles report on a reform of sex education in the German state of Baden-Württemberg. There is nothing about children being separated from their recalcitrant parents, but I can imagine that someone unfamiliar with the context might read such an idea into them – after all, attendance at the sex education classes is described as mandatory. Haik has also sent links to YouTube videos in which hidden cameras ostensibly show German youth authorities taking children from their parents' homes with the help of the police. He offers to meet me again tomorrow and introduce me to his friends so that I can better understand how they see the world of today. It would be worthwhile to talk to him some more, I think, because he listens and tries to articulate his ideas. I wonder whether he would also talk with the other young people who came out of the film screening? And would they talk with him? I won't find out, because we're leaving at the crack of dawn so that we can make a detour on our drive to Nagorno-Karabakh: some of the most moving notes Osip Mandelstam left are about Lake Sevan. After his return, at his last public reading in 1933, he was asked provocatively what characterizes his poetry and answered tersely: 'Yearning for world culture.'

Forty-Fifth Day: To Lake Sevan and on to Nagorno-Karabakh

The beach towels hung out for sale along the road to Sevan are printed with pictures of curvy women in little bikinis, the Stars and Stripes, or dollar bills – a tricky choice when you're on your way to Iran and you want something you'll be able to dry yourself with on the Caspian Sea. At the third stand I find a towel showing a smiling Mickey Mouse. That should pass. Along the lakeshore stand a dense row of children with their arms spread like Christ on the cross. What is that about? I ask. They're showing the size of the fish that they, or more likely their fathers, have caught, the driver enlightens me. The cleverest ones have propped up naked shop-window mannequins with the arms turned diagonally upwards. Some are hanging their heads, as if even the mannequins in Armenia emulated the Passion.

Then comes the disillusionment: the island on which Osip Mandelstam lived for a month in 1930 no longer exists. It is now a peninsula because the water level has gone down 20 metres, which is a catastrophe for the ecosystem, we learn: from 1933 on, Soviet engineers deliberately reduced the surface of the lake by 40 per cent to gain more fertile land along the shore and more water for use thanks to the decreased evaporation. On the hill that once formed the island, you can still draw the same salt-free wind into your lungs and walk through the tall prairie grasses, 'so strong, full of sap and sure of themselves that one would like to comb them with an iron comb'.[55] Little remains, however, of the incomparable richness of bird and plant species. And the island that is no longer an island is not nearly as peaceful and remote as it was barely a century ago. The additions of a hundred years include the Soviet Union's group recreation accommodation, capitalism's villas and holiday rentals on the opposite shore, the noise of jet-skis, the pop music of the beach cafés and, in the distance, the sound of cars going by. But Mandelstam too was woken up in the early morning by the rattling of a motor. A lighthouse was built, which seems to have been torn down again, and, during or shortly after Mandelstam's stay, a House of Writers, which still stands and is supposed to be renovated soon. 'Wherever I penetrated I met the firm will and hand of the Bolshevist party,' he wrote. 'Yet, on this journey, my eye, obsessed with everything odd, evanescent and ephemeral, has captured only the light-giving trembling of chance coincidences, the floral ornamentation of reality.' I find the church still extant, its oldest ruins dating from 301, and stand before the fire-red, nameless funeral slabs with which the earth is literally paved, as Mandelstam noted. Nature has suffered more under socialism than the temples and the graves, which have almost become nature themselves in Armenia.

We drink our morning coffee on the terrace of the club built in 1964, a seashell of glass and concrete hovering in the hillside beside the Writers' House – Soviet avant-garde, yes, a really sensational specimen this time, and still open to serve day-trippers. In the wainscoted dining room hang pictures of the authors who have stayed on the island, or the peninsula. The caretaker pronounces their names reverently, but sadly I don't know a single one. In Armenia, as the saying goes, they are world-famous. Only Osip Mandelstam is missing, whose air was taken by the Assyrian.

We drive on along the eastern shore through the treeless countryside, and then we arrive in the remoteness in which the whole lake must have lain a century ago. It is huge, still one of the largest alpine lakes in the world and, for Armenia's small geographic scale, almost the sea that Tigran Mansurian misses. And yet the water surrounds one with the clarity, the coldness and the lifeless silence of 2,000 metres above sea level. And Mickey Mouse will seldom have beamed as he does on the matte prairie grass, already warmed by the sun, that runs up a mountainside in a broad arc of the lakeshore.

The road is not in good condition – and why should it be, if practically no one drives on it? – and so noon is past by the time we reach Vardenis, south of the lake. The former workers' housing blocks are built of the same dark stone as the villages; the beautiful natural bricks must be cheaper here than concrete. Apart from that, it looks like hundreds, thousands of industrial towns in the former Soviet Union: a grid of broad streets; shops with no display windows, many of which seem to be closed not just for midday; a few snack stands; a market; few pedestrians and still fewer cars; here and there expensive SUVs. No drinkers in the streets; after the Bloodlands, their absence is conspicuous. The Russians all moved away when Armenia became independent, say the men eating kebab sandwiches at the next table.

'Because the factories closed?' I ask.

'And because they spoke Russian.'

'And the big cars?'

'Belong to very rich people.'

'How does a person get rich here?'

'Not by obeying the law.'

Somewhere beyond Vardenis we leave Armenia. We don't notice where; there is no sign that we are now on Azerbaijani soil, in the mountainous Kalbajar district to be exact, which lies between Armenia and the enclave of Nagorno-Karabakh. Before the war, the population was exclusively Muslim, mainly Kurdish peasants and shepherds. Now we encounter no people at all, and no cars. The men in the kebab shop recommended that we go with a full tank, since there would be no petrol station anywhere and rarely anyone who might help us out. Armenia has never said good-bye, and yet a sign finally turns up welcoming us to the Republic of Nagorno-Karabakh. On Google Maps, it begins quite a few kilometres further east, past the monastery of Dadivank, but, in contrast to the border between Georgia and South Ossetia, there is no one here who might sound the alarm when the border shifts. In the next valley stands a border station, but there is no customs officer by the road. The barrier is a simple wooden pole with a cord hanging from it, and it is raised. The driver parks the car to make sure we're not crossing the border illegally.

A German passport seems to be a rarity on this secondary route to Nagorno-Karabakh, and so the officer whom we find behind his desk keenly examines even the empty pages with significant nods. Without having asked the reason for my trip, he hands back the passport unstamped and says I have to apply for a visa in Stepanakert. Then he accompanies us to the car, takes his leave with a handshake, and watches long as we drive away. A curious state, I think, where you get an entry permit only after you've entered. A short time later, the mobile phone signal disappears, as it did in Crimea. I infer from that that I won't be able to use my credit card either. On the map that the driver has spread out on the steering wheel – without stopping – the next villages have different names than on Google Maps; all of them starting with 'Nor', meaning 'new': New Karachmar, New Manasha, New Brajur. Old Karachmar et cetera are probably in Azerbaijan and probably have Turkish names today.

We stop at Dadivank Monastery, founded, according to legend, in the first century after Christ. The present-day buildings, including the church, were built in the fourteenth century on a hilltop in steep, wooded mountains that look today just as lonesome and deserted as if nothing had happened on earth since then. The church itself, in fact, with its weathered walls, with moss and bushes growing on the roof and the cupola, has something of a great, ancient, bent and wildly branching tree that no longer bears many leaves. Like that of most Armenian churches, its plan imitates a cross with almost equal arms, and, like the churches in Georgia, it seems to have been restored just enough to keep the walls from collapsing. The frescoes do not hide their age, and the wiring is not plastered over nor even hidden by a wainscot. One wall is completely covered with soot; another shows the silhouette of a staircase that must once have led to a gallery. They say the shepherd who lived in the church with his family during the Soviet Union was worried that his children might fall off the stairs, and so he tore them down. The soot betrays where the stove was, which also served as a heating furnace. Many of the faithful have left their traces on the old Persian rugs that now cover the floor, as have the birds in the rafters. Once again I wonder what makes up the magic of these spaces, which could be much better restored, making them much more authentic. It is not only that they show history, all the experiences, the pain and joy, like an ancient face or the bark of a tree. It is also the aleatory, the imperfect, that the years have thrown together; even the wiring, the soot, the holes in the carpet; it is the birds and the angle of the light giving a different twist to every second, because only God is eternal and perfect.

Father Hovhannes Houhamesyan, a tall, athletically built man with a carefully trimmed beard and his hair combed back, explains to us that he has a treaty with the birds.

'A treaty?'

'Yes. They can live wherever they want, except in the church.'

'And?'

'They just don't observe it.'

Father Hovhannes has an intimate relationship with his church because, in this solitude, there is neither a congregation in the strict sense nor any monastic life: only the masses on Sundays and holidays for the surrounding villages and individual worshippers, occasionally Armenian tourists, an old woman who keeps a kiosk and the builders, who, after twenty-four years, are still not done with the renovations. Before the liberation, the whole region was inhabited by Turks. The fact that they were probably Kurds, who had suffered heavily themselves under the Turks, and that the Turks in question are not Turks at all but Azerbaijanis – the priest seems to be unaware of such nuances, or the war has blurred them. 'There is no country called Azerbaijan,' he insists when I ask why he calls the Azerbaijanis Turks.

He finds it only logical that the inhabitants had to abandon their houses; after all, Armenians had already lived here long before the Turks. You only have to compare the ages of the churches and the mosques, almost 2,000 compared with at best 200 years, to know who this land belongs to. I try in vain to coax a compassionate word out of Father Hovhannes for the people who lost their home, simple farmers and shepherds. Home? asks the priest, who served at the front as a chaplain. Yes, home, I say; for an individual a place is home when they are born and raised there, no matter what happened 200 or 2,000 years before. But Father Hovhannes doesn't want to talk about individuals; he speaks of the Turks only as a group which expelled and massacred the Armenians. I try love for one's enemies, which is actually specific to Christianity: what did that mean at the front? As if in the pulpit, the priest raises his voice and declares solemnly that a Christian must never start a war.

'All right,' I say, 'but once you are at war – does loving your enemy have any meaning then?'

'We had to defend our country against the enemy.'

'But did you love the enemy?'

'There is a rule,' says the priest slowly, and leans his upper body backwards, standing, as if to let off steam: 'The enemy has to leave at least a chance for you to love him. But the Turks don't. They are raised to hate us, to kill us. They don't give us a chance to love them.'

'That would be too easy!' I exclaim, not very reverently. 'If the enemy gave you a chance to love him, he wouldn't be an enemy. The special thing about Christ is that he says thou shalt love not just thy neighbour, but thy enemy. In other words, love him who hates you or wants to harm you, or in some way rejects you. That's who you're supposed to love. Is that possible?'

'Yes, if we were to live with them in peace, the different religions I mean, then we could love them. But in wartime it doesn't work.'

'Why not?'

'You can't kill a person you love.'

'And what was it like for you when you were at the front?'

'If you say to yourself, in the moment when you're aiming at someone, that you love them, then you can't pull the trigger; you just can't. That's how it was for me. That's how it is in war.'

On the map we look for Khojaly, but we don't know the present name of the little town where the biggest massacre of the war occurred in the night from the 25th to the 26th of February 1992. The Armenian troops had cut it off from Aghdam, the next city in Azerbaijani territory, in October 1991, leaving Khojaly with no electricity, running water, heat or telephone and supplied only by helicopters, which rarely came over the enemy lines because they could be shot down at any time. The 160 Azeri soldiers who had remained to defend Khojaly with small arms had no chance when the Armenians, supported by Russian armoured cars, sounded the charge. The Azeri commander told the inhabitants to flee on foot to Aghdam, and so 3,000 civilians, with a few soldiers ordered to accompany them, set out late at night in a heavy snowstorm. At dawn they were marching across open country when they were fired on from a hilltop. The Azerbaijani soldiers returned fire, but they were hopelessly outnumbered and without cover, and they were quickly killed. When international reporters reached the field a few days later, it was covered with bodies, including those of many women and children. The figure of 485 dead that was determined by an Azerbaijani parliamentary commission is called realistic by Thomas de Waal in *Black Garden*, the authoritative book on the war in Nagorno-Karabakh. Up to then, the Armenians had been widely seen as victims, and their fight for Nagorno-Karabakh had the halo of a liberation struggle, particularly in left-wing circles. The news of Khojaly, and a year later the conquest of Kalbajar, which had never belonged to Nagorno-Karabakh, and in which regular Russian troops were again involved, led to a swing in worldwide public opinion. The Armenian government at first denied the reports but ultimately admitted that civilians had been killed, although not such a great number. The most open statement was that of the Armenian military leader and later minister of defence Serzh Azati Sargsyan: 'Before Khojalu, the Azerbaijanis thought that they were joking with us, they thought that the Armenians were people who could not raise their hand against the civilian population. We needed to put a stop to all that. And that's what happened.' The government meanwhile insisted that the attack had been committed by irregular militias, including refugees from Sumgait. There a pogrom had occurred in 1988 in which, by an official count, twenty-six Armenians had died; de Waal calls this figure realistic too, but it grew over the years in the Armenian public discourse to 450. There have to have been more killed in Sumgait than in Khojaly – just as Azerbaijan, conversely, claims Khojaly as a genocide of its own.

But it is not only a conflict over numbers. Hardly anyone in Azerbaijan, especially among the younger people, knows anything specific about Sumgait, and certainly not that Azerbaijanis beat, tortured, raped and humiliated their Armenian neighbours, killing at least twenty-six of them. Those who do remember the rampage attribute it to Soviet agents provocateurs. Hardly any Armenian knows of Khojaly. Like lovers, nations long remember what they suffered and forget their own guilt all the sooner. They don't even deny it – they simply forget it, and that is much worse, because in time not even a scar remains. The Iranians, for example – to take the other nation I belong to – the Iranians cultivate the myth that they have always been attacked: by Assyrians, Babylonians and Greeks, by Arabs and Mongols, by Turks and Russians, by British and Americans, by Iraqis and Wahhabis. Only on this journey, centuries later, when the memory doesn't hurt anyone any more, do I realize how many people my forefathers themselves killed in the Caucasus, how many they kidnapped as slaves, how many churches they desecrated.

With the help of Thomas de Waal's *Black Garden*, which has become my travel guide in Nagorno-Karabakh, just as Timothy Snyder's *Bloodlands* guided me from Poland to Ukraine, we determine the approximate location of Khojaly and ask for directions along the way. But, the closer we get, the fewer people have ever heard the name. That is a problem with every war when you try to collate the conflicting memories: the more people have been driven out of a place, the more new arrivals there are who don't know its history. In Khojaly itself, where we finally arrive – not a real city, but a sparsely scattered settlement – we find no one at all who knows anything about the circumstances of the conquest. The inhabitants find it inconceivable that Armenian soldiers shot civilians, much less committed a massacre.

In a shop, the grocer reports that all the houses in Khojaly had been burnt down when they got here.

'By whom?'

'By the Turks, I assume.'

'Were you there?'

'No, of course not. When we arrived, everything was already destroyed.'

Until the war they had lived in Aghdam, which was then on the other side of the border and today lies in the buffer zone between Nagorno-Karabakh and Azerbaijan. Living among Azeris had always been difficult, he continues, but when the Soviet Union broke down, Armenians no longer felt safe in the streets in the evening.

'Are you relieved that the Azeris are gone?'

'What can you do if coexistence doesn't work?' the father asks me back. The conversation comes around to his military service, which he spent stationed in East Germany. In those days, the borders were closed there and open here; now it's the other way round; that's the way the world turns.

'Yes, we're happy,' one of his two daughters pitches in, standing behind the counter with her parents, and she describes the Turks' inborn hatred of

Armenians, their brutality and blood lust. She is eighteen, at most twenty, so she has no personal recollections of the war or of Azerbaijan. Turned half towards us, half towards his family, the father speaks up again, apparently finding his daughter's judgement too absolute, and tells about his recent visit to Krasnodar, where his sister lives. At a wedding, she pointed, rather in jest, to some of the guests and said they were Azeris. He didn't know what to do, he says, whether to stay or to leave; they were the first Azeris he had seen since the war.

'What would you have done?' I ask his daughters.

'They're Turks and always will be,' says the younger one, apparently in accord with her sister; 'I would have left.'

'And what did you do?' I ask the father.

'I stayed; naturally I stayed and joined the celebration, what else?'

'Did you drink a toast with the Azeris?'

'No, I didn't,' the father says, reassuring his daughters, and laughs. Then he writes down Armen's number for us: Armen is the only person in Khojaly who lived here before the war; he can no doubt tell us more about how the town was liberated.

Even I can hear the creaky voice that answers, although it's our driver who has the telephone, noting the directions, which almost take us right out of Khojaly. By a heap of rubble with bushes growing out of it we ask whether it is the remains of a mosque. Yes, replies a woman with grey hair worn loose, who seems to have been standing here a long time. She responds to our subsequent questions with a confused look. A little way further on, the street becomes a lane, and there is Armen waiting for us, a robust man in spite of his age, with thick white hair, bushy eyebrows and coarse whiskers. He is wearing spotted tracksuit trousers and a shirt unbuttoned to his navel, and has so much nicotine on his vocal cords that every cough becomes a concert. He was a shepherd, he croaks, a shepherd all his life, and he takes us with him into his house, which consists of an anteroom for lumber and a living room with darkened windows. As we enter, a woman whose hair is still black, sitting on the edge of the bed watching an Indian romantic film, turns to look at us, with no greeting. Her sleeveless pink dress could just as well be a dressing gown. Armen introduces her as his second wife, but his first love; perhaps we saw his other wife along the road, yes, where the mosque used to be. He was born in the village, he says, where there were fifteen, sixteen other Armenian houses; apart from them, only Azeris lived here. What were the weddings like? In all the decades, there were only two mixed couples,

Armen says, not more. And did the people go to each other's celebrations, or to funerals? The Azeris often came to the Armenians'; the Armenians practically never went to the Azeris'. Why? Because there was always plenty to eat at the Armenians', says Armen, and laughs so piteously that we almost want to take him to a doctor. He has nevertheless finished his third cigarette in the few minutes we've been here, and in spite of the late hour he has put a mocha on the table that is not for weak hearts. 'We were all poor, but the Azeris weren't as lavish with their celebrations; that's not part of their tradition. So it wasn't worth our while.'

Apart from the Azeris' meagre hospitality, the coexistence was more or less harmonious, but after about 1968 the authorities didn't assign any vacant houses to Armenians any more. Naturally that led to conflicts and gave them the feeling they were no longer welcome in their own country, especially since they were discriminated against in other government offices too, Armen says, in the distribution of commissions, food and jobs. In 1982, things had become intolerable, and Armen moved to a village where only Armenians lived, not far away. Here in Khojaly, only the two Armenians stayed who were married to Azeris. When the war broke out, the mayor's son killed his mother; the other Armenian had fled in time with her husband. Where Armen lived at the time, four residents were killed and 500 sheep stolen. He knew about the massacre of Khojaly, and, a quarter of a century later, he still believes the Azeris were shot by their own soldiers because they ran away. The Armenian Army had no motive to kill Azeris who were already on the way to Azerbaijan, he says; besides, Armenians never kill women and children. Then Armen reaches behind him and lays a long knife on the table. 'We only kill men.'

'With this knife?'

'Yes, with this knife,' says Armen, and holds it to his throat: 'Like this.'

He and the other men of the Armenian village captured two Azeris; whether they were soldiers or not is not quite clear. A woman from Sumgait who had barely survived the pogrom stepped forward and struck one of the two prisoners in the neck with a kitchen knife. In Sumgait she had seen how Armenian women had had their breasts and ears cut off.

'Did the prisoners have anything to do with Sumgait?'

'No, of course not; they were from here.'

'But why did the woman want to kill them?'

'That's how vendetta is,' says Armen, using the Italian word, and makes a dismissive gesture, as if one death more makes no difference.

'And then?'

'The kitchen knife didn't go through his skin; it wasn't sharp enough. So I gave her mine.'

'This knife here?' I ask, pointing at the table.

'Yes, this knife,' says Armen, and holds it to his throat again. 'Then she drank his blood.'

It was long ago, in 1930, that someone went swimming in Lake Sevan and didn't come back. An expedition was sent out and brought back the frozen but smiling swimmer. He had been found lying on a rock. The inhabitants of the island greeted the rescued man with applause. 'That was the most splendid handclapping I ever heard in my life,' writes Osip Mandelstam: 'a man was being congratulated on the fact that he was not yet a corpse.'[56]

Forty-sixth Day: Through Nagorno-Karabakh

'What do you do as foreign minister of a state no one recognizes?'

'Whether the state is recognized or not doesn't make a big difference,' says Karen Mirzoyan, who is Nagorno-Karabakh's foreign minister. 'Like any other foreign minister, I represent my country in the world. I just can't use the traditional means of diplomacy. But, on the other hand, that leaves me freer. I practically don't exist.'

'And how does not existing make you freer?'

'Well, I can communicate much more directly. I can go to Berlin and talk to people over beer and sausages. I can explain to them that we're a normal country and that all we want is to live normal lives.' Nagorno-Karabakh isn't really that special, he continues: he just spent ten days in Transnistria, where they have quite similar problems. And what does he think of other separatist movements, whether in eastern Ukraine or in Crimea, in Abkhazia or in South Ossetia, in Catalonia or in Scotland: is there a natural sympathy? Yes, of course, the Karabakhis feel solidarity with all peoples fighting for their right to self-determination.

'Why don't you found a Union of Unrecognized States?'

'That's the wrong expression,' Karen Mirzoyan replies, apparently not finding the suggestion entirely absurd: 'Union of Obstructed States would be more accurate. There are many states that have had long struggles for recognition. Even states that are superpowers today were once unrecognized.'

Karen Mirzoyan is an affable man, bearded, with professorial glasses, who would smile if he were to read here that his belly does not disguise his predilection for beer and sausages. He doesn't deny the Khojaly massacre outright but says things are more complicated than they are often portrayed as being – although it's true that Armenians are not perfect and war is dirty. Later, if there is a political solution, there will be a time to bring together the conflicting narratives. Isn't it rather the other way around? I ask. Isn't recognizing the other side's suffering the prerequisite for a solution? The foreign minister knows the historical background, having read Middle Eastern studies, yet he is not so sure. Before Khojaly there was Sumgait; before Sumgait something else; and so on, backwards in time, until you come to the tsars, the Persians or the Mongols. Just read Ferdowsi's *Book of Kings*, he suggests: Nagorno-Karabakh is already mentioned as the home of the Armenians in a tenth-century Persian poem. Well, I answer, the Azerbaijanis would point out that Nagorno-Karabakh is the birthplace of their most famous singers and poets, and didn't first belong to Azerbaijan under the Soviet Union but was a khanate for centuries. He would phrase it differently, says the foreign minister: after centuries, Nagorno-Karabakh is finally free. I remind him that many Armenians were resettled in Nagorno-Karabakh by the Russians only in the nineteenth century. Exactly, cries the foreign minister, anyone can find an episode in history that fits his interpretation. How far back do we want to go? In the end, we would arrive at the mythical conflict between nomads and settlers. No, he doubts it would be helpful to argue about history; pragmatic solutions are more important, and the Azeris moving back into their houses is certainly not one.

Stepanakert is not a beautiful city but not a poor one either. The streets show that a lot of money has flowed into Nagorno-Karabakh, more than to other Armenian small towns, at any rate. Stepanakert is small, with barely 50,000 inhabitants, although it is now a capital – small as everything is in Nagorno-Karabakh, except the mountains enclosing the high plain on three sides. Armenians in the diaspora in particular demonstrate their patriotism by supporting the young state's development; they donate, invest, spend their vacation here, or do volunteer service, like young American Jews in Israel. The names of donors are inscribed on many public buildings. There is also a motorway that runs right across the country and a new airport from which no plane has ever taken off. To our surprise, the doors nonetheless swing open, allowing us to stroll into the brand-new terminal. We can walk up to the check-in counter, take a baggage trolley, use the public toilets. The sign shows that check-in will start at 3:30 p.m., but that's only a test, the manager of the airport tells us – or perhaps he's only a well-dressed caretaker; in any case, he's the only other person in the whole building. He willingly leads us through the security barrier, which beeps although there are no officers around to care. We don't need to put our hand luggage through the X-ray machine to get to the departure lounge or to continue from there out to the equally deserted runway. The runway at least is guarded by two soldiers who wonder what we're doing here; we might ask them the same thing.

'Could an aeroplane land this afternoon?'

'Yes, absolutely,' the manager assures me – I will assume that's what he is – and he explains that an exercise is conducted once a week to practise for a landing. Then he points to the control tower, where – unbelievable! – two air traffic controllers wave down at us.

'And what do the controllers do?'

'They wait,' says the manager, and hopes that I'll be able to take a plane on my next trip to Nagorno-Karabakh: 'That's our parting wish to every visitor.'

Unfortunately, we have not been granted a permit for the buffer zone around Aghdam, which belongs to the Azerbaijani mainland and was nonetheless taken by Armenian troops in 1993. So, as I did on the other side of the border, I decide to try my luck and see how far we get. To our amazement, no one stops us, and we find neither a barrier nor a checkpoint. We can simply drive on into no man's land. To the left and right of the deteriorating track, bounded by fences full of holes, the ruins of single-storey stone houses dot the plain, overgrown with thick brush, their roofs and sometimes their walls caved in, all windows torn out; between them the occasional wrecked car, crumpled like paper, as if to save space in the vacant plain. A few lanes show traces of people still walking between the houses, and on foot I come to fields where maize and potatoes are growing. In the middle of the silence, which the sight of the hastily abandoned farmhouses and the last vestiges, such as empty tins and plastic dolls, brings virtually to a roar, in the middle of the war after which life did not return, the phone I thought was dead vibrates in my trouser pocket and emits one – no, two – no, three – a whole sequence of message signals. 'Welcome to Azerbaijan,' reads the first text message I've received; 'in your plan, each minute costs ...'. I seize the opportunity to phone home. 'Where are you?' asks my ten-year-old daughter, and I try to explain it to her.

The farther we drive, the closer together the ruins stand. There are trees that once formed an avenue or offered shade in a park, and more and more buildings have multiple storeys: those will have housed the government offices of Aghdam, which was once a provincial capital of 50,000 inhabitants. If I place the style correctly, they are from the early days of the Soviet Union. We see no prefabs; perhaps they did not survive the passage of time, although they were newer. While Aghdam's football club-in-exile, Qarabağ Futbol Klubu, has just won the Azerbaijan championship and will play in the Champions League next year, pigs run wild among the ruins of Aghdam. On an empty field which may once have been the town's central square, a troop of young soldiers are chopping wood, without showing much ambition. Probably new recruits, to judge by their age, they are wearing T-shirts with their camouflage trousers and trainers or plastic slippers on their feet. We refrain from going to talk to them to avoid any questions about what we're doing here. Fortunately, they do not seem particularly interested in us.

We come to the great mosque, built in 1868, which is protected by the state of Nagorno-Karabakh, a sign says. The sign itself is weathered, however. The mosque is comparatively well preserved, especially the two splendid minarets in two colours of brick. Of the decorations that once ornamented the prayer hall, however, only a few scraps remain. The conquerors have left their names on the bare walls; the windows, no doubt ornate, have been torn out; the floor is covered with debris. From the minaret I look down at the city, which was not bombarded, nor even fired upon, but fell to Armenia on 23 July 1993, without a fight. The surrender of Aghdam amounted to a collapse of the Azerbaijani Army, which was practically leaderless because of the power struggle in Baku. A short time later, the former head of Azerbaijan's communist party, Heydar Aliyev, emerged victorious from that struggle and with a ceasefire agreement stopped the war, but also democracy in the country. Today, Aghdam looks as you imagine cities would look after an atomic bomb or a poison gas attack. Everything that goes with people is there, but there is no human life. Hasn't Enver Pasha, who fled to Germany after the defeat of the Ottoman Empire and then carried his pan-Turkism to central Asia, falling in the fight against the Red Army in Tajikistan in 1922 – haven't his ideals triumphed after all? 'Here, as everywhere else in the world, nationalism had set to work to break up the rich, indeed profoundly religious concepts of the state into their paltry biological components,' Franz Werfel writes in *The Forty Days of Musa Dagh*. Cities filled with a Babylonian tangle of languages, countries where the peoples coexisted, not famously, but persistently; an early modernity in which cosmopolitanism went without saying; villages in which the religions were good neighbours or bad, but neighbours: in Armenia and Azerbaijan, the communities have become racially pure as almost nowhere else, not even in Turkey itself, and not even in Germany, in spite of the Holocaust. That is what I should have said in objection to the foreign minister of the state of Nagorno-Karabakh when he dismissed the khanate as foreign domination, but it is also what is wrong with the courageous proponents of enlightenment who founded a national culture in Baku; it is what you feel like reminding modern humanity when you look down from the minaret at the deserted city of Aghdam:

> The pashas of former days knew well enough that their concept of all-embracing spiritual unity – the Caliphate – was nobler than the obsessions of a few progress-mad overachievers. In the indolence and vice of the old empire, its *laisser-aller*, its sleepy venality, there lay concealed a cautious wisdom, a moderating, resigned governing principle, which entirely escaped short-sighted westerners striving after quick results. The old pashas knew with the subtlest instinct that a noble, even if ruined palace will not bear too much renovation. But the Young Turks managed to destroy the work of centuries in a breath. They did what they, the chiefs of a state comprising several races, never should have done. Their mad jingoism aroused that of subject peoples.[57]

Franz Werfel was already nostalgic to the point of indecency in 1933, and yet worse was to come.

The former street continues eastwards on the far side of an unguarded barricade, but I don't dare walk more than two, three hundred yards across the open field, because somewhere there have to be trenches, barbed-wire fences, mines, or whatever is keeping Armenia and Azerbaijan apart. So we drive north, and at the edge of Aghdam we discover a car parked in front of a house. And in the courtyard we actually find a little family, father and mother busy renovating, and their handicapped son. Five years ago he came into the world weighing 920 grams, explains the mother, unhesitatingly inviting us to coffee. Chickens are running through the yard, turkeys, and a lamb trying to escape the son. In the shed, more animals are bleating. The father says the tensions in Nagorno-Karabakh began with collectivization – before his time, that is – but he does not trace them back to the genocide, the Middle Ages or some time of legend; he doesn't think that far back. He was born in Askeran, 18 kilometres west of here, worked there as a cook, and a few years ago he found the farm in Aghdam that was the closest to being workable. No one asked him anything when he took it over as a dacha. They sell fruit, vegetables and eggs, and now milk and meat too, at the market. He didn't fight for the liberation himself – he had just turned eighteen then – but he was called up last year for the April war. So he treasures peace more than anything else.

'Do you think the Azeris will ever return?'

'I'm only a working man,' he says. 'If peace prevails, they can come back. Why not?'

'And if the owners showed up at the door – would you give them back the farm?'

'If they are good people – of course. It belongs to them. I would say I rebuilt the farm for them.'

A few hundred yards further on, we meet a blonde, most likely bleached, woman with ostentatious make-up coming the other way, her arms strong enough to carry two big water canisters. She moved to Nagorno-Karabakh only in 1998, because her husband found a job here; since his death two years ago she has been alone in the strange country, and now it's too late to go back. She lives in Aghdam because it costs nothing and she has a big garden. Besides, there are soldiers everywhere who buy the fruit and vegetables she grows; the money pays for the few things she can't grow herself. She no longer expects anything from the government, and from fate she wants only to be left in peace.

We can tell when we've left the buffer zone by the asphalt that once again covers the road completely, by the power lines, and by the houses that are not in ruins. The first village we come to is called New Maragha, and, besides a Soviet memorial – more forgotten than preserved – for the inhabitants fallen in the Second World War, there is also a memorial to the lost home-land. We ask some women sitting in front of the two shops who here is from old Maragha, and they lead us to a shack where Amirian Ruzik looks back on seventy-nine years. He knows nothing about any Azeris' inborn hatred of Armenians; they always got along well in Maragha, perhaps because the Azeris there were a small minority. Why then did the violence break out? 'It came out of nowhere!' says Ruzik, as many people do after a civil war. In his recollection, the Azeri head of the Communist Party, Abdurrahman Vezirov, went on television in 1989 and called on the people to kill Armenians, and soon afterwards their village was being fired on by tanks. The Red Army helped the inhabitants leave Maragha, and Ruzik struggled through by bus and shared taxi to Samarkand, where his sister lived. When he came back, all the houses were demolished, the village was occupied by the Azeri Army, and both of his sons were in the war on the Armenian side. The head man of the village summoned all the inhabitants he could find, twelve families, and they moved into the houses here, which Azeris had abandoned. Because he was all alone, he was assigned only this tumbledown shack, which doesn't even have running water, and he is still angry about the injustice. The wrong people are in charge in New Maragha, as in the rest of the world for that matter. The idea that the conflict dates back to collectivization is nonsense, he says; on the contrary: if the Soviet Union hadn't collapsed, he would still be living well in Maragha today and not in a windowless tip with a 60-dollar pension that barely pays for cigarettes. But smoking a bit less wouldn't hurt either, he admits.

'And the children?' I ask.

'My daughter Nune has a house in New Maragha.'

'Why don't you move in with her?'

'I go over for meals, but the rest of the day – you know, I love being alone.'

By now his daughter is here, already forty-five years old herself and willing to show us the house her father doesn't want to live in, in spite of her entreaties. Is the old cemetery still there, the Muslim one? No, says Nune, nor the mosque. There is an even older cemetery, a few kilometres outside the village; there are many tombstones there engraved with Arabic script.

'Why are they still standing?'

'Once somebody destroyed one of the old tombstones, and the next day someone in his family died. Since then, we've left the old cemetery alone.'

'And what about the trees?' it suddenly occurs to me to ask.

'The trees too,' answers Nune, who doesn't seem to find the question strange. 'The trees have no nationality.'

After we have visited the old cemetery, where the dead were buried in a different calendar – 1328 or 1305 after the Hijra – Nune takes us with her into the house where she lives with her family. It belonged to the village imam, who does not seem to have been a poor man. The green paint of the interior has peeled, the dark floorboards are worn, the window frames have never been replaced. In the garden stands an old apple tree full of fruit. 'What a beautiful house!' I exclaim, and ask why they didn't renovate it.

'My sons don't want us to.'

'Why not?'

'They think the war could break out again any day, and then we would have to run away and leave everything behind a second time.'

In parting, Nune gives us a big bag of apples from the tree that the imam, or perhaps his father or grandfather, planted.

Forty-Seventh Day: To the Armenian–Azeri Ceasefire Line and on to Iran

Shusha is much too expansive for its 3,500 inhabitants, most of whom are poor Armenian refugees from Azerbaijan. One of the most important cities in Transcaucasia as late as the nineteenth century, famous for its new churches, mosques and theatres, prosperous as the hub of the trade routes, quadrilingual with Armenian, Azeri Turkish, Persian and Russian, it was burnt down three times, in 1905, 1920 and 1992; the last time by Armenians, before that by Azerbaijanis, and the first time by both. Osip Mandelstam in his day was shocked by the broad, deserted streets that climb the steep hillside.

> And so, in upland Karadagiy,
> in that predatory place, Shusha,
> I tasted terrors
> that the soul knows too well.
> Forty thousand dead windows
> stare from all directions, there,
> and labour's heartless cocoon
> lies buried on the mountain.[58]

In 1992, when Khojaly had long since fallen, the Azerbaijani artillery held out long in Shusha – whose population was 90 per cent Azeri – bombarding the nearby capital Stepanakert, which lay 600 metres lower. The Armenians finally took Shusha on the 8th and 9th of May 1993, with heavy losses, and left it to looters and marauders. It was a conscious, publicly committed act of revenge: in the brief war between Armenia and Azerbaijan, when both nations were independent for the first time since the end of the Romanov dynasty, Azeri soldiers had run amok in the city for three days, destroying the Armenian quarter and massacring hundreds of Armenian civilians. The fact that the two main mosques are still standing is the work of a group of longstanding Armenian inhabitants who stood up to the tanks after the fall of the city and then barricaded themselves inside the city museum for seven days to protect the precious carpets, paintings and vessels. Many of the stone buildings that survived have since been restored to attract visitors, but residents are also lacking. The churches shine as if they were just built, and the two mosques bear signs saying they were restored with Iranian help, although evidence of it is hard to find. But so are the pigs reported in Azerbaijani newspapers, for that matter.

The young press officer with whom we drive towards the front explains to us that not even he is told in advance what sector reporters will be taken to.

'Why not?' I ask.

'Because the Azeris eavesdrop on our communications.'

'Aha.'

'But we intercept theirs too! Once we heard a general making a date with his mistress. Then he told his wife he was going to be late on account of an important meeting. So then we called his wife and told her where her husband was.'

'So that's how you win the war!'

'That's called psychological warfare,' says the officer, indicating by his laughter that it was more a boyish prank – if the story is true at all.

The atmosphere in the barracks at Martakert in northeastern Karabakh is relaxed because today is Sunday, and hence the soldiers get permission to leave the post. Outside, parents are waiting to spend the day with their sons; inside, the loudspeakers are playing Armenian pop music and the recruits are playing football. The major orders coffee for us on the condition that we have a drink with him after our visit to the front. We get a Merci chocolate as a bonus. When I mention that I also visited the border from the Azeri side, everyone in the office wants to know what it looks like over there. I report on my visit to Tap Qaragoyunlu, and that shots are exchanged there every now and again.

'Yes, they're always the ones who start it,' says the major.

'The Azeris say the same thing.'

We are taken along cart tracks 'to the northern ceasefire line', as I am instructed to write to avoid mentioning the exact location. In any case, Tap Qaragoyunlu lies somewhere along the silhouette of buildings and trees maybe two, maybe four kilometres away. In spite of the ceasefire, skirmishes occur regularly, says the soldier, handing me his binoculars; only yesterday the Azeris fired another twenty rounds, without the Armenians returning fire. Usually no one gets hurt; you just have to pay strict attention never to leave the cover of the sandbags and trenches. Until the year 2000, they used to talk to the other side on the telephone; they even met for meals. But now they can only observe the enemy's movements; that increases the risk of unintended incidents.

In contrast to the front in Georgia or in eastern Ukraine, the position is obviously meant to be a permanent one: the trenches are carefully propped up and floored with stone slabs, and there are roofed chambers along them for rest or meals. The soldiers are posted here for two weeks at a time, then they return to barracks. Military service is for two and a half years, and recruits go to the front after six months' training. Do they think they'll live to see the opening of the border? I ask the recruits who have joined us in the little coffee room. No, not their generation, says one; their grandchildren perhaps. Asked about their goals, they give the usual answers: work, family, security, a decent life; some hope to go abroad. I ask whether they think young people in Azerbaijan today have different goals – for example, the recruits doing their military service in the trenches on the other side. Yes, says one of the recruits, he thinks people his age on the other side have different goals. They, the Armenians, want to build houses, he says; the others want to destroy houses. Do they really believe the life ambition of young Azeris is to destroy houses? Yes, the recruit confirms: even the children there are raised to hate. I tell them about the historic revanchism between the French and the Germans and that, when I was a schoolboy, it was hard for children in my class to find a host family in France because many grandparents refused to have a German in the house. And for young people today, 'revanchism' is just a word they learn in history class.

'There is a big difference,' the commander chimes in, who is ten or fifteen years older than the recruits.

'What's that?'

'The Germans and the French are both Europeans. But we here, right here in this trench, are on the easternmost edge of Europe. Over there' – he points his hand in the direction of the silhouette of buildings and trees two or four kilometres away – 'over there is where Asia starts.'

'And that means?'

'That means we are dealing with sheep.'

I ask to make sure I have understood the interpreter's translation correctly. *Sheep*? Not *ship*, or something else?

'They are sheep,' the commander says, to put any misunderstanding to rest. 'They are told which way to run, and they all run that way. That is the difference.'

Not only is it always the other side that shoots first, probably in every war, it is also always the others who hate, while everyone on our side only wants to live a normal life: work, family, security.

For the rest of the day we drive in switchbacks up and down the various mountain ranges, first along the main route back to the Armenian mainland, then towards Iran. The further south we go, the more Persian signs we see by the roadside – for hotels, restaurants or 'disco dancing' – and the shabbier the socialist housing blocks look. The most Middle Eastern thing about the cities and towns are the bustling crowds in the streets and on the pavements, the like of which I didn't see anywhere north of the Caucasus, although the architecture was the same. The streets look like village scenes, in part because of the few cars and the black clothes of the old women. I imagine what people's first impression is when they arrive from the opposite direction: sobering, because they do not associate poverty with Armenians, who belong to the middle class in Iran, and because the image evoked by 'disco dancing' is quite different from a dive in the ground floor of a high-rise estate whose vestigial façade is mercifully hidden by washing hung out to dry.

When we reach the River Aras, the limit beyond which imperial Russia repulsed Iran, I see a different landscape, the one so familiar to me: the warm brown of the broad, bare slopes, lit up in the evening sun, sharply divided from the glowing green of the valleys, traversed by the rushing water like a silver chain. The Caucasus, with its deep gorges and steep mountains covered with forests, bushes and grasses, could not have a more natural border than this one, no matter how arbitrarily it was drawn in the nineteenth century. After the Armenian passport check, I walk all alone with my suitcase, as if in a spy film, across the wide bridge at whose far end awaits, not a black limousine, but a pair of border agents such as you could only find in the Islamic Republic of Iran. While the younger one, the one in uniform, with narrow sideburns and his hair gelled up into a roof ridge as if he were on his way to an MTV appearance, types my data into the computer, the older one, evidently his superior, lounges in his chair in an Adidas tracksuit and seems to be reading along on his screen, unless he is watching YouTube videos. Both of them are clean-shaven, which in itself was for a long time unthinkable for Iranian civil servants, because the revolutionary ideology called for at least a three-day beard. Soon they'll be putting on ties too, and then the revolution will be on its way out.

There's something not right about my data, so the superior shuffles away on his sneakers. When he returns, he asks me to follow him. The informal mode of address between the state and the citizen, a radical break with the baroque set phrases of Persian conversation, is a feature of the revolution that still persists. In the entrance area of the office to which I am led, the carpeting has been cut away so that people can take their shoes off as they would at the entrance to a mosque. Through the open door, I spy two legs in the next room lying on the desk in pyjama trousers. Peasants, I think in my bourgeois arrogance, not even a state of workers and peasants, but just peasants: I am sure the customs officials, both the dapper MTV star and the casual athlete, and most of all the devout fellow who owns the two legs in pyjama trousers, and likewise the ministers, ambassadors, generals, secretaries of state and the millionaire directors of the state and religious enterprises, have all retained, two, at most three generations after urbanization, their provincial customs and lifestyle. Their informal address is not that of the comrade but that of the village.

'Yā Ali!' I hear, the invocation of the Shiites' first imam, and shortly thereafter a bearded officer enters the room, without a uniform jacket, his greyish-brown service shirt half out of his dark trousers, and begins by apologizing for my having to take off my shoes. If that is a problem for me, he would come outside, but, he says, we are more comfortable in the office. Then he invites me to be seated on one of the sofas and asks me, with the placating formal form of address and in the obsequious tone required by the Persian ritual of politeness, for my occupation, education, family, itinerary, address in Germany, address in Iran, telephone number in Germany, telephone number in Iran, and so on. These are the routine questions, I realize right away, not an interrogation. I inquire whether I may charge my phone while we talk, and the officer pulls the plug of the television set on which the state news channel is trying to imitate CNN, except that the anchorwoman is wearing a black chador. Once the officer asks me to advise him what else he might ask about, and I tell him the year my parents emigrated from Iran. Why is he writing all of this down? I ask. It is the rule in the case of Iranians living abroad, unfortunately; he begs my forgiveness for taking up my precious time. Apparently the most recent rule also requires giving a pleasant reception to Iranians living abroad. The bourgeois one once berated is now the citizen one aspires to be.

This was the last border to cross on this journey, I realize, as I ride into the night in the first taxi I can find on the south bank of the Aras. A few kilometres further on, it is no longer Armenia on the opposite shore, but the Nakhchivan Autonomous Republic, which would be a chapter in itself. For all the advantages of European unity, for all the difficulty of the living conditions and political circumstances to the East and South, there is also something beautiful about borders that are still borders, and the difference it makes whether you are on this side or that, a real difference not just of languages, but of systems, ways of life, cultures and experiences, such a radical difference as there no longer is within the European Union, nor even within the Western hemisphere. Only the borders must be open, otherwise we will never know the differences, and hence never know ourselves.

Forty-Eighth Day: Via Jolfa to Tabriz

Just when I was emphasizing the diversity between countries, Iran begins as Armenia left off: with a church. Far from so-called civilization, which seems coarse in comparison, reflecting the rugged brown of the mountainsides in the middle of the green, it is a warning of the wilderness in the middle of Paradise. The Church of Stephanus, ostensibly founded by the Apostle Bartholomew, demonstrates that Christianity is a Middle Eastern religion. The stalactite vault in the portal, the continuous ornamentation inside the cupola, evoking the infinity of Heaven, only look typically Islamic; they are just as much Christian and, if they are typical of anything, then of Middle Eastern sacred architecture as a whole. Will it one day be said that Christianity *was* a Middle Eastern religion? Mass is said in St Stephanus only on holy days because there are neither monks nor congregations round about; but the church is in a better state of preservation and more carefully restored than the monasteries I visited in Armenia itself. And, in Europe, synagogues are valued only now that there are few Jews left. A genocide is not necessary for the minority to be suddenly missed; there can be other reasons as well for their disappearance – expulsion, contempt, disenfranchisement, general distress. St Stephen is of course a very desirable saint for a Shiite country, revered as he is in Christianity as the first martyr. Christianity is the real, the earlier religion of blood witness: that is also part of what the Church of Stephanus recalls, standing so to speak at the entrance to Iran.

In Jolfa, the first city across the border, I imagine a visiting Armenian's first impression of Iran. First the usual, of course: the women's headscarves, or the boxy little cars that look as if they were designed after a child's drawing – no wonder no one wants to import them. No 'disco dancing', but at least Coca-Cola, burgers and the return of the pizzeria. Next, the Armenian will think: more traffic and better roads; more goods and more advertising; more wealth and more poverty. Those who are fighting for the preservation of historic architecture in Yerevan will notice the brutal functionalism of the architecture in Jolfa, which easily rivals communist housing blocks in ugliness. I have no consolation to offer the Armenian: where nothing is left of

278

their history – and that is much less than in the modern West – small towns are equally dreary everywhere in Iran, that is, dreary in the same way: along a multi-lane thoroughfare, a row of shop fronts in two- to three-storey cubes built of concrete blocks, often not even plastered, or else covered by a façade of bright-coloured plastic. At least Jolfa has a new pedestrian zone: no doubt someone in authority brought back the idea from a business trip to Europe – in the Islamic Republic, such travel is a bonus for loyalty to the party line.

The well-built motorway takes me in less than two hours to Tabriz, once half a day's journey away. Some summers we drove, with my parents and my brothers, from Germany to Isfahan by car: in those days there was something almost cosy, contemplative about the city, in anticipation of the next stop, Tehran. Now Tabriz is another megalopolis, a behemoth eating into the desert, marbled with motorways, hemmed by modern apartment blocks, larded with shopping malls, surrounded by commuter towns. In those days, Iran had 30 million inhabitants; today there are over 80 million, and urbanization continues – so this is how noisy population growth is, how unpleasant it smells.

I flee from the summer heat and the smog into the labyrinthine bazaar, which is still the same as in my childhood memories and has thus become much more exotic in forty, forty-five years in comparison with the changes all around it: the miraculously cool air and the aromas that change every metre, herbs, spices, soaps, dairy products, fishes, meats, carpets and work-shops, the dulled rays from the tiny skylights, and the displays that glow nonetheless in every colour. In a tea house I order baklava and a hookah, only to set my head spinning with the first puff. The shisha cafés along Eigelstein in Cologne have evidently weaned me off the strong, unperfumed tobacco. I bravely draw in the smoke until a pleasant rapture sets in, slowing down the life around me by 10 per cent, the already sluggish innkeeper with his lazy assistants, the likewise lethargic merchants, and also the old people hurrying through the narrow, crowded aisles with two-wheeled handcarts as if they were paid for every second saved. I don't understand a word of the conversations at the surrounding tables – not because of the hubbub, but because everyone is speaking Turkish, Azeri-Turkish to be exact. About 16 million Azerbaijanis live in Iran, twice as many as in the Republic of Azerbaijan. Thus, if the innkeeper acts a bit paternalistic towards me, as if he had to explain to me how to drink tea, it is because he sees me not as a foreigner but as a Persian.

What am I writing? asks the man whose hookah is next to mine on the table. I'm a writer, I explain. I take notes all the time; that's part of my job.

'Are you writing about us?' he asks with amusement, indicating the men beside him with whom he has been talking.

'I would like to, but I don't understand a word,' I admit candidly, and ask him the first question that comes into my head, now that he has addressed me in Persian: 'Would the people here rather belong to Iran or to North Azerbaijan?'

'That can't be answered in one sentence,' answers one of the men, leaning towards us from the other table.

'Then answer in two.'

'I used to be proud to be Iranian. But now I'm *untarafi*.' This is the first time I've heard this usage: literally, the word means 'beyond', 'belonging to the further side'; here it seems to be a fixed expression for supporters of a union with the north.

'But you control the country,' I say, and point out that even the bazaar of Tehran, the economic heart of the country from time immemorial, is in Azeri hands, and Azeris also occupy critical posts in the government, right up to the Leader of the Revolution, Ayatollah Khamenei.

'No!' my neighbour protests, 'the Leader is not Azeri; that's just a pretence. In reality, his parents immigrated from Iraq.'

'Even if they did – there are so many Azeris in the bureaucracy.'

'They repudiate their Turkishness; they don't speak Azeri, or, if they do, then only at home.'

'Just look at the country,' another of the men groans contemptuously, as if that were enough to explain why he has become *untarafi*.

'*Untaraf* there is just as little freedom as here.'

'But *untaraf* you can at least enjoy yourself. Here you have neither freedom nor joy.'

'Just look at what they do to you if they catch you with a bottle of whisky.'

'And if you say anything, you get *kun-chubi*.' That is another new expression that seems to have become part of the language of the Islamic Republic. Literally, it means something like 'backside-wooding', in the sense of 'shoving a stick in a person's backside', and it refers to a customary treatment of political prisoners, as the law-enforcement agencies themselves had to admit after the mass protests of 2009, when the son of a high conservative official was inadvertently so tortured along with the other prisoners. But the reality also includes this: this man *is* saying something, loudly and clearly, to a stranger, who is taking notes, while seated with half a dozen men in the bazaar, which has a thousand ears.

I ask my way to the House of the Constitutional Revolution, which is in front of one of the doors of the bazaar, and which everyone in Tabriz still knows. It is the two-storey palace of a wealthy merchant, built in 1868 with brickwork, wooden balustrades, slender columns, multicoloured upper windows and the obligatory fountain in a green courtyard. The portraits of the constitutionalists who assembled in this house in the early twentieth century are hung on the walls, and their personal effects and weapons are displayed in glass cases. The newspapers that were exhibited in the literature museum in Baku are also on display here, including *Molla Nasreddin*, the magazine that satirized the religious establishment, and a printing press that was not faster in its day, but more effective than Facebook and Twitter were during the 2009 rebellion. The opposition between modernists and religionists that escalated at the end of the Ottoman Empire was less acute in Iran's constitutional movement. The modernists cut a fairly traditional figure, with their Middle Eastern robes and robust moustaches, and many ayatollahs, including those ranking highest among them, supported liberal reforms. A large photograph shows the first Iranian parliament in 1906, whose members wore either fezzes or turbans but adopted a constitution that was progressive even by European standards. The Armenian resistance fighter Yeprem Khan is commemorated as a reminder that some Armenian units fought for Iran's first democracy, and half of a room, including a bronze bust, is devoted to the American Howard Baskerville, who got caught up in the political maelstrom while teaching at the Presbyterian mission school in Tabriz. In spite of all the American consul's efforts to deter him, Baskerville not only supported the revolution but became one of its military leaders, helping with his regiment to defend Tabriz under siege by royalist troops in 1909. 'The only difference between me and these people is my place of birth,' he once said to a countryman, probably the consul, 'and this is not a big difference.'

When, after ten months – the inhabitants had begun to eat grass – the American tried to break through the siege line with a group of students on 20 April 1909, he became a martyr of Iran at the age of just twenty-four. Half Tabriz made the pilgrimage to the Armenian cemetery for his funeral, where a member of the parliament said, 'Young America made this sacrifice for the constitution of Iran in the person of young Baskerville.' Five days later, Tabriz fell to the royalists, whose mobilization was backed by Russia and Great Britain. Shortly before, the two great powers had divided Iran into two zones of influence in the Anglo-Russian Entente and agreed on Mohammad Ali Shah as their joint puppet. Nevertheless, the constitutionalists counter-attacked in the same year and drove out Mohammad Ali Shah. When the parliament returned to its work in November 1909, the session began with a eulogy to Howard Baskerville. His rifle, wrapped in an Iranian flag, was sent to his parents in Minnesota: 'Persia deeply mourns the loss of its dear son, honourably fallen for the cause of freedom, and we swear that the future Persian nation will always remember him as a Lafayette and will always protect his sacred grave.'

Another room is devoted to the women who participated in the revolution, and not just in spirit. They regularly defended the meetings of oppositional clerics by sit-ins in front of the mosque, and in just one battle there were twenty women among the fallen constitutionalists. Another woman partisan killed a loyalist cleric who was speaking in support of the shah in Artillery Barracks Square in Tehran; she was executed on the spot. There is Bibi Khanoum Astarabadi, whose pamphlet *The Shortcomings of Men* had turned the dominant image of the sexes on its head before the turn of the century, and who opened Iran's first Muslim girls' school in 1907. There is Zaynab Pasha, who led the protests against the tobacco concession in Tabriz. In 1890, Nasser ad-Din Shah, who reigned for almost half a century, had granted a British businessman a monopoly on the production and export of tobacco, one of Iran's most lucrative industries before the discovery of oil. The opposition thereupon proclaimed a boycott, and the clergy issued a fatwa saying smoking was a sin until further notice. Zaynab Pasha and a group of armed women stormed the shops that persisted in selling tobacco, as well as the state department store in Tabriz. 'If you men have no courage to fight the oppressor, take our veils and get lost,' she shouted at a meeting. 'Just don't claim to be men. We'll fight in your place.' Then she pulled off her veil – an unheard-of provocation at the turn of the twentieth century – and threw it at the hesitant men. After her example, several women of Tehran stood in front of the convoy of Nasser ad-Din's successor Mozaffar in 1906 and recited a declaration of protest: 'Beware the day when the people shall take away your crown and your robe of state.' There is the first Iranian woman's magazine, *Dānesh* ('Knowledge') from 1910, followed by others, *Jahān-e zan* ('Woman's world'), *Shokufeh* ('Blossom'), *Zabān-e zan* ('Language of women') and *Zanān-e Iran* ('Women of Iran'). There are the banners of the women's organizations that formed all over the country in the course of the revolution: Society for the Freedom of Women, Secret Union of Iranian

282

Women, Ladies' Patriotic Association, Society for the Welfare of Iranian Women, Women of Iran, Union of Women, Association of Jewish Women, Ambassadors of Women's Prosperity, Society of Christian Graduates, and so on. When Russia issued a forty-eight-hour ultimatum to the elected government of Iran in late 1911 calling for the expulsion of the chancellor of the treasury – William Morgan Shuster, an American customs official and writer who had reformed the country's feudal tax system and dissolved its oppressive foreign contracts – 300 women forced their way into parliament, tore off their veils and demanded that the representatives resist the pressure: the American must stay, otherwise they would kill their husbands, their children and themselves. And in fact the parliament refused Russia's demand. All the text there is to read about early Iranian feminism is incredible enough, but now I see the photos of the revolutionary women, and I am still more perplexed: they are all heavily veiled – that is, not just with headscarves, but with the traditional chador that covers the whole body. Of course they are veiled, I realize, otherwise they couldn't have torn the chador from their heads in protest.

Because there are few explanations accompanying the exhibits, I ask whether someone can guide me through the exhibition. No, there is no guide. Nor are there brochures, a plan of the museum, or a catalogue. There is no information at all about the Constitutional Revolution. 'What kind of a museum is this, with no explanations!' scolds a gentleman with a tie resting in the courtyard.

'We should be glad they've left it here at all,' I console him.

'If you look at it that way, you're right, we can be grateful.'

I want to visit the houses of Tabriz's most famous writers, but give up after the first one. The house of Parvin Etesami – my mother's favourite poet, which is why I know her poems – is arranged with such abysmal carelessness that I am ashamed vicariously for my mother. The exhibition is limited to some cheaply enlarged photos, copied poems and a transcript from the American School in Tehran, displayed in two chambers in the basement of the old house. The doubtless splendid salon in the ground floor, which opens on the once flourishing courtyard, is not accessible because the museum director resides there.

In the evening I am the guest of the historian Rahim Raisnia, a scholar of the old, pre-revolutionary school, although he is not all that old and may have been a student himself in 1979. What is old-fashioned about him is rather the type of the silent, naturally secular historian endeavouring to put the past in order regardless of the storms raging all around. For the *Encyclopaedia of the World of Islam* he oversees the culture and history of the Turkic peoples, and so, in the basement of his house, which is stuffed to the ceiling with books, we talk first about the advocates of enlightenment and socialism who were active from the Caucasus to Iran. No, the expulsion and murder of thousands of Iranian communists under Stalin has never been studied in Iran, Raisnia says, shaking his head over the historical blindness typical of all ideologies, not just the Islamic Republic.

And his work for the encyclopaedia? It is relatively unfettered, says Raisnia, although the editor, Gholam Ali Haddad-Adel, is one of the leading conservatives and closest allies of the Leader of the Revolution. After the suppression of the Green Movement in 2009, Haddad-Adel called together the staff of the encyclopaedia to assure them that he made a division between his office as chairman of the parliament and his function as editor of the encyclopaedia; they were to go on with their research as before. Haddad-Adel has mostly kept his word, Raisnia says, and the limits that exist also apply to the other Islamic encyclopaedia. There are two Islamic encyclopaedias? Yes, says Raisnia, the reformists have their own. And the limits? For example, the Bāb and the Baha'i religion, which is persecuted in Iran today, can be mentioned only in negative terms, regardless of which camp you are in. At most, you can keep the tone moderate or the passage short. In his own field, on the other hand – Iran's Turkish-language history – there are no major restrictions. And the Constitutional Revolution? It's more or less fair game since the radical Mahmoud Ahmadinejad is no longer president, but not in the tone the other encyclopaedia takes. The difference is more visible on the anniversary of the Constitutional Revolution: the reformists always gather in the museum, while the conservatives hold a conference elsewhere in Tabriz on Sheikh Fazlollah Nuri, who attained the crown of martyrdom by being publicly hanged in 1909, after he had declared all supporters of the parliament heretics.

What about Mohammad Mosaddegh, the democratically elected prime minister who nationalized the country's oil and was overthrown by the CIA in 1953? Getting better, gradually, says Raisnia. Including the role of the clergy, who supported the coup? If you formulate it very academically and reservedly, you can work the topic in, says Raisnia, although only in an inconspicuous place, a journal article or the like; after all, Ayatollah Kashani, Khomeini's teacher and Mosaddegh's opponent, still gets honoured with street names and postage stamps. I remind Raisnia that Barack Obama, in a speech on the Iranian New Year in 2009, was the first American president to address the Iranian people directly and appealed for a reconciliation; and then Khomeini's successor Ayatollah Khamenei rejected the initiative with the argument, among others, that the United States had overthrown Mosaddegh. Yes, says Raisnia, for Iran the 1953 coup, even more than the failure of the Constitutional Revolution in 1921, was the traumatic political event of the twentieth century, and is therefore instrumentalized even by those who otherwise would never pronounce the name Mosaddegh.

The early feminists? They're all the rage now, Raisnia finds, although not at the universities, where serious research in the social sciences is rare anyway. Every small town nowadays has at least one university, and academic titles have declined in value because of the numerous for-profit colleges that award diplomas in return for money or favours. As if all the politicians and military leaders who pride themselves on their doctorates had even studied in earnest, to say nothing of writing a work like that of Dr Mosaddegh, who was a first-rate legal scholar with a doctoral degree from Switzerland. Add to that, of course, the various waves of dismissals, most recently in 2009, and the emigration of the very cleverest researchers and the most committed teachers. The mathematician Maryam Mirzakhani, Raisnia continues, recently deceased at the age of forty, who was the first woman anywhere to receive the Fields Medal and emigrated to America because she saw no future in Iran, was only one of thousands, tens of thousands; Iran is the country with the highest brain drain in the world.

I ask him about separatism. On his inauguration, President Rouhani promised an academy for Turkish language and culture, but, as with so many other things, he hasn't been able to deliver it, Raisnia reports; the nationalism that is common to all of Iran's religions and ethnic groups is more and more strongly linked in the dominant discourse to Persianness, although only half of Iranians speak Persian as their mother tongue. The culture and literature of the Azeris are studied only in private associations, through privately organized lectures, readings and courses. The result is a dangerous gap. The schools are not allowed to teach in Azeri-Turkish, but at the same time every Azeri, every single one, watches Turkish television; after all, the Iranian channels are intolerable; they mistake the TV studio for a pulpit. Meanwhile, in Turkish television the nationalism is increasing, and as for the Republic of Azerbaijan, they support the separatists, not very secretly, with propaganda and money. Many Azeris are still *intarafi* – that is, all they want is a reasonable autonomy within Iran. But more and more are turning to pan-Turkism, or are *untarafi*. And because many Azeris boycott the elections, Raisnia continues, the Azerbaijani territories vote to a large degree for the conservatives who reject any cultural autonomy: a vicious circle.

And himself? When the borders were still closed, he once watched a bird flying away towards the north, and he thought he would give an eye to see what it looks like *untaraf*. But in the late 1980s, when he was one of the first to go to North Azerbaijan, he was glad he'd kept both his eyes, to be able to see both the progress and the backwardness. Music, for example, was very strong because of the conservatories; that was impressive. And the fact that literature was funded – funded! – was almost unbelievable; there were stipends for writers and residencies for writers in the countryside, not prison cells! But, on the other hand, a lot of what the writers there wrote was pointless; he noticed that too. No wonder, since they were paid by the word: that doesn't encourage rigour. And what did he find backward in Azerbaijan? Books about the Azeri race on display in the bookshops; intellectuals railing against Armenians, replies Raisnia. 'Our job is to put out fires, not to kindle them,' he reminded Anar, then the best-known writer in Azerbaijan and now still president of the association that expelled Akram Aylisli. 'You are right, but that doesn't work here,' Anar answered, and told Raisnia of a lecture in which he quoted a line of an old folk song: 'I love you even if you hate me.' The listeners were outraged, gave voice to their displeasure, just because of this one line from a well-known song, so that he was obliged to say something against the Armenians to get out of a difficult situation. Thus, in Azerbaijan too, loving one's enemy was both an ideal and an impossibility.

In the taxi that takes me back to my hotel, I notice that all the radio communication between the dispatcher and the drivers is in Persian. That's a new rule, the driver explains: anyone who speaks Turkish into the microphone gets reprimanded by the central office and can even be fired for persistent violations. And yet they're all Turks, even the dispatcher, and sometimes he simply doesn't understand her Persian.

Forty-Ninth Day: Via Ahmadabad to Alamout Castle

It's no easy matter to find breakfast along the motorway. The service areas, built after the European model plus minarets, offer sandwiches and croissants, pizza and hamburgers, but nothing my driver would call edible. He can't believe there is no mutton head and mutton foot in aspic between Tabriz and Tehran, the *kalleh-pācheh* that fortifies workers and travellers for the whole day, so he stops at one motorway café after another. While he is asking in yet another restaurant, my gaze falls on a gardener watering the lawn between the car parks with extreme care. At first the situation looks normal, but, the longer I watch, the more surreal it becomes. The gardener seems to be watering each blade of grass individually; he is talking to the lawn as he moves his garden hose in slow motion. Then I think: no, he is real, this gardener is only doing what a gardener does extremely carefully, while all around him the country is going mad: minarets at the motorway services, but no *kalleh-pācheh*, just pizza and hamburgers. In the end, my driver contents himself with a tomato omelette, although he knows before ordering it that it won't be cooked right – not the way they do in Azerbaijan. 'The tomatoes should have been fried longer,' he complains after eating.

'Then you shouldn't have said to hurry when you ordered it,' the waiter says in his defence.

'He's got a point there,' I say, to the driver's exasperation.

'You Persians are all in cahoots,' he wails in his Turkish accent, which in itself is enough to make Persians laugh.

Towards noon we turn off the motorway, which is as straight as the highways north of the Caucasus, although here not even grass covers the endless plain.

'Which way is Ahmadabad?' the driver asks four young men who are waiting at a crossroads, although there are no other cars in sight. The state is so displeased by the memory that the village cannot be signposted.

'To Mosaddegh's tomb?' the men ask in return. They know immediately why we want to go to Ahmadabad.

'Yes,' says the driver.

'God rest his soul,' the men say almost in chorus, pointing us the way.

We look around: in this windy wilderness, arable only where it is heavily irrigated, Mohammad Mosaddegh spent the last years of his life under house arrest; here he lived with his staff, the peasants of his village and 150 guards; here his wife and children were allowed to visit him once a week; here he lies buried; and I would have thought at least nature was no longer his enemy. Here he wrote to his son on 9 February 1962: 'The solitude torments me. I spent most of the summer out of doors and spoke a few words with anyone who passed by. But in winter, when it's cold, I stay in my room and it's very bad. I haven't been able to find anyone trustworthy whom I can talk to. To tell you the truth, I don't care to go on living.'

The pictures of the Iranian prime minister who nationalized the country's oil, taking it away from the British, were printed all over the world in the early 1950s: the recalcitrant leader of a developing nation breaking valid contracts with a world power, sitting up in his bed over papers, in his shirt and pyjama trousers of cheap Iranian material like those the simple people wear. It was his preferred place to work. He received visitors at this bed, including foreign emissaries and even ministers, and that was not just a signal, as it was understood in Iran, that he would no longer stand at attention for the West, nor was it the impertinence of a madman trying to play at world politics, as it was represented the Western press – including left-leaning magazines such as *Der Spiegel* by the way, which put Mosaddegh's head with his mouth contorted on its cover, photographed from below so that the perspective gave him a giant hooked nose like those of Nazi iconography.

Mosaddegh was sick; he suffered from a strange nerve disorder that was never identified; he had frequent fevers and could spend hours discussing his stomach ulcers that no doctor had correctly diagnosed. He also stayed away from his official workplace because he was importuned there by too many people with dubious interests. In spite of his exquisite politeness, to which all eyewitnesses attested, he had little tolerance for the foppery of receptions and balls. Indeed, he despised the affectation of the aristocracy as only an aristocrat can. As a scion of the Qajars, he fought his own class, and even his own relations, during the Constitutional Revolution. He was actually afraid of big rallies, which he organized time and again to explain himself publicly when his opponents intrigued against him – although he was such a moving speaker that he could bring hundreds of thousands to tears. Then the tears often came to his own eyes, or he sank to the floor unconscious behind the lectern. In parliament he once grew so angry that he broke a wooden armrest off the head of government's seat of honour and gesticulated with it wildly. Even today the Iranians call him 'the Lion' for his strength. Yet he complained constantly about his infirmities, his age, his weakness; he read his medical report out loud at international conferences, threatening to shake off once and for all the burden that his office was to him if his demands were not met. And, in fact, in his long political career, which he began at the age of fourteen when the Qajar king appointed him treasurer of the huge province of Khosaran and which led him several times into prison, into exile, and just as often into ministerial posts – in fact, Mosaddegh more than once spontaneously declared his resignation on the open stage because something didn't suit him, got into his turquoise Pontiac and had his chauffeur take him at full speed to his

288

country house in Ahmadabad, where he didn't even answer the telephone for weeks.

On 19 August 1953, the forces supporting the coup d'état besieged Mosaddegh's house in Kach Street, Tehran. The radio station was occupied, there were tanks in the streets, yet the prime minister could have found ways to appeal to the people. As so often, tens of thousands, hundreds of thousands would have poured into the streets and chased off the ragtag crowd from the south side of Tehran who were not advocating their own cause. He made no such appeal; he had surrendered. Some books say Mosaddegh wanted to prevent bloodshed; others see him in the tradition of the Shiite martyrs who accept defeat as their destiny. 'It has all gone so badly, so badly!' sighed one of his ministers as they hid out in the cellar of a neighbouring house. 'And yet it is so good – really good,' Mosaddegh replied. He was put on trial, and defended himself and democracy with the precision of a lawyer and the rhetorical force of an experienced parliamentarian.

Seated: old and bent over the balustrade of the defendant's bench. Speaking: still a snarling lion, lashing out with his index finger and with irresistible arguments. He refused to beg for the shah's pardon, as he was repeatedly urged to do, and to promise he would retire in exchange for a verdict of not guilty. He insisted he was in the right and was sentenced to three years' imprisonment followed by house arrest in Ahmadabad, some hundred kilometres northwest of Tehran.

The Iranians saw from time to time in photos how the man who had once been their hope sat, ever weaker, but unbroken, on his bed or walked laboriously, leaning on a stick, through the courtyard of his country house. He died in 1967, eighty-five years old, of a stomach ulcer, the same illness he had regularly self-diagnosed in public since his student days in Switzerland. The shah prohibited all displays of mourning. Less than a month after the shah was deposed, on 5 March 1979, over a million people travelled in buses and cars, on lorries, and many on foot, to Ahmadabad to observe the anniversary of Dr Mosaddegh's death for the first time.

The property is easy to find because it is the only one in the village that is still surrounded by a clay wall. A woman in a chador who sees us knocking on the iron gate shouts from the other side of the street that we can obtain admission with the help of Mr Takdustar, whose house is in the first street to the right. Mr Takdustar is a slender, tall man with snow-white hair, moustache and stubble who has bound his dusty trousers around his wrinkled shirt with a clothes line. His father was one of the peasants whom Mosaddegh asked to wash his corpse; he himself cooked the lentils that Mosaddegh ate as his last meal. That's enough, said Mosaddegh when the plate was empty, and died the next day.

'That's intentional,' the cook says in answer to our question about the missing signposts. 'This man sacrificed everything for his nation: his fortune, his health, his freedom, even his daughter' – who went mad with worry and agitation during the coup. 'He didn't even want to draw a salary as prime minister, not even money for petrol; while under house arrest he paid for the meals of the 150 soldiers guarding him out of his own funds so as not to cause any expense to the public – and now look what the nation gives him: not even a name plate on his door.' Not even his village is to have a sign. The neighbours are still being punished fifty years after his death.

When Mosaddegh's son, who was also his physician, told him that his illness could only be treated in Europe, and the shah had authorized his travel, and a visa was already issued, Mosaddegh refused. He would rather die than insult the Iranian medical profession by getting treatment abroad. Mosaddegh was so respectful of the law, the cook recounts, that he was careful when walking in the garden not to step over the boundary of his land, even where the wall ran a few yards beyond it.

'It makes you ashamed, when you say all this; it makes you ashamed to be an Iranian.'

The cook has often been questioned after guiding visitors and told not to let any more into the house.

'I have eaten this man's bread. As long as I have the key, I will let anyone into the house who wants to enter it.'

The owner of the little shop across the road, who also ate that bread, now earns some extra bread by writing down the number plates of the cars that park in front of the house. When another of the villagers who was an employee of Mosaddegh's – like all the villagers at the time – once complained of having been beaten by one of the two secret service agents, a Mr Shahidi, Mosaddegh called the agent to account in the living room. The peasant is a drug addict and a nuisance to public morality, Mr Shahidi said in his defence. The cook, who was peeking through the door left ajar together with other servants, remembers that Mosaddegh hooked the handle of his walking stick around the agent's neck and pulled him back and forth through the living room.

'I know myself that the peasant smokes opium, but that is none of your business,' Mosaddegh shouted. 'You are here solely to guard *me*.'

'I made a mistake, I made a mistake,' the agent wailed.

Although he swore never to bother a peasant again, the master, still a ruler although he was an old man, a prisoner and a democrat, was not satisfied. 'No more meals for the secret service agents,' he ordered the cook.

For a week, Mr Shahidi and his colleague, Mr Yusofkhani, had to make the long drive to the city for food supplies, which they cooked themselves, or beg the soldiers to spare them something, until Mosaddegh lifted the ban. The sick and destitute from all over the country made their way to Ahmadabad because they could count on Mosaddegh giving them a little money and assuring them of treatment in the Tehran hospital headed by his son.

'I have only told you what I saw with my own eyes,' says the cook before taking us to the house.

There are trees in the grounds that may have been planted by Mosaddegh himself. A gravel driveway leads to the two-storey red brick house with the now unusual pointed roof, which has just four rooms, a terrace and a balcony. During the brief political spring of the late 1990s, at the beginning of Mohammad Khatami's presidency, Mosaddegh's granddaughter built a little museum on the site. There are even plastic rubbish bins, like those in German parks, along the gravel path, and the house that no one is supposed to learn of today was placed under a preservation order. Behind plate glass we can see the Pontiac in which Mosaddegh sped away from Tehran whenever he declared his resignation in the middle of a meeting. The shutters and the doors of his house have exactly the same turquoise colour, I notice. Mosaddegh is buried under the living room, a bare room with a beautiful carpet and simple ceramic tiles. He was not allowed to leave Ahmadabad even as a corpse. The walls are hung with documents, quotations and photos: Mosaddegh with his stick during his courtroom defence, which became an indictment; Mosaddegh with his stick during a walk, from behind; Mosaddegh with his stick sitting on the ground, exhausted. In the middle of the room is the tombstone, covered with an embroidered cloth, with the Quran, flowers and candles upon it. One after another we lay a hand on the tomb and recite the Fatiha three times. Why does Iran continue to accuse America even today of having toppled Mosaddegh if it doesn't even allow signposts to his village? And there is not a single street named after Mosaddegh in all Iran, my driver adds. But, in 2009, countless demonstrators held Mohammad Mosaddegh's picture in the air. Some of them got *kun-chubi*.

The sun is still high, and in my suitcase I have the beach towel from

Armenia that I bought expressly for the Caspian Sea so that I can refresh another childhood memory. Besides, I wouldn't be doing the country justice if I looked only at its desert, and I'll have plenty of time to spend in Tehran, which was already a behemoth in my childhood; what will it be now? The map shows a track leading up into the Elburz Mountains and down the other side to the sea. Along the way are the ruins of Alamout Castle, which is likewise historic and recently found its way into the German cultural supplements: it is the legendary impregnable retreat of the Assassins, who murdered political and clerical dignitaries all over the Middle East in the twelfth and thirteenth centuries without a thought for their own survival. After 11 September 2001, countless articles appeared characterizing Mohamed Atta and the other suicide attackers as successors to the Assassins. Parallels were drawn between the Assassins' leader Hassan ibn Sabah and Osama bin Laden, who also had his fortress in the mountains, and a phalanx of Western writers and journalists travelled to Alamout to learn more about 11 September in New York. As I recall, they had nothing enlightening to say after seeing the place, except that the landscape up there was gorgeous.

And how: from the first foothills, the colours multiply, not yet soaked with streams and snow. The mountain crests, sparsely covered with grasses and brush, each higher than the last, are set far apart, forming almost monochrome paintings, each with its own types of rock and vegetation, the narrow asphalt path winding through them. And the deeper we go into the mountains, the more often we look on that green in the valleys that can glow as it does only in contrast with the dry mountainsides above them. We come through rice fields too, reflecting the sun, and the landscape before Alamout is dominated by fruit orchards, especially cherry trees, glittering red. Although the foundation walls are all that is left of the castle, it is worth the climb – especially if you arrive after the day trippers and have the peak to yourself. It towers over the pretty villages, forests and fields scattered like colourful pieces of a mosaic in the brown mountains all round. If you walk around the castle, you have a view of one of those canvasses of the Creator on the opposite hillside, but this one polychrome. The shades of brown alone, depending on whether or not water flows beneath the ground, or the progressions in the grass from green to ochre and yellow, and also red, red everywhere, the fundamental tone of the rocks. I think I even see orange, although it seems to be only an optical illusion created by the interplay of the other colours. Red, yellow, green, brown and orange – all the colours of a palette except blue, but there is plenty of blue in the sky.

On the way down, I meet a busload of Dutch tourists going up, their guide saying something about 9/11. In Iran itself, the Assassins are completely forgotten: just another cult among many that proclaimed the beginning of the end of days, without the world's ending. The fact that their name has survived – 'the hashish smokers', in the sense of 'the intoxicated', a clearly pejorative name – is due solely to the polemics of the contemporary scholars, to whom the cult was a paragon of evil, a conspiracy to abolish Islam. Marco Polo and other travellers brought those polemics to Europe, whence they entered fantasy novels, Hollywood films and computer games, except that the Assassins appeared no longer as enemies of Islam but as the epitome of violence.

We find accommodation for the night in the village that lies at the feet of Alamout. The landlady of the bed and breakfast has everything under control: her three sons; her daughter-in-law bandaged after cosmetic surgery, which seems to be *en vogue* in the villages too now (in the big cities, young women with plastered noses are part of the scenery); three French and two Turkish backpackers, with whom the landlady converses in spite of having no common language; a group from Tehran who have talked too long over their tea and hookah and now have to drive back in the dark; the kitchen; her youngest boy's homework; and her private housekeeping. She cooks, commands, calculates, educates, receives and reassures as if she were a whole staff. The father is 100 kilometres away, working in Qazvin, says her youngest, fourteen years old, who takes me along on a walk through the orchards and over the hilltops, for which he is allowed to finish his homework later. No, the farmers are not so badly off here; fruit trees are the most profitable kind of agriculture, good income with less work, so they can spend most of the year earning money in the city. A kilo of cherries sells in Tehran for 12,000 toman and brings in 7,000 here – 3 and 1.70 euros respectively; every family here has two, three trees at least, and those who have none help with the picking for 70,000 a day. Although tuition is not cheap, no one is illiterate except among the old people; the parents take education seriously – all parents, the boy says; that's normal here. Corporal punishment has been abolished, but classrooms are still teacher-centred and schools are still segregated by sex, so that the boy is flabbergasted to hear how differently children learn in German classrooms. Next he wants to know what it looks like inside a church. He has never heard that there are Jews in Germany, or of the Holocaust. But, in every village we walk through, black-and-white photos of the martyrs are hung along the main street, enlarged ID photos, often in soft focus, as the fashion was in the early 1980s, so that their skin looks lily-white, the rural haircuts still in the styles of the 1970s, shoulder-length, or with sideburns. More than half a million Iranians died in the 'Holy Defence' of the country when Saddam Hussein attacked Iran, with the approval of the West, to stop the revolution. Instead he stopped democracy, of which the first rudiments had been present under Abolhassan Banisadr. Elected by 70 per cent of Iranians, the first president of the Islamic Republic barely made it across the border in time with a chador over his head when the war fell into the Islamists' laps. Shortly thereafter, women were once again required to wear the hijab, which had been lifted by the 1906 revolution.

I talk to an old man sitting in front of his house in the neighbouring village, but he understands only Tusi, as the language in these mountains is called, and shrugs his shoulders. But I do manage to strike up a conversation with a group of cherry-pickers, who have the usual questions and complaints: how things are in Germany; how corrupt they are here, the inflation and despotism. I ask whether there is anyone who supports the regime. No, no one for miles around; the villages here all voted for Rouhani – as if a vote for the president were proof of resistance against the regime.

'But you all vote?'

'Yes; we vote for the lesser evil.'

At least the reforms that are making no headway nationwide have already taken place in the countryside with the introduction of local parliaments under President Khatami. Yes, say the fruit-pickers, it's an improvement when you know the people running things and you can vote them out again.

As we move on, I ask whether the villages have their individual characteristics. Do they ever! the boy cries: in the village we just left, they all have long noses – didn't I notice that? – and in that village over there, the people talk endlessly; we'd better not go that way. It's plain to see he enjoys the summer in the mountains more than the other nine months of the year; it's a Railway Children kind of life, except that the danger is of running into bears rather than trains.

'What do you think,' I ask: 'Were things better in earlier times, or are they better today?'

'You mean, in the village?'

'Yes, before people went to town.'

'The houses used to be better built, because of the winter, obviously. But there was also great poverty, in the stories my grandfather tells me. There were no schools, no doctors, no electricity, and the winters were really bad. No, I think things are better now than they used to be.'

Well, he's young yet, the museum director Fikrat Abdullayev would say, walking as he does among the petroglyphs of Qobustan every day. It would be disastrous if people thought the past was better than the present at the age of fourteen.

In the evening I sit on the balcony in front of my room and listen to the quacking and cackling in the courtyard and, mixed in with it, the mother's voice still giving orders – is that why her husband has made his getaway? Just when I want to turn out the light, a yellow taxi drives up with a sack covering its whole roof. The boot too is so full that the lid is tied down with a rope. I go to the railing and see that the father has arrived from the city with supplies, thin as a reed, his back bowed, his face marked with such exhaustion, apparently incapable of joy, incapable of more than a creaking *Salām*, his eyelids half shut, heartbreaking to see from above. He is not young any more.

Fiftieth Day: To the Caspian Sea and on to Tehran

Through gorges and over grass-green alpine meadows, past glaciers and many bands of wild horses, we cross the Elburz along a caravan road that has remained unpaved since it was built in the early seventeenth century under Shah Abbas as part of a nationwide network of overland routes. The rest areas – caravanserais – are still well preserved by the wayside, without minarets. The only people we meet are beekeepers who have pitched their camp for the summer with their hive boxes. A pint jar costs 10 euros or more: that would be a handsome producer's price even in Germany; honey would seem to be another profitable branch of agriculture. However, the beekeeper from whom we end up buying – because he is a regular bee freak and expert – complains that unfair competition is making life difficult for him: honey that is cut with sugar, dyes or cheaper supermarket products is being sold in the markets as pure natural Elburz Mountain honey. The honest beekeepers often complained, and the food inspectors took samples, but then nothing happened in the end, probably because someone had connections or belonged to a martyr's family, or some money changed hands. Now the complaints aren't even accepted any more.

The coast, which in the memories of my childhood consists of virgin forests, fields of maize, isolated beaches, fishing villages and here and there a villa, is now, seen from the mountains, a single city going on forever, with a motorway running through it. In the noisy holiday places, the women's manteaux and headscarves look all the more unreal because the rest of the family is walking through the streets in beach attire, the children in shorts and T-shirts, the husband with an inflatable crocodile under his arm. At a private swimming beach, which I hope will be somewhat less littered than the public beaches, I take my Mickey Mouse out of my suitcase. There are three narrow areas, almost like tubes, screened off from one another by plastic sheets higher than my head extending far into the water: one area for men, one for women, and between them the family area. While I swim my laps on the open sea, so as not to have to turn every 50 metres at the plastic barrier, a commotion begins on the beach. Two men are shouting something, waving their arms wildly; others are standing around them. They are too far away for me to understand the words, and without my glasses I can't discern much. Is someone drowning? It takes a while before I begin to realize that the shouts are directed at me, but I am so glad to be swimming after all the hours and days in the car that I pretend I haven't noticed. Besides, I'm not about to drown. After a few more laps, a swimmer, gasping and gesticulating, approaches and shouts something at me until there's no way I can ignore him any longer: I have to go back to the beach immediately or they'll call the police. On shore the stout lifeguard, who is not exactly in shape for rescue action, is waiting for me, red with anger or exertion: what do I think I'm doing, swimming in the women's area?

'Women's area?' I ask, with my German accent. 'I was way out to sea.'

'Yes, but you went past the barriers!'

'I'm sorry, but on the sea there are no barriers.'

'My God, you have to imagine where they would be if they went that far; that can't be so hard.'

'What nonsense! Then I would have to turn every 20 yards! What would I go swimming in the sea for?'

'You were looking at the women, I saw you!'

'I can't see anything from that distance,' I assure him, producing my glasses case from under Mickey Mouse as evidence.

'All right, all right,' the lifeguard says, finally satisfied. Apparently I do not make the impression of being a sex offender who needs to be carted off by the police: I'm too old, I'm from abroad, and now with my glasses on I look the intellectual. 'To be honest, I don't give a damn, excuse my language, where you swim. You can swim to Baku for all I care, sir. Only we have to be strict because of the Morality Police. They'll close us right down if someone here isn't following the rules.'

I had best not confess to the lifeguard that I really did look into the forbid-

296

den zone. And, I have to admit, women in swimming costumes are in fact shocking when you otherwise see women only in coats and headscarves in the street. It's just too bad I wasn't swimming with my glasses on.

We cross the Elburz Mountains again, passing the traffic jam that extends more than a hundred kilometres on the opposite side of the road, heading towards the sea. The last day before the weekend is a holiday, one of so many: in addition to the Islamic and the national holidays, there are also the Shiite days of mourning, each of them commemorating a martyrdom – the martyrdom of the first imam, or the second, third, fourth through eleventh, and the disappearance of the twelfth imam, whose return the previous president Ahmadinejad probably wanted to hasten by precipitating the end of the world with his threats against Israel. No wonder Islam can't govern a country if the people are constantly being given days off to weep! And I haven't mentioned the New Year's celebration with no fewer than thirteen more holidays, which no Persian will give up, no matter which government says so. Oil exports, it would seem, are not conducive to a Protestant work ethic.

It is thanks to Reza Shah that this road is here at all, leading through the most difficult terrain: he put an end to democracy in 1925 but connected Tehran with the coast. The roads and railways, the power stations and dams that are still the backbone of Iran's infrastructure today date mainly from his time, which ended in 1941 because England and Russia, plus the new world power America, thought his young son Mohammad Reza more pliable. Before a weekend, the trip now takes as long as it once did by camel, since two lanes are not nearly enough for Tehran's present population of 10, 15 million. The Islamic Republic has been working practically since its founding on a parallel motorway. Building shrines all over the country for the descendants of the imams goes quicker: we pass signs for one after another.

'Wherever an Arab fell during the conquest, they declare him a descendant of an imam,' the driver complains. He is from Tabriz, and *intaraf* or *untaraf* is all one to him, as long as he doesn't have to be governed by clerics. 'First they invade us, and now we're supposed to worship their soldiers.'

To avoid the city traffic, we turn off before Tehran onto the ring road that will take us in a wide northerly curve along the slopes of the Elburz, overlooking the sea of buildings that look colourless in the haze of exhaust fumes. This is an impression that surprises every visitor, whether arriving from Armenia or by air: that Tehran seems to consist exclusively of modern buildings, the oldest of them dating from the 1960s, four- or six-storey blocks of beige brick, and countless office towers and blocks of flats twenty, thirty storeys tall, plus

297

the high-rise estates, new or still under construction, that encircle the city like a ring. And the network of eight-lane urban motorways is so dense that it reminds the visitor more of Los Angeles than the Middle East.

A visit to a once high-ranking official, now sidelined. Still wealthier than, say, the president of the Bundestag in Germany, who lives in a terraced house in Bochum. Two Afghan servants who work from morning prayers until bedtime, the latest Italian espresso machine, German china – these are still musts, although sinfully expensive in Iran. The old miniatures adorning every wall, on the other hand, are simply spectacular; I have never seen such an exquisite, aesthetically outstanding collection in any museum. The official was just released from hospital a few days ago and is therefore in pyjamas, over which he wears a glossy-green Afghani coat. Like Hamid Karzai! the little assembly teases. The servants are happy when he puts it on, the former official explains; they brought him the coat from their visit home in Afghanistan. The friendly, familiar conversational tone between master and servants is noticeable; it is not the rule. He speaks slowly, with long pauses, not because of his illness, or not only, severe though it must be – there is a humidifier on the sideboard for easier breathing – but because he has always been a meditative, indeed a melancholy person. People often forget, because the Islamic Republic's practice often turns out so hamfisted, that the revolution of 1979 was a truly ideological one, prepared by decades of thought and based on a critical examination of Marxist, Islamic, philosophical, postcolonial and existentialist theories. Afterwards, it was not rare to meet revolutionaries in government offices who were remarkably cultured, religious intellectuals who complained that they would rather be reading Rumi or Heidegger than grappling with economic planning or diplomatic bulletins. Many of them have long since landed in prison or are under house arrest; still more are in exile; my host at least continues to lead his private life, on a grand scale, and so he is a host for others who amassed less wealth under the regime; his children are doubtless abroad. One of the country's best-known journalists is now a trout farmer. It's going all right, he says; the fish are in high demand, as his articles used to be. The guests don't meet until nine, half past nine, after prayers; dinner is about eleven; the ambience is deeply religious; shoes are left at the door; but the servant assures a woman visiting from abroad that she can be relaxed, by which he means she needn't wear a headscarf and manteau in the house. The visitor has kept both on because she couldn't imagine the religious milieu would be so relaxed, and she is surprised that the former official cordially shakes her hand in greeting. There is another lay guest at the table, perhaps a mystic – not a member of the regime, in any case, since he has longish hair and sideburns, like an aging rock musician.

What the little nocturnal gathering has to say about the state could not be more explicit: corruption, fraud and mismanagement, open and institutionalized; Islam used as a lubricant to oil the machine run by the security establishment; the propaganda and funding for unabashed superstition as opium for the remaining supporters, who are urged to produce more offspring; access to birth control cut; to hell with overpopulation, water shortage, pollution. The rulers themselves probably don't believe they'll still be here tomorrow, so they squander the future. Sidelined, the high official hardly speaks any differently from the others who never had any say. Separation of state and religion goes without saying, assuming anything is left of Islam. They talk about the Baha'i who was murdered a few days ago in Yazd: the murderer honestly didn't understand what he might be guilty of. He will get off lightly, prophesies the official, who was never allowed to mention the Baha'i when he was in office; in any case, the murderer won't have to pay any compensation, since the Baha'i are not protected by Islamic law.

Assuming anything is left of Islam: when I interject that the young people, including those who are politically active, are abandoning Islam altogether, the official says, yes, that's true, but it could be worse. It's more important that the young people's hearts are pure. After all, the murderer of Imam Hussein, Shemr, said his prayers zealously, and it didn't make him a better person. Yes, the younger generation: that's where everyone at this gathering places their hopes. It's other people's turn now, says the journalist who is banned from publishing, younger people's; this generation has failed, sadly, to reform the Islamic Republic. Nonetheless, he is as optimistic as ever; only more patience is called for than just one generation.

The official doesn't want to keep the miniatures for himself; he wants to transfer them to a museum; that is the dream he has been collecting for these past thirty years. We look around, jaws dropping. As we stand in front of a pair of works from the Qajar dynasty, he predicts that we will never forget them. Saying it makes it true: four great waves of plants and birds, movement captured. A metaphor for the world, existing and at the same time passing.

Fifty-First Day: Tehran

I have often thought: my relatives who stayed in Iran, few as they are, have a kindness all their own, a warmth I don't find among us expatriate Iranians. It is hard to describe – the feasts that follow one upon the other, the days taken off work to receive visits, the indulgence of our quirks and kinks, the glass of fresh, cold melon juice ready on the table in the foyer as soon as we come in out of the hot, bone-dry city air – and harder still to explain. Is it the more severe turning points of a life with revolution and war, and not just a life, but also the collective memory of oppression and vain protest, sacrifices, always leading to a new decline? Yes, the futility is probably it; those who emigrate – especially those who emigrate to the New World, like most of my relations – pay perhaps more attention to the opportunities, start at zero, and then it's all uphill. Here, you live fifty years, or sixty, or, like my aunt, ninety-five, and you have at least the subjective feeling that every hope has been vain. Perhaps that also creates a friendliness towards those who nonetheless take an interest, the tourists and relatives from abroad. Naturally our family is hardly representative, belonging as it does to the bourgeois class, whose opinions, daily routines, furniture, gender relations, readings, and American series are not so different from those of a Western bourgeoisie. In the better restaurants you can even bring alcohol along, not labelled, of course, but in a water or soft drink bottle, and pull it out of your plastic bag to pour it. Thus you don't even have to fly to Baku or Tbilisi, Yerevan or Antalya to go out in European style. Along the motorways in town, the lighted billboards announce a Gipsy Kings concert.

Visitors may be just as surprised to find that the big cities bear the stamp of the middle class as they are by Tehran's modern city centre, but in fact the anti-Western revolution was only possible, of course, in a country that was Westernized as no other in the Middle East. By now, though, most of every middle-class family has emigrated, and the worst thing is that almost every-one looks for a way to send their children abroad for university at the latest. That's easy enough for the wealthy; Iranians are well received in Canada and, until very recently, the United States, where they have the most academic titles, the least unemployment, and incomes well above average among all population groups.

And those who do not have the assets and the grades to go overseas can still claim to be a Christian or a homosexual to go to Germany. While churches, gay associations and the asylum authorities are still racking their brains for a way to identify a true confession, there is hearty laughter in Iranian living rooms about the mass coming-out abroad. For the actual Christians, who belong predominantly to our class, emigration is openly organized, supported and rewarded by an efficient American organization that apparently cooperates smoothly with the Iranian authorities, with the result that Armenian life in Tehran and Isfahan is now collapsing. The state is glad, because that leaves more room for its poor people, many of whom are now driving through Tehran in SUVs and moving to the wealthier north side of the city; they have become rich and need the flats of the middle class, although they still have their poor people's culture, with its rituals of penitence and mourning. The nouveau middle class find it perfectly normal that the gigantic lake created on the outskirts of Tehran is named, in literal translation, 'Lake of the Martyrs of the Persian Gulf', and they are happy to unpack their blankets, thermos bottles, barbecue gear and hookahs by the water, which grows ever scarcer for agriculture.

In Tehran itself, the rising classes can be found in a new park along both sides of the motorway, crossed by a three-storey pedestrian bridge illuminated in neon green called the 'Bridge of Nature'. Under a tentlike construction reminiscent of Munich's Olympic Park, the crowd carries on until two in the morning on weekends. It is good, on the one hand, that people are mixing: that the chadoris are now where the skateboarders jump back and forth with their daring haircuts; that the urban space no longer belongs solely to the old bourgeoisie. But then we go looking in the Food Corner, which is as big as Munich's *Viktualienmarkt*, for an appetizing meal – appetizing to us, I mean, the bourgeois class – and all we find are steaks, nachos and Western fast food. And the police, in various formations, hold their clubs at the ready in case the crowd becomes an assembly.

The writer Amir Hassan Cheheltan hasn't been able to publish a book in Iran for years now. Sad as he is to be an Iranian writer with no books in Persian, he lives well on the foreign editions. I advise him to give up hope of an imprimatur in Iran and to publish his Persian originals in an exile publishing house or online: then the interested readers would read them, and there's no money to be made with books in Iran anyway, at least not with good books. Sales have dropped dramatically; instead of 3,000 to 5,000 copies, the first printing of an ambitious work is now sometimes as little as 300 – three hundred copies, for a population of almost 80 million. Only the uneducated multiply.

The state has become much cleverer: if it went on killing writers, as it last did in the serial murders of the late 1990s, there would be an outcry, a resistance, an uproar; instead, it kills reading, teaches Ferdowsi and Hafiz in the schools often only as predigested information, and modern literature not at all; keeps the best writers away from their audience until they are eventually forgotten. Meanwhile the Internet is now largely free – another way to break the reading habit. Information is not suppressed; instead, thinking is brought to a halt. The next person I visit, the editor of a literary magazine, concedes that that's what's happening. Nevertheless, he is optimistic, because he observes that awareness continues to grow broader. Nothing remains under the surface any more; thanks to the Internet, every villainy is uncovered and publicized even in the villages – the news at the moment is the Supreme Leader's Quran reciter, who abused his students one after another. After the students' families – the poorest people of all – ran themselves lame trying to bring the Quran reciter to justice, they plucked up their courage and turned to the exile broadcasters, spilled everything, every unsavoury detail and every act of violence, exposed every door they had knocked on in vain, every attempt to intimidate them. Grand Ayatollah Makarem Shirazi may proclaim it a sin even to mention the affair, but the country is talking about nothing else, especially the poorest people of all. The abused students, now adolescents, have become heroes, really and truly, instead of being blamed for their own abuse, as the custom used to be. And the jokes that are circulating! To take just the latest animal GIF that's running on millions of smartphones: a cute marmot gently massaging another marmot's back in an endless loop, with the Persian caption 'Law enforcement's treatment of the accused Quran reciter Said Tusi'. And that's just the more harmless part. All the mass executions, the murdered writers, the persecuted Baha'i, the torture jails, the war that was waged six years too long for no rational reason after the Iraqis had long since been repulsed, the child soldiers, the corruption, the censorship, the destruction of the environment and the water shortage, the outrageously wasteful spending, for Ayatollah Khomeini's tomb for example – there is nothing that isn't discussed on the satellite channels and attested by pictures, audio, documents.

'But what are the consequences of that awareness?' I ask.

'Not much,' the editor concedes.

'Are the people content with the appearance of freedom?'

'They're not becoming politically active, in any case.'

'Are they thinking critically about the ideology – are they developing an alternative?'

'It's true that the masses had no books in 1979 either, but there were intellectual leaders in all directions; there were many resolutely political intellectuals, there were children of the bourgeoisie taking up a partisan struggle, there were alternative visions to the status quo. We go on drinking our tea because all the alternative visions have long since come to naught.

No, not because they came to naught: because the grand visions have been disastrous.'

In the film museum, the poster of Jafar Panahi's *Taxi Tehran* hangs prominently, boasting the Golden Bear of the Berlin Film Festival. After Panahi had been sentenced over a documentary on the 2009 protests to six years' imprisonment, a travel ban and a twenty-year filmmaking ban, he was released from prison early on bail and shot *Taxi* in secret. The film was smuggled to Berlin on a USB stick and premiered in the festival competition. The Iranian government protested vehemently against the screening, almost to the point of a diplomatic incident. But in Tehran, in the state film museum, they are proud of the Golden Bear that Jafar Panahi won, and everyone I ask has streamed *Taxi Tehran* or watched it on DVD.

Fifty-Second Day: Tehran

Tehran is unbearable, a really horrible city, exciting though many of its parallel worlds are said to be: the arts scene, the film scene, the techno scene, the rock scene, even the fashion scene; the literary scene no more, sadly. The biggest, however, is the drug scene, and most of your time is spent sitting in traffic anyway, so why the hype? But: if you drive an hour, an hour and a half into the mountains, not more, then the asphalt ends, then the road is blocked, and a ranger explains that, apart from the local inhabitants, only authorized vehicles can drive on: it's a nature preserve.

'And what kinds of animals are there here?' we ask.

The ranger reels off the list, well practised and at the same time a little proud; I don't know all the names, but I do understand 'bear' and 'tiger'. Bears, okay; but tigers? Yes, there are! Tigers, an hour, an hour and a half from Tehran.

Back in the city, at the entrance to one of the modern apartment estates on the north side, I give my name and that of Mahmoud Dowlatabadi, who became world famous for his novels about the Iranian village. Born in 1940 in a village in northeastern Iran, he earned his living as a shepherd and a farm hand; he has been a builder, a cinema ticket-taker, a cobbler's assistant, a bicycle mechanic, a barber, a cotton washer and an advertising canvasser. Then he made it into the Tehran theatre academy and acted on the stage for a time, until he began writing and couldn't stop. His epic *Kelidar*, about a dusty mountain in the northeastern desert, fills five volumes, 3,000 pages – a tremendous panorama of rural Iran in transition from feudal rule to the land reform of 1963, to the urbanization that resulted in slums such as those on the south side of Tehran. These slums, in turn, formed the masses that Ayatollah Khomeini called upon in 1978 to take to the streets. Although the revolution was originally driven by the middle class, whose economic rise had not brought them political franchise, by liberals, socialists, Marxists, Trotskyists, left-wing Islamists, communists, nationalists, religious reformers and most of all students, in the end it was the poorest people who toppled the shah. Dowlatabadi's books contain something like a deeper history of Iran since the coup against Mohammad Mosaddegh, a history that runs beneath the political events, or produces them, in the literal sense: from *Kelidar*, the monument of Iranian rural life on the threshold of its destruction, to *Missing Soluch*, which tells of a rural family after the father's flight, to *The Colonel*, the most severe reckoning imaginable on the revolution.

Yes, says Dowlatabadi, only he could write the history of the Iranian village, because only he among writers experienced it, because it is his own history, although in his case it took a different course since he began reading like a fiend and moved to the city before the land reform. 'I had to get out of the village; I simply knew too much.'

Today Dowlatabadi lives, with his wife and his almost eighty years, which he doesn't show in the least, next to Evin Prison, where he was incarcerated under the shah, like most of the important writers of his generation. When his wife picked out this gated community twelve years ago so that they could take evening walks in peace and buy their everyday needs nearby, his only condition was that the windows face the other side. To write, in any case, he retreats to the little plot of land he bought an hour or two south of Tehran.

Dowlatabadi wants to hear first about my trip, since Eastern Europe is more remote to Iranians too than Paris, London or the United States. When I come to the officers at the border where I entered from Armenia, whom I found more quaint than unpleasant, he shakes his head contemptuously. He gets annoyed all over again every time he encounters the familiar form of address in a government office, as if he had never left the village shop seventy years ago, and once in the departure lounge of Tehran airport he turned around and went home because he was so angry at the passport officer who asked him jovially, 'So, Haji, where are we off to?'

'I am not a haji!' the writer replied, 'Save your small talk!' and he got into such a dispute that he was led away for interrogation. By the time he was given back his passport, he no longer felt like travelling, least of all having to present his passport again on coming back.

'I've always been a bit too impulsive,' Dowlatabadi admits, having led me into his little study, and from the Iranian border agents the conversation turns to the 1963 land reform, which was the most disastrous of all the shah's mistakes: 'He himself created the class that would hound him out of the country.' Those in power now are the grandsons of the peasants who were given a little piece of land in 1963 but soon had to sell it cheap and try their luck in the city. There they found only misery – not only misery but, worse, alienation too. They gave up their lives, which had been arduous, true, but the same as their fathers' and their forefathers' lives; they had had a culture, a 2,000-, 3,000-year-old tradition, and a connection with nature. And what did they exchange it for? A sheet-metal shed beside a drainage ditch.

Dowlatabadi doesn't say the land reform was wrong per se, but the shah should have proceeded more skilfully, more intelligently, and spent more money too. Instead, he curried the favour of the middle class with the income from oil while fobbing off the peasants with a patch of ground that was too small to live on and too big to die on. There were no efforts to organize the peasants, in cooperatives or otherwise, and not even the left had time for the rural population; the left were too busy discussing Bakunin.

I ask what gave the shah the idea of land reform in the first place. The fear of a peasant uprising like those in China and South America, Dowlatabadi replies. Besides, the shah wanted to weaken his rivals, who included not only the clergy but also the big landowners. In the event, the two groups formed an alliance against him. When he was in prison, Dowlatabadi continues, he looked around at his fellow inmates. Only two of them were workers from the countryside; all the rest were sons of the bourgeoisie, the descendants of the landed gentry who had moved to the cities at the beginning of the modern era, sent their children to the secular schools or abroad, and managed their land remotely while living in town. Practically all the ministers, after the Constitutional Revolution, were landowners, likewise Mosaddegh, or Amir Kabir before him, and the other reformers of the nineteenth and early twentieth centuries; they were, for good or ill, true patriarchs, whose word had absolute legal force. Even Reza Shah, for all his tyranny, had advanced the country through his rigid authority, built schools, dams, railways, refineries and roads, while his son Mohammad Reza Pahlavi, city born, palace born, ultimately only distributed a little money, of which the poor invested nothing but instead paid for their pilgrimage to Mecca.

And his novel about the contemporary epoch, *The Colonel*, which tells of the failure and death of a former officer in the Islamic Republic – a colonel of

that national army that Reza Shah had created to unite all the nation's peoples and classes in one institution? Dowlatabadi shakes his head again, more
resigned than contemptuous now, because copies of a bootleg edition were
sold throughout the country, a retranslation into Persian from the German
translation. Still under shock, he tells how it happened: after Mohammad
Rouhani was elected president in 2013, the vice-minister of culture invited
Dowlatabadi to a meeting and sent an official car to fetch him. Great book,
the minister said about *The Colonel*: he read it on the plane to Karbala – on
the pilgrimage, of all things! Dowlatabadi says, hands on his head. It simply
must be published in Iran, the minister continued, and announced his plan.
On the eve of the New Year's feast, when no newspapers appear for a fort-
night, it would be distributed in secrecy, then it couldn't be stopped. Until
then, the author should keep silent. Dowlatabadi gave his assent, only to be
called by a newspaper the next day: they had heard that *The Colonel* would be
published; was that true? 'Ask the ministry,' Doulatabadi answered, already
furrowing his brow.

His publisher nonetheless prepared for publication, but the first printing
was hardly finished when the market was saturated with the back-translated
bootleg edition – a catastrophe to a writer whose work lives from its original
Persian prose. The ministry offered to burn all the copies of the pirate
edition it could lay hands on, but burning books – try as he may, a writer
cannot reconcile himself to that, especially when he knows that the bootleg
book came from the ministry itself, or from some part of the regime, as did
the news leak to the press, to sabotage the publication of the novel. But from
then on there was no question of an official imprimatur. 'They will never
officially allow *The Colonel* to be published, never. Why? Because it exposes
forty years of their lies. They would rather distribute a bad retelling of it, so
that no one likes it.'

I ask whether he nonetheless voted for Rouhani's re-election in 2017.

'What else can you do?' Dowlatabadi asks in return, and points to the wars
in the region, in Iraq, Afghanistan, Syria, and to the escalation in relations
with Saudi Arabia, the electoral victory of Donald Trump. 'At the moment,
the only objective is to prevent the country from exploding. Nothing else.
So everyone had to vote for Rouhani. They only put up such a hard-liner as
Raisi to scare people and drive up the voter turnout. And it worked, yes, and
they can go on claiming we have a democracy.'

Dowlatabadi suggests we go out to eat; after my excursion I must be
hungrier than he is; his regular place isn't chic like the new restaurants but

has the best kebab in town. It's not for nothing that the owner is the head of the rôtisseurs' guild.

'Shall we take your car?' I ask, because I have heard about Dowlatabadi's legendary Chevrolet.

'Of course; that's half the fun.'

While we wait in the street for Dowlatabadi to come out of the underground garage, his wife recounts that she's still afraid every time he leaves the house in the evening. That's another reason why she chose a walled estate: because her husband is safer here, and all the neighbours know him. I notice that immediately, when Dowlatabadi comes gliding out of the garage with the red limousine, an ocean-going tanker compared with the compact Iranian makes: on all sides the mothers with their prams, the adolescents, the old people all call reverently, 'Salām, Mr Dowlatabadi.' The writer waves, almost benevolently, out of the open window, returning their greeting. Not only the old Chevy, but also his bushy moustache, high forehead and deep voice are quite impressive. He gets along even better with the simple people, says his wife: with tradesmen, waiters, shopkeepers and servants.

Dowlatabadi demonstrates a broader repertoire, however, when he talks to the caretaker of his country house on the phone as he drives: the man has done something wrong again with the water, the workmen or the garden. From Dowlatabadi's tirade, you might think the caretaker has never done anything right in his life.

'You have to talk that way with these people,' Dowlatabadi says apologetically, after ringing off with a curse; 'otherwise they don't understand you.'

'You would have made a proper patriarch yourself.'

'Absolutely,' Dowlatabadi laughs, in good spirits again from one second to the next. 'I had opportunity enough to see how our squire did it.'

The restaurant really is very simple – metal plates, plastic tablecloths, close-set chairs – and yet full. Over dinner, Dowlatabadi tells how, having brought his parents after him to Tehran, he returned to his village only once. When his father died, his mother wanted to see her relatives again; the loneliness of the big city was hard for her to bear. Dowlatabadi drove his mother there but couldn't find their old house, couldn't find his way around at all, so much had changed. Dowlatabadi had a fit of rage – 'I told you I'm too impetuous' – and brought his mother back to Tehran without having seen anyone. 'I'll never forgive myself for that,' he says today, 'for not making more of an effort.'

'When was that?'

'It must have been 1980, and five years later she died. I think the loneliness in Tehran was one reason for her death.'

Fifty-Third Day: Tehran

I dreamt I discovered a narrow, very high tower from which I could watch the city, the people going about their important business, or gathering for sports, the cars looking like toys. I don't know whether it was Tehran; it could just as well have been any other city, or just an imaginary one. I only know that I was visiting, and fell in love with the tower, so that I climbed its stairs again and again; other people had travelled to the city with me, and they were surprised that I kept going back to the tower and stayed up on top of it for who knows how long. I almost missed our departure, in fact – our flight, I believe – because I could hardly tear myself away from the lookout platform, which was so tiny, with such a low ceiling, that I couldn't move or stand up straight, much less walk around; I could only kneel or lie down. Nor was there any fence or railing; perhaps the slight danger was part of the fun. Yet it wasn't superiority or power that I felt as I looked down on the people from above; I was aware that I was enjoying the view only for the moment and would have to go down again as soon as I needed to relieve my bladder or got hungry or my travelling companions began to get nervous, and then I would dissolve into the crowd that I was now looking at as if at a painting, a canvas with movement in its fine details, or perhaps just a shimmering because of how the light struck it, and with such a broad perspective that the details were barely discernible, and life looked like a static image, a miniature or a carpet.

The mausoleum of Ayatollah Khomeini, situated in the extreme south of Tehran, among his most loyal supporters, is not at all as sumptuous as I imagined it. Well, from the outside, of course: a golden cupola and a sky-blue one; four golden minarets; the whole complex with hotel, offices, restaurants, theological seminary and conference centre; they were thinking big. But then you see the ugly cranes and wonder why, if the state's founder is so revered, his shrine still isn't finished after thirty years. And, in the shrine itself, it is the dimensions that are imposing – the size of the hall, the height of the ceiling, the massiveness of the pillars – but not the decor, which indulges in a strangely uninspired, almost careless, nouveau-riche rococo Orientalism: a cream-coloured plush carpet and cream-coloured walls with gold decoration printed on them, as in a Louis XV salon, and glittering mirrors for that added touch of kitsch. And the guards: in dark blue knee-length livery with gold buttons, as if they belonged to the staff of a grand hotel, except that they are in their stockings, not all of them free of holes. In their hands they hold great dusters of colourful plastic feathers that recall a fair more than a mausoleum. Through the middle of the shrine runs a wall of corrugated steel, which does not separate a women's area; no, it has been put up to permit repairs – and no wonder, when you look at the workmanship of the doors, windows and stuccowork. Although today is yet another holiday, one of the eleven martyrdoms, the shrine is only modestly filled: a few women in black chadors; fathers praying while their children romp; here and there a group of Shiites from Pakistan (white galabiyyas), Iraq (black robes) or the Iranian provinces (coloured chadors). The visitors' mood is not one of reverence, much less ecstatic grief as in Mashhad, Karbala or wherever else an imam is buried, but soberly businesslike, as if they were completing an agenda item.

Perhaps the popular Shiite religious feeling doesn't relate strongly to someone who died of natural causes. But, at the same time, the scene confirms the impression that Ayatollah Khomeini is an uncomfortable memory for the Islamic Republic, not only because his most loyal followers are fighting each other tooth and nail – many of today's political prisoners were once members of the revolutionary leader's closest circle, and if anything has been heard from his sons and grandsons, it is sharp political criticism. His funeral, which set off a mass hysteria in Tehran, completed the country's awakening from the frenzy of revolution and war. For all the charisma that even his opponents ascribe to him, Ayatollah Khomeini has not gone down in the collective memory as the luminous figure that the state propaganda mythologizes him to be. Everyone knows, or could know, about the mass executions, the torture jails, the ceasefire that the Iraqis offered in 1982, when Iran's military position was better than six years later, the child soldiers. And no one can claim today that Khomeini was unaware of the mass executions, since we know that his designated successor, Ayatollah Montazeri, addressed him personally about them. Montazeri was sacked two months before Khomeini's death in 1989 and placed under house arrest in Qom, where he died in 2009. But his memoirs have been distributed throughout the country in underground editions, not least in government circles, and in 2016 his son Ahmad published online the tapes in which he speaks in no uncertain terms of Khomeini's shrugging reaction to the accusations. Ahmad was sentenced to twenty-one years in prison, but the tapes are in the world. Ayatollah

Khomeini is still respected by many Iranians as the Leader of the Revolution, and enjoys greater esteem than the state's present leaders. The supporters of the Islamic Republic revere him as well, and state propaganda stylizes him as a thirteenth imam – but beloved, as Imam Ali is beloved, as Imam Hussein, Rumi, Hafiz or Dr Mosaddegh is beloved, beloved as one whose mementoes people collect and whose words people carry in their hearts, whom people include in their prayers and to whom people turn in their inner dialogue as to a friend, father and teacher – Ayatollah Khomeini is beloved only of the most loyal supporters of his revolution. As we are leaving the shrine, I ask an official who is keeping watch from his desk whether the cupola is really gold. No, no, the official assures me, as if to allay my fears: that's only some much cheaper material.

Behesht-e Zahra, the paradise of the Prophet's daughter Zahra, is far and away more impressive than the shrine of the state's founder: a cemetery as big as a city – the second largest in the world after the cemetery of Najaf, also Shiite – with streets, bus stops, restaurants, traffic lights, shops and signposts; but a city with no inhabitants; everyone here who is alive is only visiting. Where the graves of the martyrs begin, there used to be, during the war, a great fountain whose water flowed as red as blood. Although that was laying it on very thick, very gimmicky, I still remember the sight of it from the last time I visited the Iranian cemetery that is called a paradise, when I was thirteen or fourteen. The graves are so close together that you have to walk over the stones and between the stands on which the black-and-white portrait photos – in soft focus – are hung. They go on forever, the rows of graves, roofed with sheet metal like car parks. The fallen are seventeen, eighteen, nineteen, twenty, with scattered adults among them, or occasion-ally an old man. Many tombstones show a date of death, but only the year of birth, perhaps because people in the villages didn't celebrate their birthday, and many didn't even know it. Pick-ups drive around, emanating Shiite mourning chants to monotonous drum beats almost like a techno track. In a field of honour lie parents who sacrificed several children for the nation. 'We have two and up, and five and up,' says a caretaker, as if explaining his assortment. The tens of thousands of victims of poison gas are also commemorated; the fact that it was a German company that built the gas factories for Saddam Hussein during the war is deeply engraved in the Iranians' consciousness. Thus Behesht-e Zahra is in a way another German memorial, the last on this journey, and one which no one in Germany knows about.

310

Unlike the shrine of Ayatollah Khomeini, the martyrs' cemetery is full of people, and not just the usual stalwarts with their chadors or beards, but people from all walks of life. The thought crosses my mind: the war is thirty years past, but most of the fallen are so young that they can hardly have had wives, much less children. Who mourns them? Their parents must be dead themselves by now, or at best very old.

'As long as the flames of the martyrs blaze, the furnace of the Islamic Republic burns,' says a man of perhaps fifty, pouring water on a slab and wiping away the dust with a cloth. With his jeans, polo shirt and clean-shaven cheeks, he doesn't look as though he is warming himself at the revolutionary fire. His brother fell in 1985, when the enemy had long since been repulsed. 'Almost a million martyrs, you have to imagine; a million families living on the benefits, perquisites and appointments; plus the invalids, another million or two plus their families: that's their capital. Not for nothing did Khomeini call Saddam Hussein's attack a divine blessing.'

'And yourself?'

'We don't get anything, not a thing.'

'Why not?'

'We're not *khodi*.'

That's another expression from the dictionary of the Islamic Republic: *khodi* and *gheir-e khodi* mean 'one's own' and 'not one's own', or 'insiders' and 'outsiders', dividing the Iranians into those who belong – by their social background, their clothes, their piety – to the regime and those who do not. The bourgeoisie, as a class, are *gheir-e khodi*, and therefore not so relevant, while the criticism of 'insiders', on the other hand – the reformers, Ayatollah Montazeri or the Islamic student groups that took the lead in the 2009 protests – has an aura of treason. Accordingly, *khodi* today make up the majority of political prisoners, and children of high officials are now among the recipients of *kun-chubi*.

I ask an old gentleman with white stubble on his chin carrying two watering cans about the fountain of blood. No, it's long gone, he answers, putting down his watering cans. Is this my first time here, then? He lost his son, and says it makes no difference whether a person fell at the beginning or at the end of the war. Either way, his son attained the crown of martyrdom.

'Many people say the war should have been ended earlier,' I interject.

'The many are wrong,' the old man replies. 'We had every chance of victory right up to the end.'

'But then', I ask, 'why did the Leader of the Revolution drink the cup of hemlock?', alluding to Khomeini's famous saying that agreeing to the ceasefire was for him like drinking poison.

'That's what I mean: the end came unexpectedly; victory was near.'

'Was it wrong, then?'

'The people were exhausted, that's the simple truth,' says the old man, and he recalls the severe gas attacks and the Iranian passenger aircraft shot down by an American warship in the Persian Gulf: 'We could have won, but our feet wouldn't go on. I mean, maybe that's just human, and the imam saw our weakness.'

He is only half content with the present-day state: content with the conservatives' half, to be exact; the economy is at rock bottom, he says; the country is being mismanaged – naturally it's President Rouhani's fault; he'd sell the country to the West if he could. On the other hand, no country in the world, not even America, dares attack Iran – thanks to 'our' strong military, which is loyal to the Leader.

'We have learned our lesson from history,' the old man says, glad that Iran is able to build an atomic bomb.

Imam Hussein Square, which my friend the Munich sculptor Karl Schlamminger redesigned, to the extent he was allowed, is now a pedestrian zone, as is a wide street leading to the square. One of the busiest junctions in Tehran has been transformed into a quiet space surrounded by elongated ornamental sculptures. Although interspersed with openings, they isolate the square from the noise of the other intersecting roads, and from the cheap functional architecture of the surrounding buildings. Karl's style is still recognizable, although only in fragments because most of it has been overlaid or hidden by the insignia of the cult of the martyr: a large tent for mourning assemblies, black flags and other banners. There is also a stage intended for cultural events, as a poster placed by the city explains. That probably refers to passion plays. Some joker has also created a kind of ethnological museum: a papier-mâché mountain with cave-like entrances guarded by life-sized dolls in medieval costumes, exactly the opposite of Karl's abstract art, which is much more faithful to tradition. In spite of all the chaos, the square still has a personality of its own – or, rather, the chaos gives it a personality of its own. The sudden quiet in the middle of this poor people's quarter, at what was once one of the busiest, dustiest, ugliest spots in the city, is a quality I wouldn't have thought possible, and can only be a blessing. Well, the people, most likely, would rather have a park than modern art or Shiite mourning: trees they could rest under; a lawn their children could play on.

In the side streets of the district, which look like a bazaar open to the sky, I look for a tea house where I can make a pleasant escape. Not even in this poor people's quarter do many women wear the chador – although even chadoris can have the most surprising opinions once you make their acquaintance; the young ones may not know any other attire to wear in public, or else the chador allows them to go to university, take up a profession, be more than just a wife and mother. The reformers wear the chador too, perhaps more assiduously than conservatives. Where do the chadoris live, then, if not around Imam Hussein Square? Still further south in Tehran, where the slums were in the shah's day, in the suburbs, in the small towns. Imam Hussein Square is an old neighbourhood, and old in Tehran means religious, but not necessarily in the same way as the regime.

At this time of day, only three other men are sitting here on the cushions. The innkeeper is especially solicitous towards me, as people everywhere used to be towards the bourgeoisie; as they no longer are since the revolution. I can hardly bring up politics myself, but I can already imagine what they think, and that they will complain as all Iranians do, in part because complaining is part of being Iranian. I can count on my fingers the people here who have told me in the past forty years what you often hear in a country like Germany: that they are by and large content with how things are. None of them was a taxi driver, not one, among so many taxi drivers in Iran, and even in my earliest trips as a reporter, before anyone spoke of reforms, it sometimes happened that I heard the bitterest complaints in the anterooms of a government minister. But here in Imam Hussein Square, they might have voted out of dissatisfaction for Ahmadinejad, who styled himself as an underdog, as the true representative of the revolutionary masses challenging the establishment. That is what I would ask, if it were not too awkward, to learn something in Iran. Instead, I ask about the square: are the people here in the neighbourhood happy with the new design? The square is a disaster, the men answer in unison, designed by higher-ups and built with no consideration. Why a disaster? Because no cars can drive through it any more; as a result, the merchants' sales have fallen off; many are having to sell out; the property values have dropped. If the state would at least leave them alone with its new-fangled ideas. Nobody in Iran needs a pedestrian zone.

In the evening I tour the new cafés in south Tehran. South Tehran? Yes, the artists, the cool restaurateurs and Tehran's *jeunesse dorée* have discovered the south, where the property is still affordable and the patina takes care of itself. Old in Tehran means 1960s, early 1970s; at the outside you occasionally see a building from time of Reza Shah among the galleries and trendy bars where the music is funk, the menu is traditional, and the drinks are herbal lemonades after old Iranian family recipes. In one of the single-family houses with a courtyard that has been transformed into a café, black-and-white photos of the first inhabitants hang on the walls. They look like pictures of idyllic America, the father in a suit and narrow tie, holding his dressed-up son by the hand, the son on his first bicycle, the mother in a knee-length skirt, without a headscarf of course, beaming with joy at being a housewife. The café owner found the family, who emigrated after the revolution, somewhere in America and asked their permission to exhibit their photos.

Fifty-Fourth Day: Flying out of Tehran

Two, three million pilgrims are expected to fly, drive, some of them even walk to Karbala this Muharram – two, three million who certainly have no interest in overthrowing the regime, their travel heavily subsidized, promoted by posters in the streets. I have seen for myself the shopping malls in Najaf and Karbala, built to serve two, three million pilgrims. My flight goes three hours earlier, and yet I end up in the same queue with the two flights to Iraq, conspicuous not only by the passengers' clothes, which positively smell of the Islamic Republic, the women with black headscarves covering even their chins, and of course chadors over them, and the men ostentatiously unshaven, in cheap suits and more frequently the blazers that Ahmadinejad prefers, never jeans, the dark faces still more conspicuous. Loyalty to the state seems to have an ethnic dimension too in Iran.

In the queue, the pilgrims converse about the prayer times the way other people talk about share prices: 5:18 or 5:19, and what about the prayer times in Iraq? Will we land in time, or will we do our prayers in flight? From the toilets, which are filthy even in the brand-new terminal, as if Islam did not teach cleanliness, they tramp out with wet, rolled-up sleeves, the backs of their shoes folded in so that they can slip in and out of them faster. I have hardly ever seen people praying in the glass-walled prayer room at the airport, but tonight the synthetic rugs are rolled out even in the departure lounge. The shelves in front of another prayer room are filled with women's shoes. Where are these people when they don't happen to be on the pilgrimage to Karbala? They are rarely seen in the street, never in these numbers, except perhaps at state-organized demonstrations. Where do they live? They

314

don't form part of the traditional milieu of the old city centres, which is also religious, if not nearly as zealous. Or are they perhaps not so religious at all, but only parading piety amid the pilgrims, more interested in Iraq for the shopping malls and glad of the subsidized international flight; would they never, no matter the hardships, the criticisms that they too must have, think of rebelling against a state that finances their holiday? I don't know; I haven't a clue who they are. Two, three million pilgrims, in proportion to the population and considering all the other places of pilgrimage – Mecca, Najaf, Mashhad and Damascus – and considering too that even the most faithful will not fly to Karbala every Muharram, means the regime is paying a very pretty penny to shore up its claim to rule the nation.

Visiting Family in Isfahan

The river does not flow, not even a trickle; that's the worst thing. The Life-Giving River, Zāyandehrud. What once distinguished the Iranian countryside, and earlier the cities too: the colours wrested from the desert, the plane trees that transform all the main roads into shaded avenues, the narrow canals, cool even in summer, nestling into the alleys; every house built around a garden with a shallow pool set in the middle, a mirror of the sky; the cities ringed by the lush green of the fields and fruit orchards, the turquoise or yellow, colourfully decorated domes of the mosques like flowers of paradise scattered in a meadow. Nowhere are colours so deeply moving as when you emerge from the desert. The whole 5,000-year-old civilization of Iran is built on engineering works that cleverly distribute the water from the 4,000-, 5,000-metre-high mountain ranges running though the country so that the cities can flourish and the remotest villages can feed themselves. If there was anything for which Iran was admired, emulated in the ancient world, as far away as China, as Rome, if there was anything the country contributed to world civilization, it was the art of making the earth fertile. And Isfahan shone with the greatest splendour, with the broad, here already tame, quasi-civilized, but still Life-Giving River flowing through it, spanned by the two most beautiful bridges in the world like two gold rings.

I always understood Isfahan's epithet 'Half the World', *Esfahān nesf-e jahān*, not only in a terrestrial sense as an expression of variety, age and splendour, but also in the sense that the man-made city stands for the celestial half of the universe, while the desert, the inaccessible mountains, the forces of nature constitute the other, earthly half. To take away Isfahan's river is – no, not a massacre; so many wounds have already been inflicted on Isfahan in recent decades, demolitions, thoroughfares ploughed through the historic centre, the traffic, all the noise, the bustle, the overpopulation, the emigration or inner migration of the educated classes, artists, writers – to take away Isfahan's river is the *coup de grâce*, it seems to me. Of course Isfahan will live on; at Nowruz, when the city is overrun with tourists, the water that is now being diverted to other cities that have grown just as fast is allowed to flow again for a few weeks through Isfahan. If UNESCO should threaten to withdraw the World Heritage title, or if the next Leader of the Revolution should be from Isfahan, perhaps the sluices will be opened year round; it's not impossible. Then the other cities will have to manage as best they can. But I know now what the river looks like without life; I can't shake the image from my mind. I know that I will not look forward to returning next time.

Nevertheless, I go running every morning along the river that is no longer a river. The many others who also stretch their legs in the morning, when the air is most breathable, likewise pretend the river is still there. Yet it is only a skeleton, a long, endlessly long arrangement of bones. I look at it as little as possible. I have heard, incidentally – people say all kinds of things, of course – that the water is being diverted not only for the cities that were nowhere a few years ago, not only for industrial plants that are controlled by the military or a religious foundation. The water of the Life-Giving River, allegedly, is also being diverted to a man-made lake in Qom, where the spiritual centre of this wretched regime is located.

If it were just the oppression, the lack of freedom. That is dire enough for the moment. But they are incapable of governing; they simply can't get the hang of it. Any government office, an ordinary office from which you need a piece of paper, some certificate or other, can take five days, cost five days of your life and work. To say nothing of the courts, which have become a bazaar: noisy, overcrowded, issuing judgements for money. Overpopulation or no overpopulation, now they're cutting off family planning, which until recently was still sanctioned by Islam, and for the sole reason that those who have the most children make up their clientele. The lying that is inculcated in children from their birth, by parents who behave, who talk differently at home and outside, by teachers who no longer even make an effort to be believed, by the television, which evening after evening shows a country unlike the one the children can see with their own eyes. The venality of everyone and everything, and hence the decay of values, ideals, altruism itself. Drugs spread unchecked; addiction has long since become epidemic. The wholesale destruction of the environment; whole lakes are drying up, including the gigantic Lake Urmia. To stay with water: just this morning I read on the Internet that the United Nations recommend using 20 per cent of the renewable water supply; the ecological red line is 40 per cent; 60 per cent water consumption is 'water stress' (that's what they call it); 80 per cent is a 'critical water crisis' (*sic*). Iran, however, draws 110 per cent of its reservoirs, three times the barely sustainable maximum, an exploitation for which there is, the report continues, 'no category in the international classification'. To that, add climate change, which is enlarging the deserts and melting the glaciers. No plan for what is to be done when the revenue from oil exports ceases. The minorities being snubbed, driven out of the country, or driven to rebellion. A regime that promised to govern for eternity but lives only for the day, because it evidently isn't counting on being around tomorrow.

Now, on my seventh day in Isfahan, I have the impression the air is gradually getting better. That's an illusion, of course; the fact is I'm getting used to the bone-dry, exhaust-filled atmosphere. When we took an excursion out of town the day before yesterday, I got a migraine from all the oxygen. The people say one reason why the air is so bad is because the river is gone: it used to absorb the dust. Illnesses have increased; that was even in the newspapers. The farmers protested, and took such a beating for it that they don't dare take to the streets again in the foreseeable future. They have banned the hookahs I always used to smoke in the evening in the tea house below Si-o-se Pol, the Bridge of Thirty-Three Arches, my feet almost in the water – banned them throughout the city: it's no longer allowed in Isfahan to slow life down by 10 per cent; in a way, that's only logical, actually, because it's no life at all any more.

The many new restaurants notwithstanding – nice restaurants, in the old paradise houses, as I always wished there would be. Those who eat in the restaurants have money, a family. The rich are to be appeased with a few added freedoms here and there: no headscarves on the ski slopes where the poor folk aren't around; a water bottle of vodka with your expensive dinner. Tourism is being promoted too, and at the same time channelled towards the highlights, where they now hand out audio guides, although they're just recorded on used mobile phones. No one needs the quiet little streets any more, the inconspicuous shrines, the courtyards, the city as a terrain to be discovered on foot.

But to return to the hookahs: the young people used to meet for hookahs because there were so few other places to meet – public places, I mean. They also used to meet along the river; that's all gone, unless they want to sit down beside a skeleton. If the ban also hits the poor, who also loved the river, the simple people from the other cities who camped along the banks, the men who are also banned from smoking hookahs in their own tea houses, the traditional men's tea houses, ostensibly for the sake of equality – who cares? When push comes to shove with the peasants, the state can always drag out the truncheons.

*

Minute after minute I stare into the cupola of the Lotfollah Mosque, as if intoxicated. I stand at the edge, leaning on the wall, my head back, minute after minute. When my neck hurts too much, I look around, discover something else that is also wonderful, but is not the cupola, so that I soon lean my head back again. Half an hour certainly, if not a whole hour, although I have stood in the Lotfollah so often, the first mosque I go to every time I come back. I can hardly put the pattern into words; it's not like a painting by Rembrandt or Caravaggio, after all; you don't even begin to free-associate. You begin to forget. In a way, the impression is even stronger than that of gazing into God's firmament. This man-made heaven consists not just of stars and, between them, the Void, which is also frightening, terrifying, an eternal mystery. This man-made heaven is filled at every single point with beauty. And the stars, after all, are only lights, while this man-made heaven contains many other things, a whole garden of figures, lines, colours.

I come here from time to time when I can't stand the present, I lie to a French tourist who calls out in English to me – as if heaping praise upon me personally – that he has never set foot in a more magnificent mosque. Apparently I look to him like someone who understands English. He asks me about the river too, and I tell him everything, the whole disaster, my pain. In the queue at the ticket window I was already behind him; he asked the cashier how to say 'thank you' in Persian and received in answer the correct but complicated word *sepāsgozāram*; he tried to pronounce it, but unsuccessfully. I told him the Iranians simply say *merci*, yes, the French *merci*; there are plenty of French words in colloquial Persian, because France was once the nation of culture to the Iranians; Paris to us was the big wide world. The cashier, who would also say *merci* at home, just wanted to make the Frenchman learn a Persian word, whether out of patriotism or revolutionary pedantry.

318

I tell the Frenchman what Isfahan looked like when I was a child, that I remember it as one big garden, only forty years ago; the Frenchman can hardly believe it. He is now the traveller, not I. The traveller admires what remains; the local misses what is past. And the traveller who returns to a place?

*

You begin to forget. Stop thinking, become nothing but vision, grateful. No matter what the eyes look at, nothing has a meaning, in the sense that language has meaning. Taken as a whole, it is a symbol – of what? Flowers, one might think at first, before the thinking stops; a garden. But then you forget that too. Of Creation? No, even that is too concrete; Creation is something created, hence by someone, not of itself. Listening to Bach, Scarlatti, baroque music (the same period!), sometimes Mozart's piano sonatas too, is what comes closest to the impression of the Lotfollah when I look for something analogous in a Western context. But nothing visual is so delicate, although Western culture is the culture of images.

Later, I did think of something: a body, likewise perfect, lying naked before you, a face in which everything is just right, even the tiny scar, barely a notch, like the mole in old miniatures, because unbroken perfection would not be human. There I was likewise unable to take my eyes away, could hardly bring myself to touch her, felt the allure, but the joy of just looking was stronger. Disinterested pleasure – is that what it was? The word springs to mind. It probably was, to some extent, only the expression doesn't fit; it's not only too abstract, but too weak, too restrained. You want to possess it, you are consumed with the desire to immerse yourself in it. You are captivated, not disinterested. Blissful. I try to call to mind the pattern of the cupola; I can see in my mind's eye the base colour, a careful and yet vivid yellow, like clay in the evening sun, and on it the other colours glowing, each one brighter than the next. The patterns, however, are gone from my memory, as if dissolved into thin air, though I stared into the dome another two hours. I could not have retained them, analysed them, except by stepping out of the present moment, by writing in the mosque, for example, or by referring to photographs at my desk. There is at least one great analysis of the cupola in Henri Stierlin's Isfahan book, but there are probably others as well. But that, although equally important, theoretically possible, is a different operation: understanding. It is another thing just to look. Not to understand, just to look; just for an hour, in my case, or a bit less. I wasn't lying to the Frenchman: it is like fuel; I feel revitalized afterwards, no desire this time to go from here over to the Shah Mosque, which is bigger, at first glance more impressive; as a child I liked the Shah Mosque better.

The Frenchman invited me to tea, and even tried to persuade me when I thanked him and declined. When I am travelling, I too try to strike up conversations with locals, especially if they have something to say, as I did; if they are able to translate something. I would have fit well in the Frenchman's travels. In his place, I would have struck up a conversation with me, too.

Now I am sitting by the river; I wanted to subject myself to it, the river that no longer exists. The people today still go walking along the bank, although not as many as before, I think. Older gentlemen, white hair or peaked caps, all clean-shaven, three to a bench. One man's song wafts over to me, an old song. How do you know when you're dying? And after all, everything dies sometime: every civilization, even one 5,000 years old. When only the past has any beauty, nothing new. God, that sounds sentimental. And yet it is not that way everywhere; it wasn't that way in Iran before; it's not that way today elsewhere. It's that way only where something stops going forward – living, I mean; where it no longer flows.

*

A visit to a drummer, the scion of an old family of mystics, genealogically documented back to the Middle Ages. Almost all of his order is now in Europe; the Dervish convents that still existed ten or fifteen years ago – they were just inconspicuous buildings somewhere at the edge of town, modern residential buildings with rooms like salons where men and women met, separately, but with remarkable equality; the Pir lived there with his family and taught not only on the holy days – the Dervish convents are now all abandoned, destroyed, confiscated. Many mystics were in prison, if not executed, and all that under Ahmadinejad, whose popular Shiite piety is anything but traditional: thousands of newly built *emamzadehs*, that is, tombs of relatives of the Imams whose existence no one dreamed of fifty years ago, south of Tehran the fountain where the Mahdi is allegedly supposed to appear, the Shiite messiah, remembered all of a sudden and declared a mass pilgrimage site with the wave of a hand, the poor brought there by busloads, kebab, cola, everything free, and beside the messiah's landing pad the funfair already in full swing, I assume.

Be that as it may: one son remains in Isfahan. Mystics still meet in private homes but, as the son and hence the vicar of the Pir, he had better not turn up there – too dangerous. He has other projects now, a multimedia adaptation of his heritage; he's still drumming, but now with an ensemble of young women in clouds of synthesizers and with new, invented drums, castanets too, with photos of landscapes projected on a screen, computer animation, the verses of the *Book of Kings* well recited, at least, by one of Isfahan's best storytellers. The young women move, too, their torsos sway rhythmically back and forth, they stand up, dance around each other drumming, throw the spinning drums in the air, with some exertion; the mystics once did so unintentionally, spontaneously, as the impulse took them. It's good that the drummer wants to pass on his heritage to the young people; that is meaningful work. The fact that he is involving the young women makes it politically controversial and is also a good thing. And yet it is hard to bear when I think how magnificently, incomparably and ecstatically he used to drum with his brothers and the traditional musicians, all of whom are more or less mystics, and now in Europe.

After our private concert, the drummer asks us what we felt. Because I don't want to be impolite, I answer that the music he used to play immersed me in inner contemplation, while his music now gives me a thousand ideas; at the same time, though, I think to myself: it's like the difference between the Lotfollah dome and Caravaggio – who was painting at exactly the time it was built, by the way – except that this multimedia show with drummers and pre-recorded synthesizer symphony is no Caravaggio, of course, it's just some random thing. Fortunately, the drummer finds something in my idea, runs with it. Yes, his earlier music went inwards; what he does today goes outwards, he ponders; there's a time for everything. He's unable to travel inwards today; the order in exile, himself separated from the other surviving mystics, deterred from the rites. At least his regret is perceptible; he is well aware that the tradition cannot be recreated in multimedia.

When his father the Pir died, his body was brought to Isfahan. The son was taken in for questioning ten times, he recalls, at least ten times; once the room was full of security officers. He's dead, said the drummer, why go to all this trouble? The authorities were worried about his funeral; they wanted to know every step of every participant in advance before granting a permit; they also wanted to know what would be written on his tombstone. Because they rejected every inscription the drummer proposed, because every word is an allusion, and even the name of the deceased was rich in associations, the drummer finally said, okay, then we'll have a blank tombstone with nothing on it, not even his name, just a bare surface. You begin to forget. But even nothing was too much for the authorities. After ten interrogations, at least ten, the funeral was permitted; the drummer agreed to the conditions just so his father could be buried at last. And then, at the cemetery, the mystics suddenly pulled out their dafs, their big, flat, hauntingly resonant drums, and began to dance, all of the order who were left in Isfahan, and many ordinary people danced along. The authorities hadn't counted on that, hadn't so much as dreamed that people could dance at a funeral. There weren't enough officers to collect all the drums, and no orders for that circumstance. They carried his father dancing to his grave.

The next time he was called in for questioning, the drummer was asked, almost with curiosity, what all that had been about. Why dancing at a funeral, why a concert? That was no concert, said the drummer, that came from within, the continuation of feeling. There was no intention; disinterested pleasure, so to speak. When Shiite penitents beat their backs with chains or beat their breast with their fists for hours, to the point of frenzy – that is movement too. Yes, it is, said the officers, but that's different; that comes from grief. Yes, said the drummer, but instead of beating ourselves we dance, transform the beats of the heart into rhythm, into beauty, thankful for the life God gives and takes back again, thankful for the breath with which He speaks to man, and hears us. You begin to forget.

*

Leaning on a tree trunk, I am pulling my heels up to my rump to stretch my thighs when I hear a voice behind me: *Khodā qowwat bedeh!* God give strength! – a friendly wish; the people are friendly in general in the morning when I go running, greet me, smile, something I rarely see in the streets the rest of the day, and never in Tehran. In Tehran, from your car, which is where you spend most of the day if you're a visitor, you're more likely to see fights than smiling faces; that's how strained the people are now. But what the old man whose voice I hear calls to me is more than friendly: it is subtle, an encouragement, a certain recognition, and at the same time the reminder that strength comes ultimately from God. Is he gently deriding me for stretching in broad daylight in strange clothes, something a simple man such as he would not do? Yes, perhaps there is some derision in it too, gentle of course, almost imperceptible, as you might make fun of a relative, a friend. Recognition, encouragement, admonition, edification, mockery – all in three words spoken in passing. At least greetings per se are still obligatory – two people who meet in the solitude, which can also be a riverbank in the city in the morning, greet each other. The Prophet himself said that the only permissible, indeed compelling reason to interrupt a prayer is for a greeting. From my father, who didn't like to be disturbed when he was praying, I often heard as a child that even a burglar in the house must be left undisturbed during prayers; I asked him then each time whether we might simply greet the burglar to prevent him from stealing. But there are a thousand other expressions the old man could have used which would have amounted to greeting in general terms, would have given his greeting a thousand other nuances; even colloquial Persian offers that much variety, and the religious vocabulary still more. Unthinkingly or otherwise, he said, God give strength, when he saw me in pursuit of strength. As I jog past him shortly thereafter, I again wish him a good day; I feel at my back that he is glad: at least some of these modern men still know what politeness requires and what the Prophet enjoined.

*

'There is a living rhythm in the surfaces, an oscillation in the spatial shapes and volumes of Isfahan that give this city its charm,' wrote Henri Stierlin in 1976:

It receives the visitor like a great adventure, and enchants him with an eternal interplay of light and shadow, with constant movement, as if inhaling and exhaling, as if running away or holding back, as if its volumes would contract, to explode the next moment....

In the Occident, the surface of the earth is the only plane of reference; buildings are built on it and the shapes of streets and squares can extend or contract it; but the Persian city planners drew remarkable variations from different planes, inviting surprising effects and ingenious contrasts. For other planes of reference are clearly distinguishable if you think, on the one hand, of the confusion of the bazaar, wholly enclosed and immersed in twilight, and, on the other, of the world opening up above the rooftops, where the evening breeze caressing the dense leaves all around under the starry endlessness of the firmament offers us a breath of peace.[59]

And on the mosques:

We may conclude that the Persian mosque, with its courtyard as an embedded paradise garden, its four liwans as cool grottoes, from whose stalactites water seems to fall as from an eternal spring of the four rivers of the Garden of Eden, with the vault of heaven reflected in the eternal water of the purifying basin, capturing the whole universe in its cosmic sphere, and with its cupola, finally, like the Tree of Life with its dense, shade-giving, ever fresh leafy crown – that this mosque conjures up the place of Eternity contemplated by the mystics of Shiite Islam. And this reinterpretation of the house of prayer is only possible thanks to the polychromy of the sumptuous tile decoration. From this symphony of colours, the Persian mosque takes an inexhaustible wealth of symbols which proclaims the richness of Paradise.[60]

*

On my cousin's old bicycle I ride along the river that no longer exists. Perhaps that, the river, is really the reason why I find everything sad during this sojourn. My friends in Tehran were not so hopeless; they pointed out the niches to be found everywhere and the transformation going on under-ground, below the surface of the earth, unhindered or even accelerated by the despotism. Each time, I wondered: What earth? What's left of it? The river depresses my mood, I know that; it depresses the mood of Isfahan too, weighs on the conversations, noticeably or unnoticeably, with my relatives, in the shops, in taxis. In Tehran they have no such beauties to be destroyed; that makes it easier for the new to spread. I ride and ride, past the parks, on and on, until the regular paths end below where the old fire temple stands. I consider whether to make the climb to the Zoroastrian temple to look down at Isfahan from above, from long, long ago. I decide against it; I'm already melancholy enough; I'd rather go on subjecting myself to the river that no longer exists, cycle along a gravel track, and then further when there is no more track. Earlier my route would have ended at the big factory whose fence extends into the former river; now I can push the bicycle through the riverbed and look for a footpath on the opposite bank. The way goes on, through orchards, across fields, then along lanes again, right through flocks of sheep with shepherds looking like those in old Italian films, black and white, carrying the same sticks.

That's how easy it is to get out of the overfilled city with its motorways and apartment blocks that have remade whole districts in no time at all. Especially at its former outskirts, Isfahan is hardly recognizable: where once was desert there now stands a shopping mall; where a fruit orchard was is now an amusement park. When I cycle along the Rhine from home, I end up

324

in the next borough, city or town – Porz, Niederkassel or Bad Honnef. Here, I pick my way somehow, sometimes carrying the bicycle, or crossing the riverbed to find a way forward on the opposite bank, and after three quarters of an hour I am pedalling through the pre-industrial era, except that now and then I do come past a factory, looking very old-fashioned, from the period of the shah, or see the new satellite cities in the distance, which must be the epitome of desolation. That's another thing you wouldn't see in a strictly Western European biography of my generation – besides war, revolution, oppression, fear, torture, murdered writers, dire need, flight, expulsion, brain drain, families that communicate mainly by international calls, government offices that are dealt with mainly by bribery. In Iran I have become acquainted with such a world as existed before the Russian Revolution: the severe, apparently immutable class distinctions; a cosmopolitan bourgeoisie, and then villages without electricity or running water, just a few kilometres from home.

I cycle on, further and further, take a rest in a village that is now a city with road signs, eat a hamburger that's not at all bad in one of the deserted snack stands; the burger costs 30 cents more if you want to make it yourself. The cook would like to know what kind of person I am, a bourgeois with intellectual glasses, dusty and hungry, far away from the city, with such a strange accent, on an ancient bicycle of the kind only the poor people ride, particularly the peasants, while the young, rich and hip are all hunched over their mountain bikes. I don't tell him – why should I? The mystery will haunt him much longer than its banal solution would. I come through areas that look like my childhood, donkeys, horse-drawn carts, the peasants in *sarwal*, loose drawstring trousers, women in colourful clothes working in the fields, and water, wells from which the water pours into the fields, into little channels, even water with bubbles, so much water, in one place, that the people here wash their cars. So there is still water, not far from Isfahan, in the ground, not in the river, which has been pumped dry somewhere.

On and on, in spite of the river or because of the river, I can hardly tear myself away. It wasn't deep here, a metre, two at most, not even particularly wide outside Isfahan, a brook, rather, to someone from Cologne on the Rhine. As I said, the surrounding desert made it so precious, so beautiful, the mountains on the horizon in the afternoon sun bare of all vegetation. There could hardly be a more pleasant cycle tour than along the river, if it still existed. At one point I observe two families picnicking in the middle of the riverbed; one of the two couples argues, the husband runs away, the wife sits cross-legged weeping, the others try to mediate or to console her. A picnic in a skeleton can only go wrong. Onwards, imprudently far, because I should be back in Isfahan before dark, when suddenly a nail is sticking in my tyre, a great big nail.

Fortunately, the people here still ride bicycles; even in the villages that are still villages there is always someone who does nothing else but repair bicycles. I ask my way to an old man who first has to patch the tube of a boy who was here before me – so much business today. It doesn't occur to him to ask whether I'm in a hurry, and I don't know how I might express haste in this forsaken place. Okay, if the worst comes to the worst I'll wave some pickup down so as not to have to cycle on the country road in the dark. So I stand in front of the old man, who is sitting on an empty canister, and watch his slowed but still experienced movements. A big hole, visible to the naked eye – where were you looking, sir? As if in slow motion, he cuts a strip of latex and glues it very carefully onto the tube, then tests repeatedly in a bucket of water whether any air is still escaping. In the end, patching a puncture costs 3,000 toman, 75 cents, the old man will not take a toman more, although the prices in the city are almost as high as in Europe, but the incomes only a fifth or an eighth as high, if not less. Turning the bicycle on its saddle and then back on its wheels after the work is done is my job. A-1 quality, says the old man, English model, forty, fifty years old at least; they don't make them like that any more.

By the time I reach the parks again, there is a little group of hookah smokers every few metres; there are also mixed groups and groups of young women, although there are signs posted everywhere saying they are prohibited – the hookahs, I mean, but the mixed groups probably are as well. Swimming is likewise prohibited, as are open fires, tents of course, and sleeping outdoors, absolutely. Yes, sleeping is explicitly prohibited; lying in the grass, I suppose, is at the very limit of what's permissible. And what if your eyes fall shut? Laughing is not prohibited; at least there's no sign saying so.

*

When we go exploring in the mountains east of Isfahan – at first in search of the last Armenian villages, which turn out to be just as unprepossessing as all the other villages, not at all picturesque, not at all less poor, only women sitting in front of the houses, which are more like shacks – even my aunts are amazed that so little has changed in the countryside in forty years. It is still just as it was in my childhood memories, just as squalid, except for the power

326

lines, which were still lacking then in some places, the schools, which are now a fact even in the remotest valleys and steppes, the exile broadcasters received via satellite, which report on the Leader's Quran reciter, that swine. Was the revolution not fought for them? No, not for those who have remained in the villages, but for the new cities; not for the rural population, then, but for the urban migrants, who demanded their share of prosperity, and respect at last. They were the revolutionary masses; they are still its core. The countryside has never had a voice in Iran. Less than 80 kilometres southwest of Isfahan, we see nomads' tents, real nomads; women at the petrol station whose language not even my aunts understand, their garments splendid, their hands tattooed. The revolution was certainly not fought for them, who still do not wear dull colours, who resist all progress and hence every form of ideology, and also emancipation – resist the new, whatever it may be.

*

Riding lessons. We want our youngest daughter to associate as many beautiful things as possible with Iran, and so we are going to the length of taking her to riding lessons every afternoon that we're in Isfahan, an hour's drive by taxi to the riding stables and an hour back again afterwards. At least the riding stables are quiet, idyllic no less, almost a forest except for the big paddocks, and there is a café, although there are no longer hookahs there except on the menu. And we have bought our daughter a helmet, although we don't know how we will get it into our luggage.

The riding instructor is a young woman, mid-twenties at most, slender, very pretty face, casual hooded jumper over a long shirt, her headscarf behind her hairline as usual, a very firm voice, often multitasking with her smartphone. First we watch as she gives a riding lesson to a man, which is impressive enough in itself – her clear authority and his willingness to accept it. But, then, the man is young too, just a few years older than she is; the same amazingly emancipated generation, at least in the bourgeois milieu. The way the riding instructor addresses my daughter, whose Persian is not so good and whose heart is pounding at the sight of the big grey, is just right from the first sentence: distinct, assertive, encouraging. At the same time she teaches two more adult men who can already ride on their own. Our daughter's horse, however, circles the riding instructor on a lunge line, and then, when our daughter follows the instructions carefully, the instructor turns over the line to her assistant, who is also older than she is. The self-assurance with which she calls out her instructions across the paddock, gently to my daughter, sternly to the men – no young woman ever used to speak in such tones in any milieu, especially as the other two students are not some kind of intellectuals or dandies but, to judge by their clothes, their attitude, their voices, men in the old-fashioned style, especially the one, unshaven, with a training jacket, a beer or perhaps kebab belly, and a servant of his own at the edge of the paddock, whom he orders to fetch the whip from somewhere (the car, the locker room, somewhere) because the horse is not obeying (someone's got to obey a man). Merchant milieu, I would guess, traditional, though not necessarily loyal to the regime – but who is? The young riding instructor unquestioningly treats the man as her subordinate, only her smile is somewhat awkward, but also emphatically superior when she jeers at 50 yards that a horse can't understand two commands at once; kicking it and pulling the reins at the same time – how is that supposed to work? He might think about that. There have been self-assured Iranian women in earlier ages, there have been queens, princesses, poets, mystics, Quran commentators; there were feminists as early as the nineteenth century, and even in religious families there have often been mothers who took no orders from their husbands. But the naturalness with which a young woman, multitasking with her smartphone, instructs two significantly older men in horsemanship, her tone that is nothing short of imperious and at the same time always charming – no, that would have been just as unimaginable a generation ago as women taxi drivers or women managers or single women going on thirty with no thought of marrying, instead celebrating their independence. That is the major part of the revolution that the literary magazine editor was talking about; that is what will overthrow the current regime: before the younger generation, the women.

*

A clay village in the desert: in addition to backpackers from Europe – were we that scruffy? – middle-class Iranians looking rather out of place, urban professionals, with or without little children, from hikers to hipsters and even some prim and proper, and between them the inhabitants of the desert village making up the staff who are accustomed to all kinds of customers. As if the oasis were their private home, the female guests put off their headscarves; first the Iranians, then, after a questioning look at them, the Europeans. This is not just a matter of comfort; more than that, it is a signal to take back spaces of liberty, regardless of what's happening politically, or, rather, what is not happening for the time being. After all, the headscarves here are not gradually slipping down to the shoulders, they are being taken off: that is a different operation. Apparently it doesn't bother the locals, as long as they can sell their roasted maize, boiled potatoes, date syrup and pomegranate juice, and their bast handicrafts.

The village is still well preserved, with streets too narrow for cars, connecting tunnels, wind towers that supply the houses with cooling air; several buildings have been renovated as accommodation, with courtyards, but with no furniture, only carpets and cushions. Sometimes you get the feeling that European backpackers are more accustomed than bourgeois Iranians to sitting, eating, sleeping on the floor. But, then, sometimes you don't, if I take just the two Berliners who tell us they had to justify their trip to their friends and acquaintances. The hipster nonchalance they display at their local craft-beer bar doesn't quite come off here, as they draw their plates up to their mouths, legs outstretched, instead of leaning forward over their plates while sitting cross-legged, as the more limber guests do. Be that as it may, it is an odd, mad mixture, worth the overnight stay in itself, especially when you know both languages, the foreign and the domestic, although the bourgeois Iranians are almost as foreign in the village as the Berlin hipsters.

Oddly, the Iranians, who seem to travel only in small groups, monopolize the place much more, just by their loudness, their merriment, their important-people attitude in the village; the backpackers are keen to adapt to the local situation, only they should have brought somewhat neater clothes, but we probably didn't think of that either when we were backpackers. The only language even I don't understand is the local dialect; this village, Zoroastrian up until three, four centuries ago, is completely Islamized today, although sadly with such a dry Islam, the head of the taxi service explains while driving us to the saline lake, nothing mystical, music only at weddings, otherwise mourning. What's their position towards the government? Everyone votes, because they're afraid for their pensions and the other state benefits if they don't have the stamp in their ID cards, but many people turn in blank ballots. Are they against the regime? I ask. No, they're neutral. That's an original point of view, I think to myself: neutral. There's no one left here in the villages anyway except the old people; as elsewhere, the young people have all gone away. Only tourism has created a few new jobs; on weekends there are forty, fifty coaches a day stopping at the oasis springs, plus the guests in the hotels; apart from that – and date palms and pomegranate trees – there's nothing.

All the tourism is the work of a long-bearded, long-haired man called

Maziar, the only person wearing traditional clothes. Seventeen years ago he moved to his father's home town with his wife, who is half French, and became the first one for miles around, he says with a certain pride, to remodel one of the old clay houses into a guest house. By now there are sixty of them just in this area, says Maziar, whom everyone here seems to like and to respect as a village head. Even without the jobs he has created, he would command respect by his deep, resonant voice, his strong hands and his great, almost excessive size, to say nothing of his wild hair. The summers are almost unbearable, he growls, up to 55 or even 60 degrees Celsius; he spends them in Europe with his wife and their nine-year-old son, in part so that their son doesn't forget his second language.

It is good that the Iranians are starting to discover the beauty of their landscapes and their past; traditional guest houses, tea houses, residential houses, clay villages are becoming fashionable, as are excursions to enjoy natural scenery. It keeps a few villagers from moving to the overcrowded city, allows a few more families to earn their bread; a few houses are saved from demolition; fewer commuter cities get built (no, this last is only wishful thinking; rural tourism will never create enough jobs to obviate the need for even one city). Maziar's brother, who is just as big, but beardless, has opened a tea house where he plays the drum in the evenings. When he's not playing, there is classical Persian maqam music on tape, or sometimes other ethno music. Both their wives have a wonderful mixture of worldliness and attachment to their native soil; both are friendly beyond all measure, resolutely self-assured, and at the same time discreet, more helpful than solicitous. Perhaps under the shah it would have been possible to combine worldliness with attachment for the native soil, to show by a view from the outside how precious the interior is. After all, the rulers had been educated in Europe. But, back then, the old clay villages were despised, agriculture was devastated, and with it the traditional life world; only the men sat in the tea houses, while everyone else longed for the West or for a return to something that had never existed. And all that is left today is ethno. Still better than the commuter cities, however, and definitely worth seeing for everyone. Iran is already the most popular destination offered by the Munich-based cultural tour operator Studiosus, one of the German hotel guests reports.

The young assistant who looks after everything, the goats and camels, the soft-boiled eggs, the tea and, especially lovingly, our daughter, who is getting along swimmingly with the kitchen maid's little daughter and has become her babysitter – in other words, she is now helping out in the household herself – the young assistant asks where these Europeans get so much time to travel; he hasn't left the village in his life, and never had time off either. I explain to him the essence of the backpacker and his financial situation: that four weeks in Iran, flight included, cost less than two weeks' travel in Europe. It bothers some tourists that no alcohol is served, he notices that, says the employee; on the other hand, the tourists find grass all the easier to get, if I understand the Berliners' allusions correctly, and in good quality. Many are less put off by the lack of alcohol than by the headscarf, I explain to the assistant when he asks what must be done to get still more foreigners to visit Iran. I also submit that mass tourism can disfigure a country. The people travelling in Iran today are honestly interested; if tourists were free to do whatever they liked, the business would soon be focused on nothing but partying; that would then change the culture of the villages. That's true, says the assistant; in Mesr it's already like that, out where the sand dunes begin, the latest thing in Iranian tourism; it's already all about drinking there. Really? I ask, and for a moment I suspect, against all probability, that Mesr has been invaded by British EasyJetters. But the employee is talking about Iranians going to Mesr to party.

*

I have never seen such a panorama in any desert: almost 360 degrees. We have driven with the long-bearded, long-haired hotelier's four-wheel drive into the sand dunes at the edge of the Dasht-e Kavir, the 150-kilometre-wide, 400-kilometre-long emptiness that lies in northeastern Iran: no oasis, no human life; just 400 by 150 kilometres of brownish, stony plain (and in southeastern Iran lies the even larger Dasht-e Lut). In the multicoloured landscape are two elongated hills of white limestone, gently rising on the sides farthest from each other, falling like cliffs on the long sides facing each other, one called the Princess's Throne and the other someone else's Throne. You stand on top of them and look at a world so different, so unique, as strange as the moon: the opposite cliff rising out of the landscape 10 or 20 kilometres away; the dark mountain range to the southeast, surely snow-covered in winter; the sand dunes almost artificial, like a computer animation; the gorges that become rivers when it rains; the furrows running through the sand, through the sandstone, through the limestone; the shading infinitely subtle, from white to golden brown; obstinate, spindly little trees like fearful green dots on it; and, on the open side, the endless plain all the way to the horizon. Absolute, almost audible silence: no sounds of animals, no wind; just the emptiness. Spontaneously, a wish never to see a work of human hands again, not even a work of art, because nothing can be as beautiful as this picture that has no frame.

Maziar was a potter in Tehran, a kind of professor of ceramics to be precise, training artisans. The noisier Tehran became after the revolution, the more difficult the political conditions, the stronger his wish grew to be close to nature, near the origins, his own included – instead of emigrating, as many of his friends did. He first saw the village of his father, who had moved to Tehran to study aeronautical engineering, when he was seven years old, and he always felt comfortable there, always better than in the city, although in those days there was neither electricity nor running water, and no asphalt roads for a long way, so that it took days to get there. Over a thousand people lived in the clay houses back then, young and old, with their own language, their own clothes, their own customs; lived on what they grew themselves, self-sufficient as Iran itself was until a few decades ago, in spite of the aridity, even exporting food, grain, rice, pistachios, famed throughout the East for its juicy fruit. Then gradual progress came, slow at first and then like a whirlwind after the revolution, which had the ambition of bringing the blessings of modern civilization to all Iranians instead of just to the middle class. Today Iran imports more than 90 per cent of its food.

When you have a sick child, a doctor is certainly a good thing, Maziar admits. A telephone with which to call the doctor is a good thing, too; a road that will take you to a hospital in just a few hours; medicines. Naturally the people want progress, television sets, refrigerators, and so on – what right would we have to deny it them? Besides – with or without self-sufficiency – the people used to be hungry often enough, says Maziar, not to seem nostalgic, really starved. That doesn't happen today; the people live on their pension or the *yarane*, a kind of citizens' dividend by which the state distributes oil revenue to its clientele. Naturally it is more convenient to buy everything you need in the supermarket than to grow your food with your own hands, and still go hungry if it doesn't rain, and fear every infection a child comes down with. Naturally village life was hard, often unbearable, and exacerbated by the landlord's whip, if he was a scoundrel. Naturally progress was joyously welcomed. Only the result for the village was not development, but destruction; there were only 200 people left living here, only the old people, that is. And they didn't live long.

It could have worked out, says Maziar; the village could have been brought up to the present more carefully, beginning under the shah; his White

Revolution was well intended, his courage in taking the land away from the feudal lords and distributing it among the peasants. Only the result was that chaos broke out. An example: the landlord determined who was allowed to pump how much water out of the ground for which field – that may be unjust; some landlords were good, some bad – but there was order, and, when it collapsed, no one got enough water any more. So there was another revolution, this time one from below, and since then the culture that's running the country is the same village culture that isn't even able to distribute the water in a village. No matter which government agency you look at, the offices are held not by the capable people, but by the relatives of the martyrs and disabled veterans. At least the country has remained safe, an achievement of the Islamic Republic which must not be underestimated in view of the collapse of public order in Iraq, in Syria; seventeen years without a single crime here in the oasis. At their core, the people are farmers; they have never learned to steal, unlike the people in Dasht-e Lut, where there was no proper agriculture to begin with, and the people had to feed themselves by other means – smuggling, highway robbery. If a car is stopped by the roadside here, Maziar explains, you can be sure the next driver who comes along will stop to help.

Maziar doesn't have to spend the night with tourists in the desert; he knows enough other guides and desert-loving friends from Tehran who would be happy to lead the excursions. But he enjoys the quiet, is glad to see the enthusiasm for nature that he sparks in others, is proud of his countryside. The next day he almost doesn't want to leave; he drives us to one wonderful place after another, makes us a rich gift of his discoveries, observations, insights, devotedly gives his attention to our daughter, shows her how the sand behaves when you dig formations for the wind to blow away, and lets her sit on his lap and steer his four-wheel drive all morning, even up and down the dunes, where driving becomes surfing. She finds the camel ride once round Mesr totally boring in comparison; she once rode for three days through the Moroccan desert and mounts a camel this time more for the sake of her mother, who is trying it for the first time. While waiting for them, I drink tea with a group of young people from Tehran who spent the night somewhere else in the desert, among them two regular punks, or maybe not punks, some other style, jump boots, black clothes, the young woman with her hair dyed blue. Not even Berlin hipsters could be more exotic in the desert.

*

In the city there are not many shops that patch bicycle inner tubes. Pushing the bike with another puncture, I ask around and everyone sends me 200 metres further on, always further on, always just 200 metres, then I'll be there, as if they wanted to spare me the sad truth that I'll be pushing for quite a while yet. Finally I return to the shop where I asked last and complain that there's no bicycle shop 200 metres further on, nor in 400 metres or 600 metres. Maybe it's 800 metres, the shopkeeper blithely replies, and recommends that I get on the bike and ride carefully with the flat front tyre, then it won't be so far. The result is that the old tyre is so ravaged by the many curbs and bumps in the pavement that the old bicycle mechanic tosses it in the rubbish along with the inner tube, which is beyond patching. Strangely, all the bicycle mechanics in Iran seem to be ancient, and all have the same tiny workshop, just a little room, basically – it was like that in my childhood too. The old gentleman recommends an Iranian tube instead of the cheap goods from China. The idea that an Iranian product is superior is something completely new. He is just as pleased with the English bicycle as his colleague in the village.

I give up the attempt to use the newly made cycle paths after a few blocks. The paths are there, and signs are there reserving them for cyclists, but then the path suddenly comes to an end at a shin-high kerb, or is interrupted by a metal barrier, and you have to dismount and lift the bike over it. And it often happens that there's a scooter parked on the path, so that you have to carry the bike across the grass divider between the cycle path and the pavement. The people running the country must have learned in their villages how a cycle path ought to be! But no: the people who run the country have been driving cars for two, three generations now, even the Iranian model if need be, which no mechanic in the world would call superior to a foreign one.

I didn't expect the motorists to show consideration to cyclists. But, in fact, they are mindful of every obstacle that pops up out of nowhere; they are used to that; they creep past, or step on the brake if there is any risk of a dent, or even just a road death. As a result, you can get through even the thickest traffic on a bicycle; you only have to have the courage to get in the way of the cars, and ignore their horns. There aren't many cyclists, but there are now women among them; there were none last time I was here. But cycling is spoiled for me by the exhaust fumes, the excessive car traffic; I take detours where possible through the side streets and alleys, where kerbstones, parked cars, water channels and trees in the middle of the roadway make the route into an obstacle course: quite entertaining, but too slow if you're in a hurry to get anywhere. Many cyclists wear a mask over their mouth and nose; that looks more like a hospital than fun. After my return from the pure desert air, I would put up with a gas mask too.

Everything I used to like about day-to-day life in Isfahan, all of my places, the river, the bridges, the tea houses, the bookshops, the quiet alleys along the canals, the Armenian that was spoken in our neighbourhood, is gone, as if spirited away by some demon. I would be completely depressed if it weren't for seeing my family again, my daughter having fun, and moments of happiness here and there like the desert, the Lotfollah Mosque, and the little discoveries that are still to be made in the old city centre, after so many years.

*

Not even the Poles have left a trace I can find. Yes, says my aunt, she was acquainted with several Polish women who married men from Isfahan, but after the revolution their families emigrated one after the other, no, not to Poland – the children didn't speak Polish anyway – to America, mostly. In New Zealand, of all places, there are also supposed to be many Poles from Isfahan. You just have to Google, and you find countless links, books, films, memoirs of the 100,000 or 300,000 Poles, mostly women and children, who found refuge in Iran in the early 1940s, after Stalin let them out of the Gulag in 1942. The accounts of how the desperately overcrowded little wooden boats landed on the shore of the Caspian Sea, panic, cries, how some of the boats capsized during the landing because everyone wanted to get to safety at once, how children screamed in panic, mothers carried their babies ashore soaked to the skin, local fishermen took the oldest of the refugees on their shoulders; how the dripping wet people were wrapped in blankets, how on the beach they were still paralysed with fear or euphoric at their rescue – all this describes exactly the situations Europe saw on Lesbos in the autumn of 2015. On YouTube you can watch how blond men and women, many of them barefoot, exhausted, carrying babies in their arms or leading children by the hand, their baggage in rucksacks or on donkey carts, wander through the typical Iranian landscapes, over bare mountains, through fertile valleys that aren't a brilliant green only because the film is black and white. You can watch them being fed and outfitted with clothing. The Iranians seem to have been friendly; at least it sounds that way in the Poles' reminiscences, which can be heard on YouTube in an English that still has the Polish accent. 'The debt and the gratitude that the refugees felt for their host country runs like a warm current through the entire literature of remembrance,' writes

335

a Polish author who has researched his compatriots' flight to Iran. 'There are constant mentions of the simple Iranian population's friendliness and sympathy towards the Poles.'

Three thousand orphans, I read, were sent to Isfahan and distributed to orphanages and families throughout the city. Those were the children my mother played with every Friday, because Grandmother invited them from the orphanage to our big house to romp in the green courtyard and swim in the pool, as I did too as a child, in the very same pool. My aunt reports that not all the Polish orphans in Isfahan found happiness; there were also words of anger and rejection, and more than a few of the girls later ended up in prostitution because, without parents, they naturally had a harder time of it than the Iranian children in the middle-class neighbourhood. There was something unsavoury about that: as the Polish girls got older, they were targeted, explicitly recruited, by the pimps. Iranian customers preferred to buy blonde women, says my aunt, making a disgusted face. Well, she says next, but many of the Polish girls finished school, studied, and married, while the men, the adults in general, as far as she knows, moved on as soon as they could after the war. On the Internet I find a Polish postage stamp showing a blonde child in front of a Persian rug: 'Isfahan, city of the Polish children', says the legend on the stamp, issued a few years ago. Was Poland's nationalist-religionist government already in power then, opposing the admittance of refugees?

*

My cousin teaches me how to cycle in Isfahan; he knows every passageway connecting two alleys, every little bridge, every piece of metal covering a drainage channel, every little concrete ramp that someone has poured to avoid dismounting at a kerb – great fun and, in the city centre especially, the fastest way to see the sights that are not listed in any travel guide: saints' tombs, minarets, those remote, obscure corners of the bazaar that haven't changed in forty years, exactly the same old shopkeepers, although they must be their sons, the familiar Isfahan accent that must one day die out, like every dialect in the world, the same artistic rituals of greeting – which around the bazaar are religious; that is, Arabic-enriched – when one merchant passes another, or when a good customer enters the shop. Because it is Muharram, the month in which Imam Hussein was murdered at the Battle of Karbala, many merchants have donated tea and sugar candy to be served on the street – so I listen to the neighbourhood gossip every 200 metres. I buy two bast fans to ventilate my barbecue; they're as efficient as any hairdryer. I should pray for his poor soul whenever I get my charcoal glowing in Germany, the bast weaver requests, accompanying the whole transaction with melodic basmalas.

The philosopher Abdolkarim Soroush once said that Shiite Islam is so deeply rooted in Iran that only a Shiite revolution could eradicate it, and as a matter of fact I have seen only one person praying during my entire stay, only one single person praying in two weeks in Isfahan – but here, in those corners of the old city centre where no tourist goes, piety is still the rule. At the saints' tombs and the little mosques too, every single one a gem, I am surprised to see men and women immersed in dialogue with God or reciting the Quran in their pert Isfahan accent, raising the end of every sentence up high. Religion has been so thoroughly commandeered, indeed defiled, by politics in the Islamic Republic that any ordinary public display of piety without a political intention or connotation is surprising. More typical are the blinking large-format lighted advertisements for the Leader, hanging in the middle of the world's most splendid iwan, or next to the mihrab, the prayer niche. At one of the saints' tombs, the guardians of the Middle East have defaced the Seljuk façade with two giant mosaics of Khomeini and Khamenei. The Safavids were tyrants too, my cousin reminds me – but at least they conserved what was beautiful and vied with one another in conservation. The present tyrants not only produce rubbish, which would be bad enough, but they also deface what was once sublime – as if they were envious, or conscious of their own inferiority. Did you see the shrine of Ayatollah Khomeini while you were in Tehran?

Here at least the city government has recently saved many old houses from demolition by remodelling them as museums, although with displays that always end up glorifying the Leader, no matter what the exhibition is about. The city has also replaced the asphalt with paving stones in certain alleys that tourists are likely to walk through, as in an old Italian town. Palatial homes from the Qajar or even the Safavid period – not the newfangled villas that they think old in Tehran – are now being used as hotels, or private citizens with artistic sense have bought them and renovated them for their own use. Forty years after the revolution that was supposed to take the country back to its roots, they are finally desisting from tearing up those roots, much too late of course; Isfahan is already so ruined that only strangers can be enthralled with it now: those who don't know how much has been lost in so short a time. And those responsible still haven't learned; they're finally restoring old caravanserais or baths, but they continue to tear broad swaths through the middle of the web of alleys, houses and courtyards, demolishing whole streets to make squares that are apparently supposed to compete with the old ones, but are only cheap imitations. The parks that have been established here and there in the middle of the old centre are certainly useful to the inhabitants, but naturally they too are an intrusion, which the Iranian registry of historic landmarks will need another thirty, forty years to prohibit. The *kuchehā* and *paskut-shehā*, the alleys and footpaths in which it was once possible to get lost for hours – some of them so narrow that two people can't get past each other, some of them tunnels – now lead within a few minutes, a quarter of an hour at most, to a thoroughfare or an open space. Only the bazaar – the longest in the world, at over 10 kilometres, if I remember correctly – is still intact, if no longer fully populated, since the better shops have moved to the shopping malls. The biggest of these is called City Center, even in Persian. But we're not supposed to say *merci* any more, as our grandparents did. My cousin also takes me to the house where my brothers were born – built in the mid-1950s, hence a candidate for demolition, actually; the only reason it hasn't yet made way for a block of flats is because the owner would then lose a quarter of the lot, which extends on two sides into the alleys that have long since been widened.

*

It never ceases to amaze me when I experience the mullahs without politics for a change, in their original element at *rowzekhāni*, the commemoration of the martyrs: as preachers – no, as elegists, storytellers, performers. The ceremony has just begun: so far only twenty, thirty older gentlemen sitting along the walls, the oldest on chairs, the rest leaning on cushions; the preacher is probably only the opening act. But what an act, if you don't know the show! Sitting cross-legged on the pulpit, which is as high as a door, shrouded in a black mantle, his white turban and his thick black beard up over his cheekbones like those in the caricatures of the Prophet, his hands motionless on the armrests, he tells today of Zainab, Hussein's sister, the only survivor of the massacre at Karbala; he tells of her last night beside her brother's tent and of the love of siblings; he tells of love generally, saying he who sleeps in this night is no lover; he tells of the nature of night, in which all secrets are revealed, and finally, more beautifully than I have ever heard, he tells of Majnun, waiting at night before Layla's door, an hour, two hours, until he can't bear it any more and knocks. Who is it? asks Layla curtly behind the door. It is I, Majnun – which is not a name but an attribute, literally meaning he is mad about her – please open the door just a crack, please let me see you just for a moment. Wait a little, Layla commands him, and leaves Majnun standing in front of the door, an hour, two hours, until he can't bear it any more and knocks again. Wait a little more, says Layla unmoved, and leaves Majnun standing, an hour, two hours … and so on and on, the whole night, which in the story becomes endless; Majnun waits, can't bear it any more, knocks, and must go on standing in front of the door, an hour, two hours, until, his heart pounding, he knocks again, only to be told that he must be patient a little longer. How the preacher bends forward and, whispering, imitates the pounding of Hussein's heart – whispering, just exhaling, but so loud, because he has brought his lips close to the microphone, is practically devouring the microphone, so loud that it penetrates the listeners: boom, boom, his heart, when Hussein, in the certain knowledge of his impending death, looks into his sister's tent – how the preacher moves his mouth away from the microphone whenever he raises his voice or holds his breath to heighten the tension, an hour, two hours, as he weaves other plot threads or a line of Rumi into the parallel story, making Layla and Majnun into a religious passion, constantly keeping an eye on the visitors trickling in, greeting notables individually with a blessing for the Prophet and his family, then going on with his story, or gently jibing at someone who is not following it with his thoughts and his eyes; how the preacher unexpectedly puts up his hand before a dramatic climax, and holds it still over his head, his palm spread flat, as if he were spellbound himself by the story – this is the high art of storytelling. 'They've got nothing better to do in Qom than study elocution and disputation,' my cousin mutters irritably, who would never go to a *rowzekhāni* on his own and is amazed at how suspensefully the mullah speaks, with what brilliant technique. In the end, Majnun falls asleep, and on awakening he finds some shelled walnuts in his hand. He is glad that Layla has shown him her regard and cared for his hunger, and he thanks her with emotion. Thereupon Layla opens the door and says contemptuously that he is only a child, and so she put the walnuts in his hand out of pity; if he were a lover, nuts wouldn't interest him and he wouldn't be able to swallow a thing anyway. But how can you think I don't love you? Majnun asks desperately. A lover doesn't fall asleep before the door of his beloved, answers Layla.

When the preacher was still tending the souls of his home town, a couple once brought him their son – twenty-three, twenty-five years old, a face like the moon – who was hopelessly in love with a girl. The parents were against the liaison, his parents as well as hers, for whatever reason, and isolated the lovers from each other. Although – the preacher doesn't mention whether she loved him; that's not germane; a lover loves, no matter whether his love is requited or not. The young man was ill, emaciated, pale, his beautiful face furrowed; he could hardly speak, and all he said was that he wanted to see the girl, wanted to marry her. Please talk to him, said the young man's parents and other relatives, free him of this affliction by whatever words you can. The mullah sent the parents and all the young man's relatives out of the room; they were annoyed but, hesitantly, they obeyed his instructions. When the mullah was alone with the young man, he kissed the top of his head, kissed his forehead, kissed his hands, even his feet. What are you doing? asked the young man, confused; why are you kissing my hand? Because you can teach me what love is, replied the mullah; I claim to love Imam Hussein, but look at me: I eat; I sleep at night; look at my belly. I only claim to love; if anyone is a lover, it is you. That is why I kiss your feet.

Cut to Imam Hussein's tent in the night before his death. Zainab is lying in the next tent, separated only by a few layers of cloth hanging from a pole. Now and then he looks across, knowing that he will die in the morning. Now and then she looks across between the cloths, knowing of the unequal battle that her brother will fight in the morning. When Hussein is standing by the side of her tent, the sister pretends to sleep so as not to add to his worries. And he pretends to sleep when Zainab looks in, turn and turn about, the whole night through. Unbelievable how long nights are.

From Zainab's last night with Hussein, the preacher returns to the nature of night, the secrets of the night. The night reveals who is a lover. Once, Hussein's and Zainab's eyes meet, only the pupils, flashing in the dark between the cloth of the tents. The listeners have long been in tears by this time; even the most dignified gentlemen sob. The preacher remains calm; he only lengthens the pauses between the sentences, his arms motionless on the wide armrests. Only when the hour of parting comes, his voice too catches; at the last embrace of the lovers, he has to swallow; now the tears come to his eyes too; the listeners' grief breaks out unchecked. But during the whole sermon, like an actor on stage, he has the whole house in view, including the next act; before the first tears he gives his assistant a sign with his eyes to lay a handkerchief on the armrest, and not a hidden sign, no, an obvious one. In this epic theatre, the performer's distance from the narrative does not disrupt the audience's empathy but encourages it; the concentration on the psychological process, the avoidance of superficial illusions, reinforces it.

After the climax, the preacher quickly returns to the previous flow of his story, the pace calmer now if anything. The listeners wipe the tears from their eyes, and their spirits are completely calmed when they hear something consoling, a pleasing digression. The preacher also has his eye on the time, and mentions it, stepping out of the main plot completely to say he must finish the story of Zainab's suffering before the next preacher's turn: the culmination is yet to come. But then he only digresses again with another ancillary story. The tears must first accumulate before they can really flow at the end, for the tears are what it's all about; the tears are the measure of his success. And they flow when he whispers, close to the microphone, how Hussein dies and Zainab mourns, they flow, as the river in Isfahan may one day flow again, God give strength. When they are all weeping uncontrollably on the carpets, and only my cousin rolls his eyes humourlessly, the hand that rested on the broad armrest of the pulpit shoots up one last time, but this time the index finger is outstretched. The mullah, now weeping again, withdraws his mouth from the microphone and raises his voice: 'Wipe the tears from your faces and show Heaven that you are lovers!'

*

Before its politicization by the Islamic Republic, martyrdom was defensive, as in early Christianity – the martyr did not kill but was killed. That is the core: someone gives up his life for others. The *rowzekhāni* offered something of the old experience of martyrdom as an act of sacrifice, attended only by old people, devout and from modest backgrounds, but clean-shaven, unlike the revolutionary clientele, without the habitus of the officials in their uniform suits, or blazers such as Ahmadinejad wears. In company in the evening, over whisky and the daily political criticism, my friends are almost disgusted that I attended a *rowzekhāni*, but I found it more impressive than most modern theatre performances or current films. After all, the listeners were weeping not just for Imam Hussein; they were also weeping for Majnun; they were weeping for every lover, weeping tears of their own, so that they could then go home released, cheerful. Suffering is not an end in itself; it is something to be conquered, especially since the original tradition included not only martyrdom but also fun, not only *rowzekhāni* but also *ruhowzi*, a kind of *commedia dell'arte* which, sadly, did not survive the twentieth century. One of my friends reports that a cleric recently demanded that the spectators of a state-associated or state-organized *rowzekhāni*, in any case one broadcast on television, stop their cursing Imam Hussein's assassins, something that always has an anti-Sunni aspect. Even Imam Ali forgave his enemies; on his deathbed he forgave even his murderer, the cleric admonished the people. The crowd was not to be pacified; on the contrary, the cleric himself was … well, not cursed, but insulted, and one of the listeners stood up and shouted that he didn't care if Imam Ali forgave his murderer; he would never forgive the murderer of Imam Hussein. Did that listener go home released and cheerful?

*

With a cousin visiting from America, I climb the mountain that overlooks Isfahan, Kuh-e Soffeh. I get my first disillusionment from a young, apparently religious woman to whose group we call out a *khasteh nabāshid* as they approach from above, the usual expression when someone is exerting themselves: 'May you not be tired!'

What is that supposed to mean, the woman returns snippily, *khasteh nabāshid*; that doesn't matter, or rather it's not up to us whether we're tired or not. The right thing to say is *khodā qowwat bedeh*, May God give strength, because everything depends on God. *Khasteh nabāshid* signals only atheism, nothing else. 'Wow,' my cousin and I whistle in unison when the group has passed us. It's new to him too that even the familiar, simple 'May you not be tired' is no longer on message. That puts a new light on the old gentleman who saw me stretching and wished God might give me strength.

While we gasp our way up the mountains, my cousin tells me about his military service, which was longer than anyone else's in the country because it was extended for one reason after another, first for his year of birth, then for his specialization as a medic, then for his posting, and probably for his blood type, too. At least he was never at the front, except at the beginning on a mountain peak in Kurdistan, where they lived like animals. And yet the peak was their good fortune, because the Iraqi pilots didn't aim so precisely; the slopes were so steep that the bombs only had to miss by a few metres to land far down the mountain. Besides that, the months on the peak were hard, of course, although never as hard as at the front, where many of his friends died. A friend of my cousin's who was assigned to recover the bodies no longer eats any meat and still freaks out at the sight of blood. That's the kind of friends you have if you grew up in Iran in my generation.

Only from the top do we see what has become of Isfahan, once so quiet and so green: a dirty-grey behemoth that has swallowed up the villages and towns round about. The square that is rightly called the 'Image of the

World', *Meidān-e naqsh-e jahān*, seven times the size of St Mark's, is just a spot that you try to find for a long time before you finally make it out in the city centre. The old domes too are suddenly small in comparison with the concrete sphere and the two skyscraper-high minarets of the new mosque being built. At least we can spread out the world's most delicious breakfast: tea from the thermos, a part of every excursion in Iran; fresh flat bread, sheep cheese, herbs, walnuts and tomatoes, which – at least the tomatoes! – are still better in Iran than anywhere else in the world. Not just the inner tubes.

*

I find no trace of the Poles, but in a Polish author I met at the beginning of my travels, Adam Zagajewski, I find a comment that could have been written about Isfahan, the wounded, desiccated, overrun and still enchanting Isfahan, but also about many other cities through which I have passed in the East. In fact, he is referring to Lviv, which was not on my route – Lviv of all cities, Galicia of all provinces, but, after all, they say the grass is greener everywhere else. Although Proust says, Zagajewski writes in his undated diary (what a wonderful genre!), that the imagination is always concerned with absent people, distant places, and we are unable to imagine the street we are walking along, the room we are sitting in, the person we are talking with. 'But Proust lived in the classical era, before the disaster; he couldn't foresee that one day there would be half-abandoned, half-existing cities, cities covered with a tarp of ugliness, cities lost and half-recovered.' Isfahan was mostly untouched by the great disasters of the twentieth century, except for the air strikes in the first Gulf War; its population was not completely replaced, like that of Lviv or Wrocław; it was not subjected to any socialist urban planning, only to the brutal functionalism of modern Iranian commercial architecture, the madness of the car-friendly city and the Orientalistic kitsch of the Islamic Republic; it experienced only the internal flight of the rural population, on the one hand, and the emigration of broad sections of the bourgeoisie, and especially that of the religious minorities, on the other, which, taken together, admittedly amount to a replacement of half the population; it was only transformed by the population explosion into a noisy, stinking chaos. But in the process Isfahan has lost its river, its Life-Giving River, now become a skeleton. Proust could not have anticipated that, after the twentieth century, some cities would require a new type of imagination – Zagajewski refers to Lviv, but could just as well have meant Wrocław or Isfahan: 'He couldn't foresee that in such cities imagination becomes – must be – yet another sense, half imagination and half sensory apparatus, since here the everyday medically and empirically established senses don't suffice, they must be supplemented by a half-shut eye, intuition.'[61]

*

It's a big country. It consists not only of Tehran, Isfahan, and the other ever more populous cities. There are broad areas that are barely populated, or completely uninhabited, rain forests, deserts, steppes, glaciers. From Mahan in the southeast, where we have flown for a long weekend, we drive an hour into the mountains, an hour and a half at most. Waterfalls, villages where the last bakery has closed, as everywhere in the world, and the latest generation of donkeys are a means of transport – the transition has reached precisely this point: the pack asses are still here, but the bakeries are already gone. Narrow forests in the valleys, dried-up meadows on the slopes. In summer it is as green here as in the Alps, says the hotel manager, who drives us through the area for two days in his pickup – and in spring the slopes are a painting with all the wildflowers. Couldn't more be done with such fertile soil? More fields used to be farmed, our host confirms. And why not today? There's not enough labour. How's that? Labour? Yes, the young people go away and the old people prefer to live on their pensions, the *yarane* and the bonuses that the Leader's local candidate distributes when he wins the district.

It's a good thing the oil wealth is now arriving in the villages too. Only now the fields lie fallow because it's more convenient to buy food than to grow it, and that does nothing at all for the future of the country, which in twenty, thirty years won't have any more oil income to distribute. At least around here there is still agriculture, the hotel manager adds; there is still the traditional way of life, the rich culture, the idiosyncratic customs; this area is still *bekr*, 'innocent', that's one reason why he loves it so much. And, in fact, the faces of the peasants we meet are not only friendly but laughing; the people are not only cordial but merry: please honour us with your presence, little though we have to offer you, not worthy of you in the least, the bread, the yoghurt, the tea, the fruit, the nuts, please come in. The self-assurance of the women stands out, still wearing colourful robes and their traditional headscarves instead of the uniform manteau of the revolution. Okay, they work in the fields; that would hardly be possible in a manteau.

At the second to last farm that has electricity, we buy eight big jars of honey – for whom, we'll see in Isfahan. And, after the last farm, there are more farms, women fetching water from a well, shepherds with flocks, bee-

344

hives, and then nothing for a long time until, on a plain at over 3,000 metres' altitude ringed by more mountains, we find the traces of the nomads who spent the summer here, they too perhaps the last generation. We spread out our own breakfast, flat bread, sheep's cheese, walnuts, tomatoes, honey, and even fried eggs, made by the hotel manager on a camping stove.

When we are full, we wander along the stream until the high plain narrows to a canyon. Below us, all the farmers asked why we were coming up here so late, when all the flowers are past. We love it with the fewer colours, the subtle transitions in the colouring over broad expanses, set in motion by the sunlight. It is as if we were looking at a sea, greenish brown and so calm – no, as if we were walking on the sea.

Back in the valley I stand in the bed of the pickup with my younger daughter and my older brother, leaning over the roof of the cab, our faces in the wind. Germany has no such fun to offer children – not in any climbing gym or amusement park – or grown-up children. It's like the old days when we drove to Grandfather's village, although forty years ago there were ten of us on the truck bed. In those days, grandfathers still owned villages.

*

In the Lut Desert, the wind has made the earth into spectacular sculptures, high as hills, with steeples, gables, sweeping terraces, often dropping off vertically at the edges like cliffs. The oases are watered, as they have been for millennia, by the system of underground canals, where the people take refuge in summer when the temperatures get as high as 70 degrees Celsius – the world record, confirmed by NASA. It's not just the breathtaking natural landscape. Iran is in large part also a cultural landscape, wrested from nature: the climatically ideal clay buildings with their domes that keep the heat off in summer and store warmth in winter; the wind towers that supply whole villages with air conditioning, still in use in some places; the natural medicines that are gradually being rediscovered today, the knowledge of every single herb. And every pitcher was a work of art, every old door, and every house even more so; whatever was made in the past and is still the same today – it is beautiful, not ugly. Did people feel that way back then too? They probably didn't think about it. Elsewhere too old things are beautiful, but there is also the new with a value of its own, achievements, development. What do you call a civilization in which everything new turns out ugly?

In Mahan we find something of the old Isfahan, quiet, water-rich and therefore green, a town surrounding one of the most important Sufi tombs in the world, where Sufis are no longer allowed to dance, sing, pray. Because of Muharram, the interior is also draped with black banners. At least the courtyard looks as contemplative as ever, with many trees and a big pool that duplicates the iwans and the white cupola. A little shop sells Sufi music to tourists. My brother is seriously considering buying one of the old houses with a courtyard and fountain, especially as the prices here in southeastern Iran are still affordable. We have to forget Isfahan, my brother says. Then he notices, I notice, how the home-town loyalty for which Isfahanis are often ridiculed bursts out of me.

*

It's harder to breathe in Isfahan every time I return. I try to pay no more attention to the river that no longer exists, but when I'm jogging I can't ignore the fact that I can't inhale the air as I customarily do. The main reason I have got accustomed to breathing this way is not for my health; it is the almost meditative relaxation that this breathing rhythm induces – inhaling through the nose, exhaling through the mouth, more deeply than I ordinarily breathe, but not forced; never fast, in spite of my faster pace. But when you jog along the skeleton of a river, you notice the breathlessness of life in Iran. I inhale only as far as my throat. I am certain that not only physical illnesses are becoming more frequent, as everyone observes and as the press documents with statistics, but nervousness, aggression, is also increasing. Hardly a taxi driver, no dinner conversation, no chat with a merchant lacks the complaint that the old Isfahan no longer exists.

*

The whole afternoon, uncontrollably nostalgic, I guide two friends from Germany through the old city centre, where hardly a stone has been left standing. So many new, wide streets now, squares, little parks, gentrification Islamic Republic style, so that the big families of the regime's clientele have room for the kids to run around and can drive their new compact cars right up to the house. I have to ask my way when I want to find the gems that Isfahan still offers in greater numbers than any other city in the Middle East, to say nothing of a backwater like Mahan. But they are all still there – almost all; the saints' tombs, the minarets, the old courtyards and former caravan-serais in the bazaar. It is still fun, I notice, to watch the enraptured, amazed faces of the foreigners who would never have expected such riches behind a nondescript wall, such subtlety in Iran. I would like to show them some of the twelve or fourteen synagogues in Jubare, the city's oldest quarter; I've saved the number of the chairman of the congregation in my phone, only it hasn't occurred to me until now that devout Jews don't answer the phone on the Sabbath. We'll have better luck with the churches tomorrow, then, when I take the Germans to Jolfa, New Jolfa to be exact, to Christian Isfahan.

By the time we step out onto the Meidan after a long, serpentine route through the bazaar, seeing Isfahan with foreign eyes has restored its beauty for me to some extent. Because I want to take leave of it myself, I lead my visitors into the Sheikh Lotfollah Mosque, which is full of tourists. Again I lean against the wall, my head back, and stare into the cupola, minute after minute. There is no better world.

*

For my younger daughter to have her own childhood memories of Iran was the most important reason for spending four weeks in Isfahan – for her to understand the language better, meet other children, experience beautiful moments. I want her not only to know, but to experience that she possesses a second country (no country possesses her). Her reception in the school was overwhelming; she never saw anything like it in Germany, nor in the United States, where we also lived for a few months – how her classmates immediately adopted her as one of their own and from the first day fought for the privilege of sitting next to her. All the warmth, the exuberance, the tenderness, and also the finesse of the adults in dealing with children. The school giving her a send-off with presents after just four weeks, every single teacher hugging and kissing her, her classmates not wanting to let her go – exactly that is what she will carry engraved in her mind, along with the fact that the lessons themselves are much more boring than at her Montessori school: teacher-centred, with no discussion. The school uniform, including headscarf, was more fancy dress to her, especially since the girls at the genteel private school shed their regalia on their way from the classroom to the gate. Their mothers didn't exactly look as if they would be on the pilgrimage to Karbala tomorrow, their heels high enough for the runway, all noses apparently corrected, much of the hair bleached, if not naturally blonde; as I mentioned, those who are fair don't think much of the regime as a rule. And the girls' names, my God: Elvira, Diana, Tamar, Janine. Those of us living abroad make every effort to give our children beautiful Persian names, leaf through Ferdowsi's *Book of Kings*, look in the Persian translation of the Bible perhaps for something that might build a bridge between cultures, consult books of names for something less common, and in Iran itself the girls are given names like those on ITV. A girl in a chador would hardly have been so cordially welcomed at the school, and so fawned on by her classmates, as a rare guest from Germany. My daughter is now looking forward to Cologne but has no objections to flying to Isfahan again for her next holidays.

The Journey Begins

Two generations before mine, a trip from Isfahan to Tehran was by no means an ordinary thing; the condition of the roads was miserable, the danger of highwaymen great; help in an emergency was not even conceivable. The brand-new means of transport that amazed everyone who saw it was a four-in-hand, whose horses were changed every 40 or 50 kilometres, as Grandfather wrote in his memoirs, which, sadly, have never been printed. The coach drove on right through the night wherever possible. God willing, it was possible to reach Tehran in this way in four days and nights. Today, it is four or five hours by car, although we always fly. As he was writing, Grandfather apparently did not find it absurd to mention that the coach had no roof. Hence the travellers had to bear the hot, bright sun of summer and the cold and the rain of the other seasons, and often snow in winter. Sleeping was tricky, too: because of the swaying of the carriage, it was usually limited to minutes or half-hours. With fatigue or pain, heat or cold, the travellers spent more of the time in a kind of semi-consciousness that precluded conversation and reflection. As a rule, nothing worse happened than a hat falling out of the coach or a cloak falling on the floor. Only if the coachman fell asleep, disaster threatened. Then the horses might leave the track, the carriage might overturn, one traveller might fall on another, and the heavy conveyance on top of all. Grandfather himself experienced such accidents often, and the reader can imagine, he writes, how uneasy the travellers were in the wilderness, in the steppes, in the desert or on the mountain passes. The trip cost one rial per person, plus five shahi for the ostler of each caravanserai where the horses were changed, and one or two toman for the postman who took charge of the coach. What did these sums mean?

Seventy years later, Grandfather described the scene of his first departure from Isfahan, which would only draw a laugh from readers of today, he wrote, although at the time it was very dramatic for the family, but 'they are nothing more than names now,' say his memoirs, which, sadly, have never been printed. The aunts, cousins and other relatives who stood in the entrance hall to take leave of the boy and give him their prayers – nothing remains of them all but the names. Three times the surah Ya-Sin was recited; the Quran was repeatedly held aloft and Grandfather pushed under it. The relatives accompanied him to the bazaar, where the coach would depart, a throng of fifty, sixty people. Where to? the neighbours, passers-by and merchants wondered. The boy is going to Tehran! one of the throng cried back; he's going to attend school, the Franks' school! Franks, *farangihā*, is what the Iranians call people from the West even today. The late Norouz Ali Gomashteh lifted him onto the carriage. The boy quickly stowed his luggage and found a seat. There he sat now – it would be a while yet before the coach departed – surrounded, it seemed to him, by all his relatives in tears, the loudest sobs those of his mother. 'And why should I keep it from you?' writes Grandfather in his memoirs, which, sadly, have never been printed. 'Although it was my own wish to travel to Tehran, I could no longer control myself. I cried like a little child.'

As it happens, sitting on the seat beside the coachman, which is considered a loge seat – Grandfather uses the French word; today it would be called business class – is an Englishman, Mr Allanson, if I have transcribed the name back into English correctly (in Persian script, the vowels are left to the reader's imagination), a teacher at the Bishop's school in the Jolfa district, where my aunt lives today; her parents' home is not far away; because of the remaining Christians, it is one of the preferred residential districts in Isfahan. When Mr Allanson sees the boy crying, he brings him up front beside him, puts his arm around his shoulders, and begins to comfort him and distract him. Look, have you ever seen such muscular horses? And look at that uniform. His Persian sounds so funny to the boy, so stilted, that, under other circumstances, he would have laughed at it, perhaps would even have ridiculed the foreigner in the group. But now he is grateful for the arm he feels encircling his shoulders, more like that of a brother than a father; yes, like a big brother, although Mr Allanson is much older, a regular gentleman. The coach has long since departed; they have left the city behind, the fields and orchards; they are driving along the gravel track through the desert, and he continues to talk to the boy encouragingly. Don't worry, he says; first, God willing, we'll come to Kashan, where we'll rest in the paradise garden; it's more splendid than the Forty Columns Park in Isfahan, you'll see; then Qom, where, God willing, you'll pray for your father and mother, and then, God willing, we'll soon be arriving in Tehran; you'll like Tehran.

God willing. *Enshā'allāh*, the teacher from the Bishop's school will have said in his British accent.

Not that Mr Allanson had known the boy or his parents or his relatives or teachers before; he took him under his wing out of pure kindliness, the boy will write seventy, eighty years later, out of human kindness. Although Grandfather was still politically a nationalist, an ardent supporter of Dr Mosaddegh, who opened hostilities against the British by nationalizing the Anglo-Persian Oil Company, and in his old age a demonstrator against the shah, mainly for an end to America's hegemony, even as a child I noticed the reverence with which he spoke of the West, especially Europe, most emphatically France of course, the nation of culture, which, unlike Britain, America and Russia, had left Iran in peace (although of course he made a distinction between the states and the people). Respect for the Armenian Church in Jolfa and the foreign priests, nuns and missionaries who built hospitals and schools was likewise unshakable in his house. There was something cosmopolitan about him; the awareness, to put it more simply, that there are all kinds of people wherever you go. If we have something of this awareness, if I have it, then it is not, or not only, because we have travelled the world or been enlightened by Kant and *Das Kapital*. It also has other, more remote origins, a long history, which I am now reading. It is thanks to my grandfather, who travelled by coach from Isfahan to Tehran; it is thanks to my great-grandfather, the man in the photo I have brought with me to the office where it hangs beside my desk, the man in the middle with a turban and a gap between the teeth in his smiling face, who sent the boy to learn at the American school, although he was as tearful at their parting as anyone else – and he also had to bear the question whether he had made the right decision for his son – it is thanks to Mr Allanson, whose kindness kept the boy his whole life long from seeing a person as an enemy just because his state was hostile.

When I sat in the State Theatre at Darmstadt, front row centre, and the president announced my induction into the German Academy of Language and Literature, I felt, in spite of all the banality of the circumstances – behind me a resentful colleague, seated on my left a politician's wife, before me three photographers, one of them literally on my lap to get a better picture of the celebrity on my right – I felt a shiver of emotion and pride. It seemed to me as if not I had been distinguished, admitted, but my ancestors; their thirst for knowledge, their longing for the world, their courage to discover it, their ambition as well as their virtue and, for all of me, Grandfather's earnestness and his lack of humour, which they passed along from generation to generation, until ultimately one of their sons would be admitted to the Franks' academy. Now I see Grandfather sitting in the coach crying, about to leave for Tehran, and I think: that was one of the places, the moments; it was there and then that our journey began. The boy wipes the tears from his face and gradually regains the confidence with which he packed his bag yesterday afternoon. Now he wants to show something of his abilities; he is not a cry-baby after all; wants to say at least two, three sentences in English, only the English vocabulary that Mr Armani so laboriously pounded into him at the Aliye School has evaporated. Mr Allanson doesn't laugh; he smiles. Finally the boy manages to say in English at least that he is travelling to Tehran to attend the American School. Ah! I have to go there too, cries Mr Allanson. Dr Jordan, the head of the American School, has invited him. I shall intro-duce you; you'll like it there, God willing. *Enshā'allāh*. Mr Allanson's return to Persian loosens the boy's tongue once for all.

I will never forget how we stayed in Nezamabad the first night because the road was unsafe. The caravanserai, where we had been supposed to change horses, not to pass the night, was half dilapidated. We found ourselves a corner under the roof of the one wing of the building that was still standing, and spread out our blankets side by side. As long as I was awake, this honourable Frank with the strange accent in Persian chased away my cares, telling engrossing stories and equally enthralling news of Tehran, the school, England, the Franks, until, God be praised, I finally fell asleep.

Towards evening of the fourth day, the coach arrives in Lalehzar Street in Tehran and stops in front of the post office on Artillery Barracks Square, then the heart of the city, today a colourless junction among many in south-ern Tehran. The travellers unload their luggage and take their leave of one another. Mr Allanson makes sure the boy has accommodation. Yes, says the boy, my father wrote down the address for me. He waits until Mr Allanson disappears in the crowd, then calls a porter and takes the letter with the address on it out of his shoulder bag. It is a letter of recommendation from the head of his previous school, Mohaseb ol-Dowleh, to his friend Mirza Abdolwahhab Khan Jawaheri. Although he already knows it by heart, the boy is studying the address anew when suddenly the letter is whipped out of his hands. The boy looks up and sees a stout police officer standing before him, blue uniform, sparkling cuffs, spiked helmet and twisted moustache, alternating his menacing gaze between him and the letter. This letter hasn't got a stamp, says the officer accusingly; that is an infraction! Not daring to make an objection, or to point out that he has just brought the letter with him from Isfahan personally, the boy pays the fine the officer demands. Then he sets out with the porter to Mr Jawaheri's.

Sunset is long past when at last they are standing in front of the house: it is Mr Jawaheri's shop, a sweet shop, the shutters closed, the door locked. In the dark, the boy asks around until he finds another porter who knows where Mr Jawaheri lives: at Qazvin Gate, at the other end of town. Fortunately, his father has given him enough money. It is night by the time the boy, almost out of his senses with excitement, fear and exhaustion, finally knocks on the door. Mr Jawaheri, who is from Isfahan himself, doesn't need to read the letter before taking in a boy from his home town and a student of his old friend Mohaseb ol-Dowleh. He gives instructions to unload the boy's luggage and brushes aside the boy's objections as he pays the porter's fee. Mrs Jawaheri, who has thrown a chador over her nightgown, leads the guest into the living room. The boy has no sooner sat down on the carpet when – in the middle of the conversation – he falls asleep. When the Jawaheris wake him, the next day's dinner is already waiting for him. The boy does not know who undressed him and put him to bed, but he is so comfortable that he closes his eyes once more, and immediately falls asleep.

— From the novel *Dein Name*

ACKNOWLEDGEMENTS

The journey recounted in this book consists, to be exact, of several trips that I took between September 2016 and August 2017 for the news magazine *Der Spiegel* and a four-week sojourn in Isfahan in October and November 2016. I also returned to Belarus in April 2017 for a long weekend to research the consequences of the Chernobyl nuclear disaster; that report appeared in the weekly *Die Zeit*. The original publications in those periodicals correspond in all to a little less than one third of the book. The novel *Dein Name*, whose threads I have continued to spin in other books as well, furnishes not only the prologue and epilogue: the middle part of the Forty-Ninth Day described here is also based on impressions I have recorded in *Dein Name*.

My greatest thanks go to my editor at *Der Spiegel*, Lothar Gorris, who thought up the journey with me and supervised the editing of many instalments. I also thank the other colleagues in the cultural section, documentation, and archives of *Der Spiegel*, as well as the photography editors, the Moscow office, and the travel service, for their fantastic support, especially Gordon Bersch, Andrea Curtaz-Wilkens, Christian Esch, Sebastian Hammelehle, Ulrich Klötzer, Walter Lehmann-Wiesner, Nadine Markwaldt, Christian Neef, Elke Schmitter, Claudia Stodte and Anika Zeller. Of course I could have travelled on my own, but without an editorial structure, without specialists supplying both expertise and enthusiasm, and without the financial resources that an individual traveller can hardly muster, it would have been a different book: less dense, less informative, less relevant and with many more mistakes. May there long continue to be institutions such as *Der Spiegel* which are able to perform tremendous work for reporting, work which is often invisible to the reader. The public would be much poorer without them.

353

I would also like to thank my assistant Florian Bigge, who kept me supplied with information and contacts before and during my trips. I thank my editor of many years, Ulrich Nolte of C. H. Beck publishers, and his assistant Gisela Muhn. My heartfelt thanks also go to my informants, companions and advisors in Germany and along my route. In addition to those mentioned by name in the book, they include the following persons: Katajun Amirpur (Cologne), Mariana Sadovska (Cologne), Illias Uyar (Cologne), Osman Okkan (Cologne), Mikhail Shishkin (Basle), Nilufar Taghizadeh (Heidelberg), Marcus Bensmann (Essen), Milos Djuric (Berlin), Nora Bossong (Berlin), Almut Sh. Bruckstein Çoruh (Berlin), Ekkehard Maas (German-Caucasian Society, Berlin), Daniel Göpfert (Goethe-Institut, Cracow), Georg Blochmann (Goethe-Institut, Warsaw), Ruth Leiserowitz (Warsaw), Vitautas Bruveris (Vilnius), the late Leonidas Donskas (Vilnius), Detlef M. Gericke and Aukse Bruveriene (Goethe-Institut, Vilnius), Frank Baumann, Vera Dziadok and Nelly Golenishcheva-Kutuzova (Goethe-Institut, Minsk), Oleg Aizberg (Minsk), Sashko Sadovsky (Lviv), Rüdiger Bolz (Goethe-Institut, Moscow), Irina Sherbakova (Memorial, Moscow), Kerstin Kaiser and Vladimir Formenko (Rosa Luxemburg Foundation, Moscow), Golineh Atai (Moscow), Ernes Mambetov (Simferopol), Alexandra Podolskaya (Krasnodar), Tatiana Kamynina (Krasnodar), Stephan Wackwitz and Tamta Gochitashvili (Goethe-Institut, Tbilisi), Tamara Janashia (Tbilisi), Elvin Adigozel (Goranboy), Khalida Khalilzade (Baku), Altay Guyoshov (Baku), Nazik Armanakian (Yerevan), Vaghinak Ghazaryan (Yerevan), Behzad Veladi (Tabriz), Fariba Vafi (Tehran).

NOTES

1 Primo Levi and Leonardo de Benedetti, *Auschwitz Testimonies: 1945–1986*, trans. Judith Woolf, p. 99.
2 Adam Zagajewski, *Another Beauty*, trans. Clare Cavanagh, p. 35.
3 Adam Zagajewski, 'Some Advice for the New Government', trans. Clare Cavanagh.
4 Andrzej Stasiuk, 'In the Shade', trans. Irena Maryniak, pp. 72–3.
5 Stasiuk, 'In the Shade', p. 73
6 Zagajewski, *Another Beauty*, pp. 207–8.
7 Czesław Miłosz, 'Campo dei Fiori', trans. David Brooks and Louis Iribarne.
8 Siegfried Lenz, *The Heritage*, trans. Krishna Winston, p. 454.
9 Adam Mickiewicz, *Pan Tadeusz*, trans. Kenneth R. MacKenzie.
10 Timothy Snyder, *Bloodlands: Europe between Hitler and Stalin*, p. 190.
11 Valentin Akudowitsch [Akudovich], *Der Abwesenheitscode: Versuch, Weißrußland zu verstehen* [The code of absence: towards an understanding of Belarus], p. 140.
12 Akudovich, *Der Abwesenheitscode*, p. 61.
13 Akudovich, *Der Abwesenheitscode*, p. 117.
14 Akudovich, *Der Abwesenheitscode*, p. 130.
15 Svetlana Alexievich, *Chernobyl Prayer: A Chronicle of the Future*, trans. Anna Gunin and Arch Tait.
16 Akudovich, *Der Abwesenheitscode*, p. 107.
17 Akudovich, *Der Abwesenheitscode*, p. 98.
18 Akudovich, *Der Abwesenheitscode*, p. 70.
19 Thomas Stompe, Kristina Ritter and Hans Schanda, 'Die Spuren der Gewalt: Suizid- und Homizidraten in den ehemaligen Bloodlands' [The traces of violence: suicide and homicide rates in the former Bloodlands], abstract (modified for clarity).
20 Zygmunt Haupt, 'Totenmahl im Winter' ['A wake in winter'], trans. Esther Kinsky, p. 20.
21 Haupt, 'Totenmahl im Winter' ['A wake in winter'], p. 21.
22 Wolfgang Kemp, *Der Oligarch*, pp. 10, 47, 99.
23 Kemp, *Der Oligarch*, p. 23.
24 Leo Tolstoy, *Sevastopol*, trans. Isabel F. Hapgood.
25 Karl Schlögel, *Ukraine: A Nation on the Borderland*, trans. Gerrit Jackson, p. 147.
26 Schlögel, *Ukraine*, p. 148.

27 *Letters of Anton Chekhov to His Family and Friends*, trans. Constance Garnett.
28 Neal Ascherson, *Black Sea: Coasts and Conquests; From Pericles to Putin*, p. 49.
29 Anton Chekhov, *Three Sisters*, trans. Peter Carson, p. 251.
30 Leo Tolstoy, *Hadji Murat*, trans. Paul Foote, p. 431.
31 Tolstoy, *Hadji Murat*, p. 422.
32 Alexandre Dumas, *Impressions de Voyage: Le Caucase*, p. 214.
33 Dumas, *Impressions de Voyage: Le Caucase*, p. 87.
34 Kurban Said, *Ali and Nino: A Love Story*, trans. Jenia Graman, p. 113.
35 Said, *Ali and Nino*, pp. 113–14.
36 Ascherson, *Black Sea*, pp. 49–50.
37 Giwi Margwelaschwili, *Kapitän Varusch*.
38 Said, *Ali and Nino*, p. 52.
39 Said, *Ali and Nino*, p. 91.
40 Said, *Ali and Nino*, p. 149.
41 Akram Aylisli, *Stone Dreams*, trans. Katharine E. Young.
42 Said, *Ali and Nino*, pp. 170–1.
43 Said, *Ali and Nino*, p. 84.
44 Franz Werfel, *The Forty Days of Musa Dagh*, trans. Geoffrey Dunlop, rev. James Reidel, p. 509.
45 Werfel, *The Forty Days of Musa Dagh*, p. 141.
46 Werfel, *The Forty Days of Musa Dagh*, pp. 145, 148, 271.
47 Werfel, *The Forty Days of Musa Dagh*, pp. 27, 39–40, 159, 266.
48 Werfel, *The Forty Days of Musa Dagh*, pp. 159–60.
49 Werfel, *The Forty Days of Musa Dagh*, p. 87.
50 Osip Mandelstam, *Journey to Armenia*, trans. Sidney Monas, p. 98.
51 Mandelstam, *Journey to Armenia*, p. 73.
52 Mandelstam, *Journey to Armenia*, p. 72.
53 Mandelstam, *Journey to Armenia*, p. 43.
54 Osip Mandelstam, *Complete Poetry*, trans. Burton Raffel and Alla Burago, pp. 184–5.
55 Mandelstam, *Journey to Armenia*, p. 38.
56 Mandelstam, *Journey to Armenia*, p. 41.
57 Werfel, *The Forty Days of Musa Dagh*, pp. 456–7.
58 Osip Mandelstam, 'The Carriage-Driver', trans. Burton Raffel and Alla Burago, pp. 200–1.
59 Henri Stierlin, *Isfahan: Spiegel des Paradieses*, trans. Hanna Wulf, pp. 69–70.
60 Stierlin, *Isfahan*, p. 192.
61 Adam Zagajewski, *Slight Exaggeration*, trans. Clare Cavanagh, pp. 20–1.

BIBLIOGRAPHY

Valentin Akudowitsch [Akudovich], *Der Abwesenheitscode: Versuch, Weißrußland zu verstehen* [The code of absence: towards an understanding of Belarus]. Frankfurt am Main: Suhrkamp, 2013.

Svetlana Alexievich, *Chernobyl Prayer: A Chronicle of the Future*, trans. Anna Gunin and Arch Tait. London: Penguin, 2016.

Neal Ascherson, *Black Sea: Coasts and Conquests; From Pericles to Putin*. London: Vintage, [1996] 2011.

Akram Aylisli, *Stone Dreams*, in *Farewell, Aylis*, trans. Katherine E. Young. Brighton, MA: Academic Studies Press, 2018.

Anton Chekhov, *Letters of Anton Chekhov to His Family and Friends*, trans. Constance Garnett. Library of Alexandria, 1920; https://ebooks.adelaide.edu.au/c/chekhov/anton/c51lt/complete.html.

——, *Three Sisters*, in *Plays*, trans. Peter Carson. London: Penguin, 2002.

Thomas de Waal, *Black Garden: Armenia and Azerbaijan through Peace and War*, rev. ed., New York: New York University Press, 2013.

Alexandre Dumas, *Impressions de voyage: le Caucase*. Paris: Michel Lévy Frères, 1865.

Zygmunt Haupt, 'Totenmahl im Winter', in *Ein Ring aus Papier: Erzählungen*, trans. Esther Kinsky. Frankfurt am Main: Suhrkamp, 2003.

Wolfgang Kemp, *Der Oligarch*. Springe: zu Klampen, 2016.

Navid Kermani, *Dein Name*. Munich: Hanser, 2011.

Siegfried Lenz, *The Heritage*, trans. Krishna Winston. London: Methuen, 1987.

Primo Levi and Leonardo de Benedetti, *Auschwitz Testimonies: 1945–1986*, trans. Judith Woolf. Cambridge: Polity, 2018.

Osip Mandelstam, 'The Carriage-Driver', in *Complete Poetry of Osip Emilevich Mandelstam*, trans. Burton Raffel and Alla Burago. Albany: SUNY Press, 1973.

——, *Journey to Armenia*, trans. Sidney Monas. London: Notting Hill, 2018.

Giwi Margwelaschwili, *Kapitän Wakusch*, 2 vols. Berlin: Verbrecher, 2010.

Adam Mickiewicz, *Pan Tadeusz*, trans. Kenneth R. MacKenzie. New York: Hippocrene, 1992.

Czesław Miłosz, 'Campo dei Fiori', trans. David Brooks and Louis Iribarne, in *The Collected Poems 1931–1987*. New York: Ecco Press, 1988.

Kurban Said, *Ali and Nino: A Love Story*, trans. Jenia Graman. New York: Overlook, 2000.

Karl Schlögel, *Ukraine: A Nation on the Borderland*, trans. Gerrit Jackson. London: Reaktion, 2018.

Timothy Snyder, *Bloodlands: Europe between Hitler and Stalin*. Hachette UK, 2012. New York: Basic Books/London: Bodley Head, 2010.

Andrzej Stasiuk, 'In the Shade', trans. Irena Maryniak, *Index on Censorship* 35/3 (2006), pp. 72–7; https://doi.org/10.1080/03064220600903489.

Henri Stierlin, *Isfahan: Spiegel des Paradieses*, trans. Hanna Wulf. Zurich: Atlantis, 1976.

Thomas Stompe, Kristina Ritter and Hans Schanda, 'Die Spuren der Gewalt: Suizid- und Homizidraten in den ehemaligen Bloodlands' [The traces of violence: suicide and homicide rates in the former Bloodlands], *Neuropsychiatrie* no. 2 (2013), www.springermedizin.at/die-spuren-der-gewalt/14931998; Eng. abstract: www.researchgate.net/publication/233931381.

Leo Tolstoy, *Hadji Murat*, trans. Paul Foote, in *The Cossacks and Other Stories*. London: Penguin, 2006, pp. 335–464.

——, *Sevastopol*, trans. Isabel F. Hapgood. Library of Alexandria, 1869; https://onlinebooks.library.upenn.edu/webbin/gutbook/lookup?num=47197.

Franz Werfel, *The Forty Days of Musa Dagh*, trans. Geoffrey Dunlop, rev. James Reidel. London: Penguin, 2018.

Adam Zagajewski, *Another Beauty*, trans. Clare Cavanagh. New York: Farrar Straus & Giroux, 2000.

——, 'Some Advice for the New Government', trans. Clare Cavanagh, in *New York Review of Books*, 24 November 2016; www.nybooks.com/articles/2016/11/24/some-advice-for-the-new-government/.

——, *Slight Exaggeration*, trans. Clare Cavanagh. New York: Farrar, Strauss & Giroux, 2017.